TOWARDS JUSTICE

Studies in Critical Social Sciences Book Series

Haymarket Books is proud to be working with Brill Academic Publishers (www.brill.nl) to republish the *Studies in Critical Social Sciences* book series in paperback editions. This peer-reviewed book series offers insights into our current reality by exploring the content and consequences of power relationships under capitalism, and by considering the spaces of opposition and resistance to these changes that have been defining our new age. Our full catalog of *SCSS* volumes can be viewed at https://www.haymarketbooks .org/series_collections/4-studies-in-critical-social-sciences.

Towards Justice

A Critical Theory of Global Society and Politics

Marek Hrubec

Haymarket Books
Chicago, IL

First published in 2025 by Brill Academic Publishers, The Netherlands
© 2025 Koninklijke Brill NV, Leiden, The Netherlands

Published in paperback in 2026 by
Haymarket Books
P.O. Box 180165
Chicago, IL 60618
773-583-7884
www.haymarketbooks.org

ISBN: 979-8-88890-785-6

Distributed to the trade in the US through Consortium Book Sales and
Distribution (www.cbsd.com) and internationally through Ingram Publisher
Services International (www.ingramcontent.com).

This book was published with the generous support of Lannan Foundation,
Wallace Action Fund, and the Marguerite Casey Foundation.

Special discounts are available for bulk purchases by organizations and
institutions. Please call 773-583-7884 or email info@haymarketbooks.org for more
information.

Cover design by Jamie Kerry and Ragina Johnson.

Printed in the United States.

Library of Congress Cataloging-in-Publication data is available.

Contents

PART 3
Limits of Liberal Liberty

PART 4
Experience of Recognition

PART 5
Global Perspectives of Justice

Acknowledgements

The formulation of my theoretical conception of society and politics has been a gradual project. First, I articulated an outline (Hrubec 2011) which was commented on in several journals and then a selection of these articles appeared as the books *Contradictions and Alternatives to Global Capitalism* (Solik 2015) and *Intercultural War and Peace* (Svoboda, Stech 2012). I am indebted to those whose comments and articles were published there. I have also presented parts of my theory in various European countries, the USA, China, Brazil, Cuba, Ethiopia, Nigeria, South Africa, and other countries, and, reflecting on feedback from many colleagues, I have gradually reformulated, expanded, and updated my theoretical position which I am now publishing for the first time in this book in English.

My gratitude for the many years of discussion and inspiration belongs first and foremost to friends in the Global South who have opened my insight into fundamental local and global injustices and pathologies. Then, I would also like to thank specifically Nancy Fraser (New York), Axel Honneth (Frankfurt and New York), G.A. Cohen† (Oxford), Leslie Sklair (London), Jerry Harris (Chicago), William Robinson (Santa Barbara, California), Lauren Langman (Chicago), Wei Xiaoping (Beijing), Tong Shijun (Shanghai), Liu Zuokui (Beijing), Chen Xin (Beijing), Zhou Suiming (Guangzhou), Emil Sobottka (Porto Alegre), Alessandro Pinzani (Florianopolis), Enrique Dussel (Ciudad de México), Fabricio Pereira da Silva (Rio de Janeiro), Ernesto Dominguéz López (Havana), Alexander Chumakov (Moscow), Alexander Lukin (Moscow), Achille Mbembe (Johannesburg), Binyam Mekonnen (Addis Ababa), and Robert Fine† (Warwick). I am grateful for long-lasting friendly discussions with colleagues from our Prague Centre of Global Studies, namely Martin Brabec, Oleg Suša, Josef Velek, Martin Profant, Erazim Kohák†, Dominika Dinušová, and other local colleagues in Prague, especially Jan Svoboda, Josef Zumr, Jiří Loudín, Pavel Baran, Emil Voráček, Zdenka Mansfeldová and Petr Agha, and in Bratislava Peter Dinuš, Ladislav Hohoš, Ľuboš Blaha, Richard Sťahel, Jozef Lysý† and František Škvrnda. I would also like to mention my thanks to all the debaters from the World Social Forums and other social and civic movements, the political community, and my students.

Tables

About *Towards Justice*

Marek Hrubec has long been a top international thinker on global interactions and social justice. His new book deserves close attention by all those concerned with contemporary world tensions and alternatives to hegemony and authoritarianism.

> JERRY HARRIS, National Secretary, Global Studies Association of North America, Chicago, USA

• • •

Marek Hrubec has given us a theoretical and historical *tour de force* on critical social theory in relation to the epochal events of the past half a century and the struggle for global social justice. Coming at a time of great suffering worldwide in the face of acute crisis in the world capitalist system, his theoretical and analytical formulations on global social justice will be of great importance for those seeking to make sense of the world-historic conjuncture we face at the quarter-century mark as well as for activists from the diverse social movements, both South and North, struggling for a better world.

> WILLIAM I. ROBINSON, Distinguished Professor of Sociology, University of California at Santa Barbara, USA

• • •

In this book, Marek Hrubec gives Critical Theory a global perspective. He accurately analyzes the unsustainability of imposed conservative liberalism and counters it with global justice and democratic socialism that takes the Global South seriously.

> EMIL SOBOTTKA, Professor, PUCRS University, Porto Alegre, Brazil

• • •

This impressive book draws on the very important issue of global social justice, related to the historical events of the 20th century and the major international conflicts of this century. Marek Hrubec analyses the issue of global justice dealing with a perspective of critical theory and further formulates an alternative theory of global social justice for anticipating the future. This book is full of insightful thinking and is worth reading and necessary reading.

WEI XIAOPING, Distinguished Professor, Institute of Philosophy, Chinese Academy of Social Sciences, Beijing, China

• • •

In a context of structural, and arguably civilizational crisis, understanding the complexity of the global civilization and the nature of its multiple components is a pre-requisite for meaningful action. Marek Hrubec's work offers an explanatory framework and a set of tools that allow for a critical examination of that reality and a deeper appreciation of imbalances, injustices and power dynamics. This book is a must-read.

ERNESTO DOMÍNGUEZ LÓPEZ, University of Havana, Cuba, and Visiting Professor, Stanford University, USA

• • •

Marek Hrubec's monumental work represents a profound insight into the problems of social criticism. The theory of global social justice is important precisely so that a kind of global consensus can emerge, and sharp international conflicts do not have to be resolved by wars. Hrubec generalizes the experience of his global research, not only in Western countries but also in Latin America, Africa, and China.

LADISLAV HOHOŠ, Emeritus, Comenius University, Bratislava, Slovakia

• •
•

Introduction

In the post-socialist context of Central Europe after the 1989 revolution, particularly in Prague, I was very surprised by what we began to learn about the mainstream Western political philosophy at university, particularly about paradigmatic John Rawls's *Theory of Justice* (1971). Since we were familiar with Marxism, whose obvious basis was its historical dimension, it was a surprise to discover that Rawls' theory almost does not work with time and is ahistorical. It seemed to us like an incomplete doctoral thesis, unable to answer basic questions, which meant for us mainly the problematic question of the 'transition to democracy'. We said to ourselves that economic and political power – and not the level of knowledge – determined what was relevant knowledge: The West won the Cold War, and now the ahistorical, politically innocuous theory from the U.S. will be the mainstream theory here. It was only when I came to Oxford for my doctoral studies that I gradually began to understand that Rawls' liberal theory also contained important aspects that I had to study thoroughly and come to terms with to criticize it properly.

This book deals with theoretical issues of (in)justice from different territorial and time perspectives. It examines society and politics in a European and more generally Western context, as well as in the environment of the Global South and global interactions. It analyses the topic primarily in recent decades within the broader framework of the centuries of modernity but also approaches it partly against the backdrop of long-term civilizational development.

If we distinguish between the three main ideologies and their associated theories, namely liberalism, conservatism, and socialism in the broad sense,[1] we may say that the last half-century has seen a gradual global rise of liberal tendencies, their subsequent crisis with conservative implications, and a confrontation with revitalizing socialist demands now. This book explores these developments by offering primarily critical analyses of liberal and libertarian theories and their conflicting implications, and by charting their alternatives in the forms of democratic socialism or socialist democracy, drawing on critical social theory and other currents from other parts of the world.

---

1 A more detailed breakdown brings a more complex approach, of course. The term liberalism in the general sense, for example, can be divided into, on the one hand, right-wing neoliberalism, which has been pursued mainly in practice and is associated freely with libertarianism in theory, and, on the other hand, left-wing and centrist liberalism, which has been pursued mainly in theory.

The collapse of the Eastern bloc since 1989 has meant a weakening of socialist theory in the East, the West, and elsewhere in the world, although many of
these theories in the West and the South have not been linked to the Eastern
bloc. It is more accurate to say that the collapse of the Soviet version of socialism in Central and Eastern Europe and other associated countries has brought
about a process of global mainstreaming of Western neoliberal practice and
libertarian and liberal theory, but the effects of the 2008 Western financial and
economic crisis have influenced structural changes in Western countries today
and trends for future developments, which in their contradictory overcoming
of different forms of liberalism in the broad sense contain new fragmenting
and conflicting threats and hopes. These tendencies have recently clashed with
the strengthening influence of the Global South and its various alternative
social perspectives. The alternatives began to be heard most strongly through
emancipatory waves in Latin America with social forums and demands from
the global poor and other marginalized, while, at the same time, they began to
take shape through market socialism in East Asia.

From the 1990s onwards, there was a need to come to terms again, and this
time fundamentally, with how to theoretically approach the weakened socialist conception of class conflict and find adequate perspectives. Critical theory,
which originally established itself as a Western version of Marxism, came up
with a way out. While Karl Marx's conception of the class struggle was considered by most authors to be too narrow and economically reductionist,
Georg Wilhelm Friedrich Hegel's conception of the struggle for recognition, as
received also by Marx, offered a basis for a possible actualizing reformulation
with a more complex (economic, social, political, cultural) scope, which could
also include a redefined class conflict conception, since conflicting social
classes and groups had understandably not disappeared. Jürgen Habermas
formulated this shift as "a historical step backward from Marx to Hegel to re-
establish the programme *from Hegel to Marx*" (Habermas 2009).[2] This historically required reckoning with older motives to use them in an updated form
and overcome them in a new critical social theory of recognition seemed to
many writers to be the hope for an update of democratic socialist theory. In
other words, to attempt something similar to what Marx himself, and, after
him, several waves of leftist authors who followed Hegel and Marx, such as
Herbert Marcuse, tried.

More social and political philosophers and social scientists have addressed
the topic of recognition. While Johann Gottlieb Fichte and Jean Jacques

---

2   This interpretation is related to Axel Honneth's book *Freedom's Right* (2014).

Rousseau had opened up the subject, Hegel elaborated and made it known with his conception of the struggle for recognition (*Kampf um Anerkennung*) between master and slave. Marx, Georges Sorel, Alexandre Kojève and Jean Hyppolite continued to analyse it, and it was dealt with not only in scholarly but also in literary works, for example by Jean-Paul Sartre and Simone de Beauvoir. This has made it possible to examine both an existential and social level of the subject as well as a structural level of economic, political, and other analyses. In this book, I am mainly aligning myself with contemporary inter-disciplinary analyses, mostly by authors of critical social theories.

Critical social theory of recognition, while offering the promised more complex theoretical foundations, has remained too closely associated with liberal theory and has fallen far short of reestablishing the program *from Hegel to Marx*, let alone further updating it for the current era of global interactions, including conflicts. Therefore, in this book, on the one hand, I build on the critique of liberal theory in terms of a critical social theory of recognition, and on the other hand, I reformulate this critical theory with various critically oriented theories around the world and move beyond it to a more challenging theory of global social justice.

In doing so, I also draw partly on selected supporting motifs of critical social theory that were developed in the Czechoslovak environment mainly during the participatory revitalization of Eastern European socialism since the 1960s. I further rearticulate critical social theory through selected updated compatible elements of analytical Marxism, which articulated higher claims for social and economic justice than contemporary critical theory. I also build on a critically oriented theory of global capitalism given that since the 1990s, struggles for justice have also been more strongly fought at the regional and global levels. Since a cultural and civilizational dimension is also necessary in the analysis of these issues, I also draw on a theory of civilizations. In this sense, I articulate a social theory that will be able to (a) be complex with economic, social, political, cultural, security, and environmental aspects, (b) not underestimate economic and social motives, (c) take into account the local and national as well as the macro-regional, transnational and global levels of analysis, and (d) also integrate civilizational and intercultural aspects of analysis.

Concerning clarifying the background and interactions with different parts of the world, I formulate my theoretical standpoint in dialogue with various critically oriented social theories not only from the Global North but also from the still marginalized Global South. In this book, I draw on my background in European critically focused social theory, especially in Central Europe, influenced by the experience of former state socialism and contemporary capitalism. The local environment may be a bridge between East and West, but today it is mainly one of the semiperipheries of the West, more precisely a part of the marginalised Global South in the Global North. Of course, I am presenting my European or Central European perspective to people from other systems, cultures, and civilizations only as a theoretical standpoint for our further discussion, starting from the experience that authors from other parts of the world are doing similar things, i.e. articulating their social theory, in dialogue with perspectives from other parts of the world, so that, while respecting the plurality of conceptions in different parts of the world, we can mutually inspire each other and at the same time move towards a common formulation of a conception of global social justice. While I am aware that the categories of the Global South and the Global North are not impermeable essences, this should not relativistically prevent us from recognizing the unjust fact that the majority of people in the South are exploited, oppressed and discriminated against.

As I indicated at the outset, in general, my main concern in this book is to critique and explain liberal and libertarian theories and the implications in terms of critical social theory and other critically focused social theories around the world, and to formulate an alternative theory of democratic socialism or socialist democracy from local to global justice. I also show how social and political philosophy and related disciplines have their sources in social and political practice. I use here the general term social theory, which encompasses the other sub-analyses mentioned above, but because of the emphasis on the political significance of this analysis, I also use the term social and political theory.

While most analyses in contemporary political philosophy and related disciplines focus only on current academic debates and neglect larger historical arguments, I would like to focus specifically on a longer time horizon that goes back to the origins of our European civilization in the context of other civilizations and human civilization in general. However, I analyse mainly theoretical discussions from the fall of the Eastern Bloc in the early 1990s to the present, within the broader framework of the last half-century. Their temporal embeddedness in the historical development of the Western capitalist system in particular can be succinctly captured as a cyclical alternation of emphasis on different structures of this system, even if this system remains. Specifically, this is the alternation of social or socialist tendencies (three decades of the welfare state from World War II to the 1970s), neoliberal tendencies (from the 1980s to the first decade of the new century), ordo-neoliberal and, thus, also (neo)conservative and populist tendencies (after the 2008 crisis from the 10s through the current 20s and perhaps into the 30s) and, then, in the next era, again potentially (neo)socialist tendencies on a new, higher plane.

In this timeframe of about a century, the liberal theories of the 1970s with their social concessions can be seen as summarizing the modest demands of the then-receding welfare state era, which were subsequently considered by many accommodating authors as the maximum possible in the neoliberal era. In contrast, critical social theory and other socialist theories can be seen to make more demanding social demands that still hold in mind not only from the welfare state era and the social revolt of the 1960s but also from an earlier period, so that these demands can be picked up again in an updated version when cyclical changes, after their global contradictions, potentially reach another era in the Western framework.

• • •

The theme of the book requires some territorial and temporal clarifications already here in the Introduction. It is necessary, first, to define a territorial exploration in which struggles for recognition, or more generally for justice, take place. Specifically, it is necessary to distinguish between the exploration of classical international issues that deal with individual nation-states and international relations that emerge through them, on the one hand, and the exploration of global issues, on the other. If in this book I conduct a discussion between international approaches and global approaches, and in some places, I do not specify the term 'global', I include – except international relations – all other relations beyond the nation-state, i.e., transnational, transnational, macro-regional, intercultural, extraterritorial, global and other interactions. To suggest at least some concepts, it can be said that – as the terms themselves suggest – international relations refer to contacts between individual nation-states (usually through national governments); transnational activities, mostly economic activities, transcend nation-states and do not refer to individual states as a whole; supranational issues are conceptualized as a set that includes multiple nation-states or territories that together form a supranational regional, macro-regional or networked or extraterritorially integrated whole, and these wholes are based on international relations, in which they can also be included; intercultural relations refer to the interaction of cultures and civilisations; and finally, narrowly conceived global relations are themselves a kind of supranational entity, but in contrast to macro-regional or selectively integrated networked entities, they are an entity at the level of human civilisation or, more generally, at the planetary level, including human beings as well as nature.

In case I am transcending the controversy between these terms, I use the term global also in a general sense, whereby I include all lower territorial levels of justice (macro-regional, transnational, international, national, local, etc.) under the term global justice, just as when we write about national justice, we also include all lower levels below the national level (local, district or regional).

As I show the current serious limits of international relations in the environment of corporate and political pressures of global capitalism and explain the macroregional and global orders, I focus on struggles for recognition, and more generally for justice, that emerge from international relations, but do not stay with them, transcending them in various ways and shaping new tendencies of development beyond the borders of nation-states. In this sense, I analyse in particular intercultural dialogue, universal rights, social extraterritorial recognition, and macro-regional strategic socialism with its global interactions. Just as on the general level, I build on a critical social theory of recognition and move towards my own theory of social justice, on the territorial level of analysis I mainly build on national, international, and cosmopolitan theories and move towards my theory of global social justice.

There is also a need to clarify how to conceptualise different social changes. This brings us to several kinds of crises both at the global level and especially at lower levels. The more superficial changes are structural crises in which the structure changes (for example, neoliberalism becomes established) but the whole social system (in this case capitalism) remains the same. Deeper systemic crises lead to a change in the whole system, for example, historically the fall of feudalism and the establishment of capitalism or then socialism. Complex crises can then lead to a civilizational crisis in which an entire civilization or civilizations in plural can fall, for example in the colonial conquest of the Americas by Europeans.

Changes are realized through gradual or dramatic transitions, which has led to a conflict between reformist and revolutionary approaches. However, these approaches are usually applied not independently of reality but depending on the social possibility or blockage of historical development, since revolutionary changes usually occur only when the possibility of development through transformation is blocked. However, in addition to transformation and revolution, it is also necessary to identify the more complicated concept of transformational revolution, which refers to the gradual implementation of important changes.

In social processes, transformations, revolutions, or transformational revolutions do not merely bring progress or regress, but more complex developmental trajectories. Progress in one level of structure, system, or civilization in a given territory in a given period may be accompanied by a parallel regression in another level or another territory of the same period. Similarly – and understandably more complicated – is the case with the complex development of contradictions on a global scale.

From the long-term historical perspective of thousands of years, globalization has proceeded as a contradictory dramatic process of ever-expanding territorial integration, part of the evolving technical rationality of human civilization, involving, among other things, communication, transportation, economic, social, political, and cultural integration. The territory of tribes gradually expanded into the territory of states, then the larger territories of empires, then, the territories of empires with colonies, to result in progressive planetary, i.e., global, integration. The European conquest of the Americas was a milestone in this bloody conflict-filled process, when for the first time a long-term global integration of humanity was achieved.

The expanding global interactions did not proceed linearly. A wave of global integration is usually followed by a partial global disintegration, which is then followed by even more global integration. Deglobalization causes not only administrative fragmentation of states or empires but also economic crises, wars, and environmental destruction. This cycle also repeats itself at a higher level, where the collapse of some empires or entire cultures has meant more deglobalization steps backward after which global integration has been revitalized again on an even larger scale. Thus, from an overall long-term perspective, so far in the course of the history of human civilization, dialectically, through global integration dynamics and subsequent partial corrective deglobalization regressions, ever-greater territorial integration has occurred, accompanied by ups, downs, and upward waves of social structures, systems, and civilizations that have so far resulted in global integration.

In my interpretation, I map global interactions and conflicts in such a way as to capture as much as possible the integration tendencies not only to shed light on their shape in the decades following the collapse of the Eastern bloc but also to show the areas and modes of the following potential future global integration processes that could be realized after temporary disintegration adjustments. The identification of these areas and modalities is a prerequisite for the problems of post-conflict societies after the disintegration phase of development to be more harmoniously managed and for a more equitable social order to be achieved in the subsequent new phase of global interactions with integrative tendencies.

• • •

As the title of this book, *Towards Justice*, indicates, I have been working on a theory of justice, primarily in the last half century, and aware of its long tradition at least since Plato and Aristotle. Its subtitle then specifies that my conception of justice stems from a critical theory of global society and politics. Following the interdisciplinary and transdisciplinary approach of critical theory, in this book I focus mainly on social and political philosophy, formulating the philosophical underpinnings of social and political theory, using mainly sources of sociology, political science and global studies. It is clear, however, that in the scope of one book, I can only outline the basic ideas of a theory, not fully develop them.

The main outline of my exposition is divided into five parts, with the first two explaining my foundations and methods (in general terms in the first part, and in a historical trajectory in the second part) and the following three parts applying these methods to the exposition of the topic.

More specifically, this means that, in the first part, I explore types of social critique in discussion with alternative critically oriented social and political theories, and I carry out the founding of critical theory using the methodological trichotomy of *critique, explanation, normativity*. This trichotomy, which is the underlying principle of my interpretation, expresses the argumentative dynamics of struggles for justice that progress from critiquing negative moments of social reality, to explaining positive fragments of reality, to developing these fragments in a normative conception of society for the benefit of people. I further develop this foundation through approaches to inquiry that include transdisciplinarity, realism in social development, and a conception of the relations between structures and actions of actors in practical-inert structures and history, including transformations, revolutions, and transformative revolution, which allows for an understanding of longer-term fundamental changes. In the second part, I then identify elements of methodological trichotomy and other approaches in the formulations of critical theory from its original founding programmatic documents to contemporary authors and reformulate them concerning the main paradigms at each stage of critical theory. In sum, I thereby offer methodological foundations for a more general theory of global social justice.

In Parts 3–5, I then use the methodology outlined above to analyse the theme of the book by focusing on the discussion of liberal theory and partly libertarian theory with critical social theory and other socially oriented theories to arrive at my theory of global social justice. Specifically, I first develop a critique of the deficits of a liberal conception (Part 3: Chapters 5 and 6), then I develop an explanation of the dilemmas of a critical conception of recognition (Part 4: Chapters 7 and 8), and finally, I develop normativity by specifying the crucial moments of the critical conception of global justice (Part 5: Chapters 9 and 10). This division is indeed basic and central but not exhaustive, as the book moves towards a more complex account, where the remaining two trichotomies can still be applied within each of the elements of the methodological trichotomy. While I also apply the trichotomy to the specific problems themselves, since developing a theory at a higher level of analysis ultimately requires coming to terms with alternative theories, their deficits and dilemmas, my analysis moves in this direction.

In my critique, I deal primarily with John Rawls's liberal theory, while at the same time critically clarifying its foundations and some of its consequences concerning Robert Nozick's nonegalitarian libertarian theory, elements of which have become powerful in an ideological version in political practice. I analyse an intersubjective deficit in the foundation of liberal and libertarian theory and the consequences in the social and participatory democratic spheres and in the impossibility of developing the theory in transnational planes. In analysing social theory, I draw on analyses put forward by Axel Honneth, Nancy Fraser, Charles Taylor, Iris Young, G.A. Cohen, Wei Xiaoping, and other similarly oriented authors. In this sense, it is not just a dispute of partial theories, but also a dispute of two theoretical or interpretive strands: the liberal theoretical stream in the broader sense and the critical social theoretical stream, each of which draws on its own rich history of scholarship.

In the case of both liberal theory in the third part of the book and critical theory in the fourth part, I always focus first on the local and national level (Chapters 5 and 7), and then on the international and transnational level (Chapters 6 and 8). I examine the developmental tendencies that emerge from international interactions and transcend them to global interactions mainly in the last, fifth part, with an emphasis on mapping the problems and outcomes, especially in the Global South where the most challenges need to be faced: in Latin America, Africa, and Asia. I divide Part 5 into two chapters according to their focus on intercultural and inter-civilizational dialogue in the face of the dispute over universal rights (Chapter 9) and on extraterritorial recognition of the global poor as well as socialism with Chinese characteristics linked to strategic interactions, which entails issues of social and economic justice (Chapter 10). In doing so, I map both the actions of the actors and the structures in which they operate and which they co-create. Then, at the end of the last, tenth chapter, I consider the possibilities and threats of global hegemony, authoritarianism, and war in light of potential conflicts.

To avoid the pitfalls of either political or economic reductionism in the aforementioned Parts 3, 4 and 5, I address issues of social and economic justice as well as cultural and political justice while also mapping security and other aspects. In the Conclusion of the book, which summarizes my theory of social justice (democratic socialism or socialist democracy), I present and explain a systematic normative proposal of its social justice principles.

While this systematic layout of the book provides the basis for an analytical understanding of its content, intuitive insight into the significance and various dimensions of the topic may be aided by the inclusion of an exemplary case study. In *Hegel, Haiti, and Universal History* (Buck-Morss 2009), critical theorist Susan Buck-Morss argues that in the developing modern thought of the eighteenth century, the concept of slavery played an important role in Western practical philosophy as a symbol of unfree power relations among people, while the practice of slavery was paradoxically at its height in the colonial economics and politics of the time. The violent geographical bifurcation of the demand for justice, replicating the boundary between Western countries and their colonies, was passed off as necessary, proper, and legally codified. In this authoritarian context, most Western intellectuals did not consider it appropriate to write about the unprecedented revolution that had just been carried out in Haiti by slaves, beings who were not then ascribed the capacity for freedom and education. It was the first successful revolution of black slaves in America, which led to the establishment of a state. The event was consistently glossed over and largely silent in the West. At the same time, Hegel became famous for his critical analysis of slavery and the associated inspirational concept of the struggle for recognition between master and slave in *The Phenomenology of the Spirit* (*Die Phänomenologie des Geistes*, 2018), but although we can suspect various connotations associated with contemporary slave struggles for recognition, there was no direct reference to the events in Haiti at the time. To be sure, this was a philosophical book and slavery was discussed in the abstract, and the political restrictions on free speech at the time were not kind to the author on this matter, but even so, one must be impatient to be critical of the time that passed before Hegel, in his late *Philosophy of Mind* (*Die Philosophie des Geistes*, 2010), pointed to the ability to educate the former Haitian slaves and their ability to create a state. Most other authors, however, remained silent about this watershed event until the 20th century.

One cannot help but wonder whether we find ourselves in a similar situation today in the milieu of Western social and political thought, given the hundreds of millions of poor, especially in the developing countries of the Global South. However, these are not the only marginalised people who are ignored by most European and more generally Western social and political philosophies and theories. From the perspective of the Global South, Enrique Dussel points out in his book *Politics of Liberation: Critical Global History* (*Política de la Liberación: Historia Mundial y Crítica*, 2007): the "Eurocentrism of political philosophies that, out of contempt and ignorance, forget everything that other cultures have achieved practically or politically, even in theory."

Respecting people in non-Western contexts requires overcoming egocentrism and requires recognizing their needs, abilities, and interests, as well as the differences in their social, economic, political, civilizational, and cultural systems that crystallize from different world contexts. It also means recognising their claim to their paths of development, 'multiple modernities', but this does not imply a relativist position and the dominance of particularism. At the same time, the necessary respect for other people requires an understanding of our common situation, our shared world framework, to which we have been seduced by many unjust and just events in history and in the present. A global universal commonality in a positive sense would require that mutual recognition in many aspects be realized, and thus global social justice.

PART 1

Founding a Critical Theory

∴

Social Critique

> Concepts, which comprehend not only the given reality but, simultaneously, its abolition and the new reality that is to follow.
> HERBERT MARCUSE

• •
•

A critical social theory stems from social critique. However, the elaboration of this premise differs from author to author. I aim to deal, first, with critical social theory which I will increasingly formulate in the context of other critically oriented theories around the world to articulate a more inclusive global social theory that goes beyond contemporary standard critical theory. I will analyse three fundamental elements of critical theory – *critique, explanation,* and *normativity* – which can be identified already in the initial programmatic documents of the founders of Critical Theory (the Frankfurt School), and consequently mapped in texts of their followers up until today. Although these elements have been present in Critical Theory since its beginning, and their existence was an implicit precondition for Critical Theory, they have been articulated only vaguely in their complex mutual relations. This is because only some of these elements have as a rule been addressed and because just a few of the relations between them have been discussed. Only an articulation of all three elements in their mutual constitutive relations will enable them to take a crucial place in critical theory.

I will proceed in the following way. In the first section, I will clarify the need for an internal characteristic of critically focused social and political theory. In the second section, I will clarify the essential importance of the trichotomy of critique, explanation, and normativity for this kind of theory, and will concentrate on relations between individual elements of the trichotomy. In the final, third section, I will deal with external social criticism and will examine the possibility at least in some cases of redefining it from the internal perspective. This sequence of argumentation will hopefully lead to a better understanding of the fundamentals of a theory that is based on internal social criticism and, which as a result, can be able to work out a critical concept of in/justice, and confront the pitfalls of theoretical approaches which are widespread in various versions of capitalism. In this sense, it is possible to start by saying *Marx Matters* (Fasenfest 2022). It is a part of the complex contexts which I analyse in this book. Building on one of the first programmatic texts of Critical Theory, the essay 'Traditional and Critical Theory', which as implied by the title formulates the difference between traditional and Critical Theory, one may say that there is a need for differentiation between a critical social theory and an uncritical asocial theory, both traditional and contemporary (Horkheimer 2002a; Adorno et al. 1950).

1   Internal Social Criticism

Clarification of the constitutive elements of Critical Theory requires comparing relevant alternative social and political theories, specifically theoretical social and political criticisms, which for brevity's sake I will denote as 'social criticisms'. I will start with an analysis of the theoretical approach to social criticism presented by Michael Walzer and followed by other critical theorists, and by analysing theories of other authors, will then show its limits and introduce my own standpoint.

Despite offering an inspiring insight into the issue, Walzer by mixing up parts of a multi-dimensional explication and overlooking others fails to provide sufficient reasons for the bases of social criticism (Walzer 1980). However, an analysis of his viewpoint helps to clearly articulate viable social criticism and distinguish Critical Theory from other forms of social criticism. Walzer considers social criticism to be as old as society itself, and an adequate response to it to be 'one of the essential forms of mutual recognition' (Walzer 1988, 3). In the interactions of showing, refusing, and acquiring respect, a social critic may in a symbolic fashion say: I criticize, therefore I am. And yet, the complaint he or she raises is a mere beginning, similar to the position in which Descartes declares, I think, therefore I am. With that in mind, it may be said that by challenging the behaviour of his fellows Socrates made social critics exemplary experts on 'complaint'.

Walzer conceives of social criticism as a kind of social practice characterized by a challenging interpretation. In this, he coincides with Critical Theory, which also is a kind of social criticism that is closely related to critical practice. Walzer presents a definition of social criticism against the background of other conceptions which from a moral perspective he considers to be less appropriate and to correspond less well to people's everyday experience. Primarily, he distinguishes three categories of approaches: *discovery, invention,* and *interpretation* (Walzer 1980).

The first category, discovery, refers to the kind of approach that focuses on a given area of analysis, analyses it, and reveals its problems. Such an approach relies strongly on description and explanation of the given study area. It defines the already finished value structure and clarifies its shortcomings. The second category, invention, takes a more active approach compared to the first. It does not discover and work with some already finished subject of its interest but invents the subject. It attempts to construct values that can be widely shared, 'a universal corrective for all the different social moralities' (Walzer 1980, 13). This universalistic corrective can then serve as a source of correction of the prevailing problematic practices. As an example, one might mention Rawls's principles of the normative theory of justice; these do not occur in practice, but rather are formed by the theorist from behind a veil of ignorance.

According to Walzer, the person who performs the interpretation plays a role similar to that of a judge. As social criticism occurs not only in the area of philosophy but also very often in everyday life, it does not need to be discovered or invented. A social critic engages in dialogue with other members of his or her community and contributes to assessing the conditions for their common activities: a common speech performs an *internal criticism* in the form of 'a collective reflection upon the conditions of collective life' (Walzer 1980, 35). This reflection is an interpretation that assesses the situation in which members of the community carry on discussion among themselves for their common good. Unless the critic identifies with the major values of a given society, he or she cannot define social problems and cannot focus on issues of injustice that occur in the society without enforcing his or her point of view on the society and acting as an authoritarian (Decker and Türcke 2019).

This argument is encountered in two versions, either epistemological and moral, or practical philosophical. Richard Rorty, as a representative of the first variant, agrees with Walzer that interpretation is an essential phenomenon for understanding social criticism. However, Rorty expands this argument toward the theory of knowledge, stating that knowledge of the truth can be realized only within local language games. Criticism cannot exceed its context of understanding in a given language community. If it does so, it may lose a sense of understanding of the issues, and open itself up to the danger of authoritarian abuse (Rorty 1989; Honneth 2000b; Allen 1998). By contrast, the contextualistic approach that Walzer takes within practical philosophy does not begin with epistemological argument, and when accepting it, finds the practical implications within it that are suppressed by Rorty's proposal for a division of labour between private philosophy, sensitive-oriented literature and political reforms. Walzer's practical philosophy stems from the moral assumption that the validity of norms is based on the established horizon of norms of the given community (Walzer 1980). If the social critic ignores this horizon, then he or she stands in the position of an alien who is unable to offer relevant critical reminders of the shortcomings of community life. Without a sensitive consideration of the case, the social critic imposes on the community the rules of some foreign life-form, acting toward the community in an authoritarian fashion.

Iris Young and other Critical Theorists agree with the main idea of internally grounded social criticism, represented by both the practical philosophical and epistemological perspectives (Young 1990; 2007a; Oliveira 2010). In doing so they reject a non-historical invention of theory separated from the specific society, such as is produced by the mainstream of contemporary political philosophy, that is, mainly by liberal theory such as that of John Rawls. In contrast to the approach taken by Rawls, Young talks of the model of an internal critic, such as Albert Camus, George Orwell or Mahatma Gandhi, thinkers who are followed also by Walzer. She states: 'The social critic is engaged in and committed to the society he or she criticizes. She does not take a detached point of view towards the society and its institutions, though she does stand apart from its ruling powers' (Young 1990, 6). Critical Theory, according to Young, must reject attempts to form the kind of universal theory that would be isolated and alienated from society. Such an external point of view would run the risk of succumbing to authoritarian elitist dealing or at least to accepting responsibility for a seemingly neutrally worded expertise. The internal critic, on the other hand, is connected to unjustly repressed members of the community and may risk censorship or stronger institutional repression by governmental power, which may stand against a minority or even a majority of society, including the critics. Sources of repression may come from commercial, ideological, bureaucratic or other sources (Hrubec and Višňovský 2023), as we have seen in struggles against capitalist repression, for example. This can be a situation of the birth of dissent, exile, or even guerrilla resistance.

An important contribution comes from Axel Honneth, a former director of the Institute for Social Research in Frankfurt, who defines social criticism from the point of view of Critical Theory. Honneth's concept of social criticism differs significantly from that of Walzer but shares its basic structure of argumentation. (Honneth 2000a; Brink and Owen 2007). Honneth reformulates Walzer's conception using a different terminology, redefining invention as construction and defining interpretation as reconstruction. In doing so, Honneth differs from Rawls's constructivism in emphasizing the reconstructivism of Habermas. He also agrees with Walzer's prioritizing of an interpretative model of social criticism, recognizing the crucially important role of actors who are under pressure from social pathology and who formulate their criticisms. Honneth, however, has two reservations here.

First, Walzer's social critic, who reconstructs the conditions of the shared life of community members, is exposed to the pitfalls of relativism which have to be solved also within Critical Theory (Behhabib 1986). This internal critic derives his or her standards of judgment exclusively from the internal resources of the community, and tends to react to complaints against injustice based on other, external sources in an ignorant manner which confirms the status quo: This is how we do it here. Walzer's relativism is visible, for example, in the conclusion he draws in his book *Interpretation and Social Criticism*: 'It is a mistake, then, to praise the prophets for their universalistic message. For what is most admirable about them is their particularistic quarrel' (Walzer 1980, 93). However, this approach ignores the fact that criticism also requires an explicit corrective without which it falls into the relativism of particular disputes which can only be arbitrated based on temporal and local coincidences of the opinion of members of the society. Honneth adds that any real social criticism must be based on internal criticism but must formulate it in a way that also reflects some non-relative scale (Honneth 2000b; 1995; Sobottka 2013). For Critical Theory, which from its outset has followed the left wing of Hegelian thought, this criterion is represented by the identification of elements of emancipatory social development in the long-term perspective, from the past through the present to the future. The criterion of progress, especially the progress of reason, can be seen as a constructivist element, but only – and this is crucial – in the context of social criticism.

This basis of social criticism, according to Honneth, is necessary but not sufficient. Honneth's second objection to Walzer arises from the observation that the first generation of authors of Critical Theory did not give sufficient consideration to the formulating of solely internal and particular disputes of a given community within the overall frame of reasonable historical trends. Critical Theory in Honneth's view also requires the application of the second criterion, which is missing from Walzer's classification. The second criterion is conceived with Nietzsche's genealogy. Critical Theory sees not only positive and progressive elements in history but also negative ones that embody the social pathologies in historical regressive development (Allen 2016). An exemplary model of this approach is represented by Horkheimer and Adorno's *Dialectic of Enlightenment* (Horkheimer and Adorno 2007; Habermas 1987). As mentioned earlier, the concept of discovery defined by Walzer seems at first glance to be a variant of Honneth's genealogy. Honneth, however, rejects this similarity because he considers discovery in connection with the redefined positivist approach, while considering genealogy to be an approach separate from the mapping of pathological social norms.

In Honneth's view, Critical Theory requires that social criticism connect the earlier-mentioned components of construction, reconstruction, and genealogy. He states that it is desirable to link the formulating of the moral foundations of criticism with the construction of the progressive development of recognition in history, and thence to genealogical methodology, to show especially the paradoxes of society (Honneth 2000a; 2000b). However, Honneth's analyses and this approach in general contain several shortcomings.

2 The Trichotomy of *Critique, Explanation,* and *Normativity*

Problems with both Honneth's and Walzer's interpretations are apparent when we analyse them from the perspective of a more appropriate conception of social criticism and its elements. In the programmatic theses of Critical Theory formulated by Horkheimer and Marcuse and in subsequent texts we can already identify a more appropriate, even if not properly developed, layout based on the internal connections of three elements: an identification of problems by individual and collective subjects, a description of the related reality, and a derivation of desirable social norms. This approach is based on internal *criticism,* formulated by social agents, which makes it possible to focus attention on descriptive *explanations* of relevant topics and, on this basis, also on the formulation of *normative* conceptions of society. I consider the trichotomy of *critique, explanation,* and *normativity*, which has been partly developed and updated in the history of Critical Theory by Marcuse, Horkheimer, Habermas, Honneth and others, to be a more adequate specification of social criticism in terms of Critical Theory than other alternatives. Herbert Marcuse, for example, in one of the founding texts of Critical Theory from the thirties, speaks of the need to link critical, explanatory and normative moments using dialectical concepts that include the given reality, its cancellation, and the new reality as well (Marcuse 2009, 107). When using terminology that reflects both the content of terms and the approach of social agents to reality, we can say that these terms should not only include an explanation of the reality but also criticism of it, and a normative articulation of the new reality. An outline of this idea has also been formulated by Iris Young. She talks about ideals and arguments that have simultaneously to analyse the shortcomings of societies and to include a vision of the possibility of transforming them (Young 2000).

I will seek to articulate the trichotomy which is based on three basic approaches of social agents to a reality, specifically to a problematic reality and to its overcoming. The first approach is *rejection* (*negation*), the second, contrasting one is *adoption* (*affirmation*), and the third is *formation* (*creation*). Rejection represents a critical attitude of the social agent to a problematic reality; adoption focuses on those elements of the reality that crystallize as positive fragments of it in the background of the criticized parts of the reality; and creation concerns the development of the positive fragments of the reality into a set of desired standards and a normative complex of social arrangements. Nevertheless, this sequence of steps is not a one-shot approach. It is an iterative process through which individual actions are increasingly specified; it represents the dynamics of historical development. The trichotomy contains the basic elements which in their mutual connection perform the dynamics of social struggle, starting with negation of an undesirable situation, going on to identify positive fragments of reality, and subsequently developing them into the desired state.

Concerning the modes of discourse, traditional designations such as *narration*, *description* (including exposure) and *argumentation* can freely conform to the earlier-mentioned trichotomic approach to reality. However, a better linkage is provided by a more theoretically focused triad of terms derived from the concept of 'scribere' (to write): *proscription* which refers to denial, accusation or condemnation; *description* which relates to what exists; and *prescription* concerning what should be done. These terms have a common basis and thus make clear their mutual connection. Concerning the theme of social criticism, which is both theoretical and practical, they nevertheless have disadvantages firstly in their one-sided focus on writing, which emphasizes the theoretical side of criticism, and secondly in their lack of anchorage in social and political theory. The terms *critique, explanation* and *normativity,* by contrast, have both subtle connotations in social and political theory and also refer to its practical dimension.

In Table 1, I set out my further understanding of the trichotomy *critique, explanation,* and *normativity* in relation to the individual forms of Walzer's and Honneth's approaches. On the one hand, my division corresponds more with Walzer's differentiation of kinds of approaches, while on the other it refers to the line of thinking of Critical Theory which aims at linking critique with other approaches. In this respect, it comes closer to Honneth's analyses. Walzer covers various kinds of approaches relatively well but does so in a way that promotes only one kind of approach (interpretation) and rejects the other kinds. Honneth meanwhile employs a more complex analysis concerning the individual kinds of approaches and understands the need to reformulate them and integrate them into the overall framework of social criticism.

TABLE 1   Forms of approaches according to authors

Forms of approaches	Authors
Critique	Walzer – interpretation
	Honneth – reconstruction
Explanation	Walzer – discovery
Normativity	Walzer – invention
	Honneth – construction
	Honneth – genealogy

Walzer rightly prefers the kind of approach that emphasizes internal criticism that derives from the understanding of oppressed social subjects and from their historical and current problems, and not from external sources that can be remote from the needs and interests of community members and which can generate authoritarian practices. However, Walzer is not able to explain why internal criticism should be represented primarily by interpretation. The role of interpretation in human life is significant, as evidenced by Taylor's interpretation of human beings as interpreting and self-interpreting beings (Taylor 1985a; 1989). However, an interpretive approach to the world does not necessarily mean a critical approach. The interpretations may be various and may highlight the contradictions in reality, but this approach can confirm the status quo and show alternatives to be much worse than the current social arrangement. Furthermore, since internal criticism is not only a theoretical act, particularly in Walzer's version in which social criticism is a kind of social practice, it is not adequate to conceive of internal critique primarily as interpretation, because the common practice of internal social criticism often has a form which is not for the most part implemented in the mode of interpretation. Such criticism may well be deficient even if it is still internal, and concerning the other aspects, completely sufficient. Internal criticism should follow primarily from a rejection of negative phenomena, and should not simply represent the formulation of a point of view on an issue. The judge, who is noted by Walzer as performing an act of interpretation, speaks with members of the community, but his or her judgment may be uncritical and may confirm the status quo.

The two remaining kinds of approaches are explained by Walzer more convincingly, even if he rejects both of them. As I explained above, the second type of approach, discovery, explains the given situation and focuses on its description. The last kind of approach, invention, is not limited to passive acceptance of a given state of affairs but actively introduces new norms for a desirable future.

I would now like to attend in more detail to the problem that I outlined above in connection with Honneth's criticism of Walzer, and that consists specifically in the fact that Walzer's categorization of approaches favours only isolated internal criticism and does not gain any inspiration from other approaches (i.e. discovery and invention). As I have already explained, Honneth rightly warns of the dangers of relativism, which creates a particular voluntaristic point of view from this kind of isolationist internal criticism. Nevertheless, I will explain that Honneth's solution to the problem is also deficient. My analysis, together with more adequate approaches to the articulation of the problems, is summarized in Table 2, which lists the mutual relations between the elements of the trichotomy of social criticism. While the nouns in Table 2 refer to the core or essence of an approach, the adjectives complement this essence by listing its main characteristic.

Focusing first on reductionist approaches conceived separately, as shown in the left-hand vertical column of Table 2, we can say for example that *critique,* separately conceived, corresponds with Walzer's social criticism. Independently conceived *explanation* represents a reductionistic approach that occurs in representative form mainly in (quasi)positivist theories within the social sciences, i.e., in the current social science mainstream. Independently conceived *normativity* is usually a characteristic feature of contemporary normative theories in the sphere of moral and political philosophy.

TABLE 2   Mutual relations between elements of the trichotomy of social criticism

Combination of approaches	Critical characteristics of the approach	Explanatory characteristics of the approach	Normative characteristics of the approach
Critique	X	Explanatory critique	Normative critique
Explanation	Critical explanation	X	Normative explanation
Normativity	Critical normativity	Explanatory normativity	X

Axel Honneth rejects separate types of approaches, and in his general formulations considers it desirable that the elements of his version of social criticism should be linked. Various forms of interconnection of elements of social
criticism can also be found in formulations by other Critical Theorists, but the
roles and interconnection of the elements have not yet been developed.

While I have already mentioned that the terminology of the trichotomy *critique, explanation,* and *normativity* allows its use both in Critical Theory and
in the sphere of critical practice as well, further analysis requires a conceptual
trichotomic differentiation of the reality to which social agents relate. I specify
this differentiation as follows: a practical critique of bad reality, good activity (positive fragments and progressive trends of reality), and normative standards proposed in practice. Individual Critical Theorists differ as to which of
these elements or which relationships between them they emphasize. Nancy
Fraser, for example, agrees that it is crucial to establish the right sort of relationship between social description, social criticism, and normative theoriz-
ing (Fraser and Hrubec 2004). According to her formulations, an articulation
of this triple relationship points to how she understands Critical Theory. She
also distinguishes between the theoretical and practical levels of analysis of
the relationship (Fraser and Honneth 2003; Olson 2008). At the *theoretical
level,* she speaks of philosophical and social-theoretical reflections that allow
an explicit formulation of the paradigms of different theories of justice. This
theoretical reflection differs from the *popular conceptions* of justice which
provide members of civil society with various ideals that need to be analysed
by theorists to keep their theories from falling into non-situated standpoints
that would ignore the practical issues of injustice. These popular conceptions
are not often examined explicitly, and for the most part they are supported
only implicitly by agents of civic movements, social movements, multicultural
activities, etc. The conceptions refer to two directions, critically to bad facticity
with its causes of injustice and positively to possible solutions of injustice, and
from here to derived political requirements regarding justice. To be specific,
in modern society, the ideal of equality in popular conceptions represents
an exemplary model of good *facticity.* The possibility of developing equality
becomes an inspiration for the critique of wrong facticity and a source of
required norms. By explaining these issues, Nancy Fraser formulates her ideas,
especially in the form of *explanation* from which she derives *critical explanation* and *normative explanation* (Fraser 1996). These types of explanation may
have both practical and theoretical forms.

Fraser emphasizes the importance of linking the popular conceptions that
occur in practice with philosophical and social scientific concepts. Thus, in general, she differentiates Critical Theory from traditional theory which does not

require legitimation by citizens and which judges society in elitist and author-itarian ways 'from the top down', i.e. independently of society. Linking theory with practice, however, represents only the first definitional step of Critical Theory, because Critical Theory also of course requires a further step in the form of a critical approach in theory and practice. The second step in Critical Theory is already presupposed in the first step since practice refers here to the critical social agent who seeks to remove injustice. Our concepts need a start-ing point in social practice; they have to be derived at a basic level from pop-ular concepts. Because of that, they can become critical concepts (Fraser and Hrubec 2004; Fraser and Honneth 2003). Meanwhile, critical analysis of these concepts will allow for transcending the given reality and opening a space for critique which will provide criticism with immanence and transcendence. In this sense, Fraser in illuminating fashion begins her entire commentary in the form of *critique*, and not *explanation*.

However, this approach also has its limits because once Fraser moves on one of these levels, whether theoretical or practical, she starts from the form of *explanation* from which she then derives *critique* and *normativity.* More specif-ically, she then derives both theoretical and practical criticism of bad facticity and theoretical or practical political normative demands. This means that her meta-reflexive consideration of the connection of theory with practice pro-vides her approach with a priority of the form of *critique*, while at individual levels, namely theoretical and practical, the form of *explanation* effectively acquires primary status. The connection of the forms of approaches is there-fore incomplete because critique is realized only in the most general mode without specification in terms of *explanatory critique* and *normative critique*. Similarly, normativity occurs in the framework of the form of explanation. Nor, in the case of Fraser, does this appear with specifications in the form of *critical normativity* and *explanatory normativity*. Thus, the position presented by Fraser in her theory can be summarized as follows in Table 2: (1) *critique*, (2) *critical explanation,* (3) *normative explanation.*

Axel Honneth takes a position very different from that of Nancy Fraser. In his response to the theoretical connection of critique, explanation, and normativity, he proposes an analysis that explains the 'hermeneutic circle between normative premises and social-theoretical explanation' (Honneth and Hrubec 2007, 327; Honneth 1994b). This circle, which reminds one of the hermeneutical position in the sense in which it is employed by Gadamer, is considered by Honneth to be adequate. Honneth understands that each ele-ment of social criticism should not be isolated and should contain relations to other elements. Although he does not perform a precise conceptualization of these interrelations between individual elements, his standpoint in this case is clear and fully understandable. It also shows the parts of his argumentation on which Honneth places the greatest emphasis.

Where good facticity in social arrangements is concerned, Honneth argues that we should always consider facticity 'in light of the normative principles' contained in our analyses of society. He also says that normative principles should not be specified without social-scientific – i.e., descriptive or explanatory – analyses of the practice of social reproduction (Honneth 1995; 2000a). In this way, Honneth articulates a connection between elements of social criticism using the characteristics and forms of approaches that I described in Table 2 as *normative explanation* and *explanatory normativity*. Honneth thus formulates these claims, but as will be exposed, he can meet the claims only partially, as he incorporates only one of these two elements into his theory.

The situation is similar to his concept of critique. Here, however, he places the biggest demands on the interconnection with the other two elements of social criticism. He agrees that 'the critical experience of negativity ... is what puts a circle of normative formation of principles and social-theoretical analyses into motion ... not only in the genetic sense but also in the logical one, at the beginning of every social criticism is the diagnosis of negative social phenomena' (Honneth and Hrubec 2007, 328). He thus starts from the 'bottom', in an anti-authoritarian way, from the situation of the socially misrecognized. Firstly, misrecognition based on bad facticity, that is, on injustice and social pathology, leads us to try to formulate norms that will allow us to express the experience as misrecognition. Secondly, this conception of norms is at the same time related to social-theoretical assumptions of social reality in which good facticity is the starting point of practice that goes beyond this reality. Thus, while Honneth in the context of the second point again maps *normative explanation* and *explanatory normativity* (while in fact developing only explanatory normativity), in terms of the first point he discusses what I set forward in Table 2 as (1) *critique*, (2) *normative critique*, and (3) *critical normativity*. In the process, he gives priority to critique, and subsequently connects it with approaches of other forms. Here we come to the most challenging and inspiring ideas of Honneth's Critical Theory.

A problem arises, however, as soon as Honneth has to specify in more detail how to begin critique or to formulate normative critique. It may be said that analysis of the differences between Honneth's general demands on Critical Theory and his own realization of Critical Theory leads to the conclusion that he reduces critique and normative critique and replaces them with an approach of normativity because he underestimates the role of an agent of social change; then, he commits to normativity, i.e., to a transition from the priority of critique to the priority of normativity. Honneth considers that in the 20th century, the role of social agent in the theory was problematized so strongly that binding to this agent is now impossible. Therefore, he analyses in particular the moral conditions of social criticism, and in setting out his formal conception of morality, largely performs a transition from critique to normativity.

When Honneth discusses his ambition to develop the foundations of social theory which have a normative content, he formulates *explanatory normativity*. This ambition cannot be read as an attempt to develop social theory in the social-scientific sense of explanation that would be complemented by normative content. Here we have the *foundations* of social theory which is not primarily social-scientific. These foundations are developed in close relation to Honneth's announced moral content, and are especially morally normative. As suggested by the subtitle of the book in which he first tried to formulate his theory, 'Moral grammar of social conflicts', this is a *normative theory* that expounds a moral basis for social theory. The term social theory is to be read here primarily as a reference to the school of thought of *Critical Social Theory*, and not as a reference to social science theory. Critical Social Theory is then a general term that includes both empirical and theoretical moments, elaborated by an individual author who develops her or his version of Critical Theory with an emphasis on social science or normativity.

When Honneth talks about social criticism as a reconstruction which is a form of internal criticism based on the local community, he does not mean critique of particular social agents. The problem is that he rightly draws attention to the historical decline in the 20th century of collective subjects of change, especially the proletariat, but does not attempt to identify at least partially positive aspects of such contemporary subjects of change as social movements. For the most part, he merely replaces them with his own moral considerations in the normative terms of internal criticism. Such disillusionment, resulting from the failure of various subjects in the struggle for recognition in the 20th century, means ignoring the various unrecognized and misrecognized groups of people. With his moral reflection on the normative conditions of criticism, Honneth implicitly incorporates a critical approach of reconstruction into the approach of normativity which he complements with a neo-Hegelian and neo-Nietzschean background.

In clarifying his standpoint, he talks about the development of reason in history and presents the historic development of patterns of recognition as an explanation for the development of normative patterns. Such a position can be understood in two ways, either within the form of explanation or within that of normativity. This means that it is possible to consider either a description of norms– what I call *normative explanation,* or else analysis of norms themselves, i.e. what I call *explanatory normativity*. According to whether a preference is shown for the first or the second, the standpoint becomes either explanation or normativity. Honneth favours the second variant, normativity, and makes normative theory his priority.

Similarly, Honneth proceeds to examine the case of genealogy. The critical mapping that he provides of the development of negative normative tendencies, such as the neo-Nietzschean mapping of the spread of the negative features of instrumental rationality, can as in the case of Horkheimer and Adorno's *Dialectic of Enlightenment* be taken as a critical approach in four ways. Where normativity is concerned, we can either talk about what I designate as *normative critique* within the form of critique, or we can mention what I refer to as *critical normativity* within the form of normativity. Alternatively, with respect to explanation, it is possible to consider the choice between *critical explanation* within the form of explanation and *explanatory critique* within the form of critique. While Horkheimer and Adorno focused on critique in general and on explanatory critique, Honneth concentrates primarily on the partial negative norms (paradoxes of capitalism), and selects a critical normativity within the form of normativity.

This connecting of elements of social criticism does not limit approaches exclusively to one or another of them and provides some analyses of their relationships, but the entire project is carried out within only one form of approach, specifically within normativity. Although the normative part of the approach cannot be neglected, limiting the approach to this part is problematic. Honneth raises some initial expectations by promising an explanation of the development of standards that, within interdisciplinary and transdisciplinary research, evokes description in the framework of the social sciences. His references to social science literature appear to signify the form of normative explanation. However, he does not meet this expectation of description of the relevant facts. Similarly, Honneth does not deliver on the promise of critical analyses of negative trends as critical explanation or normative critique.

Critical normativity and explanatory normativity are important components of approach, but Honneth's conception of Critical Theory is made vulnerable as a normative reductionist approach by its limitation to only these two components. Of course, this is not a pure reductionism, operating under only one form of approach. It is a version of limitation which, in its inaccurate determination of relationships between forms of approach, gives one of them priority while the other two, critique and explanation, are taken into account only partially. Thus, we cannot talk about an interconnection of three components of social criticism, as Honneth states is his intention, but only about a normative theory which also includes certain aspects of critique and explanation. To what extent, though, is such a normative theory still a Critical Theory?

Additionally, it may be considered that any normativity is essentially a critical approach because the very fact of commitment of a normative approach means a recognition of interest in alternative social arrangements, and thus implicitly a dismissive detachment from reality. This appendix of normativity, however, suffers from several shortcomings, at least in terms of the weakness resulting from the speculative formulation of this critique, which is not based in a critique of concrete social agents. Like isolated normativity, this normative quasi-critique thus lacks a firm basis.

Concerning Table 2, Honneth's position may be summarized as follows: (1) *critique,* (2) *critical normativity,* (3) *explanatory normativity.* Though he starts in an adequate way from critique, Honneth in his theory then concentrates almost exclusively on normativity. This unbalanced focus on normativity, together with the underestimation of critique and explanation, has important implications for the formulating of Honneth's theory. His omission of the articulation of critique carried out by specific social agents and consequent lack of explanation of the empirical facts associated with the phenomena being criticized results in problems with the formulation of a desirable normative vision. With such a focus, the theory formulated in this way lacks a critique of serious problems, and at times leads to a reorienting of research into secondary subtopics. Honneth's absence of a sufficient critique and description of the social and political inequalities between North and South in the context of globalization processes is just one example of this problem.

Walzer's reduction of critique to interpretation, Honneth's partial reduction to normativity, and Fraser's partial reduction to explanation show that these authors are proceeding in the right direction but that their formulations remain at the midway point, and there are no guarantees that they will not go astray. Individual positions concerning the relations between elements of the trichotomy of social criticism become clearer if we also note other authors and the places they occupy in this arrangement. While Habermas in his early critical-theoretical writings at least tried to combine approaches of all forms, the late liberal Habermas focuses in his theory mainly on normativity, though sometimes also connecting it with the form of explanation. Michel Foucault operated in the modes of critical explanation and explanatory critique, along with Karl Marx and also Max Horkheimer and Theodor Adorno in their writings in the thirties.

I do not say that an adequate Critical Theory must necessarily apply all six of the approaches to the mutual relationships between elements of social criticism that I indicated in Table 2. However, I think that every Critical Theory should include *each* of the three forms of approach to carry out the three types of activity expressed conceptually in the Table using the nouns *critique, explanation* and *normativity*. The question of accent, expressed in the Table using the words *critical, explanatory* and *normative*, taking into account the relationships between the elements of the trichotomy, can then be a specification of the individual theory depending on the preferences of the author. However, reduction to one form of interpretation (whether critique, explanation or normativity) or partial restriction to two of the forms is a deficient version of social criticism that is not able to fully realize the requirements placed upon it.

3   External Social Criticism

The efforts of Nancy Fraser to address the above-mentioned problems open up further areas of investigation for us. Fraser is aware of the problem with Honneth's approach, but she does not solve it through a better-adjusted relationship between normativity and explanation. Examining the form of explanation, she differentiates between the more internally conceived approach of Honneth, who begins his interpretations by referring to psychological analyses and who emphasizes the psychological suffering of social agents, and her own approach, which extends into the public sphere and is more external or sociological. Fraser understands this more external approach as a characteristic that "is better suited to a Critical Theory that seeks to promote democratic struggles for social justice in a globalizing world" (Fraser and Hrubec 2004, 886).

At this point, it is necessary to distinguish between two meanings of the concepts of outer (or external) and inner (or internal), because mixing them up could lead to misunderstandings. Firstly, the terms internal and external can be understood from the point of view of internal or external criticisms, i.e., internally from the point of view of the respective social agents or externally based on opinion that assesses problems independently of the agents, allegedly from a 'neutral' perspective. Fraser and Honneth would agree here on the need to prefer internal criticism which comes either from popular conceptions, which according to Fraser are then developed by theorists, or from defining the moral conditions of the critique of misrecognized subjects, as in Honneth's analysis. But they do not agree on how this internal criticism of social agents can be processed from the perspective of philosophy and the social sciences. This perspective brings us to the second meaning of the terms internal and external. While Honneth prefers internal access through moral philosophy and the philosophical bases of psychology and microsociology, Fraser takes a more external, sociological and political science perspective which focuses on the public sphere and the role of social agents within it. But as I indicated, this external approach is still pursued in terms of the internal social agent.

Generally, all internal criticisms may be said to be connected by the view that rejection of injustice and the formulating of demands for justice need to stem, whether directly or indirectly, from a social agent within the community. Following Honneth, it is possible to say that struggles for recognition in a given community are based primarily on the articulation of people who experience misrecognition. Internal criticism requires an involvement in internal matters. This means that internal criticism prevents anyone from outside from intervening in an alienated, authoritarian way in the community's decision-making.

I would now like to make the difficult step to the external type of criticism. Although this attempt must start from internal sources, the possibilities here include considering not only the just-mentioned external point of view expressed from an internal perspective but also an external criticism in the first sense, that is, a point of view of an external kind voiced from an external perspective. In its very realization, the role of social critic provides the necessary degree of distance from the rest of society without which criticism could not be properly formulated in a reflected way. However, this distance may be more a problem of the perception of this state by the critic or his or her fellow citizens than a problem of its institutional segregation from the rest of society.

The weakest version of external criticism is that which merely takes the form of external criticism but is in fact internal criticism. External criticism in this case may be only fictive and pretended because the author is, for example, at risk of being persecuted for his or her internal criticism by censorship and repression. Externality can help here to make the critical voice allowable and to spare it persecution. A famous example is Montesquieu's *Persian Letters* (2011). These show that if the internal norms of the community are legitimate and very binding, then a social critic often cannot express a fundamental criticism without losing legitimacy with the majority of the population or without being socially punished or criminalized. But the critic can let someone else voice the criticism, and can also conceal his or her otherness by pretending that the author of the text is a different person (a pseudonym).

However, there are also stronger social pressures. Under certain conditions, the attempt to implement internal criticism can become unviable. Such a situation arises in the case of a community which succumbs to strong pathological tendencies and becomes Nazi, Stalinist, or McCarthyist, for example. This danger is especially great when the majority of the population shares these tendencies, often in a cultural context that obscures the unjust tendencies and mixes them with historical trends that were not problematic in the past. Achille Mbembe argues that people are currently being systematically manipulated by the societal system to such an extent that they are transformed into "ready-made abstract forms" that are "characteristic of the civilization of the image and of the new relationships that it establishes between fact and fiction, and capable of absorbing any content." (Mbembe 2017, 4) Under these and similar circumstances, social criticism becomes a weak voice of marginal groups whose opinions are heard in the local community – if at all – precisely as external, like the opinions sent home by an emigrant in a regressive age. Ultimately, such social criticism can only be a 'message in a bottle', and it is very uncertain that it will reach potential readers who will really identify with the criticism and consequently try to transform society. Max Horkheimer, Herbert Marcuse, Theodor Adorno and Michel Foucault were very close to this variant of social criticism in some of their periods.

Honneth is also considering external criticism. According to him, the conditions of internal criticism differ from the conditions of justifiable external criticism basically in the fact that the former is related to problematizing common injustices, whereas the latter is related to problematizing a more serious set of problems, specifically to criticizing the overall historical direction of society. While the first set of problems can be linked to the term "unjust", the second set can be specified by the terms "pathological", "anomalous", etc. (Honneth 2000b). In terms of other theories, it can be said that Honneth distinguishes between critiques of two kinds of injustice in this sense, reserving for the former the term 'injustice' and for the latter, the more serious kind of injustice the term "pathology". Pathology refers to the disturbance of the conditions of the good life which are not defined here substantively, since the plurality of different conceptions of the good life is respected, but only formally in their basic layout. The justification for this critique of pathologies stems first and foremost from society's need to admit a specific means of social diagnosis that would play the role of "therapeutic self-criticism." If deprived of it, society may probably be more stable in the short term, but in the long term it would deprive itself of the correction of its own development, which may go astray.

This diagnosis, which transcends the usual injustices within society, has special forms of expression in the given exceptional situations. If it is to go beyond this framework, it should contain transcending forms of expression which, on the one hand, take the addressee out of the context of his society, but, on the other hand, do not take her or him completely out of the reach of that society but on the contrary, lead her or him along a steady path from which it is possible to look at the society in question from a distance and to make a therapeutic self-criticism. Honneth speaks here of a revealing form of social critique, i.e., an external critique that reveals the world to us in such a fundamental way that we transform the values we still share with the pathologically formed society.

Corresponding to this is a form of expression that can take on a more artistic form, specifically, more narrative or essayistic, for example. However, this does not only mean style but also the subject of analysis, i.e., works of art or culture that can convey analyses of specific problems and themes of social criticism.

The topic of externality, however, becomes more complex if one asks the vexing question of who is really an external critic? Is not the real external critic rather an internal person who is part of the majority population which has adopted a pathological system, such as the Nazi regime? One can ask whether a majority – or a substantial part – of the population has not been alienated and has not taken an alienated, external attitude to itself and its culture. Although the social critic in this situation could act as an external critic, his or her value framework may reflect the internal value system of the society at the time before the pathological regime came to power.

It is also necessary to consider such misrecognized social groups as the Jews or the Roma in such a pathological society as, for example, the Nazi system. The experience of such groups would also be a source of criticism that the social critic could develop. To take another example, when a critic declares that black slaves are also people, he or she then brings an external element, the claim of the slave, into the value horizon of the slave regime. While we talk about internal criticism from the point of view of slaves, in terms of the society of the slave regime this is external criticism. Therefore, there is no reason why we should talk about externality in connection with a person misrecognized by the pathological society and a critic who criticizes the misrecognition and who is not linked to the pathological aspects of the society.

If it were a society or community in which its members were not the primary ones being misrecognized but the members of other communities that the first community misrecognized through imperial expansion, colonialism, or economic global exploitation to increase the consumerism of elites or even broader groups of the population, for example, then a critical subject would be the members of these misrecognized communities. In this case, a social critic should base his or her critique on the resistance of these subjects. If the critic's own society is moving in a fundamentally pathological direction, the social critic may prefer to take up the foreign value patterns of victim communities in other countries and also internal victims in his or her country: i.e., Jews and other social groups in Nazi Germany, for example, who were not recognized as German citizens by the majority of the population. Moving on to another example, I can mention this: when the critic says that black slaves are also human beings, he introduces an external element, the claim of slave, into the value horizon of the slavery community. From the point of view of the slave, we are talking about an internal critique; from the point of view of the slavery community, it is an external critique. Similarly, Walzer mentions a critic in the form of a judge who has studied in Paris or Oxford and then returns home to the periphery to practice (Walzer 1980). The judge brings the new impulses and external criteria of judgment formed during his studies but the judge should, according to Walzer, be guided above all by the desire to base his judgment on the norms of the local community and to link the newly acquired external norms to them. Walzer's interpretation is persuasive, but it overlooks the possibility of a situation of an unjust community undergoing a fundamental pathological development. Indeed, such a social critic, who has learned external values in his foreign studies and has a desire to understand the local community, would in this case be the ideal example of the critic his or her community needs. His or her external critique of societal pathologies could be guided by a victim perspective and an effort to shape a value horizon that is contextualized within the selected value patterns of the indigenous community.

The famous thesis "no one is a prophet at home" (*nemo propheta in patria*) has its origins in Jesus, who, in Nazareth, where he spent his childhood and youth, used this thesis to refer to his experience of unwittingly uprooting an originally internal social critic who had been rejected by the local people and, implicitly, to his dependence on a foreign environment outside the home (Bible, Luke 4, 16–30). Misrecognition by rejection can be refused outright or transformed into a struggle for recognition with the global scope of the critic's action, as seen in Jesus' statement: "Go into all the world and preach the gospel to all creation." (Bible, Mark, 16,15) Moreover, the global character of our time further strengthens the possibilities of this territorially unrestricted destination of social criticism, and, thus, weakens the polarization of home and world.

But the argument also has its flip side because the preference for foreign authorities is, of course, problematic. The imperial character of foreign interventions, which was legitimized in the Crusades by the very statement cited above, in turn often makes the domestic internal critics of the conquered territory a symbol of protest against foreign authoritarianism. Hence the demands for respect for local cultures in contemporary intercultural interactions which becomes a necessary condition for their dignified – or even physical – survival. Respect for local cultures or local systems in a global age requires transcultural and global rules of intercultural interactions, thus, a transcultural consensus on quasi-universal values.[1] The transnational and global nature of interactions, whether economic, social, cultural or others, should have a parallel in a territorially appropriate model of responsibility for the actions and behaviour

---

1   See my interpretation in Chapter 9.

of persons (Young 2006, 2007a). This requires a supranational and global legal order, which is currently the subject of efforts for socio-economic recognition not only in Western countries but also and especially in developing countries in the Global South.[2]

It may seem that the only real external criticism is criticism of all of human civilization, whose members pursue the pathological trends of development of the human civilization. In this case, the social critic would have to speak from a position outside of the human civilization. But if such a critic, intent on voicing external criticisms, tried to establish his or her approach firstly based on internal criticism which through no fault of his or her own was unrealizable, then from a methodological point of view even his or her external criticism would not in principle represent an external approach. The main criterion of justification here is the starting point in internal criticism, though due to historical and territorial circumstances, the subsequent attitude of a social critic may end up as external. If the starting point is internal, then the social critic can in an intercultural fashion monitor the long-term historical progressive trends in various communities, trying to articulate the criticism of social pathologies that people formulate in their practical struggles. In this way, the critic may exceed his or her territorial limitations, coming to inhabit the entire planetary crisis of human civilization. Using analysis of the long-term historical trends of criticism, the critic may succeed not only in maintaining his or her general standpoint but also in remaining located within certain historical stages of the development of certain communities and in the long run as well, may function within the bounds of internal criticism. This means to ask what tendencies and lines of development are progressive and which are not. In this sense, the above-mentioned types of external criticisms that come from internal sources and from long-term historical trends are in fact, in their intention, internal criticism. However, circumstances of serious crisis may in practice force the social critic to undertake external criticism. This may be oriented internally, but amid strongly negative circumstances, its internal character may for some time be quite uncertain.

To conclude, all internal critiques are linked by the view that, directly or indirectly, the rejection of injustice, the formulation of positive elements of reality, and the normative requirements for justice must be articulated from below. Critical theory can offer an appropriate beginning approach to this kind of task.

---

2   See my interpretation in Chapter 10.

Critical Methods

1   Transdisciplinary Approaches

In this chapter, I will focus on methods of critical theory and, more generally, of critical humanities and social sciences, which I will then apply in the rest of the book.[1] First, it should be noted that the individual critical methods have been developed in response to various research disciplines in their interdisciplinary and, in particular, transdisciplinary cooperation. Also, the complementary realization of all three aspects of the trichotomy analysed (criticism, explanation, normativity) requires, in current research, exemplification concerning the academic disciplines and sub-disciplines and their mutual cooperation. In an ideal scenario, philosophy would be set the task of providing a general (critical, explanatory/descriptive, normative) definition of the basis for research, and the social sciences (the term I use to include also the humanities) would concretize this research. In today's distorted situation in which the social sciences, especially sociology, in contrast to the conditions at the beginning of its establishment, have all but lost their normative pillar and are generally limited to a description of selectively chosen components of reality, to a description which is not thoroughly justified and often pseudo-objectivistically conceals support for the societal status quo or, at best, only the unreflected fragmentation of the empirical research, it is necessary, however, to define the tasks of philosophy and social sciences differently. If we want to exploit existing knowledge at least in part, we must be aware of this distorted situation and approach social sciences as disciplines with fragmented cognition, often without the benefit of a critical approach and without developed normative reflection. Therefore, social sciences are currently limited primarily to the description and explanation of fragments of reality. Philosophy, specifically moral and political philosophy, is often distorted as well, as it currently only supplements the state of affairs in that, in the absence of cooperation with the social sciences, it is limited to the role of mere isolated normative reasoning.

---

1   See a critical global comparison of research distortions which, in the last decades, analyses the situation in Western countries, India, Russia, Africa, Latin America, and China (Hrubec and Višňovský, 2023).

Many other sub-disciplines of practical philosophy, such as economic philosophy and cultural philosophy, are often developed within the scope of political philosophy and moral philosophy, which in recent decades have become perhaps the most significant streams of practical philosophy. One problem with many analyses, which is similar to the situation with the social sciences, is the fragmentation into various sub-disciplines or even into isolated analyses of individual problems. Unless incorporated into a broader framework of interpretation, analyses serve no purpose and disintegrate into mutually unrelated texts.

Therefore, efforts at a more satisfactory approach to research must face two challenges. First, it is necessary to deal with the fragmentation of research. Secondly, it is necessary to abandon the path of both the direct and indirect ideological focus of research via pseudo-positivist analyses which consciously or, simply as a result of their narrow specialist horizon, conceal their normative position. Efforts, though flawed, to address these two problems can be found in research in specifically grounded social philosophy, which envisages the further interdisciplinary and transdisciplinary development of such research via analyses conducted by the social sciences, as attempted in the programmatic documents of Critical theory by its founders (Horkheimer 2002a). As far back as the 1930s, at the University of Frankfurt, on the occasion of the establishment of the Institute for Social Research, where critical theory was formed and continues to be nurtured, the chair of a professor of social philosophy was set up; incidentally, this was the first-ever position for social philosophy in Germany.

This kind of social philosophy is primarily critically focused, facilitating the selection of topics for description and the development of normative arguments. Unlike critically focused political philosophy, however, its scope is considerably broader. While political philosophy generally only analyses the issues of freedom, equality, etc., in narrow political terms, social philosophy, within the scope of critical theory, has developed step-by-step criticism of fundamental social shortcomings, such as criticism of social and political injustice and criticism of instrumental reason from the beginnings of European civilization. This kind of social philosophy is not just one of the sub-disciplines of practical philosophy but is conceived as a basic and general path for the philosophical research of critical theory. It encompasses other sub-disciplines of practical philosophy, or at least their foundations, in its exploration. Even political philosophy is built on the foundations of social philosophy, even though many of its authors, aloof from critical theory, are often unaware of this in their writings or knowingly – much like legions of contemporary liberal authors –settle simply for the "free-floating" arguments of political theory, which are not anchored in any way. On the other hand, we should not underestimate political philosophy formulated in the context of social philosophy and conjunction with the social sciences, particularly political theory, because societal developments in the 20th century showed that ignoring or marginalizing the role of an actor, his liberty and participation in political organization, was associated with authoritarian regimes. For this reason, I discuss the need for a critical theory of society and politics.

The cooperation between social philosophy and various component philosophical sub-disciplines and social sciences largely depends on the central theme of the paradigm. While the paradigm of work was, for obvious reasons – like Marxism in its entirety – most linked with economic and sociological analyses, the paradigm of instincts largely responded to psychoanalysis and sociology. Similarly, the paradigm of communicative action is associated with linguistics and sociology, while its subsequent development in the theory of democracy and justice has led to cooperation with political science and jurisprudence.

The paradigm of recognition, one of the key concepts of this book, is developed on several different fronts. Although Charles Taylor is now developing his theory of recognition, in particular, concerning egalitarian communitarian and egalitarian liberal currents of thought, his early analyses drew on Marxist arguments whose traces can still also be found in his loose inclination towards authors and university circles associated with critical theory. He elaborates on his theory of recognition mainly in connection with moral philosophy and political science, while his main focus is on political philosophy. As the paradigm of recognition refined in critical theory seeks to overcome the flaws of other theories and the bias of current critical-theory paradigms, it is interlinked with more disciplines than other paradigms. Axel Honneth, in his critical theory, attempts to formulate a theory of recognition primarily as a project of social philosophy; in his analyses of the private plane of human life, he at least refers, in particular, to social psychology and sociology, while in his research of the public plane he picks up, to some extent, on other disciplines. However, his commitment to general social philosophy in the spirit of early critical theory is rather declarative, since it is in fact conceived only as a focus on moral philosophy and history of ideas. Honneth's theory had been flawed by the lack of political theory for most of its development which has been partially compensated in its late development (Honneth 2014; Honneth 2020). There are also important practical reasons for the emphasis on legal analyses in that, in the period since World War II to the 1970s, social and political movements achieved, in many respects, the progressive development of the law, and at a time when attempts are afoot to restrict these rights, social and political progressive groups are striving to reconnect with the earlier trends and reformulate the legal recognition that had been achieved to align it with the new global conditions.

In general, it is worth adding that, today, this does not and should not concern only interaction between the separate disciplines and sub-disciplines, which has been supplanted by transdisciplinary research into certain relevant issues that cut across established disciplines and sub-disciplines.

2 The Realism of Societal Development

Transdisciplinary research requires the interlinking of the different approaches and content of research, including concerning the arrangement of combinations of forms of interpretation, which I have analysed in the previous chapter. Research should center not only on reality itself, i.e. an explanation of reality but also on the reality of norms, i.e. the type of interpretation which I have called normative explanation.[2] This kind of explanation, normative realism, is a significant means of interpretation in critical theory and in other interpretative streams, not only in static terms, but also with regard to the clarification of historical developments; there is both a synchronous and diachronic aspect to research, or to the concept of history. Normative realism, which has nothing to do with realpolitik,[3] is not content merely with normativity, which the theorist constructs solely based on his own subjective beliefs about the correctness of certain ideas. Such subjectivistic normative idealism is overly influenced by the arbitrariness of the theorist since it is a priori a theoretical structure of, supposedly, the best norms, albeit as would be optimal from the point of view of a theorist, who does not take into account the practical development of norms in his interpretation. Moreover, this approach, for example, in most theories of liberal political philosophy, is grasped ahistorically. In contrast, normative realism is based on an explanation of the development of real norms in practice, and, on the theoretical level, draws on concepts of such practical norms. It provides a theoretical explanation of how norms are formulated in struggles for recognition of various social groups in the long-term historical development of specific practice (Honneth 2002, 88–109). In this respect, a critical theory of society, in which the concept of normative realism uses normative explanations, differs from the subjectivist interpretation of theories

---

2 Cf. Table 3.
3 Normative realism may involve moral, legal, political, or other. Realpolitik uses only the same term realism, but the content is different.

that do not take into account the real efforts of oppressed groups of people to promote norms in history.

However, read more narrowly – as moral realism among certain authors, such as Honneth and, in one part of Taylor's theory – normative realism, by design, constitutes explanatory normativity rather than any normative explanation. Although Honneth holds normative explanations to be of genuine importance, in his theory they are mainly just inspiration, as almost all of his attention in exploring normative realism is guided solely from a position of normativity. In general, in his interpretation of realism Honneth admits a similarity between his realism and realism in the liberal theory of John Rawls (Honneth 2015, 265–285), at least concerning one aspect, although if we characterize this aspect in more detail, significant differences come to light. Rawls differs in that, although he constructs his normative theory independently of norms in practice and draws on his own thinking about norms, he is also keen on a certain realisticness in his normative theory. He accedes to theories of realistic utopias, which, on the one hand, transcend reality with a certain normative vision, but, on the other hand, limit normativity by considerations of the realisticness of its design. This means that the degree of normativity in these theories is limited in the name of implementation. Rawls observes that "Political philosophy is realistically utopian when it extends what are ordinarily thought of as the limits of practical political possibility" and "the idea of this society is realistically utopian in that it depicts an achievable social world." (Rawls 1999, 6). The concept of a realistic utopia is constructed for "reconciliation" with the social world. However, this tenet of reconciliation, which leaves all conflict out of account, can, understandably, also be interpreted as political conformism.

Although Rawls keeps to this conciliatory definition of a realistic utopia, in the background of his reasoning lurks another idea, which, while not directly included in the definition of a realistic utopia, is an integral component of Rawls's political theory. At play here is not merely a pragmatic consideration of feasibility simply trying to avoid excessively cumbersome requirements and establish an adaptive solution but also the element of civil legitimacy which is another important part of Rawls's concept of a political utopia.

This element is also close to Honneth, whose moral realism, however, contains more than just legitimacy. Honneth does not just concentrate on the integration of normativity, first, into the framework of its potential for delivery, and, second, into the framework of legitimacy in the eyes of citizens, but also views it systematically within the framework of moral realism (Fraser and Honneth 2003, 238–247; Honneth and Hrubec 2007), which enables his theory (at least from a moral standpoint) to disengage from a given reality and achieve the desired structure or, theoretically speaking, potentially attain the interconnection of the descriptive and normative aspects of his theory. Honneth also declares that the descriptive part of the theory, the empirical facticity, should not be separated from the normative part, from normative considerations, since adequate normativity requires an understanding of society's real contradictions.

The norms analysed by Honneth could, at first glance, be regarded as particular norms, or more precisely as ethical norms rather than moral standards, i.e., as universal. However, their particular and universal nature is more complex. Honneth seeks to clarify this by reference to the distinction between types of current attempts to justify the ethical standards that tell us about human life (Honneth 1994b, 9–70). Although this explanation does not specify with any precision the particular and universal nature of the norms of moral realism, it does provide an inspiring basis for an analysis of the context of more exact assessments.

Honneth identifies the first type of justification in procedural ethics. The actual content of ethical norms is intentionally not provided here because the main attention is focused on rules for the provision thereof based on consensus among citizens seeking such consensus through their democratically formed will. Instead of a specification of norms, one more layer of specification is set which is defined more vaguely so that citizens have the space to make their own decisions about norms. However, this does not rid proceduralism of the need to set at least some basic norms for a value-driven community to create a framework of desirable procedures to which separate internal norms will apply. The theoretical definition of norms in this model is irrelevant and can be eliminated in favour of more haphazard – and perhaps more unjust – decision-making through procedures. Honneth associates this type with ideas developed by Habermas since the 1990s, for example (Habermas 1991, 100ff).

Habermas himself offers a further type of reasoning of norms. Already in his earlier writings, he presents a social theory (Habermas 1981) which can distinguish between desirable and undesirable norms based on weak or scant anthropology. The term weak anthropology derives its importance from the contrast with anthropology which is defined "strongly", which means that weak anthropology defines its subject not substantially, but only formally. Specifically, in Habermas's version it encompasses universal characteristics of human beings in the form of speech practice. The theoretical concept of universal characteristics does not encompass the exhaustive content of human speech practice but only a definition of the formal basic conditions of human life. Honneth points out three ills of other theories that try to eliminate formal anthropology. Formal anthropology wants to avoid both the difficulties suffered by the substantially defined communitarian theories which elaborate on the content of norms in detail and, therefore, become unacceptable for otherwise defined forms of human life, and also the difficulties of the libertarian conception of the individual which is not sufficiently grounded, is atomistically isolated and is insufficiently connected to other individuals in the community, or, as is the case in liberal theories, is not subject to analysis at all. Formal anthropology also wishes to hold its own compared to the concept of the boundless fragmentation of human life in many post-structuralist theories.

This second type of Habermas's justification of norms can also be found in a certain form in Taylor's theory. Taylor's anthropology, which he himself describes as formal anthropology, presents the basic conditions of human life in a value community as a criterion of desirable norms (Taylor 1989). This concept of reasoning is also close to Honneth who endorses it himself.

Nevertheless, formal anthropology is not the only kind of reasoning of norms employed by Taylor (Taylor 1989). Unlike universalistic philosophical anthropology, this third kind of reasoning, at first glance, can be considered a historical relativism. Historically formed values shared by a particular community are a criterion for assessing desirable and undesirable norms. A similar procedure is also followed by Foucault who works only with the historically limited validity of norms, specifically with validity limited to a given time and a given territory (Foucault 2018). Although Foucault does not seek the temporal and spatial limitation of this validity, he believes that more extensive validity does not exist.

Honneth correctly notes that his opinion is similar to Charles Taylor's, but in Taylor's theory he confuses two very distinct parts and views the similarity of his standpoint with Taylor's in exactly the opposite parts. Yet this issue cannot be explained by Honneth's terminological apparatus because in this respect, unlike Taylor, he does not offer a detailed specification of moral realism. To understand Taylor's position, it is first necessary to elaborate, in his own language, on the relationship between the universalistic and particularistic elements of his theory. On the one hand, Taylor tends to be regarded primarily as a communitarian-oriented author emphasizing context and, thus, on the particular values of a community. For this reason, he could also be criticized for the fact that his concept of community is not able to cope with overly particularist tendencies. However, as indicated by the mention of Taylor's formal anthropology, his theory also contains significant universalistic elements. Indeed, in his theory, universal norms occupy an important position from which other normative definitions are derived. Taylor distinguishes between moral ontology and what I would term contextualised ethics, a version of the realism of societal development. Moral ontology, which is based on philosophical anthropology, explains the elementary moral intuitions about human beings (Taylor 1985a, 15–44; Taylor 1989, 3–107). These intuitions testify to the universal characteristics of human beings in the relations of mutual recognition in a set of values in a community. Taylor finds this universal nature of human beings primarily in a transcendental linguistic community of human beings sharing certain values. The dialogic and value-enshrined characteristic of human beings facilitates the evaluation of and distinction between goods of varying importance. While some goods are relevant only to certain areas of an individual's life, others (the constitutive goods of a culture) may have long-term significance for the community as a whole.

An important fact is that this universal moral ontology, according to Taylor, is a requirement for the possibility of specific values or norms existing in practice. An interpretation of the historical formation of these values is the subject of Taylor's contextualized ethics which explains the value emergence and evolution of Western modern identity. While a description of the constitutive values of Western modern identity could be viewed as an explanation of substantial norms, in this analytical interpretation attention is focused on more general structures of these values. Therefore, these are moral values but the overhang of ordinary particular validity concerning the validity of the constitutive elements of modern identity makes them quasi-universal moral values of modern Western society. These actually existing values are of a formative characteristic for the self of the majority individual in modern Western society.

Taylor's contextualized ethics, although a kind of realism describing particular norms, actually transcend particularism in two ways. First, at their core, they include the universalistic kernel of moral ontology or, more generally, social ontology, and thus go beyond historical and geographical relativism. Secondly, they can be considered to contain the quasi-universalistic norms of societal development which are beyond momentary historical relativism because these are long-shaped and valid norms. The compliance of the norms of moral ontology with the core values of an analysis of societal development is a criterion of the correctness of the interpretation of societal developments in the sense that it is not misled by precarious particular norms, the fulfillment of which cannot realistically be expected. In the case of quasi-universalistic norms, we encounter long-enforced norms, the strong presence of which we can expect in people's actions rather than groping throughout the range of particular patterns of conduct.

Honneth's mistake is that he considers his interpretation to be related to the second type of reasoning found in Taylor, i.e., formal anthropology or moral ontology. However, there is some distance between them. Although he does not mention formal anthropology directly, in view of the theory of personality he observes that the conclusions simply "cannot simply be derived from an anthropological theory of the person" (Fraser and Honneth 2003, 138). As an alternative, he de facto defends the third kind of reasoning when he talks positively about historically shaped recognition, which is not "something given once and for all", and underlines "the number of spheres that are differentiated in the course of social development" (Fraser and Honneth 2003, 138). Therefore, Honneth's theory is a version of the third kind of reasoning. Honneth was misled by the fact that Foucault – extensively analysed in both a positive and critical light by Honneth in his early writings – also regarded the third type of reasoning as his own (Honneth 1988). The interpretation of Taylor's version of contextual ethics, however, differs significantly from Foucault's version in its internal structuring and by the separation of several levels of analysis. Although Foucault anticipates contextualized ethics, apart from his refusal of universalism he does not clarify them too closely. However, as Taylor's version of contextual ethics involves quasi-universalistic norms that have crystallized in an area over a long time, it is also possible to talk about them within the scope of a sub-discipline, i.e., formal or weak anthropology, which explores the different types of universalism. It may be added that, despite the name, it is actually not so much a sub-discipline of anthropology as a form of reasoning which is similar to the type of inquiry used in anthropology. Nevertheless, Honneth does not admit this in his terminology because he contrasts formal anthropology and contextual ethics or societal realism, and moves on, as I have mentioned, to the sphere of contextual ethics.

If I am now to summarize and interpret this study more satisfactorily, several types of analysis are identifiable. First, although Taylor talks about moral ontology as entirely universalistic norms, this is another case of a type of quasi-universalism because the analysed norms do not only stem from the biological properties of human beings but also from the very fundamental social characteristics which people gradually assumed in historical evolution when they were being formed as social beings.[4] The term universalism could be used only with a knowledge of these relationships in a very limited sense, i.e. for the characteristics of humankind at a maximum covering the timeframe of human civilization, namely in the order of thousands of years or maximally twelve thousand years, during which a certain constant, limited set of value-based dispositions of man in a community has held true. Therefore, in this limited time, we are referring to universalistic human characteristics. However, moral

---

4 Moreover, in the very long term, concerning gradually acquired properties, only quasi-universalism may also be discussed from a biological standpoint.

ontology is only a type of contextualized ethics or, more generally, the realism of societal development.

Secondly, at issue are contextualized ethics or, more generally, the realism of societal development which, based on analyses of the historical crystallization of constitutive values of a culture in a given period (in the case of Taylor and Honneth the modern epoch), also perform a comparative analysis of other cultures and arrive at quasi-universalistic norms embodying more than just the basic definition of human being as a critical being in mutual relations of recognition in a community. This interpretation shows the elementary conditions of human life concerning the need for the recognition of the equal rights of groups and individuals, while recognizing the right to respect for the specific differences of these persons as these normative conditions developed in human cultures. In this sense, these are more extensive norms than those which are the subject of moral ontology. These are more demanding egalitarian requirements in respect of the social, political and cultural participation of people in a community without inclining towards particular values of this or that culture or civilization. This level of norms, following due transcultural formulation, could therefore be transculturally acceptable for all human beings. The starting point is the consideration of a specific culture because everyone has to start somewhere and it is necessary to reflect on their own cultural background, but the path is a comparison of cultures and the result is transcultural norms.

Thirdly, a further level specifies the societal norms of the second level concerning this or that culture or civilization. This level is not transcultural but applies only particularly to a given culture. These are historically and geographically more limited quasi-universalistic values.

Quasi-universalism obviously has several forms and is not static. However, its dynamics, as outlined above in the chapter on social criticism, still need to be clarified. The development of quasi-universal values is determined by reflecting on errors and further development, and by criticism of shortcomings and the controversy surrounding such shortcomings. The problem of the crystallization of norms raises the question of how norms are transformed and how we recognize that desirable, rather than undesirable, norms are being asserted. Honneth considers transcending the current state of norms and overcoming them by transforming them or introducing new norms based on the inspirational dynamic of immanence and transcendence. Two ideas, which I have explained in other contexts, are combined here. First, because Honneth shares the position of moral realism, he draws on criticism of the actually existing norms of society. Second, as he primarily defends the position of internal critique, the transcending of the existing social order should not take place primarily through the external introduction of norms but through an immanent critical attitude (Fraser and Honneth 2003, 238ff) towards society, i.e., by means of internal challenges presented by individuals within the value-based order of society. According to Honneth, applying this reasoning means a "quasi-transcendental justification of critique in the structure of social reality" (Fraser and Honneth 2003, 244).

The interpretation of moral ontology and quasi-universalistic ethics also requires the presentation of one of Taylor's very important distinctions that is also linked to the analyses of ontology. This is the distinction between the ontological level and the level of defense, by which Taylor means political defense (Taylor 2003, 195–212). By making this distinction, Taylor wishes to explain why a separate analysis of the political level does not lead to an understanding of political issues and why ontological analyses are necessary. The terminology employed could lead us astray by implying a difference between the levels of philosophy and political science, but this interpretation would be misleading. Taylor analyses the two planes within the scope of political philosophy, with an emphasis on moral philosophy, although this overlaps with more general social philosophy. First, he formulates an ontological analysis focused on determining the relevant factors fundamental for an interpretation of the life of society. In contrast, Taylor's second level, the level of political defense, refers to the accepted political line (Taylor 2003, 195–212). A political line sets out the reasons for the correctness of individual or collective rights, freedom or goods. Further to this distinction, we can say ontology conceived in this way is ontology in the broader sense, as it comprises the two parts that I have just discussed: universalistic moral ontology and quasi-universalistic contextualized norms. This interpretation is complementary to the interpretation of political theory. However, I would like to stress that I make these distinctions in the interest of analytically clarifying the interpretation, not to separate the individual planes and their arguments entirely. Of course, the arguments are interlinked, just as social and political phenomena are interwoven in the life of human beings.

Nevertheless, an important point is an already indicated need for the fundamental redefinition of moral realism or contextualised ethics because the current interpretation is insufficient for two reasons. First, authors tend to reduce this kind of realism or contextualism solely to moral norms and only marginally touch on other norms in society. Honneth focuses on the development of the moral foundations of political philosophy, economic philosophy and legal philosophy but does not engage in proper analysis of the themes of these philosophical subdisciplines. Taylor provides a broader interpretation, focusing particularly on political philosophy, although even he does not elaborate on economic philosophy either, which becomes a problem when explaining socio-economic issues. At the same time, however, he reduced political philosophy, to some extent, to dealing with the cultural and ethical issues of different minorities. Therefore, it is necessary to extend the investigation and analyse norms and institutions of recognition to a wider scope, not only morally but also from the aspects of political philosophy, economic philosophy, legal philosophy, etc. In this respect, there is a need to develop general philosophy, or social philosophy as it is referred to by early critical theorists such as Horkheimer, so that it encompasses not only moral philosophy. As I already mentioned, although Honneth uses the term social philosophy, he reduces the original meaning of the potential broader reading of the term almost completely to moral philosophy. We should also redefine moral realism as social or societal realism, or more precisely as the realism of societal development. In this respect, moral ontology and both of the above types of contextual ethics should be redefined as normative ontology and contextual normative theory, and these should include not only moral and ethical norms but also political, economic, legal and other norms so that they are consistent with the normative structure of society as a whole, as discussed by the realism of societal development and, more generally, social philosophy, in cooperation with the social sciences, which, although in the form of requirements also exist in reality, but have yet to be assert themselves.

For my discussion in the next section, it is important, first, that a reduction to moral norms means underestimating or ignoring the majority of normative institutional structures (apart from moral ones), and thus taking the position of an actor supposedly acting almost independently of other institutions. These problems are particularly evident in the lack of articulation of economic and legal institutional structures that define the individual's sphere of action. Second, in mainstream normative philosophy, a normative approach is often reduced to an interpretation of norms and normativity which can be viewed only as a desirable norm, not as a norm grounded in reality. Realism, however, as its name suggests, incorporates not only desirable (yet non-existent) norms but primarily the reality of norms. Therefore, it should include not only the articulation of what is desirable but also a description of normative institutions and their structure.[5] The opening of these two issues requires articulation of the ambiguous relationship between the two factors that have a significant share in the formation of individuals and society: between the

---

5   Fraser criticizes Honneth for overestimating the importance of the moral order (Fraser and Honneth 2003, 278, 254ff; cf. Kocka and Offe 2000).

actions of the actor or social groups, on the one hand, and the real and desirable social and economic structures and institutions, on the other.

3   Structures, Actors, and Processes in History

Whereas, in the last decades since 1989, analyses of structures (particularly economic structures) have been played down due to the dominance of liberal political theories in favour of the idea of the actions of an almost isolated individual whose economic structural restriction of freedom remained almost unconsidered, more balanced attention is starting to be paid to the theme of structures again since the 2008 financial and economic crisis and disillusionment with the prevailing theory and practice (Balibar 2011, 17–22; Giddens 1984; Bourdieu 1977; Elster 1989).

The dispute between E.P. Thompson and G.A. Cohen is highly insightful concerning these themes (Thompson 1968, 9–10; Cohen 2000, 73–77). Thompson states that common experience provides a group of persons with the potential to form as a class. A class arises in a situation where a group of people create their own identity based on their own interests, not only between the individuals but also concerning the persons in contrast to which the group defines itself. On the one hand, it is recognized that social groups are largely defined by relations of production, i.e., the fact that the experience of persons is specified in this way; on the other hand, it must be noted that class consciousness is not specified only in this way.[6] Class arises only when people are conscious of it, which is dependent on several factors. Thompson introduces this reasoning in response to the interpretation by certain Marxists who talk of class as a thing. However, this interpretation forces social groups to reification and deprives them of the opportunity to act.

G.A. Cohen summarizes Thompson's argument with the proposition: "The connection between production relations on the one hand and consciousness, politics and culture on the other is not simple. There is logic in it but not law." (Cohen 2000, 74) This means that the economy does not inevitably or "mechanically determine" the consciousness of a social group. It should follow that class cannot be defined by economic relations alone. However, Cohen claims that this reasoning is flawed because a social group may be exposed to economic conditions that determine it without its being aware of its identity.

---

6   Here and elsewhere in this book, determination is viewed as necessary but by no means sufficient condition; I draw attention to this because determinism is sometimes interpreted as fatalism – fateful inevitability.

According to Cohen, this is also why Marx, in relation to Hegel's tiara "in itself" (*an sich*) and "for itself" (*für sich*) introduces the term "class-in-itself" (*Klasse an sich*) (Cohen 2000, 76, footnote 1). Already in Hegel's thinking, these terms describe two phases of development, with the first referring to potency and the other to realization or actuality. For Marx, class-in-itself is a social group, which, although determined by economic relations, does not yet articulate its identity, and therefore is not conscious of itself.

Nevertheless, the standpoint of both Thompson and Cohen shows signs of bias. Cohen is right in that class or an otherwise defined group of persons in that sense may already exist in a situation where it is not yet aware of itself. On the other hand, it should be noted that Cohen's quoted reference to Hegel means that it makes possible to say that a class formed in this way represents only the potential of full realization, rather than the fact of the class. This is because Cohen asserts only one reading of Thompson's tenet that class cannot be determined only by economic relations. But there is also the second reading which explains that the first reading envisages only partial class, class not yet fully developed, because it is only class in itself but not for itself. However, class may become a genuine actor only if it is aware of itself. Thompson, unlike Cohen, places more emphasis on the active, conscious actor and the opportunities it takes itself than on an entity that only subliminally responds to external stimuli. Therefore, Thompson comments only on class as a whole and not on its undeveloped part, which, however, due to the concept of *class*, are inaccurate observations. On the other hand, Cohen, however, understated freedom and choice, although they are indeed limited, and places too much emphasis on determinism. In his later period, he realizes these limits and makes an ideological shift.[7] Based on an analysis of the collapse of the working class

---

7 Awareness of these dilemmas is exemplified by the opinion of G.A. Cohen, who, in his late period, arrived at a position extending beyond his early structuralist-functionalist theory. Although he does not directly synthesize his early and late positions, the standpoint in his later period can be interpreted as the integration of his earlier interpretation of the structures within the paradigm of work into the subsequent broader interpretation of structures and actions within the concept of intersubjectivity which leads to the paradigm of community and recognition. He emphasizes the mutual relations of action within the institutions of the community between equal individuals, i.e. in contrast to the relations of action of largely isolated individuals in minimal and insufficiently egalitarian or completely non-egalitarian institutions. In terms of the trichotomy of criticism, explanation, and normativity, Cohen's late position is important normative compensation for his early position because even though Cohen always adequately emphasized social criticism, his early, almost entirely descriptive and explanatory interpretation of the structures did not analyse much the importance of norms. Cohen's later view can be regarded as a position with the potential to redefine and incorporate arguments on structures into his later sketch of theory which can be

as a subject of change in the 20th century, he concedes that entities are not economically determined as much as he previously thought. In this context, he speaks of the need also to consider normative influences that transcend economic determinants, such as critical analysis of the influence of nationalism or religion (Cohen 1995). Therefore, he starts placing greater emphasis on the possibility of the conscious choices of actors and develops a normative theory incorporating the formulation of a normative social order that is not completely determined.

Thompson, who wants to avoid the reification of class in economic givens, talks about class as a free conscious process. Cohen understands this objection but knows that the consciousness and freedom of a given class are largely determined and limited by the system, and therefore emphasizes the primary definition of class by means of economic structures. He also asks whether it is more appropriate to say that class passes through a specific process than that it is that process.

Thompson is mistaken because he does not acknowledge that there are also unconscious classes; he does not expect them to be rooted in a structure in which their actions and subsequent consciousness occur. Thompson underestimates precisely that which Cohen overrates, i.e., he underestimates the economic conditions behind opportunities for the freedom and choices of different groups and individuals. Although this underestimation can be found primarily in liberal theory which clearly emphasizes individual choices, the tendency towards such thinking has expanded significantly in other aspects of political and social theory in the past decades.

This discussion distinctly points to two extremes. On the one hand, there is the concept of class as a thing, as a static structure; on the other hand, there is the voluntaristic concept of class as a conscious act, a criterion of which is the existence of consciousness thereof and not economic conditionality. Although Cohen and Thompson do not reach so far in their arguments, their opinions are indicative of such contradictory interpretations.

The question is how to synthesize the two lines of argument. Honneth's recognition theory is the first, albeit inadequate, step towards this connection. It is based on internal, specifically intersubjective, sources, and therefore it primarily emphasizes the aspect of the actors. This starting position for actors intuitively

---

described as critical egalitarian communitarianism when he develops his theory of equality and community against a backdrop of criticism of libertarianism and liberalism. A contribution to this synthesis is also made by his analyses of the relationship between inclusive and restrictive materialism which show the interaction of structures and actions of individuals and social groups. (Cohen 1995; Cohen 2000; Cohen and Hrubec 2009, 751–759).

and consciously acting in the struggle for recognition allows him, based on such struggle for recognition, to identify institutions in which the patterns of different types of recognition were gradually established (Honneth 1996). Honneth is evidently not inclined to either of the extreme positions in the dispute on structures and conscious processes behind the actions of actors. First, although he follows up on Thompson's analyses, he is aware of the fact that the struggle for recognition is not always conscious but sometimes takes an intuitive and emotional form. Second, in his analysis of social pathologies, while he is opposed to structuralist interpretations, he does identify causes of reification in pathologies originating in intersubjective relations that are embedded and articulated in various institutions of misrecognition, i.e. institutions that Cohen would call structures (Honneth 2008). Therefore, although Honneth himself does not integrate the idea of structure into his theory, these two points show that he took a step towards the synthesis of both lines of argument.

The problem with Honneth's approach, however, is that it merely tends towards synthesis without engaging in synthesis itself, and the above-mentioned problem that, in his moral realism, he conceives of institutions only as moral conditions of actions, and does not identify the economic and other social causes or conditions of these moral norms. Although Cohen's early structural functionalism is not without its flaws, as I have mentioned above, his theory, in comparison with Honneth's theory, contains the necessary analysis of economic structures that are not only the result of action but, at the same time, are also conditions indispensable for further action, where the struggle for moral recognition, as described by Honneth, takes place. This framework is the necessary but insufficient determination of institutions of recognition and the action of actors therein.

Another (this time quite deliberate) step towards synthesis in the interpretation of the structures and conscious actions of actors is taken by Iris Young (Young 2001, 1–18; Young 2002, 410–428), whose efforts to integrate these interpretative lines are crucial to the whole argument. On the one hand, Young discusses the actions of actors and is aware of the importance of the possibility of their free speech, for example. On the other hand, she criticizes the libertarian approach to freedom for ignoring the fact that people cannot express themselves entirely freely, as they are limited by structural inequalities that are created or co-created by social institutions. This criticism of libertarianism is based on the overestimation of the individualistic aspect of persons, which can also be found – although to a lesser extent – in liberal theory. For example, although John Rawls, in his theory, speaks of the importance of the basic structure of society in which individuals act, his interpretation deals with the fundamental systemic limits of individual action only marginally.

In her critical theory, Iris Young draws on the post-liberal concept of Jean Hampton, who warns against the potential tyranny of the state and emphasizes the freedom of individuals, and who also analyses the oppression of individuals, by reference to certain social and economic institutions of the regime (Hampton 1997). Young argues:

> It is certainly misleading, however, to reify the metaphor of structure, that is, to think of social structures as entities independent of social actors, lying passively around them easing or inhibiting their movement. On the contrary, social structures exist only in the action and interaction of persons; they exist not as states, but as processes.
>
> YOUNG 2001, 13

Therefore, it is necessary to analyse the economic and social structures while recognizing that the concept of structures is criticized as static and unable to explain changes, and, thus, we need to focus on understanding structures as a process.[8] For this reason, she explains structures as processes – not random processes but structured processes and structures in a process.

Structures, however, cannot simply be grasped as a direct result of the actions of actors. The formation of structures has caused deeper than just the direct, individual, and conscious action of actors. Manifestations by individuals are not absolutely unlimited and free because individuals always find themselves in certain conditions that are defined by certain structures. Therefore, they act in an environment that is usually the result of long-term and collectively shaped structuring, with conscious and unconscious, coordinated and random components. This kind of social structuration is called by Jean-Paul Sartre, followed by Iris Young, the practico-inert (Young 2001, 13; Sartre 2004).

The relationship between the actions of actors and structures is, therefore, a complex relationship, the interpretation of which involves transgressing the unilateral interpretations of both structural functionalism and the theory of action of the individual actor, developed in particular by liberal and libertarian theories. Emphasizing the excessive influence of structures or of free action of individuals leads to illusory views either of the escalated determinism of the system or of concepts of the arbitrary acts of individuals. An adequate view is an interpretation of the actions of social groups and individuals in structures of

---

8   In her interpretation, Iris Young builds primarily on Blau, Giddens, Sartre, and Gewirth (Cf. Wendt, 1987, 335–370).

society and economy; such actions contribute to the formation of these structures but only to a limited extent due to their long-term and socially situated
nature. This processual version of practico-inert structuration encompasses
both conscious and unconscious acts, and its concrete form is determined by
the dynamics of efforts toward mutual recognition of social actors and by the
historical and socially contextualized structures of institutions of recognition.

Let us now turn to a general differentiation of four planes of historical interpretation linked to the articulation of the relationship between the subject
and structures. Of course, everyone can recall connections to historical materialism and other emancipatory currents (Honneth and Jaeggi 1977.) but the
past period has shown that many of the earlier key methodological disputes
have largely lost their relevance and the focus has shifted to other aspects of
the analysis of critically focused social theory. An appropriate approach is an
updating and a greater degree of generalization of the supporting aspects of
the materialist theory of social development (*die materialistische Theorie der
sozialen Evolution*) from the perspective of critical social theory and other critical social currents.

In the following interpretation, I follow up on analyses of already mentioned moral and societal realism, or more precisely on its historical dimension. While the actual content of historical development is discussed primarily
in the seventh chapter on recognition, here I will make a general distinction
between the planes of historical interpretation.

The first plane is the interpretation of the actions of group and individual subjects seeking recognition. This kind of interpretation is convincingly
presented by Honneth's normative theory of intersubjective relations in
response to E.P. Thompson, although I will engage in reformulation and will
not draw solely on the moral foundations of social theory but on the broader
field of social theory. In this way, I will add further normative social aspects to
moral theory and extend the descriptive and critical components of the theory. This plane of interpretation, although mainly focused on the conscious
activities of entities, also affects other alternatives, as well as their emotional
behaviour. Activities may, therefore, be both conscious acts and the unconscious behaviour of actors in the implementation of various activities, of the
realization of which they are conscious.

The second plane is the interpretation of social institutions which have
long been shaped by the actions of subjects; I take into account practico-inert
structuration which points to the structural conditionality of the actions of
subjects or to the complex relationship between subjects and structures. Here,
Honneth's theory of moral realism and Taylor's contextual ethics offer a model
interpretation insofar as it is linked to the supplementary precondition as that

applied on the first plane of interpretation, in the sense of a transformation extending into wider social theory.

The third plane is the interpretation of social institutions that primarily chart (also in the long run) economic institutions. This interpretation focuses on economic structures in economic realism. A model example here is Cohen's early theory based on the concept of economic structures which are the causes, contributory causes, or at least conditions of moral and other norms, structures, and institutions. While the second plane is normative, the third plane is the material basis for norms, with the norms, in return, also able to influence that basis (Cohen 2000, 364–388). The second and third planes together form an integral unit, which includes social institutional structures. Their influence on the actions of individuals and social groups is different, however, because normative institutions are a more loosely shaped structure of societal expectations, i.e., only a "context, not a straitjacket".[9] It should be added that economic structures are linked with economic norms.

The fourth plane is the interpretation of the technological and other structures of human civilization which are material conditions for the other planes of structuring and action. An inspiring example of interpretation here, despite certain limitations of this text, is Horkheimer and Adorno's *Dialectic of Enlightenment,* which charts the history of the negative effect of instrumental reason from antiquity to World War II (Adorno and Horkheimer 2007). While other planes of interpretation involve arguments on intersubjective theory and, in that framework, are linked to the theory of action subjects and their feasible opportunities to have a relevant impact on societal structures, the fourth plane of interpretation, focusing on complex development, reveals very long-term historical developmental trends and structures of human civilization; although they also result from the actions of subjects, these actors have so far had only a minimal direct and conscious influence on such trends and structures.[10] Therefore, it is a kind of analysis that I present as an analysis defining the boundaries of the subject of my research in this book and inserting such research into the broader topic of scholarship. It provides my arguments with context and a definition of the conditions in which these arguments exist.

---

9   A conceptual interpretation of this issue based on a practical example is provided by (Scott 1985, 198ff).

10   Although individuals and groups of persons contributed significantly to the emergence of the telephone, for example, this invention was preceded by numerous other technological innovations, and in this respect, the invention of the telephone was a continuation of previous developments rather than an entirely new technological innovation.

However, there is another reason why I address this fourth plane of interpretation. The main focus in the analysis of this plane is devoted to Adorno and Horkheimer's *Dialectic of Enlightenment*, one of the important works in critical theory and which highlights important dangers and risks in the development of Western civilization and, to some extent, the whole of human civilization. Although Adorno and Horkheimer's diagnosis is not able to step beyond the confines of subject-object approach, it points out major shortcomings stemming from this deficit framework of Western civilization in the paradigm of work.

The boundaries between the four types of planes are not absolute and in effect is used to enhance the transparency of different types of social institutions and structures that are not isolated but mutually permeated. The first plane charts the actions of individual and social groups which is the source of all the activities, institutions and structures of the other planes of interpretation. The other planes could not have been created at all without the actions of the subjects. But this does not mean that, as soon as they were created for the purposes of practico-inert structuration, they could not significantly influence and limit further actions of subjects. Individual forms of structures are of a long-term nature which the actions of individual subjects and social groups can change only with great difficulty. For example, the existence and development of a normative ideal of equality or freedom and its enshrinement in the normative institutions of modern society may be changed temporarily in the wake of fundamental reforms or revolutions but in the longer term it persists in less institutionalized models of action and after the temporary duration of regimes that suppress this ideal, the influence of this ideal is reasserted. However, this ideal may lose momentum or take on an even bigger or completely different kind of power after the transformation of modern society or after the ascent of a different kind of society. Similar to this is the existence and development of longer-term economic structures that are associated with the existence of particular social systems, such as capitalism. It is not a completely determined historical development, nor is it a completely random development according to a relativist interpretation. The very complex development of societies and civilizations throughout history has so far only allowed us to make basic theoretical abstractions of empirical knowledge of history with its stages.

The various types of structures in different historical periods are interdependent, so – to provide an extreme example for the sake of continuity – the primordial level of developments in technology and the "economy" was inconsistent with the modern structure of parliamentarianism. In contrast, the current level of technological development does not guide the majority population back to a primordial level of development in the (pre-)economy or norms of society. Nevertheless, the individual planes of structures are not entirely strictly interlinked but have relative autonomy. As already mentioned, this means refusal of both absolute randomness and relativism, on the one hand, and fatalism, on the other. From this perspective, the planes of normative structures and economic structures need not correspond completely but may to some extent be developed at different levels. Individual planes may relatively differ in terms of whether they develop progressively or regressively. The progress of one plane may coexist with the regression of another plane. On the whole, this means complex historical tendencies which may be a combination of different or unevenly advancing historical trajectories.

This development may entail either only gradual structural systemic modifications or even the replacement of the system itself, because in long-term historical trajectories changes sooner or later lead to the replacement of the system. This need not be just the classic polarity between revolutionary reversals and progressive reformism. The question, after closer examination, is based on considerations of the problematic features of both reforms and revolutions. Reformism, which, with slight modifications, affirms the entire system, or even its current structures, allows for partial positive changes without a commitment to fundamental changes, but its disadvantage is that the changes are only slow and may contain substantial shortcomings in the structure or system, or, in the unsecured ordering of the current situation, may prompt a return to earlier stages of development. As for revolutions, while some revolutions may result in real positive changes in structures, or even in the entire system, other revolutionary events may only give the appearance of systemic (or at least structural) changes without actually giving rise to genuine changes, or changes may be made only during the revolution, after which the old order is reinstated. Alternatively, there may be real regime change but the regime established does not meet the ideas and expectations because of which the revolution was carried out, which means that the desirable revolutionary change did not materialize. In contrast, there may be certain gradual comprehensive transformations that can result in bigger changes in the structure and system. For this change between transformation and revolution, Nancy Fraser introduces the term "affirmative transformation" (Fraser 1997, 11–40). Although the structure or system is transformed by way of reform in the longer term, fundamental change is genuinely introduced.

Moreover, there is no need to consider only one model. For example, universal basic income, which, although it is only one of the partial solutions, and may remain as such, could, if reinforced, deliver an impact of such magnitude to system structures that the system could gradually change. The payment of regular social or civil benefits, which would be entirely unconditional for all citizens, and would be in such an amount significant enough to cover citizens' basic and other needs, could achieve such an altered quality of life for many citizens that even the system could be redefined. Of course, this is especially true of systems in which structures are deliberately introduced strategically in the form of foreshadowing institutions that lead to system change. Then, this kind of change is a revolutionary change. In this sense, in reference to our book *Social Transformations and Revolutions*, I use the term *transformative revolution*, where the term refers by the noun to a core and by the adjective to a complementary characteristic: it is a fundamental, revolutionary change implemented gradually, in a transformational way (Arnason and Hrubec, 2016).

This opens the question as to what we currently consider a revolution. According to G.A. Cohen, four basic definitions have been established in history (Cohen and Scannella 1997, 38–42; Cohen 2000, 101–115). Revolutions have been primarily conceived as a change that is: (1) violent, (2) unconstitutional, (3) sudden, and (4) comprehensive. These characteristics of revolution are relatively independent and historically it was often enough only for one of them to exist to talk of revolution. Some revolutions may, thus, also take the form of a non-violent, constitutional or gradual change.

As regards violence and constitutionality, the overthrow of tyrants and unjust regimes established by military occupation, for example, which cannot be successfully resisted non-violently, there is the possibility of legitimate violent change. For example, the violent resistance during World War II is generally regarded as legitimate and just, including the rejection of the unjust legal order established by the Munich Agreement, which is regarded as invalid *ab initio*.

Another example is the October Revolution of 1917, which also took place violently, unconstitutionally, suddenly, and comprehensively; from various aspects, the subsequent development was so inadequate that, after the collapse of the Soviet Union in 1991, there was a return, in many respects, to the situation from which the revolution had been born. In this case, it is clear that from the longer-term perspective, certain revolutionary changes and established new systems are only temporary stages, despite transforming significantly the lives of many individuals and social groups and become the main drivers of international and national policies for many decades. The actual comprehensive implementation of fundamental change that is not removed over time is a more challenging project.

Cohen says that past revolutions were often the result of en-masse open oppression and exploitation which then, therefore, were also violent, unconstitutional and sudden, whereas later the system was introduced and established in what was usually a more complicated and ideologically more covert manner. However, these classic revolutionary characteristics also applied to the Romanian dramatic change of system in 1989, for example, but not to the Czechoslovak change, which, although carried out suddenly, was non-violent (velvet) and basically constitutional. And it did not meet much the expectations of citizens who had their own notions of comprehensive systemic change during the 1989 change and the following years.

I believe that, while the ideal is to remove an unjust system quickly, peacefully, constitutionally and comprehensively, the main characteristics of successful transformation to a more equitable arrangement lie in comprehensiveness and sustainability. Such a change requires the intensive preparation of conditions for implementation within the scope of both short-term and long-term obtained value-based patterns in the struggle for the recognition and justice of individuals and social groups. From this perspective (i.e., in terms of the realism of societal development and its short- and long-term normativity), it is important, yet only secondary, whether the process is transformative, revolutionary or a combination thereof in the form of transformative revolution, as the primary focus on the time aspect of the change could lead to superficial pseudo-revolutions or pseudo-transformations.

At the end of this chapter, it is possible to concretise the approach to history and to outline selected developmental tendencies, which will then be analysed later in the book. If we look at the issue from the empirical and conceptual perspectives of the three basic ideologies of conservatism, liberalism and socialism (Freeden 1998; Heywood 2021), it may be said that the conservative exercise of traditional values and interests has been displaced by liberal values and interests in the West and some other countries with the gradual assertion of capitalism in modern times in recent centuries. However, this long-term development is of course not linear. The promotion of liberal and partly socialist tendencies during the French Revolution, for example, was followed by a conservative counter-revolution but this was subsequently reversed again by liberal trends. The gradual assertion of capitalism with liberalism had a series of cyclical reversals, just as the assertion of feudalism had before (Hobsbawm 1996a; Hobsbawm 1996b).

A closer look can chart the development within one system without overthrowing it, but with its various cyclical crises and eras. In this way, we can link the development of capitalism in Western countries in the era from World War II to the 1970s with the tendencies of the welfare state (social and socialist demands of the workers, social movements, student revolts, etc.), which attempted to correct the anti-social trends of the World War II and the previous economic crisis, and in competition with the socially oriented Soviet Union.

Then after three decades (as a consequence of the oil crisis and the financing of the Vietnam War, the abandonment of the gold standard, and the introduction of speculative capitalism), we can describe another era of tendencies that were characterised by a reduction in the social aspects of development. These tendencies began to gradually establish themselves in Western countries from the 1970s onwards, especially in the 1980s with the formulation of neoliberal concepts and practices (Kotz 2017) when modest liberal theories (reflecting some of the demands of the waning post-war welfare state era) began to be seen as the maximum possible in the eyes of some people. These trends then, after the collapse of socialism in the Eastern Bloc in 1989–1991, resulted in neo-liberal triumphalism and the global expansion of capitalism in the 1990s. Since liberal tendencies in a general sense have largely asserted themselves in their libertarian (neoliberal) version and significantly damaged the welfare state, in the following decade from 2000 onwards they sparked protests against neo-liberal capitalism, culminating in the 2008 financial and economic crisis. This marked the end of an era after three decades, but the consequences of which still define our present.

However, at the beginning of the next era, in the following decade in the 2010s, there was no fundamental reflection on the causes of the crisis and on the establishment of a new, more equitable order. As socialism was still marked by its previous crisis (1989–1991), populist, conservative and social conservative politics began to assert itself as the only strong alternative to liberalism and neoliberalism in real politics (Jones 2023; Hazony 2022).[11] This has not been a replacement of the whole liberal system in a broader sense but only of some of its dimensions. The newly established ordo-neoliberalism[12] has preserved some aspects of global neoliberalism and ushered in a new era with defensive demands for strategic sovereignty through greater closure of regional blocs in interactions of global confrontation. Here, conservative and neoconservative tendencies can be identified that put limits to the previous expanded neoliberal and liberal trends.

In the decade of the 2020s, this structural change establishes regional variants of strategic sovereignty primarily in the major powers of the USA, China and Russia, and partly in the European Union and other countries and regions of the world, implying ambivalent efforts to secure basic regional

---

11   Since approximately 2016, the USA has been exemplary of these populist and rhetorically socially conservative tendencies, which have also emerged in other Western countries since this period. In the USA, they grow out of the dominant socially conservative self-identification of citizens in recent decades.

12   Ordo-neoliberalism is a neoliberal order enforced by the state.

self-sufficiency vis-à-vis global competitors. This approach opens up space for multiple future scenarios.

On the one hand, it may positively provide some certainty and lead to a strengthening of the trend of a bigger regional self-sufficiency within a global cooperation, but, on the other hand, a bigger closure of regions within a global adversary would be de facto a delay in the resolution of global tensions, which in the coming period in the late 2020s and 2030s may even result in more extensive conflicts than have occurred from the World War II to the present (more intense or more extensive wars or a world war localized in more places in the world), as I explain in the last section of Chapter 10.

Without a timely solution, it is probably only after this period of conflict that the opportunity for establishing a new structural, and perhaps deeper, systemic change that would provide the basic framework for socially just arrangements within national, regional and global frameworks could come in the next era. Thus, the neo-socialist alternative (democratic socialism or socialist democracy in its updated version) is waiting for a larger crisis of its competitors, after which it could once again offer its newly articulated starting points in several nation-states, in some regions and macro-regions, and, with a larger planetary consensus, also at the global level. In the long run, socialism can be expected to make use of the positive elements of liberalism and conservatism but to update and overcome them in its own system.

This is not a fully determined development, but rather only a part of usual cyclical tendencies within one system in the medium term and a potential subsequent change of the whole system in the longer term. However, given the accelerated historical trends, the cycles may shorten. Below, I outline historical eras from the 1930s to the mid-21st century in Western countries, with significant global influences:

Conservative nationalism

    1930s and 1940s – the economic and political crisis and the world war

National welfare state

    1950s – post-World War II development of the welfare state

    1960s – welfare state

    1970s – multidimensional crisis

This era had its parallel with the development of state socialism in the Eastern Bloc, and in some other parts of the world partly dependent on these developments.

Globally promoted neoliberalism

    1980s – the rise

    1990s – triumphalism

    2000s – criticism, the 2008 crisis

Regional strategic sovereignty
  2010s – ordo-neoliberalism, populism, social conservatism
  2020s – strategic conception and sovereignty
  2030s – potential major crises and armed conflicts
Conflict scenarios: ongoing conflicts and collapses
Peace scenarios: potential neo-socialism
  2030s and 2040s – potential beginnings of a new system of social justice
    from local to higher levels

These trajectories, which map historical trends mainly in Western countries, have parallels in various trajectories in non-Western parts of the world, which, due to global interconnectedness, partly overlap with Western ones. For example, Eric Hobsbawm's interpretation of the short 20th century, which follows the long 19th century from the French Revolution to the beginning of World War I and which also applies to Western countries, is strongly defined by non-Western developments, specifically the birth and fall of the Soviet Union (Hobsbawm 1996c). The short 20th century charts the relevant milestones mainly for Eastern Europe, which is associated with socialist experiments.

With the end of the short 20th century, however, the capitalist system in Western countries did not change, nor even fundamentally the structure of neoliberal capitalism, which continued its development. My schedule above, therefore, shows a different, second view of trajectories in Western countries and countries associated with them. These perspectives are not mutually exclusive, but complementary. Another perspective can be identified since 1978 when China began the reform and opening up to the world that has made it the world's second-largest economy and an influential global country. The gradual intertwining of production and trade between China and the USA, and subsequently other Western and non-Western countries, opened a new stage of development, which I will discuss in Section 3 of Chapter 10.

This phase has continued to the present day, although it has undergone its share of changes, notably the partial weakening of China-US relations and the parallel strengthening of China's relations with the countries of the global South. While the model of the Soviet Union has ended, the model of "socialism with Chinese characteristics" and its significant linkages with other parts of the world now influence the main dynamics of contemporary global interactions. It is possible to say that the next century with the Chinese model effectively began in 1978 and then, by the late 1980s and early 1990s, overlapped with the waning "Soviet" short century. Thus, multiple parallel complementary developmental perspectives can be put forward to interpret certain macro-regions networked with other parts of the world.

PART 2

Development of Critical Theory

∴

CHAPTER 3

The Programme of Critical Theory

The critical theory of society is, in its totality, the unfolding of a single existential judgment.

MAX HORKHEIMER, "Traditional and Critical Theory"

∵

A thorough understanding of the analysed trichotomy of critique, explanation, normativity, and other aspects of critical theory requires identifying them in the founding programmatic documents and other texts of Critical Theory in the development of the various paradigms from the founding to the present. First, I will focus on the initial programmatic theses of Critical Theory as formulated by Max Horkheimer and Herbert Marcuse, and then on the major reformulation undertaken by Theodor Adorno and Max Horkheimer some ten years later.

Although the basic ideas of critical theory go back to Hegel and Marx, Critical Theory was first explicitly formulated by Max Horkheimer and Herbert Marcuse. The connection between Critical Theory and these influential figures in philosophical and social theory and the turbulent public life of the second and third quarters of the 20th century is strong. If we track their work in line with their intentions, it is evident that Horkheimer and Marcuse both directly undertook their studies as part of – and indeed as the foundation of – this project. Therefore, I discuss Horkheimer and Marcuse in the context of the roles they played as complementary co-authors of the programme theses of Critical Theory in the 1930s, without which this critical-theoretical project could not have been born.

Of course, one should bear in mind the distinctions between the various stages in the school's development: at the very least the initial reception of Marxism motivated by the Soviet developments of the 1920s, the guiding role of Critical Theory in the research programme proper in the 1930s, the pessimistic change in the 1940s, the revitalized practical impulse culminating in the student revolt of 1968, the theory of communicative action, and several stages in the initiatives of later years (Fraser, 2010; Honneth, 2014; Young, 2010; Linklater, 2007).

In 2023, it was already a hundred years since a research institute was founded in Frankfurt am Main in February 1923 and gradually institutionalized as the Institute for Social Research (*Institut für Sozialforschung*). After its establishment, a group of researchers began to form within its institutional and political framework, first under the heading of materialist theory and then in connection with a critical social theory, or Critical Theory, also known after World War II under the external but still most famous designation from the city of its origin, as the Frankfurt School. In this article, like the founding documents, I will stick to the most appropriate name, Critical Theory, (the school of Critical Theory), but it should be noted that none of these terms exhaustively describes the research project, as its focus, as will be seen below, cannot be reduced to materialism, nor to criticism, nor even to Frankfurt – whether we are defining the research in general as a research paradigm, or determining the research intent of a group that could be more narrowly defined as the members of the Institute and their collaborators outside the Institute, or more broadly to include like-minded scholars (Jay, 1996; Held, 1980; Wiggershaus, 1986).

Over the many decades since the programme's definition in the 1930s, not only a Critical Theory of the Frankfurt School but also a critical theory, in general, has developed much and been a thorn in the side of many power holders. That is why I will refer mainly to a critical theory in general. With its social critique of capitalist, Nazi, and Soviet power practices, it would become an indisputable subject of contention in all the influential political regimes of the last century. In the capitalist order it was marginalized and at extreme moments accused of subversion; in the Soviet system, it was considered a bourgeois ideology as a Western Marxism; and under Nazism its authors and supporters had to emigrate (Wiggershaus, 1986).[1] In terms of content, its focus has been well demonstrated by its prominence in discussions about the possibilities of democratic socialism mainly in the period of social emancipation in the

---

1   Even as the Institute for Social Research was being named, some of the proposals that were considered rather provocative (too leftist) in the German environment of the day had to be abandoned. Alas, in the years that followed the situation was much worse. In 1933, on the day Reich President Hindenburg appointed Hitler as Chancellor, the house where Max Horkheimer, director of the Institute for Social Research, lived was occupied by a Nazi SA unit and turned into military quarters. A month and a half later, the Institute was closed down by the police and the building was confiscated, with part of it being handed over to the Nazi student association. After the transfer of the Institute to American exile in 1935, conditions were created for the research to continue, although its members refrained from using some of the terms in the Institute's vocabulary. On the positive side though, after the war, in the 1950s, the Frankfurt Institute was rebuilt as a result of Horkheimer's and Adorno's efforts, and a new institution called the New School for Social Research was built in New York as well.

1960s, associated with the student revolts in Western countries and with the reforms aimed at democratic socialism in Czechoslovakia that culminated in the Prague Spring. However, critical theory also maintained a certain reflexive distance from these potentially promising, yet specifically ideologically limited activities, which were eventually suffocated by those in power. The gradual development of critical theory, from its inception to the present day, can be seen as a testament to the change in critical thinking about society and the key dilemmas and tensions of the 20th and 21st centuries, according to the influence that Marxism, psychoanalysis, and cultural studies had on critical theory, along with that of phenomenology, existentialism, feminism, postmodernism, multiculturalism, egalitarian liberalism and communitarianism, post-colonialism, and critical global studies.

In this chapter, first, I will focus on Horkheimer's foundations of Critical Theory. Second, I will specify Marcuse's. Then, third, I will examine Adorno and Horkheimer's redefinition of Critical Theory. In what follows, I look at the founding of the Institute for Social Research; at the guiding role played by Critical Theory in shaping the Institute; and, at how its ideas evolved. I will outline a methodological trichotomy underpinning the authors' approach.

1   Horkheimer's Foundations

Horkheimer's essay "Traditional and Critical Theory" (Horkheimer 2002a) and Marcuse's study "Philosophy and Critical Theory" (Horkheimer and Marcuse 1937), introduced in Horkheimer's five-page address, are generally considered to be among the fundamental programme documents of Critical Theory. Although these studies were not the very first pieces of writing by the group of researchers that gradually assembled around Horkheimer at the Institute for Social Research, they introduced the term Critical Theory at a time when the group was intensely debating the need for a new social theory. Their immediate publication in 1937 in the Institute's journal *Zeitschrift für Sozialforschung* (Schmidt, 1970)[2] is proof that they are a kind of manifesto, which, while maintaining a certain plurality of opinion among the members of the group, sets out its orientation in an original manner. The conceptual focus and argumentational foundation of Critical Theory are well documented in these studies and in several other texts by Horkheimer and Marcuse from that time. Although

---

2 Horkheimer had published the journal since 1932, and from 1939 to 1941 it was known as *Studies in Philosophy and Social Science*. See Schmidt's study on "Zeitschrift für Sozialforschung", attached in the form of a preface to the journal's republication.

these older texts belong irrevocably to the era in which they were created, it is possible to identify ideas that retain their appeal and are far from obvious.

Max Horkheimer anticipated the content of his essay "Traditional and Critical Theory" in an inaugural speech delivered in January 1931 on the occasion of taking over the position of director of the Institute for Social Research and professor of social philosophy at the University of Frankfurt (Horkheimer 1931), a move that brought together the two isolated professorships of philosophy and sociology for the first time in the German-speaking world. Referring to Marx in his speech, Horkheimer emphasized that two important factors – the culmination of German classical philosophy in Hegel's social philosophy and the subsequent development of industry and science in the 19th century – had allowed society as a whole to become less unpredictable and unjust towards individuals (Horkheimer 1932a; Horkheimer-Regius 1934a).[3] Thus, according to Horkheimer, the task of contemporary social philosophy is to help bring the two factors into accord on the basis of philosophical inquiry and through interdisciplinary cooperation with sociology, economics, history, and other sciences.

Although a research project formulated in this way meant for the Institute for Social Research the following of the research of social issues set out by the first director of the institute, Carl Grünberg, especially in his journal *Archiv für die Geschichte des Sozialismus und der Arbeiterbewegung*, it was a transition from social history to social theory related to *The Crisis of Marxism*, which was the title of the book Horkheimer was working on.[4] By emphasis on interdisciplinary theoretical research of contemporary society, Horkheimer referred to the programme being pursued by one of the founding figures of the Institute, Kurt Albert Gerlach.

However, in the time that elapsed between the writing of the inaugural speech and his programmatic article, Horkheimer's views evolved. They did not change fundamentally, but in writing the article, he framed his ideas primarily within materialist theory, seeking to expound on the aforementioned project of implementing Hegelian-Marxist philosophy in fair social practices, emphasizing the use of existing research knowledge and industrial potential.

---

3   Horkheimer's contribution to Grünberg's 70th birthday anthology suggests that this solution to the problem necessitated a revision of Hegel's philosophy to separate its fruitful legacy from its metaphysical beginnings. Horkheimer's critique focused on Hegel's conception of the absolute spirit. Cf. Horkheimer's earlier collection of shorter texts written from 1926 to 1931 and published under the pseudonym Heinrich Regius.

4   The plan was to publish Horkheimer's work as the sixth volume of publications by the Institute for Social Research.

However, the tense pre-war situation and the fact that some of Marx's predictions failed to materialize led Horkheimer to revise his thinking in 1937 and to focus on Critical Theory – while maintaining the materialist grounding of the theory.

Although the impetus for Horkheimer's study "Traditional and Critical Theory", written after emigration from Nazi Germany into exile in New York and published in Paris, was the 70th anniversary of the first volume of *Capital*, as an émigré in a new work environment his options were limited and so there is no explicit mention of Marx.[5] However, Horkheimer left obvious clues and references, thereby eliminating the need to be more explicit. As the title suggests, the article focuses on the distinction between traditional and critical theory. While traditional theory attempts only to describe the existing state, for the most part impartially, in the spirit of Descartes' *Discourse on the Method*, especially within established positivism, inadvertently conservative in accepting the supporting pillars of power and the structure of the given social order, whereas critical theory rejects such an alienating affirmative approach to social reality (Horkheimer 1932c).[6] Horkheimer, who agreed with other researchers working on the programme ideas of critical theory at that time, declares that "Critical theory maintains: it need not be so; man can change reality," and points to the social engagement of critical theory: "the critical theory of society is, in its totality, the unfolding of a single existential judgment" (Horkheimer 2002a, 223–224); it unfolds a practical judgement that enables the struggle for a just society. In broadly conceived interdisciplinary research, this social critique is linked to the historically formed connection between the validity of individual theories and the interests of individual social groups as representatives of the social order. On that basis and with an analysis of natural human needs, he develops a practically committed theory in which the stress is on the political economy, and which opposes exploitation and discrimination. Thus, critical theory combines theory of knowledge with theory of society, and theory with practice in general. Hence epistemology has to be linked to social theory and to the social subject. This subject of "critical thought and its theory" is "a definite individual in his real relation to other individuals and groups, in his conflict with a particular class, and, finally, in the resultant web of relationships with the social totality and with nature" (Horkheimer 2002a, 211).

Dialectics forms an internal part of this project. In his article "Zum Problem der Wahrheit", Horkheimer lists the characteristics of dialectical thinking:

---

5 In the introduction to his article "Philosophie und kritische Theorie", Horkheimer mentions the title of his book at least, although he initially refers just to the subtitle.

6 Cf. his ten remarks on the crisis of science and society (1932c).

the unifying principle of regressive and progressive moments, preservation and overcoming, of good and bad aspects of moments in nature and
human history; an attempt ... to try to analytically achieve concepts in
relation to each other and through them to reconstruct reality – these
and all other features of dialectical thinking correspond to a form of complex reality that is constantly changing in all its details.

HORKHEIMER 1935b, 351

In short, it is an "open dialectic" that should be capable of reflecting a historically changing reality (Horkheimer 1934b, 25; Horkheimer 1941a, 121–123).[7]

Horkheimer does not attempt a literal reception of Hegel's or Marx's conception of dialectics but expresses the intention to incorporate his theory into a
particular stream of thought. The dialectical movement from thesis via antithesis to synthesis has its parallel in the relationship analysed earlier among the
three elements of critical theory – critique, explanation, and normativity – and
it is within this implicit framework that Horkheimer sets out the basic theses
of critical theory in "Traditional and Critical Theory" and in his other writing
from the 1930s, much of which was published in *Zeitschrift für Sozialforschung*.
Although Horkheimer does not sufficiently articulate or distinguish these, it is
possible to at least partly identify them and show how they are linked in terms
of their arguments.

In his study entitled "The Social Function of Philosophy", Horkheimer
defines the first element of critical theory, i.e., critique, as not a mere negation but an

effort which is not satisfied to accept the prevailing ideas, actions, and
social conditions unthinkingly and from mere habit; an effort which aims
to coordinate the individual sides of social life with each other and with
the general ideas and aims of the epoch, to deduce them genetically, to
distinguish the appearance from the essence, to examine the foundations
of things, in short, really to know them.

HORKHEIMER 2002b

Horkheimer develops a critique of knowledge that rejects the acontextual and
ahistorical independence of ideas, in which ideas perpetuate and fulfill only

---

7   In the programme's notes on the work of the Institute for Social Research, Horkheimer
    defines the characteristics of concepts to be used in the Institute's previously modified
    research in the early 1940s using the adjectives *critical, historical, "inductive"* (denoting a spe-
    cific meaning) and *integrative* (1941a).

ideological functions, in the sense of politically serving the self-centered partial interests of certain social groups, either as a consequence of insufficient reflection or the conscious concealment of reality. In *Anfänge der bürgerlichen Geschichtsphilosophie*, Horkheimer builds on revelation of the ideological contradictions between ideologically proclaimed ideals and social reality (Horkheimer 1930a; 2002a, 77, 87; 1930b; 1933a, 13–14; 1937).[8] He points out that while ideology creates the illusion that an ideal is identical to reality or for example promises the freedom of the individual, in practice the ideology suppresses it. Thus, his approach is also a critique of a given social practice.

This type of critique does not require any external criteria, since it is satisfied with the subject of its examination, in which it finds contradictions. However, for Horkheimer, it is not just a matter of critiquing the discrepancy between words and deeds. He does not seek to critique the practical nonfulfillment of racist ideals, for example. Although even in this case there is a contradiction between reality and the proclaimed politics, critical theorists do not consider this discrepancy undesirable. He is not just concerned with the contradiction between reality and ideas but with the contradiction between reality and the *correct* ideas. The premise is to critique the failure to pursue the correct ideas, such as the failure to achieve the promised freedom of the individual referred to above. This brings us to the question of how to determine which ideas are correct and which are not. Since immanent criticism, as I have already indicated, would be existentially dependent on the contradiction in the relationship between any words and deeds, any less unspecific examination of relations would end in relativism. Although Horkheimer states that, at the most general level, no invariant criteria are desirable, that does not mean that critical theory has no criteria and that it gives itself up to relativism. In the article "Montaigne und die Funktion der Skepsis", we read that Horkheimer rejects relativistic and skeptical approaches that are barely able to fulfill their restorative function in contemporary conditions as they were in late antiquity or the Renaissance (Horkheimer, 1938).[9] The weighty foundations of critical theory must therefore be borne by immanent critique with the help of a closer specification expressed by some other critical-theoretical moment.

The second element is description and explanation, which is linked primarily to the materialistic foundations of critical theory. As indicated earlier, the

---

8 Horkheimer also articulates this contradiction as a conflict between the early bourgeois formulation of the ideal (e.g., in Kant or Hegel) and the late bourgeois reconciliation with the given reality, e.g., in positivism (1930b).

9 More precisely, scepticism fulfils a beneficial but only limited function as a one-sided part of the dialectical whole.

practical commitment of critical theory and the interconnection of critique, explanation, and normativity protect critical-theoretical description against the pseudo-neutralist temptations of positivism.

In his articles "Materialismus und Moral" and "Materialismus und Metaphysik", Horkheimer sees a human being as a being entrenched in nature and society who adapts his surroundings to his work (Horkheimer 1933b, 185; 1933b, 223–224). The world is transformed by historically conditioned human practice, specifically by work in society. Since people are active subjects who participate in shaping their environment as members of historically situated social groups, they cannot be considered either a purely passive element, controlled by the environment they impartially observe, or a completely decisive factor that determines voluntaristically their surroundings. In its own practical situation, "Critical theory is neither 'deeply rooted' like totalitarian propaganda nor 'detached' like the liberalist intelligentsia." (Horkheimer 2002a, 223–224) As potential critical self-awareness, critical theory seeks to be part of the good practice in which it participates epistemologically and socially; the truth of the theory here is the moment of good practice (Horkheimer 1935b, 345; 2002a, 90). In his article "Zur Rationalismusstreit in der gegenwärtigen Philosophie", Horkheimer tries to specify good practice, stating that a theory's value is historically connected to the aims of progressive social forces (Horkheimer 1934b, 26–27; 1932c, 1). He then further defines good practice among progressive forces by introducing the distinction between partial and generalizable interest, and the general interest or the general public (Horkheimer 1934b, 32).

But which social groups, as progressive forces, promote this general interest? Horkheimer is in no doubt that this interest is primarily about the economic concerns of class society: "such a concern is necessarily generated in the proletariat." (Horkheimer 2002a, 213) Further to Marx's analysis of the struggle for recognition of individual social classes and the critique of ideology, Horkheimer concludes that the social groups most affected by the ideologically generated irrationality (in terms of the inconsistency) of the capitalist order and its social perpetuation relations have – as social forces negating the status quo – an interest in creating a rational organization of human activity, a rational society (Horkheimer 1937).

However, Horkheimer's reflections on the workers' movement are already indicated in "Traditional and Critical Theory" by the scepticism of the second half of the 1930s regarding the progressive role the proletariat should play in society: "even the situation of the proletariat is, in this society, no guarantee of correct knowledge" (Horkheimer 2002a, 213); "Nor is there a social class by whose acceptance of the theory one could be guided." (Horkheimer 2002a, p. 242) The hopes previously placed in this social class by philosophy of history

had largely been dashed, mainly because of the general trend of its disintegration in the capitalist countries, the rise of Stalinism in the Soviet Union,
and Nazi tendencies in Germany and other countries (Horkheimer 1939; 1941b;
1941c). The class-defined connection between theory and practice – a reflection of the theoretical hopes in social reality and in people's awareness – was
weakening. Here Marxism did not provide sufficient explanation, since the
proletariat, the dominant subject of social change, did not play its expected
role in the political scene. However, Horkheimer made only brief reference
to an alternative subject, be it a newly structured majority of the population
dependent on wage labour or another subject.

The descriptive materialistic dimension of Horkheimer's conception of critical theory has one other supporting element: the psychoanalytic tradition,
particularly Freud's theory of the libido, which was still not very well developed in critical theory in the 1930s. Horkheimer talks about the instinctive
drives that stimulate people into relieving tension and fulfilling their needs.
In "Materialismus und Metaphysik", this stimulus is considered a natural fact
(Horkheimer 1933a; 1936). The pursuit of happiness, satisfaction, and self-
preservation are legitimate human reactions, as they are elementary, natural
attributes of the human race, but they are suppressed by the current organization of society, especially by its economic side. According to Horkheimer,
the task of critical theory is to understand these social limitations that prevent
human being from achieving fuller self-realization and to help eliminate them.

As a result of the disappointment at the marginalization of the social role of
the working class, a normative concept of human being only in general characteristics became increasingly important for Horkheimer. This normativity
forms the third element of critical theory set out by Horkheimer. Although
Horkheimer's reference to the generalizable interest of one social group seems
to echo the role of the proletariat, which was to represent all mankind, the
growing emphasis on a generalization that includes other groups reflects
the non-fulfilment of the historical mission of this subject of social change,
particularly in the situation which led to the catastrophe of the World War II
(Horkheimer 1968, 193).

As can be seen from Horkheimer's introductory pages to Marcuse's study
"Philosophy and Critical Theory," the difficulty of finding support in the rejected
reality, which was at that time distorted by repressive, Nazi moments, renders
critical theory increasingly reliant on the imagination in formulating normativity (Horkheimer and Marcuse 1937; Horkheimer 1935a; Honneth 1994b).[10] The

---

10   Horkheimer does not go as far as Marcuse, and does not consider the use of imag-
      ination and idealism to be sufficient reason to rehabilitate the term utopia (1935a).

imagination is idealistic in inspiration, while its content, to be contrasted with the undesirable reality, acquires a materialistic critical character: "This negative formulation ... is the materialist content of the idealist concept of reason" (Horkheimer 2002a, 242). However, Horkheimer is straightforward in specifying these normative elements of critical theory. References to a community of free people are among the initial formulations that were not taken further.

All three elements of trichotomic critical theory (critique, description, normativity) require interdisciplinary research as a condition of the critical theory (Horkheimer 1932b; 2002a), not just in terms of linking up the tasks of the individual social sciences but also in connecting them with the possibilities of philosophy. However, it is not possible to rely solely on the original claim of critical theory that the most general, yet particular results of the analyses stemming from the particular standpoints of the individual sciences or disciplines will find a new position and significance in the reconstruction of the whole within the broader, interconnected theoretical framework with a philosophical examination. This claim is rendered problematic by the unreflected adaptation of positivist-oriented sciences to the given power relations. Hence philosophy acquires a fundamental significance.

2   Marcuse's Foundations

Although Marcuse's articulation of the basic theses of Critical Theory in the 1930s is largely analogous to Horkheimer's, it must be considered distinctive, being expressed from Marcuse's specific perspective. Marcuse – who joined the Institute for Social Research in 1933 on Horkheimer's recommendation to his colleague Leo Löwenthal, who also lured Erich Fromm to the Institute – was initially heavily influenced by phenomenology and related existentialism through his studies with Husserl, Heidegger and other philosophers. However, aware of the limits of these schools of thought, he gradually, beginning with his *Habilitation* thesis and then other writings, transformed his Heideggerian theory of historicity into a critical theory of history (Marcuse 1932). In his treatment of the young Marx, he stressed that phenomenology lacks completeness since it neglects the material and historical conditions of human life (Marcuse 1968, 21; 1937a, 414–415). On the same basis, he formulated his critique of the political existentialism of the time, which he thought contributed

---

Horkheimer's – but also Marcuse's – less elaborate conception of normativity is also evident when compared with his distanced and contemporaneous supportive interpretation of philosophical anthropology.

to "totalitarian political theory" rather than offering fruitful existential motives (Marcuse 1934).[11]

Marcuse's developing cooperation with the Institute is well illustrated by the study "Philosophy and Critical Theory", which he wrote together with Horkheimer (Horkheimer and Marcuse 1937). In his part, the larger section, of this text, which specifies some of Horkheimer's formulations, Marcuse focuses on the role that philosophy can play in relation to critical theory. Using the same differentiation that I have applied to distinguish the three moments of Horkheimer's version of critical theory, i.e., critique, explanation (especially of economic and psychoanalytically conceived materialism) and normativity, it can be said that the clarification of the relationship between philosophy and critical theory refers to a third moment that is particularly closely linked to the first. Within these three moments, I will focus on the basic theses of Critical Theory that Marcuse formulated in his study and in other texts from the 1930s, published mainly in the *Zeitschrift für Sozialforschung (Journal of Social Research)*, which co-formulated the key ideas for a development of critical theory.

Marcuse starts from the dialectical method of analysis, which, according to him, reflects the critical insight that given facts are negations of truth even if they appear as truth. Dialectic means that all forms of being include negativity which determines their content and development (Marcuse 1940, 411). The relationship between aspects of dialectic – specifically, the movement from negation of thesis by antithesis to synthesis – and the moments of the trichotomic articulation of critical theory is more explicitly conceived by Marcuse than by Horkheimer. In his article "Zum Begriff des Wesens" (Marcuse 1936, 37), he states that "Dialectical concepts transcend a given social reality in the direction of another historical form that is present in that reality as a tendency. ... All materialist concepts contain an accusation and a demand."[12] In this sense, Marcuse's critical theory involves a relation to the given undesirable reality that is the object of the accusation or critique, a description of the positive social fragments and tendencies that exist, and finally a normative demand for another historical form of reality that is based on these positive elements.

Without an overall view of Marcuse's writings – indeed, given the form of his expression – there remains sometimes a tension between his arguments, at times arguments that are exacerbated. Some of his expressions should not obscure the importance of the other moments he emphasizes in his other

---

11   Marcuse's distinction between philosophical and political existentialism is aimed at the
      critique of the political version, which he associates primarily with Carl Schmitt.
12   Compare with (Marcuse 1930, 304–326; 1931, 541–557).

studies. An important part of the first moment of Marcuse's conception of critical theory, which in the 1930s – in contrast to Horkheimer's conception – is characterized primarily by an indirect study of society mediated by the analysis of competing social theories, is a critique of ideology, especially the ideological function of philosophy. In his article "Zum Begriff des Wesens" (Marcuse 1936, 18), Marcuse analyses bourgeois philosophy and finds both positive and negative elements in it. He finds emancipatory potential in its progressive concepts such as reason, morality, happiness and human rights. Historically, in the ideals of the early emerging bourgeoisie, which is critical of traditional hierarchical society, he sees references to an emancipated society, in the concepts of freedom, democracy, critical idealism, or materialistically conceived human needs, for example. By contrast, in the philosophy of the late bourgeoisie, which has already taken power, he reveals a disguised contradiction between the promise of rights and freedoms and an attachment to the realisation of domination and repression. It considers the ideological proclamation of concepts that are not applied in practice as instruments of manipulation of the population and legitimation of an unjust regime.

However, Marcuse is not content with such relativism and shows that bourgeois philosophy as a whole contains, albeit in embryo, conservative tendencies that serve to consolidate propertied individualism. The disregard for the concrete conditions of human life prevents this philosophy from revealing the intrinsic connection between the exercise of freedom and 'material existential conditions' (Marcuse 1937b, 62; cf. Horkheimer and Marcuse 1937, 625–647). Given the established division of labor, philosophy itself is unable to overcome its specialisation and the overly abstract nature of its inquiry. Critical theory, says Marcuse, should also seek to reflect existing philosophy in the context of interdisciplinary research because, in times of social regression, it need not perform ideological functions, for it can embody (as I will explain in interpreting Marcuse's formulation of normativity) a more advanced form of thought.

Marcuse, like Horkheimer, analyses this situation which occurs in the second half of the 1930s when it is not possible to place too much historical-philosophical hope in the working class as a subject of social change in the West. While in Marx's time the conviction of the future positive outcome of the development of society prevailed, which also determined the resolution of the dispute between utopian and scientific socialism at that time, the reflection of critical theory in social reality through the diminishing of the role of the proletariat weakened in the 1930s. As a consequence of this process, the explanations carried out by positivist-oriented social sciences were associated with an undesirable state of society or "bad facticity".

This brings us to the second moment of critical theory, its descriptively formulated materialist foundation, which Marcuse addresses in almost all of his texts. He distinguishes between the "false materialism of bourgeois practice", which is an expression of contradictory social reality, and the "true materialism of critical theory" (Marcuse 1937b, 62). He states, "Materialist theory opposes historical relativism because it is bound to the social forces which the historical situation reveals as progressive and truly 'universal'." (Marcuse 1936, 31) Concrete history, according to Marcuse, is the opposite of abstract "historicity", which can be used relativistically by all social groups. Historically embedded progressive forces can be specified from the perspective of the economic and political concepts of critical theory, since "materialist protest and materialist critique grew out of the struggle of repressed groups for better living conditions." (Horkheimer and Marcuse 1937, 647; cf. Marcuse 1938, 55–89) Following Marx's analysis of class society, an economic specification of the abstract philosophical determination of the position of social groups in society can be made.

Marcuse proposes his further positive ideas again in a negative form of expression. He emphasizes that the absence of reflection on the unsatisfactory economic situation in liberal theory has its successor in totalitarian theory, which legitimized the realization of the Nazi state (Marcuse 1934, 185–194). Marcuse also describes a similar transformation, which lacks the necessary fundamental changes, in the field of culture (Marcuse 1937b, 1, 54–94).

However, according to Marcuse, giving importance to economic factors should neither mean reducing theory to economic social science, which is currently in the grip of a positivist fixation on an undesirable reality, nor should it lead to the economic reductionism in practice to which the commissars in the Soviet Union succumbed sometimes. Marcuse's critique of this new 'economism' is that the set of social, political, cultural, and psychological relations cannot be explained in terms of organising economic institutions and secured only through nationalisation of the means of production and economic state planning. This view is taken up in a developed form in Marcuse's later writings, in which the threat to human beings in all the systems of the time is attributed to technological dominance (Marcuse 1941, 414–439; cf. Marcuse 1991). Critical theory should be concerned with explaining the overall position of human beings and the historical change in the overall conditions of the world and life as a social being from the standpoint of a broadly conceived, albeit economically oriented, materialist social theory, and not simply with explaining human being as a component of the economic gear from the standpoint of economic theory.

Marcuse's materialist theory, again like Horkheimer's, keeps, in addition to the economic dimension, another dimension: the interest in human happiness as well as the transformation of the material conditions to achieve this happiness (Horkheimer and Marcuse 1937, 625–647). Marcuse thinks that society is dominated by an irrational system that, while not completely preventing human free expression and the satisfaction of needs, creates pseudo-needs and consequent pseudo-happiness behind which repressive interests hide. In his article "Zur Kritik des Hedonismus" (Marcuse 1938, 55–89), published a year after the publication of his study on philosophy and critical theory, Marcuse specifies the reference to human happiness by analyzing the repressed satisfaction of physical and spiritual needs under the repressive conditions of the society. This anticipates his later reception of Freud's writings and the integration of psychoanalysis into his theory (Marcuse 1955a; Marcuse 1955b).

In his treatise on hedonism, Marcuse criticizes idealistic ascetic theories that reject the fulfillment of bodily needs as an immoral position, and, at the same time, he turns against subjectivist hedonistic theories that move purely in the sphere of individual gratification without regard to the socially shaped conditions of satisfaction, e.g. he criticizes the work ethic, in which the moral habit of postponing the satisfaction of needs manifests itself as a typical feature of the spirit of capitalism, and also the affirmative character of culture, which affirms this given social order (Marcuse 1937b, 54–94; cf. Horkheimer-Regius 1934a). In this way, Marcuse links his argument about the adequate satisfaction of human needs, both sensually and intellectually defined, to an argument about the economic conditions of a just society.

The final, third key moment of the critical theory formulated by Marcuse – its normative articulation – builds on critique and explanation, emphasizing also the need for philosophical imagination at a time when social reality is not developing in a direction that could be described as desirable. The impossibility of sufficiently identifying actually existing fruitful paths of development results in the need to establish a desirable normative articulation by means of imagination, an imagination that has always been linked to philosophy and that can suggest to critical theory a picture of a better social order. Marcuse does not elaborate a normative theory of society itself, but he articulates more fully what Horkheimer merely suggests (Horkheimer, Marcuse 1937, 625–647). He illuminates how normativity may link idealism to materialism in a dialectical way. From this perspective, in which materialist critical theory also acquires a utopian character through its rationalist and idealist dimensions, Marcuse's later famous call in the late 1960s, "Be realistic, demand the impossible," becomes more intelligible.

The rationalist theory of society in its ideal form, according to Marcuse, is interconnected with the idea of reason which consists in the ability to conceptually grasp truth, goodness, and rightness. Then, a rationalist society is one that is shaped by the actions and organization of the social whole that are legitimized by the exercise of this capacity (Marcuse 1934, 170–171).

Marcuse thinks that the negative tendencies of social development lead in a dialectical way to a rationalist conception of a possible better society. In this development, the refusal of the positivist approach should not give way to the voluntarism of mere fantasy. Mere fantasy, with its rejection of bad facticity, resigns and leaves the human subject in that facticity. Imagination should be part of a materialist theory of society, reflecting at least the elements and partial tendencies of the development of society towards a rational society (Horkheimer and Marcuse 1937, 625–647). I have already stated in my interpretation of Marcuse's dialectic and materialism that one should look for selected fragments in social reality that can be understood as normative potential from which a more desirable social whole can develop.

In "Introduction to Hegel's Philosophy," Marcuse develops the conclusions of the article on philosophy and critical theory and shows, through his updating of Hegel, that the intertwining of materialism and idealism in critical theory simultaneously opens up the possibility of an interdisciplinary restructuring of the role of the social sciences and philosophy concerning practice, particularly critical thinking gets a new form because it is transferred to social practice and social theory (Marcuse 1940, 412).

3   Adorno and Horkheimer's Redefinition

Now I will focus on Adorno and Horkheimer's redefinition of a critical theory. I will introduce the topic of social and environmental conflicts, first, by articulating the main ideas of the problematic historical dialectic of Western civilization, second, of the whole of human civilization as well, and third, by a necessary transition from a monological paradigm to an intersubjective paradigm of relations among human beings and the nature to try to overcome the problematic dialectic of the civilizations. I will focus on the paradigmatic text of this kind of thinking concerning the repression of nature and conflicts which follow that repression. Even if the text on the dialectic of enlightenment has its own circumscriptions given the fact of its origin being connected to WWII, it deserves attention because it identifies long-term pathological tendencies and, at the same time, paradoxically, it is within the framework of these tendencies due to its lack of ability to overcome the boundaries of the given paradigm.

However, its skeptical explanatory critique can be the first move beyond the contemporary desperate situation which, then, can be reformulated and developed by more developed and sophisticated contemporary analyses.

The opening of the theme of a dialectic of civilization is well expressed by Claude Lévi Strauss's metaphor that our civilization is no longer the "fragile flower" that must be protected in a cultivated park against surrounding threats (2012 [1955]). Civilization is created in mass production, in monoculture. The idea draws attention to the expansion of civilization and loss of its need for this kind of protection as it has gained strength. Lévi Strauss's idea can still be considered relatively optimistic, as it only points to excessive civilizational productivism and the planetary push of civilization. This thesis is the starting point that Theodor Adorno and Max Horkheimer enriched by their explanatory criticism of this civilizational process.

The fact of brutal destruction produced by World War II led Adorno and Horkheimer, especially in their joint work the *Dialectic of Enlightenment* (2007 [1944]), to the ever-increasing rejection of the destructive technocratic rationalization and, particularly, to a criticism of repression and cultural manipulation.[13] Settlement of the system of technocratic dominance was considered the outcome of the erroneous social development since the beginning, as a consequence of expansive rationalization and related technological pathologies from the birth of our civilization to the present. They focus on the overwhelmingly negative aspects of this enforcement of civilization against human beings and nature at the very beginning when the process was not over-exacerbated. It is a refusal of civilization.

This pervasive negativism, however, leads to hopelessness. In their pessimistic view, at least an attempt to reverse this pathological development could be considered. However, a reader who does not accept their perspective can at least appreciate and follow the inspirational concept of social critique they have drawn up. Their analysis can be read as an important critical memento that is behind our everyday experience and critical approach. The picture of the negative civilizational tendencies mapped by Horkheimer and Adorno can create the background to a more subtle social criticism. It could be – but was not –supplemented by fundamental reflections on potential social and environmental transformation.

---

13   This kind of critical thinking appeared already in the last year of *Studies in Philosophy and Social Science*, which was originally a journal of Adorno and Horkheimer's Institute für Sozialforschung in Frankfurt (Horkheimer, 1941d, 365; comp. Horkheimer, 1941c, 266–388; Adorno 1941).

The consequences of technological reasoning, which has had a strong impact on our lives especially since the beginning of modern times, are a challenge that cannot be ignored and overcome. Adorno and Horkheimer's attention is focused on the long-term historical causes of the development of capitalism. They focus primarily on a general critique of Western civilization in relation to the determining role of the negative aspects of rationality. Their interpretation sees the source of pathological civilizational development from antiquity to the present in the negative moments of the rational use of natural processes. This kind of disposition is instrumental to the control of nature, and consequently to the formation of the "relations of social domination".

As stated by Karl Marx:

> Capitalism production ... disturbs the metabolic interaction between man and the earth, i.e. prevents the return to the soil of its constituent elements consumed by man in the form of food and clothing; therefore, it violates the conditions necessary to lasting fertility of the soil ... Capitalist production, therefore, develops technology ... only by sapping the original sources of all wealth – the soil and the worker.
>
> MARX 1967 [1867]

Both the authors follow Marx by reinterpreting and extending their critique from the point of view of civilization. They criticize the extensive use of reason; with its roots not only in the 18th century as is usually analysed but already in antiquity. From this perspective, their broad concept of the Enlightenment accompanies the whole history of the West. Endeavours to survive and deal with the traps of nature have led to the instrumentalization of human reason since the beginning of Western civilization. As a result of this approach and the formation of the contrast between nature and culture, there were three types of nature control and reification. First, the control of external nature, i.e., surrounding nature, in which one lives; the outer world which surrounds us. Second, the control of inner nature, i.e., the life instinct, the nature of human beings. Thirdly, in connection with the second kind of control, not only control of himself or herself, but also control of one another.

When Horkheimer and Adorno explain the problem of instrumental reason by finding it already in the canonical texts of Western civilization; in Homer, they show that the development of instrumental reason – from then to the present – has mainly negative aspects. The basis of the developmental dialectic of the formation of Western civilization is the denial of nature and the spreading of a kind of rationality which is in fact irrationality. This is a paradox, because outer nature began to be dominated through liberation of human beings who are disciplined and enslaved. There is an expansion of technical rationality and its self-serving development when it forgets its own mediating role and suppresses the original purpose it should serve. Its development paradoxically becomes a brake on the development of the human being and his surroundings and leads to crises. This evolutionary dialectic has, over time, become the dialectic of capitalism, a fact with long-lasting historical implications. The economic crisis before World War II and subsequent Nazism and Fascism are just the culmination of this long-term development, which from the beginning of human development has included the transformation of means into purpose.

The essay on Homer's *Odyssey* provides an outline of the origins of the development of pathological and crisis features of human reason (1999). Odysseus, the subject here endowed with instrumental rationality, attempts to control the environmental nature around him, his own nature, and the nature of his subordinates. Odysseus is a stray entity who controls in order to strengthen and save his own life but, through this control, he also weakens life. After the war in Troy, he cannot find his way home; he wanders, facing ups and downs, and developing technical rationality as a means for his survival and consumption. What he did not dare at home in a community of loved ones, he takes liberty to undertake on the road in a situation of isolation, promoting his own ruthless "atomistic interest". Being outside the community of his loved ones enables him to promote dictate in a competitive struggle with others. His approach to life later becomes an exemplary model of the modern Western economy, a technical irrationality that prevents people from meeting their real needs. Economic crises, mass manipulation, concentration camps, and the Holocaust are all results of an overturned technical rationality in modern times. All these manifestations of human dominance have their determining source in the spontaneous development of technical rationality since the beginnings of human civilization. The subject of instrumental reason is a subject that evolves in human history from slaver to entrepreneur and administrator.

Homer's *Odyssey* has an important resemblance to the classical parts of Western civilization, such as Hegel's *Phenomenology of Spirit* (2018 [1806]) and Marx's *Capital* (1967 [1867]). In constructing their work, both these authors come from a certain intellectual motif strongly shared in historical culture, from the odyssey. It is a motif with a relatively general and long-term validity because a journey expresses movement and life of a human being. Of course, the empowerment of an agent of modern times and the fascination by overseas trips of discovery – in fact, of colonial conquest – to the Americas, Africa, and Asia can be observed at that time. As Lévi-Strauss states, they in fact did not consider their journey the discovery of a new world, they were convinced they had re-found the paradise described in the Bible. Amy Allen shows, however, that the progress of the Western empires was a regress of colonialized subjects (Allen, 2016). In the contemporary global era, it is revived by tourist travel in a simplified commercial way which brings about sometimes the destruction of the local ways of life.

The idea of the odyssey, which was revived in the philosophical, scientific and literary works of the modern era (Kosik, 2012), consisted in the wandering of a subject in the world, in the knowledge of the world which the subject acquires for himself.[14] The subject can be an individual human being, a spirit, a collective in the form of a social class, etc. However, it is always true that the subject can only know himself through his own activity, the transformation of the world and hence of himself. The subject changes the world and transforms himself. Goethe's educational novel *Wilhelm Meister* or Rousseau's *Emil or on Education* are just other versions of Homer's *Odyssey*, Hegel's *Phenomenology of Spirit*, or Marx's *Capital*. All these works are a kind of odyssey. Hegel's odyssey of the spirit is the way in which consciousness in history passes through many forms to know what it is in itself and to become for itself. This historical "experience of consciousness" has its parallel in Marx's *Capital*, which is the odyssey of specific historical practice. It is a means whereby concrete practice goes from its basic labour product through various forms of practice to a fundamental practical act based on the knowledge and transformation of oneself and of one's surroundings. Today, corporations following their profit rationality create consumerists by pushing them into a journey of permanent economic growth and consumption, at social and environmental costs.

Although Horkheimer and Adorno's interpretation had the ambition to express their opinion on the development of the entire human civilization, it followed almost exclusively criticism of Western culture. However, following Horkheimer and Adorno's logic, it would be necessary to realize that even other cultures are not automatically seamless (comp. Eisenstadt 2002; Benjamin 1973). Firstly, non-Western cultures have been hit by Western instrumental rationality during colonialism, the Cold War, and the current global capitalism. Second, even if Western cultures were not affected by Western influences, we can identify characteristics shared by various cultures, including expansion that dominates by instrumental rationality. Western culture should therefore remain a center for criticism, but other cultures cannot be omitted. We should seriously criticize instrumental reason, not only to focus on the beginnings of

---

14   „Himself" because this kind of subject was usually considered man at that time; it marginalized and repressed women.

Western civilization but also on the beginnings of other civilizations in order to see problems in multiple modernities. Alternatives to the European Odyssey are the epics of *Ramayana* and *Mahabharata* on the territory of modern-day India, *The Epic of Gilgamesh* or the *Old Testament* in the Middle East, for example, if we follow only some paradigmatic classic texts. And the archaeological excavations of interactions between Mesopotamia (Ur) and Indus Valley (Harrappa culture) in the third millennium BC, for example, reveal mutual interactions of cultures already at that time (Kenover, Price 2013).

In all these above-mentioned works, the ways of searching and wandering are illustrated, as evidenced by the historical process of cultivation on the one hand and the historical process of escalation of instrumental control of people and nature on the other. The idea of a journey presents the subject's path to the world, both literally and metaphorically. Individual and collective subjects are recognized and matured through their deeds that change the world and themselves, i.e., external nature and internal nature. In this process, the subject changes the world, but through expansion of instrumental rationality that develops various forms of control of people and nature. However, it is necessary to point out that the interpretation is based on the illumination of the actions of the individual actors, the heroes of the epics, but the behaviour of the individual subject is only a substitute and represents the collective process of the development of whole cultures or of the whole of human civilization.

Following this analysis, we can say that the problem of instrumental rationality comes from the beginning of human history, not only in repressive systems but often also implicitly reproduced in opposition to those repressive systems. It existed in feudalism and capitalism and in attempts to overcome it. Thus, the technocratic problem is deeper due to the long-term historical evolutionary tendencies of instrumental reason within human civilization. However, because we live in global capitalism now, we have to face the systemic and structural problems mainly in connection to capitalism today.

Today corporate owners and managers within the system of global capitalism transform Western citizens into consumers, people in peripheral developing countries into producers or a useless reserve army of unemployment, and nature into the sources for production lines. It leads not only to global social pathologies and injustices but also to the destructive consequences of global climate change.

Due to the fact that the various components of human civilization come into contact with each other in the present global era, and the development of human civilization is indeed becoming a full-planetary one, the hypertrophy of the pathological aspects of instrumental rationality can cause the collapse of human civilization. For this reason, the ambivalence of global technological development may be seen as a powerful motive which may seem more promising but because it is anchored in the historical technocratic pathologies, it remains also a warning.

Martin Jay, in his classic book on the history of Critical Theory (1996 [1973]), considered the 1930s and 1940s the most fruitful decade of the Institute for Social Research. Today, however, we know already that Critical Theory in those years was strong in its *theoretical agenda setting* and its first focus on *critique* but it was not specified and there was no or at best only a very weak proposal as to what to do. Apart from the basis of critique, explanation was only partly developed, and normativity was covered only implicitly and marginally. Considering the concept of the dialectic of enlightenment in this methodological way, it included a reductive subject-object paradigm that did not allow for (1) a sufficient *explanation* of the reality and (2) a developed *normativity*. Instrumental reason as a mono-logical approach to human beings and to nature is based on subject-object relations. These relations were an adequate target of critique which, however, did not permit the description of the intersubjective dimensions of human life and its relation to nature, and to develop a normative proposal for an inter-subjective approach to solving pathologies and injustices.

It was not an adequate description and explanation of historical development with various deviations. It is important to distinguish between an unnecessarily generalizing refusal of rationality as such and a required critique of the domination of technocratic or instrumental reason (Habermas 2015; Honneth 2000b). Thus, the Enlightenment critique is problematic as a critical explanation and explanatory critique.

And it is also not adequate as a normative point of view. The position is one-sided and inappropriate because it does not illuminate the normative possibility of crossing the given state. There is no room for at least partial free action against the negative technocratic tendencies of instrumental rationality in historical development. The highly skeptical, almost fatalistic, position does not include such a possibility of critical correction.

There can at least be attempts to overcome the monological use and misuse of instrumental rationality. Instrumental rationality can be used positively but it should not be the main principle of action. Otherwise, it becomes a problematic assumption on which authoritarian non-participatory systems can be established. A redefinition of the position can be achieved by refusing resignation and attempting to carry out meaningful activities that would allow inter-subjective development by cultivating patterns of mutual relations among people (Honneth 2014), and also between people and nature, even if still against a background of pathological technocratic development, which in the 20th century resulted in the civilizational regression of two world wars, and continues to threaten humanity and the environment through planetary homogenisation, supranational authoritarian tendencies, and world war.

The analysis has to include research of systems and structures as well as of subjects. However, if we were to take only the general structure or humanity, we would miss the specific subject groups, which are mainly responsible for problems, and also social groups who resist in unjust structures and systems. In looking for positive fragments of society's development, it leads us to the question related to the *Dialectic of Enlightenment* of whether it is most appropriate to analyse only the characteristics of Odysseus. Additional interpretations also require critical points of view of the people who were subordinate to Odysseus: his subordinate men who did not have the lead word in decision-making, as well as women and other subordinate subjects, including slaves (Atwood 2005; comp. Jaggar 2005).

As for the identification of the systemic and structural problems and the specific subjects as well today in the era of global capitalist interactions (Sklair 2016; Robinson 2014; Harris 2016), I have already indicated that corporation owners and interlinked politicians, managers, and technicians follow the profit instrumental rationality and create consumers by pushing them into permanent economic growth and meaningless mass consumption, at heavy social and environmental costs mainly in developing countries. Consumerists are willing to go this way; having their part of responsibility for the negative consequences of this lifestyle too even if they still do not admit it. However, we have also to take into account that long-term historical technocratic development linked to the expansion of instrumental rationality is not directly and consciously shaped by individual agents and that individual possibilities for its correction are very difficult and weak. Action has to be a long-term inter-subjective activity that would include individual as well as collective agents in the structures and systems.

This interpretation can be framed by the present possibilities and the coming transformation of inner (human) and outer external nature. The fundamental turning point, which is likely to bring about dramatic changes in conditions in all spheres of human life, will be the situation after the technological transformation or transformative revolution associated with the fuller development and application of artificial intelligence and automation, i.e., after the considerable replacement of mental and physical human labour by external means and their blending with the internal environment, i.e., with human being. Another technological development, which will probably change the situation and human being itself in an even more complex and conflicting way, will be a practice of genetic manipulation of human beings, while we still have more or less the same genetic make-up as before the emergence of human civilization twelve thousand years ago.

It has its relevance when Achille Mbembe, a critical thinker and contemporary Africa's most influential philosopher, says:

> The world will not survive unless humanity devotes itself to the task of sustaining what can be called the *reservoirs of life*. The refusal of perish may yet turn us into historical beings and make it possible for the world to be a world. But our vocation to survive depends on making the desire for life the cornerstone of a new way of thinking about politics and culture.
>
> MBEMBE 2017, 181

Motivation and efforts to identify problems and change the status quo exist among many social groups around the world, although due to technocratic thinking they have usually been limited to more superficial changes and have not penetrated to the determinants of deeper causes among social, civilizational, and environmental processes. Nevertheless, we can see at least initial attempts to map the situation.

There are already relevant impulses for identification of the problems and improvement in practice even if these impulses mainly address intermediate superficial connections between environmental consequences and their causes in a technocratic way, and do not analyse the main causes deeply rooted in societies and human civilization in general. However, we can appreciate at least the initial attempts to improve the situation. Especially since the foundation of the Club of Rome in 1968 and the publication of its first report *The Limits to Growth* (Meadows et al. 1972), various initiatives with a public influence were organized. To mention a few in the last decade, the global community was motivated to take environmental and social development goals more seriously by the conference on sustainable development which was held by the United Nations in Rio de Janeiro in 2012, for example. "The Sustainable Development Goals", so-called *Transforming our World: the 2030 Agenda for Sustainable Development* (2012), were adopted and then discussed and some parts have already been implemented by UN member states. It is relevant to analyse critically the partial implementation of these obligations in societies and the environment and also reflect philosophically on the ongoing social and environmental conflicts and potential collapse (Sťahel and Dědečková 2023).

The United Nations Framework Convention on Climate Change adopted the *Paris Agreement* through 195 states in 2015; this included the aim of pursuing a global approach to the threat of climate change (Paris Agreement 2015). The presupposition was that such a transformation would let societies develop without dramatic negative changes. In 2018, however, the Intergovernmental Panel on Climate Change (IPCC) Special Report on Global Warming stressed that global climate change would be a much bigger problem than was expected. The IPCC stated that humanity should react before 2030, otherwise, dramatic changes were expected, the flooding of vast territories, for example. Also, the World Wildlife Fund warned in its report: "The astonishing decline in wild-life populations shown by the latest Living Planet Index – a 60% fall in just over 40 years – is a grim reminder and perhaps the ultimate indicator of the pressure we exert on the planet" (Lambertini 2018). Thus, an urgent transformative revolution of societies is necessary. A concept of the Anthropocene may be tested for an explanation that human beings are the key forces shaping the planet Earth today (Sklair 2021). The Anthropocene can be reformulated mainly as the capitalocene in the contemporary stage of global development, stressing the role of capitalism. We may ask if it is possible to avoid global catastrophe. The warning and practical recommendations are based on certain implicit presuppositions of the deeper and long-term developmental tendencies of societies and the whole of human civilization which have to be analysed to really understand the problem and its (im)possible solution (Löwy 2015; Williams 2010).

Of course, skeptics may say it is unlikely to work, just as the milder information campaigns in previous decades have not worked. If that were true, George Monbiot's scenario, which says "a people's rebellion is the only way to fight climate breakdown" (Monbiot 2018), could be considered. If this scenario were not successful as well, there would not be long to wait for a collapse. Then, there is only the hope that the catastrophe will not be too big that it cannot be fixed in the future.

Critical Paradigms

> Without that existential moment, the struggle for recognition, which permeates the whole being of man, praxis is reduced to technique and manipulation. Praxis is the making of man and the mastering of nature, and the realisation of human freedom.
>
> KAREL KOSÍK, *Dialectics of the Concrete*

∴

1   Work and Eros

Having considered the constituent programmatic documents of Critical Theory and the formulations of and challenges to the paradigm of work in the previous chapter, I will now, in quicker succession, analyse the subsequent development of Critical Theory, which has resulted in efforts to reformulate and transgress the paradigm of work and to open up other points of departure through the gradual articulation of alternative paradigms. I will focus not on an entire comprehensive explanation of paradigmatic evolution but on the core agenda. After an introductory paragraph on the crystallisation of paradigms in the 20th century, I will discuss particular paradigms as conceived by pivotal critical theorists. Whether and in what form the individual components of the trichotomy – criticism, explanation, and normativity – are present in or absent from the paradigms will be my guide.

After a stage of positivism and interpretations sharing an emphasis on the impartiality of inquiry or, at least, on the isolated descriptive nature of scientific discourse, attempts to scientifically describe social reality directly ceased to be methodologically feasible. Further, Marxism, which was critically focused but remained within the realm of too straightforward description, required revision. In the wake of social, economic and political complex problems, it was no longer possible to inquire without a sophisticated mediated approach. Wittgenstein placed an emphasis on understanding language which has been a way of avoiding pseudo-problems and poor problem-solving. The *linguistic turn*, or turn to language, introduced a new form of inquiry in the 20th century. With the linguistic turn, scholars started asking how we understand sentences containing claims about social and political issues. Yet language is a very narrow medium incapable of expressing that much. It was necessary to broaden the horizon. As of the 1960s, the *cultural turn*, along with the establishment of cultural studies, saw a focus on creating meaning, not only in language but in all human life in its cultural interactions. The initial emphasis on mass culture in cultural studies later began to concentrate more on the construction of identities. However, the inability to articulate the importance of intersubjective relationships in community and the reductionist focus on individual products of the cultural industry in particular soon necessitated a new approach to human life in society. The *recognition turn,* which does not, however, cover the whole plurality of other approaches, began to crystallise in the 1980s and has been developed since the 1990s. It has pointed to the significance of relations of misrecognition and struggles for mutual recognition of persons in various spheres of society. The dynamics of struggles for recognition in the community deliver a more systematic and more articulated understanding of social and political conflicts. As the Eastern Block collapsed, however, the topic of the expansion of global economic forces emerged. The *global turn* problematised the ability of the nation state to stand its ground under the pressures of transnational capital and meant that there was a challenge to create and institutionalise transnational, supranational and global responses, whether in the form of social forums and movements or macro-regions of large developing countries. The theme of global interactions started to transform into a paradigmatic form.

The transformation of paradigms took place in several stages over the evolution of Critical Theory and other critically focused social theories, in conjunction with the theories of key authors and their successors. If we were to limit ourselves to the main currents of thought, which, obviously, cannot capture the intellectual richness of critical research entirely, we could say that there are primarily four to five paradigms, of which the first two were developed by the first generation of authors of Critical Theory and, then, were steadily expanded by each further generation: (1) the paradigm of work or production (Marx), which was initially – following a certain redefinition and supplementation – developed at the inception of Critical Theory (Horkheimer, Marcuse) and then criticised (Horkheimer, Adorno); (2) the revitalisation of the previous paradigm by a concept of instinctive – especially sexual – nature (Marcuse); (3) the paradigm of communicative action (Habermas); (4) the paradigm of recognition (Honneth); and (5) the paradigm of global interactions (a plurality of authors). Although the authors in brackets are not the sole representatives of these paradigms, they can be regarded as the main (or among the main) authors focusing on them in Critical Theory.

Herbert Marcuse, whose opinion, compared to the point of view of Horkheimer and the standpoints of certain other critical theorists, was distinguished by relative continuity, did not abandon, like the authors of *Dialectics of Enlightenment*, a potential positive solution to the unsatisfactory situation and after the World War II tried to reformulate the existing programme of Critical Theory by grounding it psychoanalytically. Marcuse attempted to overcome the inadequacy of the paradigm of work by interlinking Marx's criticism of oppression created by economic factors with Freud's reflection on the importance of the repression of instinct for human civilization, which he achieved by elaborating on the sociological and political foundations of Freud's theory (Marcuse 1987). Erich Fromm took a similar approach (Fromm 1936, 77–135). The psychoanalytic interpretation of human satisfaction and happiness, associated with conflicts of different instincts depending on their somatic and psychological aspect (or more generally on the aspects of nature and civilisation), is incorporated by the authors into an interpretation of the historical development of society. Human civilisation here is shaped by the sublimation of instincts and by work. While Freud believes that the emergence and further evolution of civilisation is based on a repressive approach to instincts, Marcuse critically rejects Freud's fatalism conveyed by the repression of instincts and offers his own complementary alternative interpretation upholding Eros (libido) as a creative element in the evolution of human civilization. This explanation includes an allusion showing that although the history of mankind remains a dialectical kind of negation of nature, it is, in some respects, a cultivated negation which, through work, overcomes the unwanted elements of nature and embraces positive nature as the driving force for the development of civilisation. In the atmosphere of the student movement and the New Left in the 1960s and 1970s, the refusal of the existing repressive approach to instinctive nature and to work brought Marcuse considerable success and the status of intellectual leader in the then revolt against a repressive social order. Marcuse identified a source of criticism and normativity in instinctive nature, specifically in motivation by pleasure (Marcuse 1979).[1] This source can be seen as the beginning of the transcending of the existing state of society; the reformulated Freudian theory of instincts here is the basis of the overhang in the social order. Numerous authors have proceeded similarly. For example, Cornelius Castoriadis formulated a body of change closely linked to analyses of pressure in the pre-social, psychological realm. According to this interpretation, human

---

1   The transition from the economic concept of work to the concept of instinct also includes their partial interlinking. Lawrence Birken explains the importance of Freud's economic principle for his psychoanalysis, for example (Birken 1999, 311–330).

being is instinctively destined to form ever better conditions for life and to resist social oppression.

In his study of one-dimensional man, which became an essential subversive work not only of the revolts of the 1960s but of the entire New Left and the subsequent emancipatory social movement, Marcuse develops his analyses further, reformulating them to apply them to social conditions (Marcuse 1991). He explains new, sophisticated forms of the domination of people in capitalist societies and in the Soviet Union at that time. Nevertheless, he focuses mainly on the ideology of Western developed societies and criticises consumerism as a form of control and domination. He analyses the creation of artificial needs that bind, rather than liberate, mankind.

Nina Power, outlining a theory of the one-dimensional woman, uses arguments that pick up on Marcuse (Power 2009). In her objective of developing future feminism, she criticises not only the prevailing ideology that discriminates against women but also the current forms of feminism, which, satisfied with small successes in the opportunity to incorporate women into the existing unjust system of work and celebrating an individual cultural identity, have acceded to a position of excessive compromise which reproduces the status of women as one-dimensional components of the production system in the pacifying clutches of consumerism (Fraser 2009, 97–117). The analysis emphasises the need not to overlook the "objective basis" of obstacles to women's equality, the "material basis" of an ideology which makes it impossible for classic types of social organization to be successful in their protests and efforts at change. This unveiling of ideology and economy is a source of opportunity for the new political formulation of feminist criticism.

Marcuse also identifies ambivalent trends in societal development. On the one hand, he thinks that developed societies will soon be ready for a shift towards a more progressive order but, on the other hand, he also analyses the dangerous trends that hinder positive development and could threaten society. He tried to articulate an outline of prerequisites for the positive outcome of development which he thematised in connection with automation-driven rising labour productivity, generating ever more wealth as a material precondition for equitable order, and conditions for the removal of domination. Marcuse presents a vision of society which need not stray from the practices of traditional repressive sublimation to practices of repressive desublimation, as witnessed by Marcuse, but can transform itself into a society of non-repressive sublimation. Such evolution, however, requires the development of creative and critical potential of human beings, which Marcuse, in the last period of his life, searches for primarily in autonomous aesthetic manifestations which could also be applied in the social and political spheres.

Overall, it might be said that Marcuse's transition to the paradigm of instinctive nature progressed, over several stages, hand in hand with his attempts to redefine the paradigm of work. Yet, these efforts to synthesise sublimation with work did not become a model example of a fundamental paradigm shift. Furthermore, Marcuse, like other authors of first-generation Critical Theory, stayed put with specifically developed criticism and explanation, and although he shifted his analysis to the reformulation of Critical Theory, he did not develop the normative aspect of his theory, keeping instead to fragments and implicit references.

2　　Communication and Recognition

Jürgen Habermas, the leading personality of the second-generation Critical Theory, overstepped the productivist paradigm of work by original means. He tried to overcome the instrumentalistically focused conception of social theory and the pessimistic ramifications of analyses of the *Dialectics of Enlightenment*, and developed a normative concept of society by inclining towards the "linguistic turn" paradigm. The path to this transformation led through his analyses of the transformation of the public sphere and the societal crisis of legitimacy (Habermas 1989).[2] Habermas established himself by means of critical analyses of the historical inception and development of the bourgeois public in European countries, crystallised by debate among citizens in a setting where newspapers, libraries, cafes and other cultural institutions were formed. The public, in its infancy and in the early stages of its development in the 18th century, inherently continued to encompass the important factor of criticism of feudal state power. The bourgeoisie started replacing the feudal culture of representation, representing the interests of a narrow economic group of people, with the culture of participation, delivering democratic potential. Its critical dimension, however, began to fade as the influence of capitalism spread, the mass media was commercialised, information was commodified and the welfare state became increasingly permeated with society. The regressive evolution of citizens' participation in public affairs limited their involvement in the democratic decision-making process. The supposed freedoms of Western societies are severely constrained also by this growing civic passivity. Habermas interlaces these considerations with the crisis of legitimacy in late capitalism.

2　Cf. another important author of the same critical-theory generation (Wellmer 1969). Of the younger authors following up on Habermas's analyses here (Cohen and Arato 1992).

The crisis of legitimacy refers to a situation in which the government is no longer able to sufficiently justify the existing political, economic and social order. Citizens reject the current pseudo-consensus and demand change. Although Habermas increasingly focused on the themes related to the communication of citizens in public space, the line of interpretation in his analyses at this time continued to be partly inspired by the paradigm of work.

The full shift of the focus of Habermas's interest to the transformation of Critical Theory from a concept of consciousness in the subject-object relationships to a concept of language in the intersubjective relationships peaked in the early 1980s. With this transition from the paradigm of work to the paradigm of communication, Habermas provided Critical Theory with an entirely new general theoretical framework, based on which he made a distinction between instrumental rationality, connected with a functionalist description, and communicative rationality, which he normatively defined by his consensus-oriented theory of communicative action (Habermas 2015). Habermas laid these new foundations employing his analysis of the historical development of communicative action and, based on this analysis, he formulated universally applicable, general patterns of communicative action. As a result, he started shifting the focus of attention from criticism and explanation to normativity and explanation.

The political and legal implications of this interdisciplinary-steeped social theory opened up the issue of the relationship between description and prescription, between facticity and validity (Habermas 1992). According to Habermas, a theory only normatively defined, such as the current egalitarian liberalism, the representative epitome of which is Rawls's liberalism, does not take into account the realisation of ideals in real society, deformed by the imperatives of power and organisational functionalism. On the other hand, contemporary systems theory, such as that of Luhmann, which is a good example of a purely descriptive theory, reflects, in its technocratic approach to society, only the objectified structure of the autopoetic configuration of system mechanisms. In contrast to these one-sided approaches, Habermas prefers a dual perspective able to reflect the normative opinion of participants and the descriptive position of the observer of these system mechanisms. Habermas's theory is aimed at anchoring a normative designation of claims to validity in a specific environment of society while analysing the relationship between the facticity of law, which is specified by its actual birth and institutional presence, and its validity, which depends on the how it is generally recognised among citizens.

However, while Habermas's standpoint is characterised by its efforts at a balanced relationship between description and prescription, which is the basis of his theory, his attitude to criticism is suppressed. The critically exposed conflict of interests of different social groups, which was the focus of earlier Critical Theory, is now replaced by a vague prescriptive consensus of communicative action. The later development of this consensual standpoint by a stress on ahistorically conceived and effectively procedurally guaranteed individual rights introduced Habermas into the mainstream of contemporary political thinking and went a long way towards convergence with egalitarian liberalism.

Axel Honneth, one of leaders in third-generation Critical Theory, who assumed Horkheimer's and Habermas's chair of social philosophy at the University of Frankfurt and took up the post of director of the Institute for Social Research, tried to revitalise the criticism factor and establish the recognition paradigm. Following up on the original interdisciplinary project of Critical Theory pursued by Horkheimer and Marcuse, in the processing of both Adorno's and Horkheimer's radically critical approach to instrumental reason and Habermas's normative conception of communicative reason, he attempts, on the one hand, not to sink into the all-spurning pessimism of the war and post-war period, and, on the other, not to let the local affluence of the welfare state in Western countries of the 1970s and 1980s make him turn a blind eye to persistent inequalities and systemic pathologies. Although he continues Habermas's efforts to develop normativity, he realises that, in the tradition of Critical Theory, criticism has not yet been thoroughly normatively justified or developed into a form of social philosophy and theory. In this respect, he makes the association between criticism and normativity the central relationship of his theory. He thinks that social criticism, criticism of societal pathology, requires the differentiation of normality from the criticized state. Understanding social 'pathology' requires an articulation of the conditions of human self-realisation which can be expressed indirectly by negative concepts referring to social conditions (Honneth 1994b, 9–70; Honneth 1990). The theory of points of intersection of the various concepts of social normality must be general enough to allow these concepts to be incorporated into the theory, yet specific enough to shed light on their subjects. For this reason, Honneth draws up a formal concept that, not wishing to substantially dictate to people the details of their lives, articulates not the full objectives of human self-realisation but only its assumptions.

On the one hand, Honneth builds on Habermas's intersubjective turn but, on the other, he believes that normative-based Critical Theory should close the split, caused by Habermas's theory, between only positively conceived theoretical norms of communication and the everyday conflictual social action in which social norms are actually to be found. People do not criticise because they perceive a deviation from the consensual rules of communication but due to existential experience of a violation of moral norms gained in the course of their socialisation, i.e., due to a lack of recognition of their intuitively present social patterns and associated demands for recognition of their person. Lack of recognition, which initially prevents the self-realisation of individuals and social groups, is then a source of criticism and motivation to engage in a social struggle for recognition. As Honneth does not believe that it is enough to define criticism, thus conceived, in a theory of communication based on the linguistic turn, he develops, by building on the cultural turn, a more complex intersubjective concept of community which, in its very kernel, is capable of reflecting a framework extending beyond the linguistic. In his formal theory of social recognition in the context of community, he replaces Habermas's aspect of consensus with the prism of conflict, allowing differences to be uncovered and eliminated, and therefore reinforces the theme of criticism in Critical Theory, but mainly does so from the perspective of formulating the normative articulation of criticism, not much from the perspective of criticism per se (Honneth 1996).

Honneth's theory deals with the complex patterns of mutual recognition between people in a community's social institutions, specifically the synchronous levels of recognition: recognition at the level of primary private relationships, recognition at the level of legal relationships, and recognition at the level of a value community in the form of solidarity and recognition of performance. Another integral part of his theory is the diachronic part which addresses the historical process of gaining recognition in the West in recent centuries. Honneth traces this development as the historical formation of different types of norms of recognition. Although concepts of work and communication are rejected as paradigms here, they are present in the recognition paradigm as elements.

Although Honneth's concept of recognition is an inspiring theory, its benefit is overshadowed by an underestimation of descriptive specification and, thus, of the entire explanation of the phenomena. Although Honneth attempts to link normative theory with historically specified moral realism by abstracting general trends in the development of moral values from moral development – as I discussed in the first chapter – the descriptive component of his theory and, by association, the criticism of society remain only modestly developed (Fraser and Honneth 2003). In the absence of real knowledge of injustice in society, or only based on the fleeting thematisation thereof, Critical Theory can hardly articulate the main issues which people point out in their criticism and which they try to resolve (Fasenfest 2022; Thompson 2016). Overstretching a normative aspect dulls sensitivity to genuine human ailments and, therefore, the normative specification of the theory lacks sufficient grounding. Iris Young and Nancy Fraser elaborated on these arguments in their original way on the one hand, and on the other, they moved beyond them, in an inspiring way, by complementing these analyses with other motifs and by developing their theories from the aspect of arguments and concerning feminism and the global context (Fraser 1997; Fraser and Honneth 2003; Young 2000).

3 Global Interactions

As I would like to recall the Central European context from which I come, I will introduce the development of paradigms by our authors. Some of them say that they themselves are Critical Theorists, others share certain themes and research approaches with them but belong to a wider range of critical theory. The involvement of these authors in critical-theory research began to consolidate from the second generation of Critical Theory whose most prominent Czech figure was a philosopher Karel Kosík. The wider range of authors of this generation in Czechoslovakia, which was formed against the inspiring backdrop of the 1960s, includes (and I by no means claim to be making an exhaustive list) following figures proffering various interpretations. While large sociological research of the Czechoslovak society was led by Pavel Machonin (Machonin 1966; Machonin 1969), a complex social-scientific analysis of the civilization on the crossroad was made under the leadership of Radovan Richta (Richta 2018). Other affiliated authors have been active in the revived cultural output, including creative literary and theatrical works and the Czechoslovak new wave in film. Economic reforms formulated by Ota Šik and his team, aiming to market socialism (Šik 1976), and legal and political reforms formulated by Zdeněk Mlynář with his colleagues (Mlynář 1975) had the most significant economic and political influence.

The third generation of Czechoslovak critical theorists grasped those achievements and attempted advancing them in the subsequent normalisation era of the 1970s and 1980s, and tried again since the 1990s but it was also a time of new, disparately politically conflictual conditions when the fourth generation slowly crystallised in the new Western context of very widespread international cooperation and the fifth one has continued in the global context.

As I mentioned, the most significant Czech figure to develop ideas of critical theory was Karel Kosík, one of the most influential 20th-century Czech philosophers. His masterpiece, *Dialectics of the Concrete* (Kosík 2012), has been translated into many languages and greatly influenced international debate in and after the 1960s. In certain aspects, his approach was close to that pursued by Herbert Marcuse in his attempt to link the paradigm of work with existentialist themes. However, as I will explain, Kosík also contributed partly to the development of the recognition paradigm and – in his late period – also to the opening-up of the paradigm of global interactions. With a certain simplification, it is possible to say about the Czechoslovak critical social thought at that time that, while Karel Kosík updated it mainly with inspiring existentialist motives, the mentioned Radovan Richta, with his original analysis of civilizational development, was the main representative of scientific-technical solutions to societal problems. Both together, each of them by his own way, co-created theoretical bases of a revitalization of the society at that time.

If we want to understand Kosík work, we must first clarify its place in the coordinates of critical thinking and critical theory (Kosík 1997c, 18; Kosík 2012; Kosík 1958). Kosík himself provides a good guide to understanding his theory, stating that, for example, Spinozism, physicalism (or more generally positivism) and postmodernism are alien to his thinking.[3] I will build on one path of Kosík's thinking which some critical theorists continue to follow today. It is possible to see Kosík's dialectics of the concrete and his late criticism of global forces also as a contribution to a version of the theory of recognition, i.e., as a dialectic of concrete recognition. Kosík works contain ample sources evidencing that the earlier interpretation of his work as a mere synthesis of Marxism and existentialism or as phenomenological Marxism[4] can now be replaced by a more fitting interpretation that reveals the previously only partially articulated potential of his work. This new interpretation considers critical theory building on Marxist materialist theory, existentialism, and new-Hegelianism,[5] which would be also enriched by essays on global interactions in Kosík's later works.

It is instructive to examine how Kosík incorporates the Hegelian element into the centre of his Marxist materialist philosophy. He arrives at an

---

3   See, for example: "Spinozism and physicalism are the two most widespread types of the reductionist method, which converts the wealth of reality into something basic and elementary. All the world's wealth is cast into the abyss of immutable substance." (Kosík 1997c, 23). Also see: "There was a cataclysmic shift: mankind is ejected from the place where it belongs ... into philistinism and vacuity, into the one-dimensionality of a functioning system. And the postmodern ideology accompanies this decline by arguing that there is no truth." (Kosík 1997c, 27).

4   Such an interpretation (usually in connection with Heidegger-Marxism), while not wrong, only paves the way for the main historically appreciated aspects in Kosík's work to be affiliated with the work of Sartre and Marcuse.

5   For the sake of distinction, I use the term new-Hegelianism for the present, as opposed to neo-Hegelianism for the 19th century.

inclusion of new-Hegelian aspects in *Dialectics of the Concrete* at the latest. This by no means constitutes a mere return to Hegel because Kosík's materialist philosophy includes and updates certain parts of the Hegelian thought. Kosík states that the emergence of Marxism tends to be associated with the collapse of Hegel's philosophical system. Whereas Hegel's system represented unity, Marxism and existentialism – in Kosík's interpretation – are two of its offshoots. On the one hand, Kosík believes that the term "collapse" obscures the fact of the original fruitful philosophical activity which was a condition precedent to Marxism and existentialism. On the other hand, he points to the inadequacy of this interpretation, in that it renders the Hegelian system the maximum unity, and turns the following philosophical currents into mere apostate "unilateralism". According to Kosík, each of these three streams can in fact be regarded as a peak, and the two remaining ones as elements of the collapse. For Marx, Hegel and Kierkegaard could, at first glance, represent only objective and subjective idealism. Kierkegaard, for his part, could view Hegel's philosophy as an inanimate system of concepts and Marx's teachings as alienated technological determinism. This does not mean any relativism. Kosík finds the criterion of the correctness of every single opinion in philosophical activity, which can understand other positions in their contemporary conditionality and limitations by illustrating the opportunity for their historical defeat. This is a historical truth that Kosík documents with Marx, while also showing what specific historical form it may take: "Materialist philosophy may, in certain historical periods, make a distinction between the philosophy of 'absolute spirit' (Hegelianism) to which the complementary critical addition is the philosophy of existence and moralism" (Kosík 1963, 119–120).

Kosík says of his theoretical approach that it is not a simple theory, but a "theoretical *criticism* or *critical* theory" (Kosík 1963, 127–128; Kosík 2012), as it does not just illuminate certain objective given facts and their historical forms but also follows the birth and evolution of a collective subject which surpasses these historically inadequate formations in praxis. The concept of praxis emphasizes human creation. It has ontological significance because, in praxis, a human being, through his work, not only enriches an object to which he has access but is also revealed as a being that historically produces the reality of human society and, for this reason, he also understands it. Man, in this sense, is an "onto-formative" being. The reality, through the concept of praxis, is revealed to be the opposite of definiteness; it is formulated as a "shaping". Kosík depicts this argument with the principle: "Praxis ... is the determination of the human being as a shaping of reality" (Kosík 1963, 154).

What critical theory of praxis is derived from this interpretation? Kosík specifies the praxis of human beings by first discussing the fact that human

beings, based on labour, i.e., based on the objectification or shaping of civilisation, give their presence new meaning by starting to think about the future.
Through labour, human beings discover the future appears as a new dimension
of their being. In this way, they are gradually able to make out their finitude.

Building on Hegel, Kosík states that the dimensions of human existence are
articulated in the struggle for recognition. Human beings realise their finitude
in the struggle for life, in the fight to the death. Aware of how it may end, they
opt for slavery or, conversely, they fight to be recognised as the master. Through
this choice, the future slave and future master display their ability to project
the future and, accordingly, to shape the present in the struggle for recognition. In this way, human beings manifested their freedom in the past.

In the struggle for recognition, existential moments such as anxiety or
fear of death, or even joy or hope, come to the fore. It is in these that man is
formed as a free being. In the absence of this complementary element, which
is an existential moment, labor could not be a component of praxis. In summary, the motto of Kosík's critical theory of recognition can be expressed by
the proposition: "Without that existential moment, the struggle for recognition, which permeates the whole being of man, *praxis* is reduced to tech-
nique and manipulation. Praxis is the making of man and the mastering of
nature, and the realisation of human freedom." (Kosík 1963, 156; cf. Kosík 1993,
118) In this sense, praxis includes both the labour and the existential moment.
Concentration only on the labour aspect of praxis leads to manipulation and
forestalls the development of freedom because freedom cannot stem only
from objective relations with nature. Therefore, in his quest to destroy the
pseudo-concrete, Kosík places the moment of recognition at the core of his
conception of praxis: "The dialectic of master and servant is the basic model
of praxis." (Kosík 1963, 156) In general, Kosík's interpretation of the struggle for
recognition is obvious. However, various authors' different interpretations of
the dialectic of master and servant confront us with the question of which of
several paths would Kosík follow if this theme were to be made more concrete.
If we were to make a comparison, it could be said that Marx moves within the
paradigm of work and views the struggle for recognition as a conflict involving the economic self-affirmation of a particular social class. His early philosophical and anthropological considerations, however, have inspired various
authors to engage in the more fruitful development of the debate on recognition. According to Honneth, a theory in which the struggle for recognition
under the paradigm of work is identified only with the struggle for economic
self-affirmation, e.g., Marxist functionalism, is inadequate, since it reflects
only one component of the necessary recognition. Human beings cannot be
reduced to *homo faber*, although the formation of civilization and humankind

is highly structured by human productive activities. However, as work incorporates a dimension that is a source of the social recognition of a person who has achieved something through his work, an interpretation reducing the work paradigm to mere instrumental action, or even rejecting it entirely, is also unreasonable. Jean-Paul Sartre does not go that far but emphasizes an existentially conceived conflict between people and the struggle for recognition, which he perceives as the process of objectifying subjects (Sartre 2003; 1985). Alexandre Kojeve anticipates Sartre's existentialist interpretation and tracks the realisation of death in the struggle for recognition as a precondition for the freedom of a human subject (Kojeve 1980).

Regarding existentialist interpretations, Honneth states that the main significance of the struggle for recognition does not lie in the precarious cognition of human mortality (Honneth 1996; 2001; 2003; Fraser and Honneth 2003). In connection with the intersubjective interpretation, he explains that cognition of a rival's mortality in the struggle for recognition need not be crucial in many contemporary societies, as adversaries in the struggle for recognition gain the most benefit from the formation of certain reciprocal social relations. In this respect, a fundamental factor in the struggle for recognition is already cognition of a rival's opposition, whereby the adversary conveys his vulnerability. Thus, a subtle understanding of the struggle for recognition shows that mutual recognition may have a more sensitive threshold: cognition of another's existential vulnerability. Nevertheless, at the same time, it is undeniable that the escalation of conflict into mortal combat is of primary significance in many societies.

However, existential interpretations suffer from the unresolved relationship between subject and object in this redefinition. This is why an update of the concept of the struggle for recognition requires, first, clarification and, then, an intersubjective turn, i.e. a turn from monological interpretations which are too objectivist (under the paradigm of work or the subject-object paradigm) or too subjectivist (under the paradigm of the existentialistically isolated subject) to intersubjective interpretations (within the framework of the paradigm of recognition, or at least the narrower paradigm of communication).

If Kosík had proceeded along this path of reasoning, he could have resolved the problems he was attempting to eliminate. Because he attempted to elevate the problem of freedom (which, naturally, had not only philosophical but also, and above all, historically contingent social coordinates), he placed a particular emphasis on the existential moment of praxis, trying to compensate for the work moment, but a more developed balanced reformulation of the two moments was not forthcoming in his theory. The failure to complete the answer to this question shows the limits of Kosík's theory, the untapped potential of which comprises the clarification of intersubjective relations between objectivism (or rather pseudo-objectivism) of the paradigm of work and a version of existentialist heightened subjectivism. It could be said that while the fixation on an interpretation of the purely productive aspect of recognition continues to draw its strength solely from the *working* or *objective* moment of praxis, and the fixation solely on the interpretation of the purely existential aspect of recognition is based only on the *subjective* moment of praxis, the interpretation of the *intersubjective* aspect of recognition fully facilitates recognition of both the work and freedom of a human being. Therefore, the intersubjective turn is a prerequisite for a balanced concept of recognition and the opportunity to criticize a manipulative approach to human beings.

However, Kosík's contribution to the interaction of these concepts of work and existence is, in my opinion – much like Sartre's contribution, for example – undeniable. Kosík's references to the importance of conversation and the involvement of the individual in interpersonal relationships in the community are also headed in the adequate direction (Kosík 2004, 75–81; 1993, 20–21;).[6] For this reason, we can appreciate the fact that he opened up the path to the intersubjective turn, even though this was not completed in his work. Criticising Kosík for this shortfall in *Dialectics of the Concrete*, which was an extraordinary achievement at the time, would be historically unjust.

It is still important to remember that, in the long run, only the path of the servant leads to freedom, while the way of the master is blind alley. The perception of the mere immediate future proves to be an illusion while the mediated future is the truth. However, I am compelled to leave a detailed explanation of the trends in development aside here because I want to focus on the continuity of Kosík's late essays with his conception of recognition from *Dialectics of the Concrete*, more narrative essays discussing major current problems, specifically global capitalism, which also opens up the paradigm of global interactions. Here, Kosík linked with foreign authors who had started critical analyses of global interactions even earlier than he had, and whom I also discuss in this book. Although Kosík's critique of global forces in his later essays is characterised by a certain sceptical shift, it is still based on his earlier formulations. It is only through this connection with *Dialectics of the Concrete* that Kosík's later texts assume greater weight, because, as stand-alone works, they would have been deprived of deeper theoretical background.

---

6   Elements of this thinking can already be found in Kosík's early work *Česká radikální demokracie. Příspěvek k dějinám názorových sporů v české společnosti 19. století* (1958).

The essay "Our Current Crisis" shows the interdependence between Kosík's thinking in the 1960s and the 1990s. The fact that, in 1993, Kosík completed the seventh and eighth chapters of this essay, which dates from the spring of 1968, is proof that he was able and willing, in one text, to build on his earlier ideas and develop them further. The degree of shift in his standpoint could not then have been insurmountable for him.

In the added chapters of the essay, Kosík criticises the manipulative aspect of praxis. He focuses on the capitalist and real-socialist systems and tries to uncover the essence of social crisis with a critique on its fundamental determinants by analysing the market and regimentation (Kosík 1993, 49ff; 1997c, 29). The hypertrophy of these two elements, free competition and planning, brings the two systems into conflict, and thus, according to Kosík, obscures the very essence of the current crisis. The kernel of the problem is the alienated "mechanism of production and consumption", which dictates the dynamics of life of human beings. This mechanism is a special "historical formation" converted into the synthesis of economy, technology, science and other associated activities (Kosík 1993, 52; 1997c, 28–29; 1997b, 252). The fusion of originally separate spheres into a single result in the manipulative relationships of human beings to themselves and to others. Kosík reiterates and develops these ideas in the essay "Seven Autumn Stops", referring to the symbiosis of economy, science and technology as "gigantism" and "titanism" (Kosík 2004, 57–59). This conglomerate successively subordinates other areas of human life and gains a monopoly position. The essay "Morality in Times of Globalisation" deals with technology, science, finance, industry, ideology and warfare in this symbiotic unit (Kosík 2004, 90f, 96). Morality does not belong here, however, because it has been reduced to two versions of rules. The first version is a series of system standards, the other lies in "moralistic rhetoric", the task of which is to feign that morality has not yet been expelled by the system. In this situation, not even those who belong to the ruling elite can express themselves freely because they become mere service apparatus in an impersonal system of economic, military and other institutions. The manipulative moment here prevails over the existential moment.

Kosík explains the system conglomerate in his essay "Bridges Across a European River" by drawing on the struggle for recognition in its ultimate form, namely in the form of war. He states that, in the past, it was possible to stand face to face with a war adversary, to show mercy in the struggle for recognition and devote one's life thereto. Now, however, the struggle no longer takes place directly between opponents but in an alienated form without personal contact. The latest technology allows one of the rivals for recognition to have absolute supremacy, removing the need for an existential approach to the conflict (Kosík

2004, 113–114). The human dimension is lost because the system overshadows the existential dimension of human beings and, with that, their freedom. In a global era, Kosík muses, the strongest of the rivals in the struggle for recognition establishes hegemony and eliminates human freedom by employing systemic measures and the rhetorical pretense of promoting freedom.

Kosík incorporates this argument into his earlier line of reasoning. In the essay "All Power Comes from the Imagination", he recalls his idea from *Dialectics of the Concrete* concerning two moments of praxis, which comprises, on the one hand, the control of nature and, hence, the objectification of human beings, and, on the other, the realisation of freedom through recognition. This time, however, he emphasises the result of the one-sided implementation of praxis in modern times:

> There is an *ambiguity* intrinsic in the grand modern inception: the subject not only has the will to be free, but it is also encumbered with the yearning to rule over nature, to become a monopoly owner and master. ... [This] *re*-binds people, shackling them to the functioning system which transforms them into *its* accessories, *its* objects, *its* servants.
> KOSÍK 1997c, 22

Kosík highlights the instrumental power of the system and its gravitational force depriving man of his freedom. Yet he does not remain only at abstract criticism. In other essays, he discusses the form currently taken by this system. He speaks out directly against the aggression of transnational capital, differentiating it from the old forms of capital and calling it global super-capital engulfing the "modern *bestia triumphans*" (Kosík 1997c, 27).[7] Then, he intensifies this idea by criticising super-capital for the deprivation of liberty, and from this he refers to democracy:

> The planetary giant Super-capital suffers and tolerates democracy provided that it puts up no resistance. Democracy does not live with contemporary capitalism in a voluntary association and natural, equal coexistence: Super-capital *limits* democracy, reduces it to a half-hearted democracy unable to cope with many of today's fundamental problems.
> KOSÍK 1997b, 244–245

---

7 Kosík raises a similar argument about global or planetary domination or a planetary task force in his essay "Lumpenbourgeoisie and the Higher Spiritual Truth" (1997b, 250–252). Kosík revives the term *bestia triumphans* with reference to an 1897 treatise of the same name by the Mrštík brothers (Kosík 1997a, 75).

Kosík explains that the existing system is being reproduced but in new global dimensions, resulting in the ever-greater enrichment of a privileged minority, i.e., the West (Kosík 1997c, 23). He emphasises that problems accompanying the promotion of the existing order could also affect the Global South:

> If Europe, including Russia, together with the United States, fails to see through the dangerous game in which it is being drawn by an anonymous dictator in time, and the desperate population of the South begins rallying against the parasitic North, this could be disastrous: a catastrophe will occur if the rebels succumb to the fascination of the Euro-American way of life and the sole aim of their action is to rise to the ranks of the nobility ... to assume its habits and normality.
>
> KOSÍK 1997a, 236; cf. SAKWA 2017

The current crisis can be surmounted if a liberating alternative to the dominant model of global interactions is found (Kosík 1997c, 28; 1968). Kosík believes that, if we could identify and implement a model capable of harmonising the objectifying moment of work and the existential moment of freedom, we would be on the right track. He also shows that the lack of mutual recognition of people in the manipulating symbiosis of technology, economy, militarism and other parts of the existing system is pushing us only along a trajectory of declining freedom over the whole of our lives. Kosík's contribution embodies, in crystalline form, efforts to link the elements of social structure and action of the subject. Not only the main ideas of his famous *Dialectics of the Concrete* but also his outline of the paradigms of recognition and global interactions, his critique of their unjust and pathological characteristics and his normative implication of opportunities, make Kosík's considerations – despite their limits – an important theoretical work.

At the end of this chapter, it would be fitting to include an interpretation of the theme of global interactions I opened via the ideas of Karel Kosík. The concept of global interactions has transformed from a theme to a paradigm, and has been analysed by multiple critical authors, some of whom, especially members of the third and fourth generations of Critical Theory, focused on this research more than Kosík. At this point, I will only mention a few important texts which, from my perspective, have opened up the necessary questions in the context of critical theory and on which I dwell in this book.

While investigations of global interactions began simultaneously as these interactions became the truly planetary conquest of the Americas more than 500 years ago, it is important in critical social research to cite Marx and Engels's characterization of these interactions as continuing previous national processes of industrialisation, exploitation, the extinction of old needs and the emergence of new needs:

> The bourgeoisie has through its exploitation of the world market given a cosmopolitan character to production and consumption in every country. To the great chagrin of Reactionists, it has drawn from under the feet of industry the national ground on which it stood. All old-established national industries have been destroyed or are daily being destroyed. They are dislodged by new industries, whose introduction becomes a life and death question for all civilised nations, by industries that no longer work up indigenous raw material, but raw material drawn from the remotest zones; industries whose products are consumed, not only at home, but in every quarter of the globe. In place of the old wants, satisfied by the production of the country, we find new wants, requiring for their satisfaction the products of distant lands and climes. In place of the old local and national seclusion and self-sufficiency, we have intercourse in every direction, universal inter-dependence of nations. And as in material, so also in intellectual production.
>
> MARX and ENGELS 1969

As for a critical theory, Habermas's concept of post-national constellation (Habermas 1998) was a relevant starting point of analyses. It plotted not only the dilemmas of the global era but also oscillations between the answers to these dilemmas. Other authors have presented a reconstructive interpretation with an emphasis on cosmopolitan social justice. A full rundown of analyses of these themes has been also presented by Nancy Fraser in her concept of global redistribution, recognition and representation (Fraser 2010); a like-oriented interpretation was put forward by Iris Young in her concept of social justice, set out in a model of responsibility based on social relations (Young 2007a; 2010). Ulrich Beck, Alexander Wendt and Andrew Linklater also offered pivotal work on global issues (Beck 2005; Beck 1992; Wendt 1999; Linklater 2007; Linklater 1998; cf. Burchill, Devetak and Linklater 2001). Key and influential analyses were formulated in the field of global studies, mainly by Paul Kennedy, Leslie Sklair, Jarry Harris, William Robinson and their colleagues (Kennedy 2010; Kennedy 2017; Robinson 2004; Robinson 2014; Sklair 2002; Sklair 2001; Harris 2008; Harris 2016; Chase-Dunn, Lerro 2013).

Although the theme of transnational and global interactions since the collapse of the Eastern Bloc has been processed in terms of many aspects, whether transnational or global integration moments or the relationships between global conflictual and crisis tendencies and various fragmentary reactions, it has developed partly in parallel to the recognition paradigm. Moreover, the fact of the matter is that past paradigms were also mutually intertwined, and decades were needed, in the face of fluctuating conclusiveness, for them to become more or less established as a relevant discourse.

PART 3

Limits of Liberal Liberty

∵

Deficits of National Liberty

Having formulated the constituent and methodological basis of critical theory in the first part of the book (Chapters 1 and 2) and identified the elements thereof in the historical development of Critical Theory from inception to the present in the second part (Chapters 3 and 4), now I will analyse society and politics by focusing on a critique of liberalism and its nationalist consequences in the third part (Chapters 5 and 6). I will start by analysing national deficits in liberal theory, before progressing to international and transnational deficits. My analysis will consistently concentrate, first, on the political deficit, specifically the democratic deficit, and then, on the social-economic deficit. I will illuminate that the demands imposed by a liberal concept of politics on citizens in the community are at odds with the absence of a participatory stimulus for isolated and alienated citizens in a liberal theory. Insufficiently spoken national assumptions and their unintended consequences in the liberal and libertarian concepts of politics conflict with the ideals of liberty. I will conclude that liberalism and libertarianism (in practice associated with a model of neoliberalism), as a result of their contradictory foundations in political practice throughout history, cyclically lead in their dialectical anti-liberal denial in various milder or stronger versions of national neoconservatism, the establishment of which is also associated with nonegalitarian populism.

My critique of the problematic liberal concept of liberty also touches on the forward-looking promise of liberty made by liberal theory and, to some degree, practice. In the following text, I will show that liberalism is unable to keep its promise and that a more satisfactory concept of liberty is formulated by critical theory. In the first section, I will discuss the deficit arising from the constraints of potential civil participation and from limited democracy, the shortcomings of the liberal concept of the public sphere, and the crucial role played by public reason or, more generally, by public discourse, which is an organisational component of the public sphere.

Then, in the second section, I will stress the actions of individual and collective actors related to the politics of universalism. Then, in my analysis of individualism and instrumental reason, I put forward an interpretation of normative institutions and economic structures embedded in the realism of societal development and a historical understanding of autonomy as a distortedly crystallised constitutive good in modern times.

The third and fourth sections discuss the social deficit. The liberal theory seeks, in some measure, to complement its emphasis on the value of liberty with certain deliberations on the value of citizens' social welfare. I will highlight problems associated with attempts to reduce the social discrepancies thereby arising, first, by analysing the liberal concept of redistribution, specifically by examining the principle of difference. After that, I will show that liberal theory and practice, in analyses of the core values thereof, must eliminate entirely – or at least relegate to the lower rungs of the hierarchy of values – the limited concept of social welfare. The absence of sufficient redistribution in mainstream liberal arguments then prompts me to discuss solutions to external ownership. This debate calls attention to the difference between addressing the mere consequences of social problems and tackling their root causes, i.e.: property.

In my interpretation, I will focus on the paradigmatic liberal theory expounded by the most influential Western political philosopher since the 1970s, John Rawls.[1]

I argue that Rawls' conception of the public sphere is, on the whole, more demanding in normative terms than practical politics, but in principle it embodies a formulation that is an unproblematic complement of the programmes of political parties, and which reproduces the problems of political practice through the aforementioned deficits in a more moderate fashion. These deficits are also found amongst those that, for example, Nancy Fraser – independently of Rawls' work – links with current political theory and practical policy in her study *Rethinking the Public Sphere: A Contribution to the Critique of Actually Existing Democracy* (Fraser 1990). Concerning the democratic deficit, Fraser mentions the need "to understand the limits of actually existing late capitalist democracy" and discusses weak publics in an "actually existing democracy", which is not the same as democracy *per se* (Fraser 1997; Fraser and Honneth 2003; Nicolacopoulos 2008). Based on an analysis of John Rawls's political theory, these deficits can be critically articulated, themes that need to be subsequently explained can be suggested, and, following a study thereof, normative ways out of the deficits can be formulated.

---

1   If we were to sum up the content of Rawls's work in a nutshell, his *A Theory of Justice* and *Political Liberalism* are inclined towards a discussion of the wisest legitimate concept of justice for a liberal democratic society within a *nation*-state, while his *The Law of Peoples* aims to redefine and expand on these ideas to sketch fundamental contours for the *foreign* policy of this type of regime within an acceptable, just society of peoples, and for a more general purpose – the possibility of a *global* society of liberal and decent peoples.

1   Inadequacies of Public Reason

The theory of *justice as fairness*, as formulated by Rawls in his theory of justice, aims to justify normative principles and procedures allowing for the equal distribution of basic goods which are produced by society and to which individual members of society lay competing claims. The theory is based on a contractualist concept of the original position, in which people, based on their individual choices, should hypothetically make a social contract behind a "veil of ignorance", which should enable them to forget reality, neglect their social status, wealth, talent and many other dispositions, and thus independently of their problems and interests decide what principles should apply in society. Rawls believes that in such a – in a way constituent – assembly the people would unanimously opt (effectively as though one person were taking the decision) for principles of justice, to which I will now turn.

First, however, I would dwell on the idea of a hypothetical social contract and its shortcomings. Seyla Benhabib aptly formulates core objections to Rawls's contractualism by questioning his idea of the original position. She is critical of the construction of the 'original position' as a limited process of deliberation of an individual rather than as an open process of collective argumentation, claiming that the model of discursive or communicative ethics should be preferred here because it institutionalises true dialogue between real individuals, who are both "generalised others", considered equal morally acting persons, and "concrete others", i.e. individuals with irreducible differences (Benhabib 1992, 169).

This criticism provides a good basis for considerations in which several points need to be analytically separated. First, the reason for the doubts lies in Rawls's emphasis on the liberal, primly individualistic nature of decision-making, which, in a sense, renders the social contract an unsocial contract because individuals make decisions in isolation, without taking into account the opinions of others. Rawls plainly does not defend a plurality of different persons entering into the contract because, in his opinion, everyone would reach a consensus as though a single person were taking the decision. In this way, he draws only on the situation of like individuals, and therefore there is no need to engender dialogue between them or to take into account their differences, which could not be ignored in dialogue.[2]

---

2   In his theory of justice, Rawls does at least introduce the method of reflective equilibrium, designed to form balanced opinions and to justify a particular position, although this remains a relativist approach unconnected with the activities of citizens (with their criticism

Secondly, this contracting approach excludes the arguments of differently situated specific persons with various characteristics. The proclaimed desirable moral equality of persons is only abstractly declared here, and is not considered together with their real social problems and cultural differences. Another implicit assumption of the original position is its nationalistic nature, as the concept of the original position does not apply to citizens in general, but to the citizens of a given nation-state or nation. This veiled assumption, which should be conceived with regard to poor and other marginalized minorities and foreign issues, could have negative (asocial, xenophobic, violent and other) ramifications in the face of domestic and foreign conflicts inherently caused by the liberal contradictions analysed in this and the following chapter (Harris 2009).

The basic trouble with the original position within the scope of the hypothetical contract is that it ignores people's real problems and prevents them from engaging in dialogue and relationships of justice. Instead of transparent criticism of injustice, it obscures problems behind the concept of the veil of ignorance, which is designed to resolve a matter by ensuring that it is not recognised at all. Yet problems cannot be resolved by ignoring them. What is more, skirting around issues has serious epistemological social consequences. As the hypothetical contract glosses over the real problems that people face, it is unable to establish which themes should be the subject of discussion, let alone allow the decisions to be taken on them. Rawls effectively replaces people's reasoning and decision-making with his individual consideration of his themes, which need not overlap with the topics of people he is considering. In this respect, he ignores social and economic inequalities, cultural discrimination and other issues which people would otherwise act upon. An adequate approach, conversely, would be to begin by considering a *critique* of people's real problems. This alone can form a basis on which to articulate important issues that need to be addressed, and to seek out the norms according to which a solution could be realised.

As to the outcome of the social contract, Rawls argues that the conditions of the original position of choice (which I have just challenged) should deliver principles of justice which, by analogy, are fair. He believes that, in the original position, individuals would unanimously choose them, i.e., on the one hand, they should choose fundamental political and civil liberties and, on the other, they should specifically take into account the worst possible social and

---

and subsequent explanation of problems and requirements) and enabling each individual theorist to assume an opinion which may even be authoritarian.

economic status. Therefore, they would prefer norms which, while not eliminating inequalities between people, should at least allay them slightly:

(a)   Each person has an equal right to a fully adequate scheme of equal
      basic liberties which is compatible with a similar scheme of liber-
      ties for all.
(b)   Social and economic inequalities are to satisfy two conditions. First,
      they must be attached to offices and positions open to all under
      conditions of fair equality of opportunity; and second, they must be
      to the greatest benefit of the least advantaged members of society.
      RAWLS 1983, 5

Although Rawls formulates two principles, there are effectively three principles because the second principle has two parts: the maximum equal liberty
principle, the equal opportunity principle, and the difference principle. The
first principle discusses a set of equal basic political and civil liberties, i.e., formal equal political and civil liberties such as the freedom of conscience and
association, or the freedom of speech or the vote. The equal opportunity principle encompasses the civil and political issues which I will address now. I will
tackle the difference principle, which deals with social issues, later. I emphasise that, while the concept of the "difference principle" is sometimes used as
an umbrella term for the latter two principles, in line with most existing literature I will use it only for the second – social – part. The difference principle
is often referred to as the "second principle", which follows on from the "first
principle", the liberty principle.

As one of the main categories of Rawls's theory – if not the main category –
is public reason, the application of the above principles to the realm of public
reason renders their limits representative. How, then, is the position of a free
citizen applied in the public reason defined by Rawls or, more generally, discourse? Rawls assigns a privileged position to public reason, as indicated by
his works *The Law of Peoples* and *The Idea of Public Reason Revisited*: "Taken
together, they represent the culmination of my reflections on how reasonable
citizens and peoples might live together peacefully in a just world." (Rawls
1999, vi) In other words, the processing of these themes represents a certain
culmination in which Rawls completes his thoughts on international politics
in the concept of the law of peoples and redefines his general thoughts on
the political establishment by means of the notion of public reason. While he
also outlines the role of public reason in international politics, he concentrates
mainly on its application on a national scale in the context of a Western-type
country, namely liberal democracy.

The idea of public reason appeared explicitly for the first time in Rawls' second book *Political Liberalism* (Rawls 1993a, 212–254; Rawls 1999a, 131–180). Since the characteristic feature of liberal democracy is reasonable pluralism, i.e. the reality of the pluralism of different moral, philosophical, and religious *comprehensive doctrines* – (e.g. ecological, Protestant or Catholic), according to Rawls, citizens realize that in solving basic political questions they cannot – on the basis of these comprehensive doctrines – hope to reach agreement (Rawls 1999a, 131–132). Such agreement, however, can be reached with the help of public reason. In the first approximation, public reason is defined as a method to be used by a political community to formulate its plans, determine the priority of its objectives and take its decisions (Rawls 1993a, 212). Rawls states that public reason relates to "'constitutional essentials' and questions of basic justice" (Rawls 1993a, 214; in detail 227–230; Rawls 1999a, 133). In other words, "The idea of public reason specifies at the deepest level the basic moral and political values that are to determine a constitutional democratic government's relation to its citizens and their relation to one another" (Rawls 1999a, 132).

Rawls binds public reason and public discourse together in the sense that the ideal of public reason dominates in public discourse, so that public reason has a controlling influence in public discourse (Rawls 1999a, e.g., 215). He is milder in his expressions elsewhere stating that public reasoning is a type of public discourse (Rawls 1999a, e.g., 155). Since my objective is to show that Rawls' idea of public reason is conceived too narrowly, there are two options on how to proceed in terms of terminology. We can insist on the concept of public reason and expand it or think about a broader approach using a different term.[3] I think the latter option is better as it would enable us to maintain the concept of public reason for Rawls' problematic standpoint and if possible, to reserve a concept of public discourse for a more adequate stance. The conception of public discourse has already been incorporated into a dialogical, communicative or deliberative tradition of thought, which I am building on.[4]

Rawls limits the theory of public discourse by his conception of public reason where he divides citizens into two categories. By establishing boundaries, limits, or restrictions (Rawls 1993a, 214–215) on his concept of public reason, he makes a rather sharp distinction between public and non-public use of reason. On the one hand, he rather unusually assigns the public dimension of reason only to government and related activities, like government statements, parliamentary discussions, discussions in legal proceedings, in political parties,

---

3 Some authors even separate out particular strands of Rawls' idea of public reason and extend them under a different name. Cf. e.g., Cohen (2003).

4 On the history of public discourse, see e.g., Wuthnow (1989).

including election campaigns and their evaluations by citizens in the single act of election. Persons who may use public reason are government officials and candidates for public offices (Rawls 1999a, 133; c.f. Rawls 1993b, § 1–3, 132-152). Their circle is specified by the so-called public political forum that includes

> the discourse of judges in their decisions, and especially of the judges of a supreme court; the discourse of government officials, especially chief executives and legislators; and finally, the discourse of candidates for public office and their campaign managers, especially in their public oratory, party platforms, and political statements.
>
> RAWLS 1999a, 133–134

On the other hand, Rawls completely separates the so-called background culture or the culture of civic society, to which he does not assign the public dimension of reason, from the public political forum (Rawls 1999a, 133–134; Rawls 1993a, 14). Within this culture, he conceives of the non-public dimension of reason extensively in connection with discussions in different schools, especially at universities and in specialized schools, in scientific, professional and voluntary associations, churches and other associations of civil society. In this way he eliminates civic activities from public reason; citizens have no choice but to watch the performance of civil servants, or, – if they do not satisfy public reason – to try to remove them. This relationship between the two categories of citizens within the public discourse is non-communicative because there is no dialogue between them about the various problems. Civil servants either perform their duties well or they can be removed from their offices.

Amongst the activities that Rawls regards as non-public is the media, which, per its name, becomes a mere mediator between the public political culture of civil servants and the culture of civil society (Rawls 1999a, 134). Rawls denotes all kinds of media (TV, radio, newspapers, etc.) as non-public political culture. At the same time, the communication and information revolution has strengthened the influence of traditional and new media, including social networks, to such an extent that their impact on the public sphere has increased significantly. The new forms of media bring hyper-communication with corporately manipulated and chaotically acting participants, and need a restructuring.

In terms of content, it is important to note that, in his arguments on public reason, Rawls excludes certain controversial manifestations and allows for their partial integration only in situations where they reinforce public reason. This includes the presentation of various comprehensive doctrines (philosophical, moral or religious) by the proponents or opponents thereof.

Although, in certain circumstances, presenting such manifestations might not be appropriate, the thematisation thereof shows the limits of Rawls's theory and allows us to outline the entire spectrum of manifestations we might consider when trying to expand the concept of public reason in such a way as to embrace the activities of a wider range of participants than just civil servants. For instance, Jurgen Habermas convincingly argues that there is a danger of marginalisation of the various arenas of the political public, particularly social movements, voluntary associations and other areas of communication within civil society, including the media (Habermas 1995, 109–131; Rawls 1995, 132–180; Habermas 1989). These independent public forums that are not identical with state administration and economic systems are, to him, the essence of the sovereignty of the people. Thomas McCarthy offers an apt expression of Habermas' attitude in his discussion with Rawls, stating that in this conception of a deliberative decentring of power, various public arenas for debating a variety of issues relating to problems of society and politically and culturally activated publics are the key for democratic self-government of citizens.[5]

The part of public discourse overlooked by Rawls, i.e., that what he considers to be an unofficial forum of citizens, is an unmistakable cornerstone of the self-government of free citizens, i.e.: democracy. The articulation of ideas and discussions thereon in a civil society is a key building block in the formation of the opinions of a political public, without which it would be difficult to shape democratic mechanisms in parliament, courts, etc. Such articulation, however, is precluded by Rawls's idea of public reason because his distinction reductively focuses on views articulated in parliamentary and judicial spheres (Gutmann 2003).

To Rawls these arguments mean endorsing the view that policy must be anchored in a comprehensive doctrine; in the case of Habermas, it is in the comprehensive philosophy of communicative action and discourse. Although this interpretation might be considered more suitable for the cultural theory developed by Seyla Benhabib that ties up with Habermas (Benhabib 2002; cf. Benhabib 1996), it would be inadequate. Nonetheless, it contains a useful element that points to, in the concept of public reason, an attempt to go beyond the mere acceptability of opinions in the eyes of citizens; in other words, to go beyond particular arguments by universalistic justification. What is crucial for Rawls is only the general acceptability of the argument by other citizens; on

---

5   On the other hand, McCarthy quite rightly criticizes Habermas' quasi-proceduralistic conception of democracy as being too formal in character. McCarthy (1994, 49; cf. 44–63); cf. also with the analysis of Rawls' and Habermas' work on global justice: Moon (2003, 257–274).

the other hand, for Habermas, it is also the validity or real justification of this acceptability within the framework of idealized consensus, which, however, is rejected by Rawls as a boundary criterion of comprehensive doctrine. To sum up, Rawls' narrowly defined conception of public reason set limits on the democratic scope of the decision-making undertaken by citizens; nevertheless, within this narrow conception more room is left for decision-making that is not subject to the criterion of justification, to a selected group of people – certain civil servants.

Rawls' motivation for this authoritative conception of public reason is an effort to maintain social stability. According to Rawls, we reflect the fact of reasonable pluralism and we are aware that some of the reasons we would like to endorse will be unacceptable to some citizens:

> We seek a political conception of justice for a democratic society viewed as a system of fair cooperation between free and equal citizens who, as politically autonomous ..., willingly accept the publicly recognized principles of justice specifying the fair terms of cooperation. However, the society in question is one in which there is diversity of comprehensive doctrines, all perfectly reasonable. This is the fact of reasonable pluralism ... Now if all citizens are freely to endorse the political conception of justice, that conception must be able to gain the support of citizens who affirm different and opposing though reasonable comprehensive doctrines, in which case we have an overlapping consensus of reasonable doctrines.
>
> RAWLS 1993a, 24–25, note 27

Thus, we look away from comprehensive doctrines of individual citizens, we leave them behind the veil of ignorance, and we look upon the thus-created political liberalism as derived from a generally acceptable position. This is a basis of a political conception of justice linked to an overlapping consensus and thereby a public justification in a society of reasonable pluralism (Rawls 1993a, 25).

Rawls claims that since we realize that some reasons valued by us will be not acceptable to some citizens, the fact of reasonable pluralism has to be excluded from the sphere of public reason in advance and only room for overlapping consensus should be left. Participants of the discussion should try to give reasons for their views and their actions, which others could not reasonably reject. By taking this step, Rawls limits the scope of topics and reasons to be discussed. Controversial questions are thus eliminated from the decisive

political space beforehand.[6] Acceptability of opinions by others and the resulting stability wins priority over the criticism of a variety of forms of injustice.
Limitation of the discussion to the acceptability of opinions in the eyes of citizens thus puts aside the critical dimension of public reason, i.e., the dimension
which Rawls shifts to marginal debates because of his unbalanced differentiation between public and non-public spheres. The rejection of criticism and
the solving of controversial problems, however, hides the problems that might
become a source of conflicts, and these need not be solved peacefully.[7]

The separation of citizens from the official public discourse leads to their
alienation from the community and thus to a limiting of the legitimacy of the
existing order, which consequently undermines the stability of the order that
Rawls strives for. The main problem associated with this deficit is not, in my
opinion, the maintenance of a frequently undesirable stability but the misrecognition of citizens in terms of their participation in a democratic regime.
This throws doubt on the securing of the very essence of democracy which
consists in the anchoring of institutional discussions in parliament, the court
of law, and other institutions in the discussions of citizens and their life in
society.[8]

The elimination of the culture of civic society and disputes about significant
questions of society and policy and the exclusion of the media from public reason under the conditions of a mass media democracy lead to the fact that the
accumulated tension between the official and "unofficial" public is discharged
once in a while in the media-manipulated discussion, i.e. in pseudo-discourse
(cf. Garnham 1999, 359–376; Dean 2001, 243–265; Sparks 2001; Sklair 2000b,
28–30). Ed Baker studies the cultural and political role of the media and arrives
at the understandable thesis that liberals, including Rawls, should recognize
the membership of citizens in the community (or the so-called cultural structures that are deformed by the mass media) as primarily good and thus to give
it a proper meaning in the theory as a whole (Baker 2002). A more specific
analysis of the participation of citizens in a culturally and politically defined
community and the role of the media therein will facilitate the elimination
of current problems hindering the realisation of a participatory order, e.g. the

---

6   I do not argue that public reason must be able to remove any disagreements among the citi-
    zens. I think, however, that it should be able to name the key problems of society and policy
    and help the citizens to be able to resolve them. Micah Schwartzman tries to overturn this
    objection against Rawls' theory: Schwartzman (2004, 191–220).
7   Cf. with the theory of the moral grammar of social conflicts by Axel Honneth, who analyses
    the struggles for recognition as a source of criticism: Honneth (1992).
8   Cf. with Honneth's mentioned book and with Lipkin (1995).

removal of the manipulation of public opinion in the media and public space employing propagation affordable only to wealthy individuals, companies and well-established political parties, with which the legal corruption of political parties – in the form of sponsorship by financially strong corporations in a situation where many citizens cannot afford such sponsorship – is also closely related.

2   Problems of Individualism and Instrumental Reason

Although liberalism does not deliberately view the individual as an atomised unit, as the libertarians do, by neglecting an interpretation from the perspective of the social ontology it implicitly contributes to the notion of an excessively individualised individual.[9] Proceduralism and other forms instrumentalising human action that envisage the concept of an isolated individual result in a technicist and even technocratic approach to individuals, alienation and the potential reification of others. These phenomena lead to the resignation of meaningful policy, passivity, consumerism and the consequent weakening of the freedom to influence political events. Rawls anticipates such a problematic concept of the individual and such a concept of political procedures in his liberal theory of public reason. As it will be clear in later, in cyclical liberal crises, these problematic consequences are emphasized by nationalist neoconservative approaches that try to address the isolation of individuals by offering substitute concepts of community that tend to be regressive.

Concerning the actions of subjects, specifically political actors, Charles Taylor provides an inspiring interpretation of the political and cultural deficits of liberal theories by drawing on the concept of the politics of universalism which does not necessarily mean a universalist approach. While this concept is also used by liberal authors, Taylor's version is not affiliated with it but only with the pretense thereof. The concept of the politics of universalism is based on a reductive concept of the autonomy of the human individual, with an emphasis on his individual rights. Under this concept, independent individuals are expected to take decisions via impartial procedures.

---

9   I am not referring here to the atomistically individualistic concept of the individual in individualistic *methodology* ("methodological individualism"); rather, I am criticising atomism in social *ontology* ("ontological libertarianism"). Methodological (but not atomistic) individualism can analytically examine many issues to great benefit, but these must then be incorporated into broader analyses which are not only individualistic.

Although Taylor does not reject the politics of universalism entirely, he does criticise the one-sided conception thereof as offered by liberals, especially its dominance compared to the politics of difference, which – contrasted to politics of universalism – I will discuss in the seventh chapter on recognition in a local context. The fact that the politics of universalism distorts the value of autonomy with an inflammatory concept of individualism and the socio-economically and culturally unsituated individual translates into a failure to appreciate the value of authenticity associated with the unique characteristics of individuals and various socio-culturally defined groups of people. In this sense, in the interpretation of the realism of societal development, following Taylor, it could be claimed that the politics of universalism and politics of authenticity (or politics of difference) are based on two main historical con-stitutive goods of modernity: the first primarily drawing on autonomy and the second mainly on authenticity.

By ignoring the unique characteristics of individuals and groups, the pol-itics of universalism attempts to eliminate their negative discrimination, yet ignores the fact that the mere attempt to remove negative discrimination and any attempt to impose a purportedly neutral abstract perspective will not erad-icate inequalities between people induced by prior discrimination. Existing inequalities must be addressed, which means that the social, economic, cul-tural, ethnic and other characteristics of individuals need to be considered. Similarly, fundamental individual rights alone are not a sufficient guarantee that the other needs of misrecognized various social groups – which can be, and usually are, outvoted by procedural measures in the majority model of democracy – will be safeguarded. Liberal theory fails to take into account the necessary recognition and support of individuals and groups.

The subject of Rawls's theory is the largely passive and isolated individu-alistic subject who does not have much opportunity to participate in public life and submits to the instrumental reason of proceduralist tendencies. Rawls, aware that his theory suffers from a version of proceduralist characteristics, attempts to address this deficit to some extent by way of reformulation, defin-ing proceduralism simply as an unlimited procedural regime, and no longer regarding the narrower concept in the form of constitutional proceduralism as proceduralism (Rawls 2001, 222ff). However, it does not undermine criticism of proceduralism, especially when we consider that unlimited proceduralism effectively never occurs either in practice or in theory.

The shortcomings in Rawls's liberal theory largely reflect the shortcomings in liberal theory in general and liberal society in recent decades – shortcom-ings whose sources can be mapped more generally historically in modern times. Taylor identifies liberal theory problems with the insufficient inclusion of citizens in public life through critical analysis of hyper-goods, which constitute the major Western values in the modern era (Taylor 1992). In particular, he focuses on the distorted concept of autonomy and authenticity and on the dominant relationship of autonomy towards authenticity. Taken together, he identifies the causes of these problems primarily in three *malaises* of modern society: first, excessive individualism; second, the domination of instrumental reason; and third, a deficiency – stemming from those two malaises – in political life, i.e.: the risk of loss of freedom. However, this criticism is not a rejection of modernism. Rather it is a formulation of the negative aspects thereof and the articulation of positive aspects, which Taylor subsequently attempts to develop. The significance of this interpretation of the ambivalent nature of modernism lies in a research project much like that implemented (with a focus on the shorter period of recent decades) by Axel Honneth's research team under the name of "paradoxes of capitalist modernisation" (Honneth 2002).

Taylor explains the formation of individualism in modern times in his interpretation of the development of modern moral sources, and shows how it became crystallised due to the gradual modern secularisation process, which weakened the conception of Self embedded in a theistically based hierarchical social and cosmic order. The deterioration and disintegration of the traditional repressive hierarchical order triggered a desired increase in human freedom and individuality and freed up space for autonomous and authentic expressions of the individual and entire social groups. Autonomy and authenticity started to be formed as typically modern hypergoods grounding other goods. However, the premodern social order provided human beings with certain positive anchorage and security within intersubjective relationships in the community even if in the repressive traditional form. It provided human beings with specific experience, giving life meaning and integrating human beings into broader society and the world in general.

Their absence, due to the growth of modern individualism, was reflected in the uprooting of human beings from intersubjective relationships of mutual recognition in the community. Swelling excessive and self-centred individualism nudges the individual increasingly towards an isolationist way of life. In this way, excessive individualism undermines its own foundations, i.e., the position of the autonomy of the individual in the community. Freedom of human beings is decontextualised and an emphasis is placed on autonomy, though this is asocially deformed and alienated from community. As, in this process, the individual is conceived only abstractly without unique characteristics, his or her authenticity wanes. The result is an upset balance between autonomy and authenticity to the detriment of authenticity. This leads to a crisis of liberalism and to subsequent efforts to compensate for the uprooting of human beings by their substitute anchoring in a non-egalitarian traditional or pseudo-traditional community in which, however, economic, social, political and other dimensions of their lives are repressively limited.

The second modern malaise identified by Taylor, as I have indicated above, but which I have not yet historically anchored, is the dominance of instrumental reason and action. Placing an emphasis on human autonomy meant focusing, from the outset of the modern era, on independent rational knowledge and action based on an instrumental approach to people and nature. As in the case of individualism, instrumental rationality has positive and negative aspects. It enabled human beings to establish themselves in the wider world and, through its technical approach, to create an industrial and post-industrial civilisation. Consequently, human beings gradually increased their material living standards in many respects; for many people in the West, this translated into an easier livelihood, health care, housing, etc. Yet, at the same time, as I already analysed in Chapter 3, the use of instrumental rationality had negative ramifications. Taylor explains that it prompted a boom in calculative rationality, which focuses primarily on individual calculations of profits and costs, and therefore is generally more focused on the technical means of achieving aims than on the aims themselves.[10] This instrumental approach ignores aims and the associated hypergoods, and in particularly becomes oblivious to the values of human beings and nature. It is a subject-object relationship that instrumentalises and colonises inner and outer nature. This type of rationality, as well as the actions and behaviour based thereon, occurs in the handling of technical problems, where, in some cases, it may even be beneficial, and in personal relationships, in society and in politics, where, however, its manipulativeness and technocratic domination over other persons has negative repercussions, and it resulted in authoritarian and repressive regimes. Other people and nature, in the eyes of the calculator, are transformed into useable objects and budget items. Internalising instrumental rationality can guide a subject to the priority of looking at his or her own life in terms of financial and energy investments in his or her own time, investments in a life partner, investments in health, etc. Although, in his interpretation, Taylor does not arrive at conclusions as pessimistic as those of Adorno and Horkheimer in *Dialectic of Enlightenment*, the main line of critical consideration of instrumental rationality is the same, the difference being that Taylor formulates his criticism by means of a theory that, unlike *Dialectic of Enlightenment*, is confined to an intersubjective paradigm. Habermas actually proceeded similarly, but based his critique of instrumental

---

10   Cf. the impacts of this problem on gender inequality (Held 2006; Tronto 1994).

reason within an intersubjective paradigm, particularly on communicative action (Habermas 1981). Taylor also develops his theory of communication, or more precisely his theory of dialogue, but does not stop here, moving on instead towards a broader concept of community and, hence, towards relations of mutual recognition between individuals in the community.

The simultaneous consequences of the first two malaises – excessive individualism and instrumental reason – trigger a third modern malaise in political life: the danger that political freedom will be restricted or even lost. I might note critically, in relation to Taylor's hypothesis, that not only political freedoms but also economic and other freedoms should be realised. Restrictively conceived individualism, if the attempts of isolated individuals are carried out in the first place, is geared towards the enforcement of the isolated interests of citizens and the selfish privatisation of their lives. Citizens stop identifying themselves with the political community, cease taking an interest in public life and their participation therein, and also lose interest in political choice. In this context, the actions and behaviour of citizens induce the application of the instrumental rationality of a preference for the imperatives of a technocratic system and the interests of various power groups, and, due to the acceptability of the existing order in the eyes of the citizens, these only deliver the basic means for their survival and consumerist supplements for individuals as mere components of the system's gears (Langman and Lundskow 2016). Social fragmentation and a technocratic system deprive citizens of their freedom, which need not be removed from them forcibly because, in large part, they themselves surrender often it voluntarily in exchange for a certain level of consumption. As Alexis de Tocqueville declared, occasionally people accept moderate despotism if this means a less laboriously secured standard of living (Tocqueville 2002; Taylor 1992, 103ff). However, it should be acknowledged that this is not a democracy, but an oligarchy, accompanied by occasional media-manipulated elections. Unresolved problems and conflicts could then prompt citizens to accept or even prefer the rapid pseudo-solutions offered by authoritarian political leaders familiar to us from the 1930s, for example. Unfortunately, soon after the 2008 financial and economic crisis, attempts to revitalize them began.

In summary, excessive individualism, the one-sided application of instrumental reason, and the consequent restriction or loss of political freedom are issues that need to be addressed as the loss of community, meaning, and freedom, if we evaluate it first from the point of view of unfulfilled liberal promises. The sources of these problems in modern times stem from the warping and unbalanced relationship between the hypergoods of Western society: autonomy and authenticity.

To summarise the arguments so far, and to focus on the fundamental issues, in Rawls's theory it is possible to identify the problem of individuals not situated in the community. In general, it could be said that social institutions, at national level, should secure sufficiently strong norms of reciprocity so that the results of social cooperation can be divided fairly, and this cooperation should be regulated by intersubjectively acknowledged rules. Since, however, there is a lack of motivation among citizens at national level, we encounter complications well known also from the debate between liberalism and communitarism.

The problem with most liberal theories, including Rawls's theory, is that they lack the motivational stimuli which could encourage citizens to promote the values of a liberal society, which should be acknowledged also from the internal liberal point of view (Taylor 2003, 473–492; Taylor 1978, 133–154; Honneth 1995, 231–246). We may appreciate the fact that liberalism, on the one hand, tries to offer citizens the basic framework of a fair (albeit problematically conceived) politics with the security of fundamental universal rights and liberties, and that, on the other hand, it demands a certain political responsibility from them. This demand, however, can be applied only when members of the community have a sufficiently developed sense of commitment to others. Yet the mutual bond of bindingness and, thus, the motivation to conform to certain normative rules – while maintaining normative pluralism – does not arise from mere procedural adherence to the enforcement of some technical rule but crystallises among individuals in relationships of mutual recognition in the community. Not only the ability but also the motivated willingness of citizens to take responsibility for the values of the community and society and actively promote them requires citizens to identify with the demands of political institutions. The participation of citizens and their responsibility for political and social justice can be expected only if political institutions represent the citizens themselves and, thus, create an environment in which citizens identify with the political community.

3   Shortcomings of Redistribution

I will now turn to an analysis of the social deficit of liberal theory. First, we need to focus on Rawls's difference principle, which is – as I have mentioned – linked with the equal opportunity principle. The difference principle relates mainly to the idea of (un)equal distribution of primary goods. Strictly speaking, it encompasses the potential difference or potential social inequality between people, which can be justified, but only under conditions under which the worst situated citizens would also benefit from this unequal order.

In response to comments from critics, Rawls keeps to the main ideas of his principles but refines them slightly and states: "Social and economic inequalities are to satisfy two conditions. First, they must be attached to offices and positions open to all under conditions of fair equality of opportunity; and second, they must be to the greatest benefit of the least advantaged members of society" (Rawls 1992, 78).

The equal opportunity principle has its own object of analysis and does not focus directly on the removal or restriction of economic inequalities, which in theories of justice are usually termed social injustice, but rather, at most, touches only on the political context of social injustice. In contrast, the difference principle really does concern social injustice, i.e., a subject for which Rawls reserves the term "economic inequalities".

The shortcomings of this principle can be analysed from different aspects. One of the first criticisms might be the vague determination of the principle with respect to the persons whom it is meant to concern. Seyla Benhabib points out that it lacks a sufficient specification of the "least advantaged members" discussed by the principle (Benhabib 1992, 168). The principle, not wanting to be personally unfocused, focuses on a group of persons but is unable to provide a more specific definition of them. Should these disadvantaged persons be women with children, people who have lost their jobs, or someone else?

Rawls, when addressing the issue of defining these persons, lends himself communitarian assistance to some degree by redistributing primary goods. He characterises the social conditions that must be met in order for these persons to be able to realise their conception of good. The primary goods, on the basis of which we can recognise who in society belongs to the least advantaged, are fundamental rights and freedoms, freedom of movement, income and wealth, the foundations of self-esteem, etc. According to Rawls, the inequalities related to the difference principle are differences in expectations that citizens have concerning primary goods during their complete life, and the least advantaged persons are people of income class with the lowest expectations (Rawls 2001, 72–73). It would appear, then, that Rawls works with a social class defined by financial income, which, compared to the income of other classes, is the least able to obtain, or effectively purchase, such goods (Cohen 2011, 166–200; Cohen 2001). However, this definition is misleading, since the purchase of fundamental rights and freedoms is difficult to imagine in a democratic country in terms of Rawls's liberal normative theory.

The problem here lies in the merely ostensible specification of persons by means of the concept of "least advantaged members". Insufficient determination of the principle makes it impossible to eliminate the disadvantage because there is no specification of the type of disadvantage or of which group of persons is disadvantaged. The definition needs to be clarified.

Here, a problem similar to Rawls's failure to define the original position recurs – the starting point is not a critical mapping of the problems but rather their concealment with a veil of ignorance, and this also suppresses the identification of the groups of persons dealing with certain problems.[11] In his untransparent original position, Rawls disregards socio-economic and other issues and, therefore, is subsequently unable to address them using the difference principle. In this context, Nancy Fraser states that "an adequate conception of the public sphere requires not merely the bracketing, but rather the elimination, of social inequality", and: "this theory should render visible the ways in which social inequality taints deliberation within publics in late-capitalist societies" (Fraser 1997, 136–137).

Furthermore, G.A. Cohen, in his *Self-ownership, Freedom, and Equality* (Cohen 1995, 223–226)[12] criticises Rawls for his overly narrow definition of the circle of persons encompassed by his considerations. Although Cohen recognises that Rawls's difference principle *implicitly* confirms help for the socially needy who are unable to work or do not have work, he points to the fact that an *explicit* expression and justification thereof are absent. According to Cohen, Rawls's theory discusses contractual cooperation, which is intended to serve stakeholders, but those who are unable to work or cooperate and are in social need (the sick, the unemployed, etc.) are excluded from this in the main framework of Rawls's arguments. As Cohen's basis is that it is impossible to have an unlimited claim on self-ownership, and hence on the results of one's work, in his critique of liberal theory he calls attention to the unsustainability of a narrow concept of the theory which is based only on collaboration, and thus also to the unacceptability of the distribution of the results merely among collaborating persons, irrespective of or with only marginal regard to those who are excluded from such collaboration through no fault of their own.

In Cohen's view, another social limit of Rawls's theory is the incompatibility of the principle of justice (specifically the difference principle, focusing on social inequality) with a non-egalitarian expectation giving rise to contractualism or a concept of a social contract in which, in Rawls's theory, principles are to be chosen. In other words, the principles of justice that Rawls lets be determined in the situation of a social contract are contrary to the contractualist

---

11   Cf. Chapter 5, Section 1.

12   The objections relate to Rawls's main works, particularly *A Theory of Justice* (1971) and *Political Liberalism* (1993).

assumptions that are meant to precede the principles. A contractualist conception of the problem of justice as collaboration entails certain problems. Either talented people will lack the motivation to cooperate and to create a just society, or the composition of society will differ significantly from that in which we actually live today (it will be worse). These difficulties stem from a comparison of the benefits accruing from membership of potentially alternative, contractually closed associations and indicating the probability of inclusion in these associations for variously disposed persons. The first problem is that if people are unable to contractually associate with each other according to the principle of mutual benefit (resulting from mutual cooperation), the haves will evidently not want to associate with the have-nots. The motivation for the haves to cooperate with the less affluent will be too tenuous here. Another problem is related to the model in which the wealthy can form associations at will, resulting in the connection of the wealthy. Such associations, however, would create types of societies even less inclusive (societies of the haves and of the have-notes) than those in which we live. According to Cohen, these two problems cast doubt on the coherence of contractual expectations with a difference principle focused on social equality, and result in the requirement to prioritise either contractualist or egalitarian tendencies. This requirement appears to be the cost of Rawls's efforts to begin opening up space for choice prior to the defining of the principles within the framework of which decision-making is subsequently to take place.

Cohen elaborates on his criticism of Rawls's liberalism in his work *If You're an Egalitarian, How Come You're So Rich?* (Cohen 2000, 101–115), in which he proposes that the just basic structure of society alone cannot prevent unwanted inequality, because people's selfishness, shaped by a long history of capitalism, necessitates not only a change in economic structure but *also* a change in people's feelings and motivations. By making such an argument, Cohen attaches a certain importance to motifs previously presented, for example, by Christian socialists (the revolution of hearts), whose arguments were long considered overly idealistic, and subscribes to the idea now promoted in a secular version by the feminist movement, "the personal is political". According to Cohen, the difference principle, if we can hypothetically consider it adequate in this case, should also apply to personal choices made within institutions of community and society, not just to institutions. He concludes that a just society requires both a fair institutional structure and a just ethos, by the application of which, in their actions, people can support the institutional structure.

In general, Cohen discusses the topic of just ethos mainly in polemics with liberals when he addresses the question of whether wealthier people need financial incentives (such as low taxes) so that they do not start working less than they have been working, and so that they are willing, with their special taxes, to support those who are in a worse social situation (Cohen 1992; Cohen 2003; Cohen 2008). It is important to note here that if economic inequalities are to be reduced by the idea that – as I have mentioned above – economic inequality "must be to the greatest benefit of the least advantaged members of society", there is no precise specification of what is meant by "the greatest benefit". If advantaged members of society know that their selfishness is incorporated into calculations of the benchmarking of the benefit for the least advantaged, they will argue that, were taxes higher, they would refuse to work more, and that, therefore, even lesser benefit for the least advantaged should be regarded as the greatest benefit. Then, the regression of the least advantaged could still be interpreted as their greatest benefit because the wealthy would be able to insist that greater demands on redistribution from the haves to the have-nots would cause even less incentive for the haves to work and, consequently, pay more taxes, and this would result in the even greater regression of the least advantaged. A relativistic definition of the difference principle reduces the opportunity to apply its core idea. Cohen explains that, if the rich were genuinely to act according to a just ethos, they would not need any financial benefits. They could decide for themselves whether to continue working just the same without financial incentives and, thereby, contribute to those who are poorer, or whether to work less in the absence of such incentives. Justice, then, is also dependent on the choice of the individual.

This argument is based on the fact that, in this case, those who are wealthier bear responsibility for their own choices. In contrast, those who are not responsible for their plight, i.e., those who do not have the option to make arrangements so that they have the necessary social goods for themselves, need help from the wealthier. It follows that, according to Cohen, the aim of the principles of equal redistribution is to ensure that people have the necessary goods that they themselves have no opportunity to procure.

From the perspective of a theory of recognition, besides the institutional conditions of actions, a primary cause is lack of motivation, or in other words insufficient ethos, the underrated anchoring of individuals in relations of mutual recognition within a community – relations in which they could socialise and nurture the desirable ethos. The liberal absence of motivational resources is shown here to be a barrier undermining the very life of liberalism. If there is no emphasis on the mutual recognition of individuals, a supportive approach to the socially disadvantaged is not to be expected (Hegel 1991).[13]

---

13   See also Taylor's analyses in the previous two sections.

Cohen, in his opinion, promotes egalitarianism aimed at addressing the issue of injustice stemming from the randomness, from mere luck (luck egalitarianism). He does not advocate either *equality of opportunity* or *equality of resources*, but *equal access* to social welfare and resources which people are unable to secure for themselves – through no fault of their own, but because of unfortunate circumstances. While, for example, Ronald Dworkin defends his liberal concept of the equality of resources (Dworkin 1981, 283–345), Cohen rejects it mainly on the grounds that those who, through no fault of their own, have greater needs and, therefore, require more resources (the disabled, or, conversely, the highly gifted who could contribute to society with their talent in music, for example) are disadvantaged in conditions of the equality of resources (Cohen 1999, 80–100). Cohen also reaches for this argument in discussion with Will Kymlicka, who, drawing on Dworkin's theory, attempts to justify multicultural policy, which helps disadvantaged cultural minorities (Kymlicka 1995). In response to the socialist defence of oppressed social groups, Cohen defends multicultural assistance for marginalised cultural groups, while pointing out that this contradicts Dworkin's equality of resources because different cultural groups need different resources according to the degree of their marginalisation.

Now I return directly to an analysis of the difference principle. For analytical reasons, I would overlook, for a moment, the shortcomings of the difference principle and consider it hypothetically as an adequate principle, purely so that I can analyse its place in the hierarchical structure of Rawls's theory. Its place is determined primarily in relation to the first principle. Although the principles of justice – the liberty principle and the difference principle – are not equivalent, as Rawls explicitly says that the first principle always takes precedence over the other, both are prerequisites for social justice required in his *Theory of Justice*. Without questioning the value of the liberty principle, Rodney Peffer asks whether it is reasonable to elevate liberty at the expense of securing the basic social needs of the individual (Peffer 1990, 14, 10, 416ff). Social needs vary, but the satisfaction of some of them, especially biological needs (food, water, etc.), is essential for human life to survive. Could an individual whose basic biological needs have not been met exercise the right to freedom? And even if these needs have been satisfied, should she or he not also have his other social needs – conditional on implementing the first principle, the liberty principle – secured? Peffer defined this principle by stressing basic security and subsistence rights of every person which means physical integrity and a minimum standard of material well-being, including basic needs (Peffer 1990, 14).

Rawls responded to this criticism and, in his next text, made the remark that the first principle may be preceded by a prime principle, which should secure the satisfaction of basic social needs: "This principle may be preceded by a lexically prior principle requiring that basic needs be met, at least insofar as their being met is a necessary condition for citizens to understand and to be able fruitfully to exercise the basic rights and liberties" (Rawls 2001, 44, note 7).

The big problem is that the prime principle was not integrated into Rawls's theory. He presented it only as a footnote. He did not attempt to incorporate it into his theory or refine it. If he had, he would have encountered the problem of the understandable claim of the *liberté* priority in liberal theory. The adoption of the principle of basic social needs as a fully fledged principle in liberal theory along the lines of Peffer's critique and Rawls's subsequent comments would give it precedence over the liberty principle and place it in the beginning as the first principle and, consequently, would relegate the liberty principle to (at least) second place. Because Rawls places considerable emphasis on the ordering of principles and on the priority of the liberty principle, which is understandably favoured in liberal theory, demoting it to second place would mean abandoning the main principle of liberal theory. The seriously intended inclusion of the principle of basic needs would require structural changes to the constitution of the whole of Rawls's theory and the precedence of social motives over liberal motives. Yet that would mean the collapse of liberal theory and an inclination towards an alternative, socialist theory which places social motives higher than liberal motives.

Rawls recognises that if he were to reformulate the order of his principles in favour of the social motive of the prime principle without wishing to abandon his liberal standpoint, he would find himself in an internally inconsistent and untenable position. Therefore, he does not elaborate on the prime principle and does not incorporate it into his theory. On the contrary, he fundamentally restricts the importance of the social difference principle.

4   Marginalisation of Redistribution and the Problem of Ownership

Now I will move to the bigger problems of liberalisms and libertarianism, particularly to the marginalization of social redistribution and the problem of ownership. Although the difference principle includes the above shortcomings, it was at least partly an attempt to address certain economic inequalities. However, against the backdrop of the advancing increase in the influence of non-egalitarian libertarianism, which is a political philosophy of a kind of neoliberalism promoted in practice, in his final decades Rawls redefined his theory and strengthened its social deficit; this took place in the 20 years between the release of *A Theory of Justice* (1971) and *Political Liberalism* (1993). This redefinition can also be observed in Rawls's formulation of the idea of public reason,[14] confirmed in his study "The Idea of Public Reason Revisited". The publisher heralded *Political Liberalism* under a banner of three Rs: "Rawls Rethinks Rawls". What does this reformulation of Rawls's first book comprise?

Compared to *A Theory of Justice*, in which the difference principle assumed a secondary, yet still relevant, place, in *Political Liberalism* and in Rawls's other works in the political-liberal conception of tolerance it is marginalised, whereas the lead position of the liberty principle is enhanced in the constitutional framework. Susan Moller Okin states about Rawls's approach that this focus on liberties as the conditions for tolerance drowns out the redistributive aspect of his original theory of justice. The priority of the principle of liberty has become a monopoly. (Okin 1993, 1010, 1011; cf. Rawls 1999b, 473–496). Brian Barry, like Okin and other authors, critically emphasises that the difference principle is abandoned and sacrificed (Barry 1995, 913).

This criticism points out the reformulation of Rawls's "social" liberalism into liberalism devoid of a social attribute. If we realise that liberalism defined only by the first principle is broadly consistent with non-egalitarian libertarianism, it becomes clear that Rawls's reformulation acquires the nature of a transition to a completely different political direction. Although I am disposed to a similar, albeit not so acute, conclusion, it cannot be reached solely based on the rather rash arguments raised by Rawls's above-mentioned critics which we have presented thus far.

Upon reading Rawls's writings more closely, the analysed themes and the methods used to process them can be determined with greater precision. First, it should be emphasised that the main subject of analysis in *A Theory of Justice* and *Political Liberalism* does not overlap. Therefore, we can challenge the theory concerning Rawls's reformulation of his approach to social injustice in his second book. By definition, while the first book deals primarily with justice, the second discusses another matter, i.e.: political legitimacy. Therefore, the approach to the arguments should be as follows. First and foremost, it should be noted that the justice defined in *A Theory of Justice* assumes a basic conception of politics that is consistent with the principles of justice, including the socially oriented difference principle. Only at this point can we examine the attenuation of the importance of the difference principle when discussing political legitimacy in Rawls's *Political Liberalism*.

---

14   The opposite approach can be seen in (Rorty 1997, 31–34).

Rawls argues that

> Political liberalism is a kind of view. ... Accepting the idea of public reason
> and its principle of legitimacy emphatically does not mean, then, accept-
> ing a particular liberal conception of justice down to the last details. ...
> We agree that citizens share in political power as free and equal ... yet
> we differ as to which principles are the most reasonable basis of public
> justification. The view I have called 'justice as fairness' is but one example
> of a liberal political conception; its specific content is not definitive of
> such a view.
>
> RAWLS 1993a, 226, cf. 137

The main aim of political liberalism is to promote the idea of public reason
and the associated acceptability or tolerated bearability of a political regime
from the point of view of citizens, as I have already mentioned. The key idea
is that the adequacy of the theory of justice is measured by how it is acceptable from the standpoint of an overlapping consensus of different opinions
(Rawls 1993a, 229–230); thus, political liberalism is reflected in the application
of the idea of public reason. However, while the liberty principle, concerning
such application, seems to be acceptable, Rawls takes the view that accepting the difference principle is problematic because he wants to accommodate
non-egalitarian libertarianism, but not other positions such as critical theory.
Because he regards his theory of justice (as fairness) only as one kind of political liberalism (Rawls 1993a, 223, 226), all that connects it with other liberalisms
is the liberty principle. Therefore, in his general political-liberal conception
in *Political Liberalism*, he leans solely on this principle, which is a prerequisite not only for justice but also legitimacy. In contrast, he claims that the
difference principle does not belong to the constitutional basis and its accesso-
ries (Rawls 1993a, 228–229).[15] Put simply, political liberalism does not require
social justice. While the liberty principle is a prerequisite for the application of
public reason in public discourse, the difference principle in Rawls's *Political
Liberalism* is only one of the possible topics for discussion. All kinds of political
liberalism are conceptions of justice and, for example, Nozick's libertarian theory of justice without a social dimension is probably, from this point of view
ventured by Rawls, remarkably almost as acceptable as Rawls's egalitarian liberal theory of justice.

---

15   When thematising the social minimum, Rawls also omits the difference principle in the
      mentioned study "The Idea of Public Reason Revisited" (133).

Rawls, however, had already thematised these opinions, even if only secondarily, in *A Theory of Justice*, in which states:

> The first principle ... is the primary standard for the constitutional convention. ... The second principle comes into play at the stage of the legislature. Thus, the priority of the first principle of justice to the second is reflected in the priority of the constitutional convention to the legislative stage.
>
> RAWLS 1971, 199

Various authors who adopt Rawls's theory, however, have always stressed – wrongly, because they do so more than Rawls himself – the socio-egalitarian dimension of his theory. We could argue that *Political Liberalism* is not really about Rawls's reformulation of Rawls, as presented by the book's publisher and Rawls's commentators, including Susan Okin and Brian Barry. It is about the limits that were already present in *A Theory of Justice*, the deficiencies that are felt fully only in Rawls's second book (Wei 2010, 108–125). Rawls confirms his standpoint opinion in *Justice as Fairness* (Rawls 2001), in which he reformulates his theory of justice based on *Political Liberalism*. Although he is still working with both the liberty principle and the difference principle, this is only marginalised – and even becomes expendable – in *Political Liberalism*.

Political liberalism does not require justice as fairness; legitimacy does not require (social) justice. The limitation of the social exclusion of certain layers or classes of the population by the difference principle is just a possible option. Rawls's political liberalism does not require such an option, however, because unlike many egalitarian theorists and critical theorists he does not in the fact consider certain versions of non-egalitarian libertarianism as an unviable political position but rather as a position acceptable in the realm of an overlapping consensus.

Nevertheless, Rawls's liberal theory still contains significant problems stemming from the fact that, for socio-economic issues – if he explores them at all – he seeks a solution in redistributive policy, the main focus of which is further mitigation of existing economic inequalities while retaining the main elements of the unjust economic order. By reducing the problem to a question of redistribution and by underestimating distribution, Rawls fails to remove the *causes* of social inequalities. The issue of redistributive policies that partially offset the negative consequences of initial distribution often overshadows, in contemporary political theories, the fundamental question of ownership relations, which are the root cause of inequality among people. Right and left libertarians, in particular, agree on this correct but, as I will show, one-sided emphasis on ownership.

A concept of ownership is a central concept of libertarian philosophy and is based on self-ownership, i.e., ownership whereby a person owns himself. As egalitarian libertarianism addresses partly social issues in its own way (Vallentyne and Steiner 2001; Vallentyne and Steiner 2000; Steiner 1994; Van Parijs 1995), I will focus on non-egalitarian libertarianism, with which Rawls's theory has important factors in common. I will build on Cohen's critical analysis of the non-egalitarian libertarian conception of self-ownership as formulated by the influential representative of this line of thought, Robert Nozick, in his pivotal work *Anarchy, State, and Utopia* (Nozick, 1974; Nozick 1981; Paul 1981).

Nozick's conception of self-ownership grants all persons the full and exclusive right to control and use themselves, which for Nozick means the natural right of every individual not to be forced to provide things or services to any other person except where this is contractually agreed. All persons may freely dispose of themselves as they see fit. From this right to self-ownership, Nozick deduces that there is no obligation of solidarity towards others. For example, Nozick believes that government redistributive activities for the benefit of the socially needy, which are part of the order of most Western countries, are an abuse of rights to self-ownership, and, formulated acutely, a kind of partial slavery.

In response to Locke's conception of self-ownership, in his first principle of justice Nozick argues that ownership is fair if it has been freely obtained. In another principle, the principle of transfer, he similarly argues that the transfer of ownership is fair if the original owner freely transfers his ownership to someone else. However, this argument in itself implicitly contains the defence of domination formed by the accumulation of property. Owners who wish to hire workers purportedly enter into a situation in which both sides are free to decide whether or not, under certain conditions, they will conclude an employment contract. However, there is a problem in that they do not have an equal status because an employee, who is existentially dependent on wages under the contract, finds himself in a lower position in the hierarchy of power, and faces domination. In this situation, he may be forced to enter into a contract even though it is much less favourable for him than for the employer – the owner of the means of production. The extreme form of this problem is the case of a slave. If someone owns the means of production and other persons, those persons usually have no choice but to be enslaved.

Wei Xiaoping accurately structures this kind of argument in his comparison of Rawls's liberalism and Nozick's libertarianism, especially the principle of self-ownership, which is associated either with Nozick's rejection of redistribution or with Rawls's principle of redistribution:

1. 'Self-ownership' (extent of one's property).
2. The differences between the rich and the poor derived from 'self-ownership'.
3. Government redistribution – by way of taxation – cannot be justified, because it would violate individual rights.
4. All social values are to be distributed equally, unless an unequal distribution of these values is to everyone's advantage.

WEI 2010, 112–113[16]

Wei states that both theories, Nozick's and Rawls's, are grounded in the same basis; the first two points pertain to both Nozick's and Rawls's theories. They differ in the third point, where Nozick isolates the principle of self-ownership, and in the fourth point, which is related to Rawls's difference principle in *A Theory of Justice*, although, as discussed above, Rawls went on to problematise this in *Political Liberalism*.

As they both share a common Lockean starting point, they also concur in the first two points and do not address the causes of social inequalities. In the fourth point, Rawls has only partially allayed the consequences of the individual causes but does not address the root causes themselves because he does not view the unequal status of the employee and the employing owner of the means of production as a problem, for example. The position maintained by Nozick and Rawls is very apparent in the interpretation presented by G.A. Cohen in his analysis of ownership (Cohen 2000, 61–69). He distinguishes between several categories of workers, or direct producers, and their relationship to their internal and external ownership. In this context, he shows the difference between a slave, a serf, a worker/employee and an independent producer. A slave does not own either his own labour or the means of production he uses. Both are owned by the slaver. The remaining three categories of workers have internal property, i.e., they all own themselves and their labour, either wholly or only partially, as is the case with a serf. However, the difference between them lies in the field of external ownership. An employee has no external ownership, i.e., he owns no means of production; a serf owns

---

16   The first three points are clarified by Nozick in *Anarchy, State, and Utopia* (1974, 172). The fourth point is an interpretation of Rawls's difference principle (see above in this section). This interpretation is inspired by G.A. Cohen (1995).

certain means of production; and an independent producer owns all means of production.

Cohen asks what facilitates exploitation, and responds that the main problem is the fact that the employees do not own any means of production, compelling them – often for existential reasons – to enter into a work contract that is disadvantageous for them and could deprive them of payment for part of their labour. The issue of exploitation and lack of ownership do not figure solely in a capitalist regime. However, exploitation takes a different form in each system. Under capitalism, it mainly takes the form of an exchange or sale of labour, while in a slave or trade regime mode, as Cohen emphasises, it is implemented by non-economic pressures, i.e., the domination of one group over another by means of ideology and violence (Cohen 2000, 63ff., 82–83).

Naturally, exploitation need not be, and often is not, carried out by the owners of the means of production themselves, as envisaged by older theories. As external ownership requires management and a professional approach, several other types of groups of persons often work closely with the owners and benefit greatly from such collaboration, in some cases even more than the owners themselves. Therefore, managers and people in other important positions who share in the profits of ownership need not be owners in order to carry out the actual control of property to the benefit of the owners or themselves.[17] In this respect, in my discussion here on owners of external sources, I am also referring to these privileged groups of people who also appropriate profit. The term "owner" should not be grasped only formally, as meaning a person who owns resources solely from a legal perspective. This does not, in itself, guarantee the actual exercise of ownership. A more adequate concept of "owner" includes those who *actually* benefit from their ownership or from their control of property (whether their own or that of someone else). They might be not only legal owners but also, first, managers high up in the structure of corporations and their affiliated managers in other companies, secondly, politicians and senior civil servants, thirdly, highly educated specialists, and, fourthly, traders.[18]

Another aspect of this interpretation offers a critical elucidation of the relationship between the various interpretations of these issues. While, according to Marx, the equal relations of the individual employment contract parties are deformed by their different relationship to ownership, and owners/

---

17   Various conservative and progressive interpretations, having their origin in the following work, concur on this argument: Burnham, J., *The Managerial Revolution* (orig. 1941).

18   Leslie Sklair discusses these groups mainly in the current global context. He also includes the media in the fourth faction (Sklair 2001; cf. Sklair 2000a, 67–85; Robinson and Harris 2000, 11–54).

employers use their position of dominance over employees for exploitative purposes,[19] for Rawls the ownership of means of production does not constitute an opportunity for the employing owner's dominance over the employee. According to Rawls, universal rules on the free and equal relationship between persons, i.e., specifically the volitional conclusion of an employment contract on equal terms, are not infringed if the process of investing in ownership, including investment in means of production, takes place by the legal method of the unforced transfer of ownership from one person to another, as stated by Nozick's principle of transfer. Here, Wei Xiaoping follows Marx (Wei 2022) and stresses that this violation of equal relations occurs through relations of social division, i.e., through domination: "As soon as the social division has happened, the principle of 'self-ownership', and those universal rules that should be obeyed by every person freely and equally, go to its opposite." (Wei 2010, 115) Social division, which separates workers/employees from ownership of the means of production, means the separation of the employee from capital. Liberal theory and libertarian theory, drawing from a similar, Lockean, formulation of self-ownership, make no distinction between the relationship that the employing owner of the means of production has to property, on the one hand, and to people as employees, whom he pays for their labour, on the other. For him, both relationships are a single type of relationship towards a property investment. The person is here reduced to a thing, reificated, resulting in alienated labour and other consequences. This critique of the reification of the entity draws attention to the need to take a step away from subject-object relationships and the work paradigm and towards subject-subject relationships. However, Marx hardly develops this, and therefore, ultimately, it is not followed by the other steps required for the transition to an intersubjective model. In this sense, Marx's position needs to be transgressed, even if his critique of liberal theory, as mentioned above, can be applauded – provided, of course, that we incorporate it into the framework of intersubjective theory.[20]

Although ownership of the means of production plays no principal role in Rawls's theory, it should be noted that he is aware of at least certain inequalities in external ownership – and thus inequalities, which he partly attempted to restrict with his difference principle. Nevertheless, Rawls pays scant attention to these issues and, even where he does, he sticks only to vague formulations that make it difficult to form an idea of the ownership of external resources.

---

19   I do not dwell here on Marx's labour theory of value, which is questioned by Cohen and other authors.

20   Although Honneth makes this intersubjective transition, he does not achieve integration (Honneth 2005).

He himself admits that he only outlines a set of policies that should form a backdrop to justice, but does not provide any reasoning for them. He concedes that social theory would be necessary to prove that these policies would truly provide a just background but himself does not dwell on such a theory. Hence, he admitted that his proposals are only rough and intuitive (Rawls 2001).

Rawls thematises this issue to some extent when he discusses the concept of a "property-owning democracy" in *Justice as Fairness* (Rawls 2001, 135ff). He argues that this kind of democracy should be established for the implementation of a system of fairness-based cooperation. Such a system of cooperation of citizens requires that these institutional patterns have to first include a sufficient amount of the means of production which would be in the hands of all citizens. However, there is no specification of how much a sufficient amount is. We can glean more only from the passage discussing the requirement for citizens to be in a position that would allow them to manage their affairs to a reasonable degree of equality.

However, it is clear from the above analyses of redistribution and the difference principle that Rawls accepts inequalities among people as a motivating factor for the wealthy, and it is up to this group of people how much will be redistributed for the benefit of the least socially advantaged. In the distribution of means of production, Rawls's formulation is even less specific, but his vague statements about a reasonable degree of equality are directed at conclusions similar to those in the previous analysis.

A certain idea can also be obtained from Rawls's negative definition, specifically his observations on what he does not include in the right to ownership in concepts which, although he does not use them, he notes that it is possible to justify. Here, Rawls states that the right to the ownership of means of production should not be included among the principles of justice or the constitutional treaty as it is a matter to be dealt with at a lower level, i.e., it concerns the randomness of individual decisions according to the current political balance of power. However, this specification must not exceed the fundamental rights and freedoms set out by his theory, so the basic framework of his conception and its shortcomings cannot be transgressed (Rawls 2001, 176–178). Nevertheless, this draws him into circular reasoning and prevents a solution to the problem. Whereas, in classical Marxism, we could encounter underestimation of fundamental individual rights and freedoms, liberalism, on the contrary, with an almost unlimited emphasis on these rights and freedoms, restricts conditions for their actual egalitarian existence. Here, there is a direct link between the deformed concept of autonomy and consequences in the form of the deprivation of liberty, as I discussed at some length in the section before last. Exclusive freedom associated with the right of ownership among certain people leads, in liberalism and – in particular – non-egalitarian libertarianism, to the expropriation or restriction of freedom among others. As Rawls, like Nozick, closely connects his theory with a concept of ownership, which he does not limit in any fundamental way, and as the starting point of this concept is self-ownership, it requires detailed attention.

From what has been noted thus far, it is already clear why the tenet of self-ownership is also close to Marxism, which uses it as a reference point to criticise exploitation, advocating that every worker be entitled to the fruits of his labour. This statement, however, might tempt us into the simplification that every worker wholly owns himself and therefore all the results of his work. According to Cohen, the consistent advocating of this proposition would result in self-centred adherence to all the activities and products of each person, thus ignoring the socially needy (including children, the elderly, etc.), who are dependent on others. This approach, then, has libertarian and liberal consequences in relation to external ownership. Therefore, in his precise analytical Marxist reasoning, Cohen states that any strong version of the right to self-ownership is ultimately the right to selfishness. Self-ownership and public property in a socialist conception is different because people are co-owners. In such a conception, selfishness is replaced by systemically conceived solidarity among the people.

Cohen says complete interconnection with libertarianism and subsequent egalitarian rejection might appear to be a serious attempt at denying this tenet of self-ownership.[21] However, because he acknowledges that this strategy is inconsistent, he seeks to reject the tenet itself. Yet this means having to deal with Nozick's reaction, according to which such rejection entails several serious problems: first, the establishment of slavery; secondly, the arbitrary treatment of others as resources; and, thirdly, the restriction of human autonomy.

---

21   Cohen is aware of the difference between right-wing libertarianism, which is formulated most purely by Nozick, and which is refused by Cohen, and left-wing libertarianism, which, according to Cohen, also has drawbacks and the supporters of which include Hillel Steiner and Herbert Spencer in the early period. Like right libertarianism, left libertarianism also accepts unreservedly the tenet of self-ownership but unlike the right-wing version defends the initial egalitarian distribution of natural resources. It promotes the idea that people originally owned the resources together and that, therefore, should continue to have equal access to their property. In this context, Cohen criticises libertarianism, which aims to be egalitarian, for ignoring both the egalitarian community and the unwanted fact of the unequal distribution of natural dispositions and talents in the human population, and as such for blurring its original ambitions – defined by the liberty of all persons – by a separate emphasis on external sources.

Cohen deals with Nozick's objections as follows (Cohen 1995, 229–243; Nozick 1974, 31, 34, 172ff). First, he addresses the problem associated with the threat of slavery by way of an interpretation of the considerations raised by Thomas Scanlon (Scanlon 1977, 66; cf. Cohen 1995, 231–233). As a basic means of rejecting the tenet of self-ownership, they propose justifying the assumption of commitments to others. According to Nozick, however, any non-contractual obligation is a form of slavery, at least in part. In response to Nozick's argument, Scanlon contends that, just as, for example, life imprisonment cannot be compared with short-term deprivation of liberty imposed to investigate a crime, slavery cannot be equated with redistributive state taxes. According to Raz, it could also be said that, for example, I am obligated to assist a family member when he or she is ill, even if the patient tries to explicitly absolve me of that obligation. Under certain circumstances, I am obliged to help, not because someone owns my right to do something, but because I recognise the existence of a relevant obligation. This recognition uncovers a gap in ownership rights revealing that I am not the sole owner of some of my activities (those that are associated with obligations) but that does not mean that I have fallen into slavery.

While we might argue, against Raz's reasoning, that he fails to distinguish between moral and legally enforceable obligations, Cohen believes that such a claim of enforceability lacks substance because Nozick's model of a minimal state – just as the model of a redistributive state – also requires the taxation of citizens, which is enshrined in law. If, in Nozick's case, the levying of taxes to pay the police force is justifiable, the collection of taxes for the benefit of the socially needy does not seem to be any less legitimate. The existence of certain obligations towards others demonstrates the normative core of the redistributive state but in no way does it attest to the slave-like nature thereof. According to Cohen, Nozick should, moreover, explain how he justifies the possibility of a completely free decision by a person to enter into total slavery (apart from the self-contradictory reference to the contractual consent of a person falling into slavery) if he is a major opponent of the redistributive state, believing it to be a form of enforcing partial slavery.

Secondly, Cohen responds to Nozick's advocacy of this tenet by referring to Kant's principle that humans are the end, not the means. This principle, according to Nozick, means that a person cannot be used as a mere means of achieving the ends of others (i.e., for redistribution, for example) without his or her consent. Cohen counters responds by formulating: (a) a relationship between Kant's principle and the tenet of self-ownership; and (b) the difference between Kant's principle and Nozick's reformulation thereof.

(a) Cohen argsues that Kant's principle does not contain the tenet of self-ownership and that nor does the tenet contain that principle. Kant's principle from the *Metaphysics of Morals* (Kant 2017) refers to the fact that we cannot use another person merely as a means but must also treat him as an end in itself. Thus, if we use, for example, a salesperson to purchase some goods, we are also committed to providing her or him with any assistance she or he needs, e.g., for health reasons. Such an obligation would not apply if we were using a vending machine, i.e.: a mere means. Cohen, referring to Kant and following his principle, asserts that healthy people have an obligation to contribute, through taxes, to those who are incapacitated. However, this is inconsistent with the tenet of self-ownership, which would have to reject the instrumental use of healthy people (recognised as an end in itself) to help the disabled because this inherently excludes any non-contractually enforceable obligations.

On the other hand, someone might accept the tenet of self-ownership and reject Kant's principle. While the tenet says nothing about positive relations with other people, Kant's principle demands our involvement in relation to others as it postulates the obligation to treat others as an end.

(b) Cohen states that Nozick's reformulation of Kant's principle of the means and the end into a principle of consent is a deformation. Whereas Kant requires that another person (also) be treated as an end, according to Cohen Nozick requires only that this other person agrees to be treated in this way. In this light, Nozick's principle of consent may result in a situation where the other person is treated merely as a means.

Thirdly, in his final objection Nozick puts forward the argument of the restriction of autonomy, claiming that people can be autonomous beings only if they are full holders of rights concerning self-ownership. Cohen, however, argues that in our environment, where people have different dispositions and are variously talented, each person can enjoy certain autonomy or real freedom only when the rights to self-ownership are partially restricted. If they are not limited, autonomy is denied to many people (the sick, unemployed, etc.). However, full self-ownership does not mean safeguarding autonomy, even assuming approximately equal distribution of talent and health, i.e., ownership of internal resources, in the entire human population. Autonomy, according to Cohen, depends on the extent of the individual's rights over both himself or herself and the external environment he may dispose of; it is in this scope of rights – as illustrated by the problem of exploitation – that people differ substantially.

In this line of reasoning, the point is not that the tenet of self-ownership is fundamentally rejected but that the interpretation makes this tenet and non-egalitarian libertarianism sufficiently unattractive. It concerns a balanced concept of ownership and the avoidance of both extremes. While complete rejection of the tenet would mean not admitting a worker's entitlement to the fruits of his labour, and hence impossibility of the criticism of exploitation, complete acceptance of the tenet would open the door to selfish denial of the correctness of distributive and redistributive action.

To summarize, I may add that criticism of the shortcomings of liberal theory, which I divided into the deficit of participation and a social deficit, could be dissected by analysing the problems attached to the conception of public reason and related themes. In terms of citizens' participation in a democratic system, injustice of the liberal conception of liberty emerges particularly in the deformed concept of autonomy, leading to excessive individualism, problems of instrumental reason and, seemingly paradoxically, the deprivation of liberty. In terms of social justice, we are faced with an inadequate conception of redistribution in the milder scenario or with the absence of redistribution in the more serious scenario and, ultimately and in particular, with the unresolved individualistic excessive entitlement to external ownership. Therefore, the liberal promise of liberty has not been kept and the traditional problems of capitalism are reproduced. Rawls's political liberalism appears to be both less participatory and hence less democratic, and less social, than customarily presented. These pitfalls make his theory the subject of critical analyses of non-egalitarian libertarianism showing that the democratic system and the related social justice require more space for the participation of citizens and their social welfare than liberal theory admits.

Shortcomings of liberal theory have been attempted to be rescued by many authors within liberal theory, and similarly within liberal practice. However, they do not address the deficit premises of liberalism itself. Liberal nationalism, which takes representative form in Davis Miller's philosophy (Miller 2000; 1995), for example, attempts to conceive of a national grounding for liberalism and to extend social redistribution, but this does not change the nature of the problems of the liberal system if it is to remain liberal and not primarily national (nationalism) or social (socialism). Indeed, in a global framework, these problems are exacerbated as solidarity demands for distribution and redistribution come into conflict with national demands that relegate poverty eradication and relevant solidarity to a secondary place, with national liberalism confined only to some pressing responsibilities for social problems in a global scale (Miller 2007).

Since the theory is usually a more ideal version of the practice, the application of libertarian theories in practice has even worse consequences, namely the weakening of democracy and the strengthening of oligarchy. As Martin Gilens and Benjamin Page (Gilens and Page 2014, 564–581) have documented in their analysis, the existence of oligarchy in political practice in the US confirms the theories of dominance of wealthy economic groups and also theories of biased pluralism, and does not confirm the theories of majority electoral democracy, the theories of majority pluralism or more demanding theories. The US no longer meets the criteria set for democracy due to the considerable influence of excessively unequal property and other forms of power. The 2020 presidential election, for example, was the most expensive election in human history which, as in the past, was heavily distorted or corrupted by oligarchic corporations and wealthy individuals. In many countries in the European Union and many other places, this kind of plutocratic corruption is also promoted and legalized (Torres-Spelliscy 2020).

Rawls's theory, like liberal theory in general, is an ahistorical conception that is, therefore, incapable of reflecting the regressive and progressive changes that can lead beyond liberalism. This does not in principle change the fact that Rawls's theory, contrary to its foundations, also mentions several chronological motives, such as ecological aspects of development. However, the question of the historical transition of countries to liberalism or any other system is completely alien to Rawls's theory: either the system is liberal, or it is not. This ahistorical approach encounters its durability especially when the common shortcomings of liberal and libertarian theory and practice lead, after a certain period of time, cyclically to crisis and to consequences that seek a way out of liberal and libertarian problems beyond the boundaries of these theories and their practical applications.

Populism becomes often the first step in finding solutions to these problems in a situation of crisis. Jan-Werner Miler points out well that the simplification of public discourse into the conflictual binary of 'the people' and 'the elite' often results in anti-pluralism, i.e., the reduction of pluralism of opinion in the public space and the authoritarian assertion of the position of the currently ruling group of persons (Miler 2017; 2021; Langman and Lundskow 2016). But he forgets that the disillusionment of people in crisis leads to a chaotic development that requires a political art of certain simplification. If populism is realized in the name of promoting an emancipatory social approach, in the version whose initial formulation was captured by Ernesto Laclau, for example, it may be a way in which it is still possible to reverse course of crisis and not end up at the wrong end of another problematic system (Laclau 2018; Laclau and Mouffe 1985; Preciado Coronado 2021, 26–46). I will return to the hopeful normative social and more demanding socialist populist path later,[22] but for now I pay

---

22   A typical case of the hopeful tendency in the political practice is the first and second pink tide in Latin America (Ali 2008; Boron and Klachko 2023; Lampter 2023, 319–334).

attention to the non-emancipatory populist paths in the context of critique that divert anti-liberal sentiment in a non-egalitarian conservative direction towards its supposed solutions to the crisis.

Conservatism can hardly be regarded as a way out of the problems and the crisis (Franco and Marsh 2015) but, as with liberalism, it is possible to appreciate some selected dimensions of it that can be fruitful. Conservatism, first, in terms of its appreciation of a community, builds on the aforementioned critique of the concept of excessive individualism. Second, it is linked to the critique of problematic expansive trajectories that destroy the beneficial characteristics that have been present so far, as pointed out by G.A. Cohen (Cohen 2012, 143–174; Pugh, Kahane and Savulescu 2013, 331–354). Therefore, these conservative aspects appreciate rather the status quo against these negative trajectories. Third, another beneficial aspect may be the critique of the oppression of a marginalized group of people in the form of a nation and the promotion of national liberation which may have conservative and progressive features (Hroch 2000; Hroch 2015; Hobsbawm 2021). In the first case, this is an intersubjective ontological critique, in the second one a chronological critique, and in the third one a critique of group marginalization. All three can be linked to the promotion of social consideration for poor or low-income groups of people, even though in principle it is only charity and not a systemic solidarity.

Nevertheless, the problem is that the main premises of conservatism are rooted in the economic, political, social and cultural spheres in interpersonal traditional hierarchies (Hazony 2022; Oakeshott 1991, 407–437; Oakeshott 1993). A milder version of the problematic development is the establishment of a conservative structure that pursues non-egalitarian interest in an authoritarian way in the name of traditional values and interests, and limits or reverses the emancipatory direction of development, whether within a national framework alone or within a broader framework, regional or larger. A stronger version tends to be the establishment of a conservative structure that hypertrophies the hierarchical system. Its exemplary version is conservative nationalism which usually faces a critique of its ethnic xenophobic motives (Bauman 1989). Ethnic and nationalist disputes can then escalate into armed conflicts and wars, as was also the case in the escalation of the crisis of liberalism in the 1930s into World War II. After World War II as well, smaller local and national conflicts expanded into regional wars involving world powers. Such developments threaten the danger of nuclear or other extremely destructive war. I will discuss the international and global dimensions of these dangers in later chapters.

CHAPTER 6

Deficits of International Liberty

A concept of justice in the nation-state which has established itself over more than the last three centuries, has since the collapse of the Eastern Block encountered its limits and reformulation due to transnational and global interactions, including conflicts. A concept of global justice is essential at times when individuals as well as whole societies find themselves under pressure from transnational and global conflicts of different economic and political systems and civilizations. We live in a very stratified global order in which the "asymmetric interdependence between the developed and newly industrialised and underdeveloped countries", brings unreconcilable conflicts and demands (Habermas 1998, 87). This unfortunate situation could be resolved by identifying and developing an appropriate institutionalised global concept to enable justice from the local level through the national, international and regional levels to the global level. The conflicting global interconnectedness of societies and individuals requires not only international relations but also a redefined global order. I will deal with the concept of global justice with the aid of a critical analysis of the concept of international justice.

My examination will take the following direction. In four sections, I will explain, on the one hand, the insufficiency of the theory of international liberal justice and, on the other hand, the need for a theory of international and global justice. While I explicate a transition between these two stages of justice by means of the concept of extra-territorial recognition in Chapter 10, here I will focus on the main differences between the two theories. First, I will outline the main theses of Rawls's liberal conception of international relations which is not able to offer an adequate concept of international and global justice in the contemporary era. My aim in this process will not be a detailed explanation of this theory but only a focus on its supporting pillars, which later will serve the purpose of my comparison with the theory of global justice. I will be concerned with the problem that is contained in the first part of Rawls's theory, specifically in his concept of a social contract – contractualism. This problem approaches in an inadequate liberal way the relationship between an individual and the community in international and global interactions. Second, I will show the inconsistent points in Rawls's theory contained in its second part, i.e., in his principles of justice chosen by social contract. Third, I will concentrate on the consequences of these limitations for a socially distributive dimension of justice or for the approach to dealing with disproportionate international and global inequalities. In the last instance, fourth, I will attempt to formulate the causes of the limitations of Rawls's liberal theory of international justice and point out the need to transfer from international justice, which follows from Rawls' liberal nationalism, to a global justice.

1   An Inadequate Relationship between an Individual and Community

Rawls initially formulated his liberal concept of international justice in his first book *A Theory of Justice* (Rawls 1971, 377–379). Rawls considers almost only the concept of justice within the framework of a national state to be important, a view of international justice in the book is only an outline. Nevertheless, it is the foundation for a more defined formulation which is later developed by Rawls in his study 'The Law of Peoples' and subsequently in his book with the same title, *The Law of Peoples*, where Rawls develops his liberal concept of international justice (Rawls 1993b, 41–82; Rawls 1999).

From the point of view of my reconstructive summary of Rawls's famous concept of international relations, it is relevant to say that Rawls mentions that the aim of his *The Law of Peoples* is a proposal of fundamental guidelines for an international policy for a liberal democratic society. It is also a proposal for a more universal purpose, which is the aim to create a worldwide community of liberal and decent peoples (Rawls 1999, 128). The Law of Peoples, in its liberal concept of international justice, serves as a 'particular political conception of right and justice that applies to the principles and norms of international law and practice' (Rawls 1999, 3). Rawls at the same time articulates two principles and mutually interconnected themes that exist in the background of his theory of international relations (Rawls 1999, 126). The first is the idealist premise that the most serious problems and disasters in the history of humankind were caused by the political aspect of injustice. Mass murders, genocide, poverty, religious persecutions or unjust wars were caused by this kind of injustice in particular. The second premise is the idea that the most problematic and disastrous events could be eliminated providing that the political dimension of injustice will be eliminated by the implementation of fair basic institutions and by following just measures of justice. Rawls adds that if these institutions are not just, they should at least be decent to achieve the required state of affairs.

The reason why Rawls does not talk about a plurality of nations but about plurality of peoples is because he intends to distinguish between state formations with their own rational and not necessarily reasonable[1] interests, demonstrated in their sovereignty, and peoples included in the Law of Peoples that set boundaries to the internal sovereignty or political autonomy of a state. On the one hand, higher requirements are placed on peoples as opposed to states because strict conformity to human rights is required, a conformity that has been increasing since the end of World War II. On the other hand, human rights are conceived in a more limited and tolerant sense which attempts to rid them of layers of ethnocentrism, whilst respecting the differences of well-ordered nations that do not possess a liberal democratic regime.[2] This should offer the possibility of a peaceful co-existence for well-ordered societies i.e. liberal democratic societies and societies ordered in hierarchies which do not present liberal democratic models of order but which do follow the fundamental human rights and allow citizen participation in governing via a consultation hierarchy based on shared values (Rawls 1999, §8–9). Rawls argues that 'In the Society of Peoples, the parallel to reasonable pluralism is the diversity among reasonable peoples with their different cultures and traditions of thought, both religious and nonreligious' (Rawls 1999, 11). The additional element of the co-existence of well-ordered societies is the relationship of these societies gathered under the Law of Peoples to societies which are not well-ordered, and which are the source of international instability. Therefore, it is possible to say that Rawls, from his liberal perspective, is concerned with international justice which in his ideal scenario to achieve by establishing the harmonious co-existence of peoples in the Society of Peoples under the Law of Peoples, which is designed to implement the political dimension of justice. The non-ideal case has an added relationship to societies which are not well-ordered.

The explanation so far is already sufficient to point out certain inconsistencies of Rawls's liberal theory of international relations. First of all, I would like to draw attention to the problem which appears in Rawls's formulation of *original position* where individual parties of a social contract decide on the principles of international justice. For the time being, I will leave aside the question as to whether it is at all sustainable to define the principles of justice

---

1   The explication of the primary meaning of the difference between the terms "reasonable" and "rational" is presented, for example, in: Rawls, J., The Basic Liberties and Their Priority (Rawls 1983, 3–87); later republished in Rawls' *Political Liberalism* (1993a).

2   Rawls does not insist on some articles of the Universal Declaration of Human Rights, for example article 21, which is concerned with democratic government. Compare with opposing view, for example in: Archibugi, D./Held, D., *Cosmopolitan Democracy: An Agenda for a New World* (1995). Also compare with: Taylor, Ch., A World Consensus on Human Rights? (1996).

via a contractual model of an original position and whether it would be better to articulate the principles of justice with the aid of another model which is not based on social contract. Even though the model of a social contract does not present a solution for most theories, I believe that it is possible to assess the problem discussed within this model independently.

The problem occurs in the specification of subjects of justice. Whilst in Rawls's theory of justice which is formulated within the framework of a national state, individuals represent themselves in an original position, in his liberal theory of international justice, the agents are representatives of peoples or even of entire states whose task is to represent solely national or state interests. As Rawls argues in *A Theory of Justice*: 'the contracting parties, in this case the representatives of states, are allowed only enough knowledge to make a rational choice to protect their interests' (Rawls 1999, 378).

This shift from individuals, who represent their own viewpoints as standpoints of moral individuals, to problematic representatives who represent in their way *peoples' interests* significantly transforms Rawls's theory. The optimum scenario in this theory is a rationally designated defence of individual rights or a liberal nationalism which promotes national interests in the name of the members of these nations against the interests of other nations. It is the case of principles which 'govern public policies towards other nations.' (Rawls, 1999, 378) This description shows Rawls's liberal theory normatively as a theory of international relations where the centre of attention is national relations.

The reasons for this standpoint are not in Rawls's universal theory of justice. For Rawls, it is not a case of excessively communally minded liberal theory. Although it is necessary to perceive his standpoint as considerate to a communitarian principle, the defence of community on the national level is for Rawls led by other motives. The underlying principle of Rawls's theory of transnational relations is the petrification of practical politics of international relations (Rawls 1999, 112), which displays an increasingly weakened orientation towards national sovereignty.

In light of the argument presented so far, the difference between Rawls's liberal theory of international justice and the theory of global justice will now become more apparent. We may start presenting it in relation to a concept of cosmopolitan justice which will make it possible to illuminate a concept of global justice later. The basic distinction between international and cosmopolitan theories, according to Rawls who refers to the cosmopolitan theories of Brian Barry, Charles Beitz, Thomas Pogge and David Richards, is that whereas cosmopolitan justice is concerned with individuals, liberal international justice is concerned with entire societies or nations (Rawls 1999, 11.1 and 16.3; Barry 1999; Beitz 1979; Pogge 1990; Richards 1982). Nevertheless, the standpoints of the aforementioned theorists of cosmopolitanism are considerably more complex and they cannot be understood based on Rawls's theory alone.

First, it is necessary to at least distinguish between libertarian theories and cosmopolitan theories. Egalitarian libertarian theories of justice, for example, the theories of Hillel Steiner or Henry Shue (Steiner 1994; Shue 1980),[3] are actually, as Rawls claims, concerned with individuals and the human rights that are assigned to human beings based on their common characteristics. In this, they differ from Rawls's point of view where these rights ensure 'a necessary, though not sufficient, standard for the decency of domestic political and social institutions', which is required from nations as members of a worldwide just society of peoples (Rawls 1999, 80, cf. 65). If the rights of individuals are in Rawls's liberal theory only one of the conditions for the acceptance of a nation amongst other nations within the framework of the Society of Peoples, the individuals play only an instrumental role here.

However, the cosmopolitan theory is not a libertarian theory. The cosmopolitan theory can concern both with entire peoples such as in the Rawls's theory and *also* with individuals as world citizens. This does not necessarily mean that the issue of justice must be approached by cosmopolitan theorists directly concerning individuals.[4] Moreover, it is important to note that cosmopolitanism does not have to result in a global government.[5] Its implementation is equally possible with the aid of states or peoples and other institutions apart from a world government.

The principal thought behind the argument so far can be summarised with the following proposition. A cosmopolitan theory can stand between international theories which like Rawls's theory depend on the relationship between national communities and ignore individuals, on the one side, and libertarian

---

3 Here, I analyse left-wing libertarian theories which are relevant to the polemics with Rawls's and cosmopolitan theories.

4 Charles Beitz articulates the difference between institutionalised and moral versions of cosmopolitanism which questions this non-mediation. Whilst institutional cosmopolitan justice as presented by Pogge and Beitz, for example, is concerned with various kinds of super-national institutions including global institutions, moral cosmopolitanism is concerned in particular with the moral foundation on which these institutions can be justified – where each person has a moral planetary status (Beitz 1999, 287; Pogge 2001). In contrast with left-libertarian authors, Charles Jones who considers his theory as morally cosmopolitan, does not accept institutional cosmopolitanism but his neo-Hegelian concept of community offers a more adequate grounding (Jones 1999).

5 Amongst various types of cosmopolitanism, there also exists a so-called legal cosmopolitanism which strives for global governance. This type of government defines a unified legal order of the world republic in which all citizens possess the same rights and duties. Compare with Nielsen (1987).

TABLE 3   Subjects and inclinations of libertarian, cosmopolitan and liberal theories

Theory	Libertarian	Cosmopolitan	Liberal
Subject	Individual	Community and individual	Liberal community
Potential	Atomism	Individual in the world	Liberal nationalism

theories that are primarily focused on an individual and ignore anything other than global institutions, on the other.

It is apparent from Table 3 that the outcomes of mentioned theories are: a) individuals, b) individuals and communities, c) communities. With respect to this specification, the libertarian theory is inclined to a social and political atomism as it tends towards an isolated perception of the individual. The liberal international theory, on the other hand, veers towards nationalism by preferring a nation over an individual and towards an instrumental concept of individual rights. This is due to the fact that within the international and transnational frameworks, it places national interests at the centre of its attention, interests which are, in the untransparent way, represented by problematic representatives who may be only the representatives of a narrow group of wealthy and influential persons.

The distinction featured in Table 3 undoubtedly does not exhaust the explanation of complex theories that focus on issues beyond the boundaries of peoples or nations.[6] Its advantage is that it summarizes this section and, therefore, stems from the polemics of liberal international theory with the cosmopolitan theory which Rawls himself considers as a main alternative to his own theory and which he misinterprets as a libertarian theory. As to international and global issues, later, in Chapter 8, I will move on from liberal theory and cosmopolitan theory to a critical theory of recognition and, then in Chapters 9 and 10, to my own theory of global justice which includes a concept of community levels: a local level, a national level, an international level, a regional (or macro-regional) level, and a global level.

---

6   A more complex system of distinction is presented for example by Walzer (2000).

2   Comparison of the Principles of Justice

So far, I have been concerned with defining subjects (individuals and nations) of liberal international and cosmopolitan justice. Now I would like to focus on the principles that are supposed to regulate the international/trans-national relations among these subjects. For Rawls, it means which principles would be chosen in the international original position. In his *A Theory of Justice*, Rawls states that the selection of principles of justice would not be problematic: 'I can give only an indication of the principles that would be acknowledged. But, in any case, there would be no surprises, since the principles chosen would, I think, be familiar ones.' (Rawls 1971, 378) Rawls here refers to the book on the law of nations by J.L. Brierly, and merely adds that 'this work contains all that we need here.' (Rawls 1971, 378; Brierly 1963) The question remains whether peoples would and should decide to accept some familiar and well-known principles. It is highly questionable as to whether the peoples of the third world are particularly happy with contemporary international relations to the extent that they would actually prefer to preserve a status quo.

In Rawls's writings, we can identify several conceptions of principles of justice and in this way open a discussion on these principles between proponents of international and cosmopolitan or even global kinds of justice. There are essentially three concepts: firstly it is Rawls's formulation of principles of international justice (a) in its initial form in *A Theory of Justice* and (b) in its already developed form in *The Law of Peoples*; secondly Rawls's formulation of more demanding principles which are valid amongst individuals at the national level; and thirdly Rawls's implicit liberal formulation of international/trans-national principles which is rooted in his concept of principles amongst individuals at the national level, i.e., the reformulation of Rawls's principles by other authors who propose an extrapolation of internationally/trans-nationally valid principles from Rawls's principles that regulate relationships amongst individuals within the national framework because they believe that Rawls's own extrapolation of principles is not adequate.[7]

2.1   Principles of International Justice in *A Theory of Justice*
In his book *A Theory of Justice*, Rawls designates four basic principles of justice which regulate relationships between nations (Rawls 1971, 378):

---

7   For better orientation, I have marked out the keywords of individual principles in italics.

1. The principle of *equality*: independent peoples who are organised within states have certain equal basic rights which are analogous to equal citizen rights within a constitutional system.
2. The principle of *self-determination*: the right of peoples to organise their own affairs without any interference of foreign powers.
3. The right to *self-defence*: the right against attacks including the right to form alliances of defence for the protection of this right.
4. The principle of *abiding by treaties*: following treaty obligations providing they are compatible with other principles which adjust relations among states.

2.2 Principles of International Justice in *The Law of Peoples*

In *The Law of Peoples*, Rawls develops his principles of justice between peoples further:

1. 'Peoples are *free* and independent, and their freedom and independence are to be respected by other peoples.
2. Peoples are to observe *treaties* and undertakings.
3. Peoples are *equal* and are parties to the agreements that bind them.
4. Peoples are to observe a duty of *non-intervention*.
5. Peoples have the right to *self-defence* but no right to instigate war for reasons other than self-defence.
6. Peoples are to honour *human rights*.
7. Peoples are to observe certain specified restrictions *in the conduct of war*.
8. Peoples have a duty to *assist* other peoples living under unfavourable conditions that prevent their having a just or decent political and social regime.'

RAWLS 1999, 37

2.3 Principles Which Regulate Relations between Individuals within the National Framework in *A Theory of Justice*

Before I express my view on the principles of international justice, I would like to draw attention to Rawls's two principles of justice from *A Theory of Justice* which apply to an individual at a national level, and which are used by the proponents of global justice for presenting challenging trans-national principles than Rawls did himself.

1. The principle of *liberty*: 'each person is to have an equal right to the most extensive basic liberty compatible with a similar liberty for others.'

2. The principle of *difference*: 'social and economic inequalities are to be arranged so that they are both (a) reasonable expected to be to *everyone's advantage*'; with a focus on the most disadvantaged citizens in Rawls' later versions of the principle of difference.

  RAWLS 1971, 60[8]

The comparison of the two presented conceptions of international principles in Sub-sections 2.1 and 2.2 makes it possible to say that the first five principles in Sub-section 2.2 redefine mildly the four principles in Sub-section 2.1. If I compare Rawls's principles of international justice with Rawls's principles that are concerned with an individual within the framework of peoples (Sub-section 2.2), it appears that principles 1 and 2 of Sub-section 2.1 and principle 1 and part of principle 2 of Sub-Section 2.2 specify, more or less, equal rights and liberty to peoples, which are analogous to the first principle of this sub-section, i.e. the *principle of liberty* at a level of peoples.

The remaining principles or parts of principles 1–4 of Sub-section 2.1 and of principles 1–5 of Sub-section 2.2 are concerned with classical principles of international law which do not form a direct parallel with principles at a domestic level. We may add that principle 7 forms an addition to principle 5.

The main contribution of the conception in Sub-section 2.2 on international law is principles 6 and 8. The focal point of the conception in Sub-section 2.2 is in respecting human rights (principle 6) and in helping peoples to the extent that they can establish a decent political and social order (principle 8). In view of Rawls's liberal reduction of human rights (Rawls 1999, 78–81), the core of the dispute between proponents of international and cosmopolitan kinds of justice resides in principle 8, which plays a less significant role than that of principle 2 in this sub-section at an international level, i.e., the *principle of difference* from the domestic level. I would like to show how this principle of the distributive dimension of justice (which sets boundaries to socio-economic inequalities or differences) is interpreted from the perspectives of international and cosmopolitan justice.

---

8 The second principle also contains a point (b) which is not usually questioned within the framework of a discussion on justice beyond nations/peoples: „attached to positions and offices open to all." For the development of Rawls's formulation of principles of justice, compare with (Rawls 1983, 3–87).

3   Shortcomings of International Redistribution

In *The Law of Peoples*, Rawls defines the consequences of international and cosmopolitan theories concerning the redistributive dimension of justice which
is, however, usually called a distributive dimension. He develops principle 8
which is concerned with support to other peoples through a *duty of assistance*
i.e., the *principle of assistance*.[9] Rawls asserts in his liberal theory that distributive equality in the international context can be essentially considered in one
adequate and one inadequate form, i.e., as good in itself or as good which is
required under certain conditions. According to Rawls's *principle of assistance*,
'inequalities are not always unjust, and ... when they are, it is only because of
their unjust effects on the basic structure of the Society of Peoples, and on
relations among peoples and among their members.' (Rawls 1999, 113) As soon
as the demands relating to a political dimension of justice (analogous to the
domestic conditions) within the Society of Peoples are fulfilled (i.e., eradication of the basic suffering of the poor, stigmatising attitude towards them and
obstacles to the fairness of political procedures within the basic structure of
society), there is no need for further elimination of inequalities between peoples, Rawls asserts.

Some theorists of cosmopolitanism, Thomas Pogge with his global egalitarian principle, for example, proposed a system that sets boundaries to the
increasing inequalities which are not dealt with by Rawls's principle of assistance whilst showing that this proposal for elimination of inequalities follows
from Rawls's own thoughts on justice at a domestic level (Pogge 1994, 195–
224; Rawls 1999, 115, note 47). Charles Beitz related to this analysis two principles: the principle of redistribution of resources and the global distributive
principle. The first principle works with the hypothetical premise of an auto-
cratic society that is completely dependent on its own resources and on labour
and independent from trade with other societies. The principle of redistribution of resources ensures the transfer of resources from wealthy societies to
poor societies to establish political and economic institutions that will ensure
the satisfaction of the basic needs of the poor following human rights.

The global distributive principle, which is similar to Pogge's global egalitarian principle follows the principle of redistribution of resources but dis-
cards the idea of autarkic society (which is not realistic today, except for a few

---

9   In Rawls's *The Law of Peoples* (1999), see the full account in §15 pp. 105–113 and §16 pp. 113–120.
    Compare this with the note on mutual assistance between peoples on p. 38 and note 47 on
    the same page. Also, compare with Rawls's view on human rights on p. 65 and note 1 on the
    same page and with his complete thoughts on human rights in §10 pp. 78–81.

isolated tribes) and presumes the exchange of goods and services between individual societies. The resources are provided for poor societies continuously and it is analogous to the procedure by which the socially orientated *principle of difference* from Rawls's *A Theory of Justice* makes provisions for the most disadvantaged citizens at a domestic level.

To assess the distributive principles, it is necessary to distinguish between the two types of cosmopolitan justice: the continuous and discontinuous kinds of justice. Continuous justice tightly binds cosmopolitan justice with national justice which is essentially unnecessary to further define after the designation of cosmopolitan justice. An example is a theory proposed by Phillip van Parijs (van Parijs 1995) or Rawls's theory of justice with the global principle of justice added, i.e., a theory which Pogge and Beitz explain, as I have shown. However, they do not subscribe to this type of justice. Instead, they follow the second type of cosmopolitan justice i.e.: the discontinuous type. Rawls overlooks the latter, which is in contrast to the first type that is open to the possibility that national justice can be ordered according to another code apart from the cosmopolitan one.

What then is the difference between international and cosmopolitan kinds of justice with respect to the distributive dimension of justice? Rawls's liberal model of international justice requires only the political dimension of justice between peoples and does not in any way call into question the possibility that the inhabitants of societies might remain in very unequal circumstances, for example, in relation to the distributive dimension of justice. On the other hand, cosmopolitan justice in its discontinuous version similar to Rawls's theory, *does not* require simplified identification of national justice with cosmopolitan justice as is the case in the continuous version of cosmopolitan justice. Instead, via Beitz's global distributive principle or Pogge's global egalitarian principle, and in contrast with Rawls's theory, cosmopolitan justice requires institutional distributive interventions in the name of world citizens even after achieving a satisfactory relationship in the international political dimension of justice. The concept of discontinuous cosmopolitan justice differs from Rawls's international justice by its consideration of frequently drastic economic inequalities between members of various peoples. The social-economic dimension of justice in this case is not mechanically subordinated to the political dimension of justice and both types complement each other.

Rawls objects to the viewpoint that the global distribution principle must have a target and a point of limit or a cutoff point. Rawls's principle or 'duty of assistance possesses has both: it seeks to raise the world's poor until they are either free and equal citizens of a reasonable liberal society or members of a decent hierarchical society. That is its target. It also has by design a cutoff point, since for each burdened society the principle ceases to apply once the target is reached.' (Rawls 1999, 119) This could be a model for an egalitarian principle with a target which is lacking in Beitz's and Pogge's principles. If they did designate the target, according to Rawls, his principles and those of Beitz and Pogge would be to a large extent in agreement. However, this is a fallacy because Beitz and Pogge do not deny the need for a target and for the point of limit, but they differ in the question of where and how the target would be specified. One of the main differences between Rawls's international justice and Beitz's and Pogge's cosmopolitan justice is the fact that both Beitz and Pogge are not satisfied with Rawls's *political* dimension of justice, and they think that, even after its achievement, it is necessary to assert *redistributive* interventions which limit the significant economic and social problems of the members of various peoples.[10]

Moreover, whilst Rawls, as I already mentioned, formulates his approach with the aim of defining a foreign policy of liberally democratic order and for creating a Society of Peoples, Beitz and Pogge think that redistribution is necessary before the achievement of a political dimension of justice with respect to the economic and social problems themselves and not only instrumentally with respect to foreign relations (Rawls 1999, 3 and 128). A related question addresses the position of Rawls's principle of assistance in the list of principles. The chronological arrangement of principles which is adopted by Rawls at a domestic level, i.e., the first principle has a priority, the second one is secondary and so on, is not favored by most proponents of the distributive dimension of cosmopolitan justice. Rawls himself does not entirely adhere to this arrangement of principles at a domestic level. Following the liberal emphasis on freedom, he asserts that the principle of liberty has priority over the distributive principle of difference without any imposition on the liberty principle but on the next page he makes a concession to this in the footnote (Rawls 1993a, 7).[11] He admits that the priority over the liberty principle must have a principle that guarantees that the fulfillment of rights for basic security and livelihood are ensured for each human being. This redefinition transforms Rawls's theory entirely because part of the social security which the principle of difference strives for, is guaranteed by Rawls via a kind of zero principle.

---

10   India is a good example of how it is possible to implement many relatively good political institutions and, at the same time, ignore many redistributive problems that the political institutions are not able to resist.

11   Rawls does make similar formulations in *The Law of Peoples* but there is insufficient grounding in his entire argument to allow their essential evaluation or at least eliminate the inconsistency of the order of principles (Rawls 1999, 64–65 and 80).

If this adjustment was valid also at the international/trans-national level, it would change the discussion so far between the proponents of cosmopolitan and liberal international kinds of justice. Rawls does not make such a concession at the international/trans-national level even though he instrumentally demands the fulfillment of similar requirements.

As a rule, all these issues are primarily addressed as redistributive, not distributive, issues in both liberal international justice theory and cosmopolitan justice theory. Therefore, they are concerned with ways of redistributing resources that are owned or controlled by someone other than the persons who need redistribution. In the case of international justice, it is primarily locally or nationally owned resources that are redistributed to other local or national communities. However, it is already a matter of reality that the dispute also concerns non-endowed natural resources (e.g., oil, gas, water, fertile land, environmental commons, etc.) which, although still owned within territorially closed units, nation-states, are at the same time claimed (sometimes rightfully) by other population groups beyond the borders of these territorial units for egalitarian reasons. The question of supranational and global ownership of a certain part of these external resources, as well as of the environment, is not likely to wait too long. However, it should be noted that the misuse of these arguments in favour of opposite interests has been going on for a long time.

4   Unsustainability of Liberal International Order

In the final section of this chapter, I will attempt to shed more light on the main causes of the limitations of Rawls's liberal concept of international justice, causes which I only outlined so far in the analysis of individual parts of his theory. The first cause, which prevents Rawls from developing a more adequate conception of principles of justice, in particular the redistribution principle, is the underestimation of the negative impacts of the present economic and other conflicts on the global level. This shows the limitations of an international conception of social distributive justice which stems from Rawls' liberal theory. The second cause is apparent in a more general form of the first cause. The overall underestimation of a critical approach to the reality leads Rawls to an inadequate conception of basic normative elements of his theory such as the relationship between an individual and a community at a domestic level and the transposition of this relationship onto the international/trans-national level. As I will attempt to demonstrate, the limitations contained in this concept of a relationship between an individual and the community do not allow Rawls to transfer from local community over to national, international and regional communities and finally to global community. The limitations of his theory fix it in a paradox of a national inter-space which on the one hand already disregards an individual at an international level and on the other hand is not able to transfer to a global community.

First, the first cause. As I already stated, Rawls believes that the obstacles which are limiting to the economic and social prosperity of individual peoples lie in political injustice and not in distributive injustice. This is an unsustainable dichotomy which relies on a rather more internationally isolated (autarkic) society in the global integration where individual societies are significantly interlinked by global financial, economic and other interactions, including conflicts.[12] The influence of social, economic, political, and cultural interactions by various, not only political but mainly economic interventions from abroad can fundamentally and quickly worsen national circumstances, the living standard of the people, for example, even in the context of political justice at a domestic level. This deterioration of the situation could be a serious threat to such a society. Moreover, these transnational interventions are created not only by owners of corporations but also by significant international and transnational institutions (IMF, World Bank, etc.) which influence transnational banking and international exchange transactions in problematic ways (Kennedy 2010; Kennedy 2017; Robinson 2004; Robinson 2014; Sklair 2002; Sklair 2001; Harris 2008; Harris 2016). They do not operate according to Rawls's code of international justice but on the basis of the unequal economic power and influence. Rawls's code of justice is a result of its liberal origin fixed on political justice. It has its consequences concerning who is a profit-maker and who is a profit-loser here.

Over the past decades, transnational corporations and transnational financial institutions have gained control over many aspects of the economic and financial sphere and have led the structure of neoliberal global capitalism into the financial and economic crisis of 2008, during which they forced nation-states to bail out private banks and other firms with public funds. Significant social inequalities are inherent in the current global order – global capitalism. The consequences of these inequalities are reflected in the loss of human life. Some consider these losses to be merely collateral – in military terminology. In their view, these are unwanted phenomena, but they accompany to a greater or lesser extent all kinds of societal arrangements. Although these losses usually take place far from the safety of our daily lives in the European Union or

---

12   Compare with the annual UN reports, for example: *World Economic and Social Survey*;
      World Economic Situation and Prospects; *Human Development Report*. Specific evidence
      on globalisation is given also by the IMF and the World Bank.

the USA, so that most Westerners can comfortably banish them from their consciousness, even those who are comfortable with this morally minimalist interpretation should at least ask whether the level of loss has already exceeded a
tolerable limit. In the 1960s, a generation of young people in Germany began
to ask their parents what they did during World War II, and how they reacted
to the existence of the Nazi concentration camps. How do we answer the question of how we have reacted to the current global order which has enormous
casualties every year? According to statistics from recent decades, approximately 18 million people a year died from poverty and related causes; one person dies every four seconds from hunger. In 110 countries, 485 million people
live in extreme poverty. But this is not due to a lack of finance and wealth.
Oxfam said, "The number of billionaires has doubled since the financial crisis
and their fortunes grow by $2.5bn a day, yet the super-rich and corporations
are paying lower rates of tax than they have in decades." (Oxfam 2018, 2) In
another report, the same organisation adds: "The richest 1 percent bagged
82 percent of wealth created last year – poorest half of humanity got nothing."
(Oxfam 2018) In this way, the social injustice of the present societal order con-
demns millions of people to live in various forms of poverty.

Returning to Rawls's fixation on political justice, we can say, it is important
to avoid all reductionisms including political reductionism. That is why I think
that cosmopolitan justice, in its discontinuous version which could, as the first
step, solve at least the most drastic problems of the present global capitalism
by its distributive justice, is more convincing than Rawls's far too one-sided liberal idea of securing international justice only by political justice which underestimates the current global economic pressures. The mentioned version of
cosmopolitan justice allows a realisation of the more appropriate relationship
between the principle of liberty and the redistributive principle of difference.

In order to identify the second cause of the limitations of the liberal theory
of international justice, it is necessary to analyse Rawls's reason why the cosmopolitan justice including its redistributive part could not be implemented
(Rawls 1999, 112f). Rawls asserts that there would not be consensus for this type
of justice. This is an argument which seems to contradict another of Rawls's
arguments which states that individual parties in the original international situation behind the veil of ignorance (not knowing their future economic and
other security) choose accordingly to the choice in the original situation also
in the social framework. Then, the parties in the international context should
be inclined to decide for a global distributive principle in the same way as they
did before in the domestic context for a distributive principle of difference.

Even if it would be ethnocentric to try to make a mechanical transfer of
arguments from a domestic level of the Western countries to the global level,

if we consider the principle of difference apart from Rawls's theory and its Western domestic arrangements, I think that it is convincing to say that the global distributive principle would be advantageous to less developed countries of the third world to the extent that there is a high probability that they would be willing to accept it.

Discussion on Rawls's argument that there would be no consensus on the implementation of a global distributive principle leads us to problems which are present not only in Rawls's theory of international justice but also in his theory of domestic justice. Already at a domestic level of his theory, we face motivation problems of individuals discussed when implementing the principle of a difference within the framework of dealing with relationships between an individual and a community. In general, it can be argued that social institutions should ensure sufficiently strong norms of reciprocity at the domestic level in order to ensure a fair sharing of results of social co-operation whilst this co-operation should be regulated by rules which are accepted by everyone.

The problem with most liberal theories, including Rawls's theory, is that they lack motivational incentives that would lead citizens towards the promotion of values of a liberal society (Taylor 2003, 195–21; Taylor 1978, 133–154). It should be acknowledged that liberalism on the one hand offers citizens a basic framework of a just society whilst ensuring basic universal rights and freedoms and, on the other hand, it requires a certain amount of political responsibility and solidarity from citizens. This requirement can be implemented only if members of the community have a sufficiently developed sense of obligation to other people. The mutual tie of obligation and with it also the motivation of the subject to respect certain normative rules does not arise from sole insistence on promoting some neutral rule but it develops in individuals from relationships based on mutual recognition within the community. It is not only the ability but also the motivated willingness of citizens to accept responsibility for the values of a community and a society and to actively promote them which enables citizens to identify with the demands of political institutions. Responsibility and participation of citizens can be expected only in cases when political institutions represent the actual citizens and, in this process, create an environment in which the citizens can identify with the political community.

To a certain degree, Rawls accepts this argument. If he further developed his argument and explained that his standpoint follows not only from Kant but also from Hegel,[13] he would have opened up a space in his theory for a better

---

13   Rawls's standpoint is an egalitarian liberalism which, on the one hand, follows on and significantly evaluates Kant's, Hegel's and Mill's teachings but in my opinion not sufficiently.

evaluation of a neo-Hegelian and more community-based concept of society which is bound by the mutual recognition of individuals and which offers people the motivation towards solidarity (Rawls 1999, 72; Hegel 1991, §308). This does not mean that Rawls should have slipped to a *substantialist* concept of a community that defines the content of practices within the community. Nevertheless, a better specification with the aid of a more *formal* conception of community would benefit his theory. Axel Honneth follows Hegel in this respect and discusses a relationship of mutual recognition between individuals within the community as a *basic good* by which people can find self-fulfillment (Honneth 2000d, 28; cf. Honneth 1996; Taylor 1985b; Taylor 1995). From this perspective and regarding distributive justice, Rawls is correct to talk about a *good* that is to be distributed but he does underestimate the *basic good* which is a precondition of this other good and which consists of relationships based on mutual recognition between people within the framework of a just community. However, concerning the issue of cosmopolitanism, neither Honneth used and developed this argument in his conception of international relations so far (Honneth 2015, 265–285).

Insufficient inclusion of individuals into intersubjective relations in Rawls's theory means that individuals are not sufficiently willing to identify with the community even at a domestic level. It can lead to substitute forms of community which can be nationalistically xenophobic or violent, for example. Atomisation of individuals is understandably reproduced also in communities of even larger numbers at regional and global levels. If there was a better environment for grounding individuals within the community, they would be able to integrate better into relationships of the domestic community and to express their solidarity. This framework could then be transgressed, and they would be able to identify in an inter-cultural way in solidarity with regional or macro-regional communities as well as with the cosmopolitan community. Specific forms of communities can then even form across various territories.

On the one hand, the absence of grounding in relationships of mutual recognition leads the largely isolated and alienated individuals to supplementary ties of tribalism or nationalism. Because Rawls's concept of international justice follows from sources of liberal nationalism, it is in a paradoxical position from the point of liberalism because it limits a liberal defense of individual rights. As I have shown in Table 3 and in the associated argument, Rawls's liberal conception of international justice does not fully acknowledge the individual

---

This concerns in particular Hegel's conception of well-ordered societies which connects the lives of individuals with their community. (Rawls 1999, 72–73, 127; Rawls 2000, 329–372; Hegel 1991, §308).

aspect of human beings and it relies on the relationship between collective units of peoples. On the other hand, it relies on insufficiently socially bound individuals. This situation does not allow individuals to step beyond national integration and transfer to the development of relationships based on mutual recognition in wider levels of a community such as the regional and global levels. The paradox of international theory which has its origin in liberal nationalism is, therefore, in the tension between a too strong individualism within the domestic framework and nationalism within the international framework.

Cosmopolitan theories of justice have a potential to deal with this paradox in their intercultural form that does not lose sight either of individuals on the one hand or of larger forms of communities than the national community on the other. But if cosmopolitan theory was not, in relation to the above-mentioned Hegelian approach, grounded in relationships based on mutual recognition of subjects within the community, it would suffer from the same problems mentioned no less than Rawls's international theory. This is particularly apparent to neo-Hegelian proponents of cosmopolitan justice who try to revive the cosmopolitan potential of Hegel's conception which is present in Hegel's critique of cosmopolitanism that is not communally grounded (Fine 2003, 609–630; Fine 2007; Jones 2023). This is the good first step to a more demanding critical conception of global justice.

Although Rawls does partly include a Hegelian concept of community in his international theory, this influence is not projected onto other parts of his theory, not to mention a possibility that he would use it to redefine main characteristics of his theory. Despite these limitations, Rawls maintains in the tolerant and inter-cultural way that Hegel's concept of community can be a beneficial element not only for the model of Western societies but also as a model for societies that are not democratic and liberal, but which possess a legitimate status of decent societies and observe basic human rights. As I already argued, Rawls's conception of international justice is constituted as the concept of a Society of Peoples which can have either liberal democratic government or decent government which enables the realisation of well-ordered hierarchical societies. As Rawls places higher demands on liberal governments than on hierarchic governments, the concept of society of decent hierarchic peoples (which, however, stems from liberal premises) actually presents in his theory the initial attempt to formulate a minimal universal concept of community. This concept of community is compatible with Hegel's concept of community, but it would require in the more adequate version real implementation in the theory to include a people into the intercultural society of peoples. Even though Hegel's concept of community is interpreted from a different perspective in Rawls's theory of international justice, it plays a significant inter-cultural role in it because it is conceived as a connecting element between various types of societies within the framework of international justice. This role is important especially for the neo-Hegelian theories that develop the idea of cosmopolitan justice, as I will show later in the next chapters.

It is possible to summarise the main thoughts on the unsustainable theory of international justice and the need for global justice in two parts. Firstly, the political dimension of justice which is emphasised by Rawls and many other liberal theorists must be balanced by a distributive dimension of justice which is the focus of authors who realise the significance of social justice. Secondly, the addition of a distributive dimension to the political dimension would be insufficient if it was not supported by an aspect of justice which is focused more on relationships of mutual recognition between individuals within a just community. These two thoughts point to the need to move away from a theory of international justice, based on Rawls's liberal nationalism, to a theory of global justice which does not ignore current drastic inequalities in the global distribution between individuals and between communities and which enables their intercultural co-existence.

PART 4

Experience of Recognition

∴

Dilemmas of Local Recognition

> Honneth takes the historical step back from Marx to Hegel to re-establish the programme 'from Hegel to Marx'.
>
> JÜRGEN HABERMAS

∴

1   The Crystallisation of Recognition

After the critique of liberal theory at the national and international levels (Part 3), now (Part 4) I will focus on an explanation of an alternative theory, mainly a critical theory by means of an identification and redefinition of the key elements of theories of recognition at local and national levels (Chapter 7) and international and transnational levels (Chapter 8).

Injustice, particularly misrecognition creates numerous conflicts and is a source of daily criticism from many people. Although struggles for recognition have been recognised for a long time as an important motif, they only became a genuinely significant phenomenon and concept with the development of modern society and the striving to do away with traditional social hierarchies. Many people have come to realise that their subordinate social standing is not inevitably a given fact but is rather a social construct of misrecognition that they do not need to tolerate but can resist. This critical tendency may have gone through a quiet period, but it is currently again on the rise. Various interactions and crises with their economic, social and political impacts and ethnically driven conflicts between different peoples and cultures all create various misrecognitions that are hard to ignore.

First of all, it is possible to say that people often experience immediate feelings of misrecognition in day-to-day situations without themselves being more specific about the source of these feelings. The experience of misrecognition is perceived and diagnosed as the atmosphere of the given period or as the spirit of the time, the *Zeitgeist*. People – particularly in Western societies – have the justified feeling that there is constant social pressure on them to enter into the competitive struggles that oppressively surround them and those around them, and to try to achieve objectives that are of little or no consequence to them, in order to achieve recognition of their activities and themselves. This feeling is often experienced in particular in academic and journalistic circles but also elsewhere where people often turn up in these situations because they are led to it by their personal ambitions linked to the exercise of their profession. But despite this, many of them perceive this competitive pressure as unpleasant and undesirable, since by the very definition of competitive struggle the majority cannot win and those who lose are accompanied by a loss of recognition. However, these groups within the population are not those who suffer most from the experience of misrecognition.

In the global social atmosphere following the end of the Cold War and particularly following 9/11, struggles for recognition have often been associated with disputes between cultures and civilisations. These clashes, not limited just to conflicts between Islam and the West, are often disagreements covering up a struggle for access to raw materials or a defensive reaction to the remains of previous colonial regimes. Intercultural disputes being played out across national state boundaries also have their national and local parallels in the disputes between majorities and cultural, ethnic and other minorities, often in relation to migration. Disputes over whether the approach to minorities is appropriate or not and how to prevent xenophobic and nationalistic aggressive approaches represent conflicts that have already lasted several decades. The questions are delimited between extremes – liquidation and exclusion of groups of people, on the one hand, and their assimilation, on the other. Discussions are often held on what form a fair position should take, which consists of various forms and justifications of a reasonable integration within the framework of the constitutional and legal principles of the given country and culture while retaining recognition of their cultural distinctiveness. We also witness a misuse of these topics by various politicians and corporations to divert attention from key economic, social and political issues.

However, cultural conflicts are not the most serious form of misrecognition. The social destitution of hundreds of millions of starving people in developing countries is their misrecognition of the most basic of needs. The struggle of the global poor for recognition is a struggle for survival. Their daily striving to stay alive, closely linked to the right to food, water, shelter, and other social rights, is a striving for recognition of their basic human rights. Here, developmental aid and the cooperation of non-profit organisations is an attempt to resolve this hardship. There are also the development activities of the state institutions of Western developed countries even if often the flip side is their misuse to promote the political and economic objectives of the "donor" countries.

The attempts to overcome underdevelopment are also linked to the efforts by BRICS+ (China, Brazil, India and others) to free themselves from the marginal standing of developing countries, and to the revitalisation of Russia. They are also a reaction to the impact of global economic and other conflicts and struggles for spheres of influence. The overall situation is marked by an effort to redefine the economic, political and cultural recognition of the individual players in the contemporary global constellation and with a shift from unipolarism to multipolarism and multilateralism which, however, is endangered by growing bipolarism of the new cold war. Individual developing countries and whole macroregions are striving for recognition of their own Chinese, Latin American or other form of modernisation ("multiple modernities") which they do not want reduced to the development path trodden hitherto by the West.

Similarly at a national scale, where the much-needed meeting of the social rights of the socially vulnerable in some countries is applied so selectively and strictly that it comes close to control and repression of the unemployed, the low-paid, etc. It is just this misrecognition of marginalised groups that is a typical feature of the channelled tension which arises from the struggle for limited resources, particularly at a time of economic recession and crisis. Other kinds of misrecognition cut across the given categories of economic, social, cultural, political and other spheres. Questions of the relationships between men and women are both cultural and also social-economic, and indeed also political. The lower financial reward for women's work and the insufficient reward for their work at home are not only an economic category but are also conditioned by cultural models of this kind of misrecognition. The lower representation of women in political life has similar causes.

The social and political theory of recognition is based on social and political philosophy, which has long and richly been rooted in the history of ideas. It is derived from concepts developed by Jean-Jacques Rousseau, Johann Gottlieb Fichte and other authors. Rousseau, in his *Discourse on the Origin and Foundations of Inequality Among Men*, analyses the basic issues of inequality and the points of departure for tackling them, and discusses the fact that people began to "appreciate each other" (*s'apprécier mutuellement*) and thereby enter into social ties (Rousseau 2019, 115–192). This had ramifications in both the recognition and misrecognition of people. Fichte deals with recognition as the "reciprocal effect" (*Wechselwirkung*) of persons in his *Foundations of Natural Right According to the Principles of the Science of Knowledge* (*Grundlage des Naturrechts nach Prinzipien der Wissenschaftslehre*) (Fichet 1971). This reciprocal effect, i.e., interaction, is used to impose certain restrictions which individuals establish between themselves in order to form a common legal consciousness. The main source for the interpretation of recognition, however, is Hegel's concept of recognition (*Anerkennung*) (Siep 1979; Neuhouser 2000; Hardimon 1994), sourced, in their analyses of class and existential conflicts, by

Karl Marx, Gyorgy Lukacs, Alexandre Kojeve and Jean-Paul Sartre,[1] as well as Georges Sorel, Jean Hyppolite, Simone de Beauvoir and others.

Unlike the neo-Hegelian efforts which, in the 20th century, were associated primarily with existentialism, some authors do not link up solely on the famous concept of the "struggle for recognition" in Hegel's *The Phenomenology of Spirit* but also develop Hegel's early, more critical work from the Jena period (Hegel 1969), in which the social theory of recognition had yet to be encumbered by the metaphysical notion of the development of the spirit in the background. The post-metaphysical processing of the concept of recognition, devoid of illusions about the non-problematic progress of reason in history, is also associated with the impossibility of overlooking the disasters of the 20th century, especially the Holocaust. Nevertheless, post-metaphysical analyses of Hegel's concept of recognition are not limited to his early writings and their trajectory of social philosophy in *The Phenomenology of Spirit* (2019 B, IV, A), as was the case until recently. Growing interest in the recognition paradigm prompted also analyses of Hegel's other texts, including his final work, *Elements of the Philosophy of Right*, where certain positive elements are identified and then reconstructed, even if this Hegel's work limits critical and emancipatory dimensions of a theory (Hegel 1991; cf. Riedel 1975; Honneth 2000d).

Generally taken, it is possible to say that Hegel provides a philosophical basis that results in an intersubjective conception of human beings within the community. Human being is conceived as a person who, in interactions with other human beings, seeks to remove the distorting moments of his recognition. This paves the way for the question of the dynamics and evolution of recognition based on the struggle against misrecognition and for recognition.

The most important authors examining Hegel's conception of recognition and building on this in contemporary critical social and political analyses include Axel Honneth and Charles Taylor (Honneth 1996; Honneth 2014; Taylor 1975; Taylor 1979). Both draw on philosophy of recognition, which they also develop along interdisciplinary and transdisciplinary lines within the social sciences. While Honneth, in this project, interconnects the philosophical exploration of the struggle against misrecognition primarily with sociology and psychology, Taylor places more of an emphasis on analysing positive recognition and supplements it, in particular, with political-science analysis.

---

1   Lukács proceeded in detail in much the same manner as Marx, who, in his Parisian manuscripts, explained the struggle for recognition in *The Phenomenology of Spirit* from an economistic perspective and from the paradigm of work. In contrast, Kojeve emphasized the bitter struggle for life in terms of his existentialist conception of recognition and death, on which Sartre built (Lukács 1954; Kojeve 1947; Sartre 2021; cf. Habermas 1973).

More specific detailing of their analyses relies on George Herbert Mead (1934; 1982), for example.

Nancy Fraser and Axel Honneth even started their common book with the phrase: "'Recognition' has become a ... keyword of our time." Such an ambitious declaration does demand proper analysis. Honneth tries to formulate a moral conception of social conflicts, and attempts to materialise Hegel's theory while maintaining some of his idealistic elements in the sense I discussed in the third chapter. An exemplary manifestation of this seminal theoretical position is Habermas's sentence encapsulating the intent of Honneth's major book: "Honneth takes the historical step back from Marx to Hegel to re-establish the programme 'from Hegel to Marx'." (Habermas 2009), In the course of my explanation, I will illuminate that while the main intention of this revitalization was good, it has not been fulfilled much, let alone adequately updated. Other prominent authors who have engaged in original means of revitalising the concept of recognition include Nancy Fraser, Iris Young and Paul Ricoeur, for example (Schmidt, Zurn 2010). At this point, however, it is time for a more detailed interpretation.

Taylor, as part of his moral ontology, presents a basic definition of mutual recognition of persons. He does not focus yet on a substantive interpretation of the human being, which can take many forms depending on the particular types of community in which the individual is to be found. As such a substantive interpretation would be contrary to the legitimate plurality of the various types of community, Taylor formulates only the characteristics of human beings that might be generally applicable. These are the elemental characteristics of the human beings.

Taylor keeps to the two alternative conceptions of human beings (Taylor 2003, 195–212) I have discussed in the previous chapters, which can now be collectively conceived as a negative conception of the human being. First, he focuses on libertarian conceptions promoting an atomistic ontological concept of the human being which is primarily perceived in isolation without regard to other persons and their inclusion in relations within the community. This criticism applies to both right-wing and left-wing versions of libertarianism. Secondly, Taylor considers liberal conceptions to be inadequate because, although they do not explicitly advocate an atomistic concept of human being, by ignoring the ontological plane of the interpretation they implicitly identify with certain premises of the libertarian conception of the human being. This identification has various origins. Whereas elements of the concept of isolated individual make their way into certain insufficiently substantiated liberal theories because they are insufficiently developed, they enter other liberal theories because these theories a priori refuse to perform analysis on an ontological level. They rely on mere political analysis, which finds no support in the social background of a person's life (Rawls 1971). This liberal stance, however, is not only unstable, but, in particular, poorly specified if it wants to defend liberal principles that are adrift. Their authors deliberately introduce elements of libertarianism into liberal theories (Rawls 1993a).

In reaction to these ontologically deficient conceptions of the human being, Taylor presents his own approach, drawing on Hegel's conception of morality and, building on that, a concept of individual in the community. As such, Taylor formulates a holistic version of moral ontology that overcomes the deficits of the atomistic version and attempts to replace Kantian transcendental subjectivism with what could be described as transcendental intersubjectivism (Apel 1993, 149–172). While a subjective conception is unable to substantiate conditions relating to the possibility of the intersubjective validity of different norms, the intersubjective conception focuses precisely on such reasoning and demonstrates validity based on intersubjective communication and life. Language and community are defining characteristics of human beings (Taylor 1985a, 45–76). However, the linguistic foundation of human beings in the community need not be burdened by such transcendentalism, and an emphasis may be placed on supplementing it with a morally hermeneutical interpretation which is also found in Taylor's interpretation, and which develops the concept of the capacity to use language into the idea of the capacity for human beings to interpret themselves and their environment. Interpretation is conceived as an evaluating activity. Human beings interpret and evaluate themselves and others in their mutual relations in the community.

A definition of human beings through this holistic ontology requires the further specification of persons and evaluation. Taylor, like Honneth, in relation to Mead, discusses "significant others" as persons who play an important role in the lives of other people. The interpretation of these persons and other persons and their relationships is of a constitutive nature for human being as an interpreter and evaluator. It is relevant to form a value-community.

The ability to evaluate also requires a clearer distinction between different types and varying degrees of evaluation. The degree of evaluation by individuals may vary, and they may perform various types of evaluation. Compared to conventional evaluations, they also carry out "strong evaluations", whereby they attach varying importance to different goods in their life. In this way, they prove their ability to distinguish not only between various goods but also between different kinds of goods. Taylor distinguishes several basic kinds of goods: common goods, which play a role in the assumption of preferences between more and less desirable phenomena and objects; collective goods, which are significant due to the common evaluation of persons in the community; life goods, which are crucial for lives of different individuals or group of persons; and hyper-goods, which are decisive for group persons or even an entire culture or civilisation. Hyper-goods are the constitutive goods of a specific culture which, against a backdrop of the culture's value horizons or value frameworks, provide basic orientation for the culture's members. Value horizons form a complex context in which hyper-goods allow people to create a certain hierarchy of goods and understand each other.

On a meta-level, we can sum up this interpretation and, further to the Chapter 4 on critical paradigms, claim that Taylor's social ontology provides clarification of philosophical anthropology, which is not only a kind of hermeneutic interpretation but also adheres to the linguistic turn. One motif is hermeneutic clarification, which emphasises the evaluative understanding and self-understanding of human being. Another motif is the inclination towards the paradigm of communication, emphasising the role of language and its importance in human life. This is a paradigm that Taylor both develops and surpasses with a communitarian-oriented interpretation stressing the importance of community which is a larger concept then communication. Thus, in this point, he finds himself in transition from the communication paradigm to the paradigm of mutual recognition in the community; and he develops the concept of recognition in particular in his further investigations related to political analysis. Although Taylor elaborates on his theory extensively, he does not offer a summarising interpretation, as Habermas did in his theory of communicative action, for example. Therefore, his ideas need to be reconstructed, and the place occupied by individual parts in the whole of his theoretical position needs to be explicated. Reconstruction of his theoretical position indicates that there is no gradual development of ideas from communication to recognition but, rather, synchronous explanatory interpretations which are based on the philosophical anthropology of language and developed by a concept of recognition, and which are developed in his broader historical social, political and cultural theoretical position.

Taylor's contribution to the shift from the communication paradigm to the recognition paradigm is close to that of Honneth, building on certain factors of Habermas's theory of communicative action while seeking to overcome its one-sidedness by developing his own theory of recognition. However, Honneth, who is a generation younger than Taylor, makes much less of a link to the communication paradigm than Taylor. Unlike Taylor, moreover, he does not rely on a problematic transcendental determination of the human being and elaborates on his post-metaphysical viewpoint of Critical Theory. Honneth appreciates the role of communication in intersubjective interaction, placing a considerable emphasis on it, but considers the main benefit of the recognition paradigm

TABLE 4   Kinds of recognition in Honneth's theory

Forms of recognition	Primary relationships (love, friendship)	Legal relationships (rights)	Social relationships (solidarity, performance)
Mode of recognition	Emotional support	Cognitive respect	Social esteem
Dimensions of personality	Needs and emotions	Responsibility	Characteristics and abilities

to be its more general trait, i.e., a tendency towards intersubjective action which includes communication, yet does not limit intersubjectivity thereto.[2] Honneth's theory, unlike Taylor's, stands fully within the recognition paradigm which he has developed by the revitalization of a concept of recognition. Honneth, in his Critical Theory of recognition, updates Hegel's identification of three types of recognition (Table 4), which I will discuss in the sections below. Any kind of recognition includes social tension and conflicts, which, on the one hand, reveal problems, but, on the other hand, show potential opportunities for further development which would facilitate a response to these problems.[3]

2   From the Private Sphere to the Public Sphere

In various social and political theories, particularly liberal ones, analyses primarily distinguish between two spheres – private and public. Feminist criticism and criticism from the positions of other discriminated groups, however, have already shown that the virtual disconnection between these spheres leads to injustice. As these spheres overlap and, in certain parts, should normatively overlap, in my interpretation I will elucidate not only on their specifics but also

---

2   I will now leave aside Honneth's link to the normative aspect of the communication paradigm because this point is not the subject of my interpretation here. However, an answer can be found in Chapter 4, Section 2.

3   Although I am also concerned with Honneth's *Freedom's Right* (2014), my analyses are mainly concerned with his analyses written before that book, since that book more fully reproduces Hegel's late philosophy of law and tends towards less critical conclusions with an emphasis on the liberal concept of liberty.

on their interdependence (Ricoeur 2005). In these analyses, it is important to see how Nancy Fraser distinguishes between emancipatory feminism, which is not afraid of a critique of capitalism, and feminism which submits to neoliberal and other versions of capitalism and, in the alliance with it, may damage a feminist approach (Fraser 2009, 97–117).

Whereas Taylor discusses the intimate sphere primarily to distinguish it from the public sphere, Honneth offers a more specific treatise in which, on the one hand, he analyses each sphere in its characteristics, and, on the other hand, largely conceives them in their interaction within a single theory of recognition, even though his theory requires even greater and more specific interconnection. Building on Hegel, he analyses, in the private sector, the primary formula of recognition in the form of love and friendship (Honneth 1996, 95–107). In doing so, he focuses on the institutional structures of these primary relationships of recognition and on their provision of emotional support. He explains how approaches of care and love as necessary life conditions were articulated not only in the bourgeois-capitalist order but also previously, in the estate system. (Fraser and Honneth 2003). Of course, also premodern societies included forms of socialisation of offspring and, more generally, persons, who were mutually defined and thereby individualised by this process concerning other persons. Recognition in the form of love is generally defined here as the positive affective attention of relevant persons, as a positive emotional relationship between one person and another specific person, in short as a kind of emotional support (Honneth 1996, 87, 95, 96). This relationship is also described by strong emotional ties realised between a small number of persons. Criteria for distinguishing love from other forms of recognition are, therefore, in a first approximation, the characteristics of positive strong emotional bonds between people and the concretisation of these bonds between two people or in small groups of persons. Much like Taylor, Honneth relates them, in Meadian way, to persons who are "significant others" for us (Honneth 1996, 71–91). This form of emotional recognition initially appears in the form of parents' love for their child. Variations of this also surface between adults in the form of friendship, an amorous relationship, or between family members, and may also occur among other persons who positively relate to each other in similar specific intimate relationships.

Love and friendship, which Honneth sometimes refers to, for brevity's sake, simply as love, are, genetically and/or developmentally, the first forms of recognition – relative to other forms – materialising also in the public sphere. Honneth shows that, without love, individuals could not develop other forms of recognition. Here, love is also primary conceptually because, without it, the remaining forms of recognition cannot be explained. In this sense, love is a fundamental prerequisite for other types of recognition and self-realisation of the human individual. Honneth, here, also follows up on Heidegger's concept of care (*Sorge*) and concept of solicitude (*Fürsorge*) which characterise man's basic attitude towards the world (*Dasein*) (Honneth 2008, 51ff; Honneth 2003, 10–27). This existential attitude or existential type of recognition precedes all other types of recognition which are more complex and more specific about how to acknowledge all other characteristics of human beings. Existential recognition forms the basis for each specific intersubjective relationship of mutual recognition of human beings. Hegel vigorously expresses this idea by saying that, in love, everyone exists in another (*Seinselbstsein in einem Fremden*) (Hegel 1969, 425).

Intimate relationships of recognition form specific bonds between the parties thereto which are based on relationships of mutual trust. Yet love and friendship, like other forms of recognition, are not just interpersonal relations; they also play a significant role in relationship of human beings with themselves. As such, the formation of everyone's personality and individuality is shaped by self-confidence, by forming trust in herself or himself. For children, this means, developmentally, gaining confidence first in their own body and the related bodily needs and emotions. A relationship of love provides the assurance that a person's needs and emotions are recognised and are entitled to satisfaction. Therefore, needs and emotions are recognised as valuable and worthy of fulfilment. There is no need to suppress or conceal them; it is possible to manifest them and believe in oneself when trying to satisfy them. As a child matures, these relationships extend to more challenging mental processes and to esteem of the adolescent's interests and value orientation. In the broadest perspective, this encompasses recognition of a person's direction on life and recognition of himself or herself as an independent individual.

Recognition is clearly not a static condition; there is a dynamic process in the development of relationships. Nevertheless, recognition does not arise only as an act of a positive relationship. It owes its existence primarily to a person's efforts to gain recognition from others. Although parents or other carers may relate to a child very positively, a child must express its own needs and feelings and strive for recognition thereof by articulating them. The struggle for recognition of needs and feelings in a constructive environment is a struggle only in the figurative sense but the neglecting of care or deliberate disregard for the needs and emotions of a child may trigger negative developments (Honneth 1996, 131ff). The mental and physical neglect, abuse or rape of a child can have serious consequences on the mental and physical integrity of the individual concerned. If the recognition a child expects is not forthcoming, its confidence that its demands will be met is eroded, as is its trust in parents or other caregivers. Forms of misrecognition ultimately also undermine a child's confidence in itself. Prolonged or severe forms of damage to a person's integrity lead to the pathological development, deformation or blocking of the growth of the personality, and cause the individual's psychological or somatic integrity to malfunction.

Here, in their philosophical analyses, Honneth and other critical-theory authors expand primarily – as is usual in critical theory – on psychoanalytic studies and engage in critical reading not only of Freud but also of later generations of authors. Honneth prefers, in particular, the analyses of Donald Winnicott and Jessica Benjamin (Winnicott 1965; Benjamin 1988), and concerns himself with a developmental analysis of the child, focusing mainly on the process of obtaining identity through the loving care of a parent. He demonstrates the initial unity of a parent – still mostly the mother in Western society – with the child, and the gradual reduction in their mutual dependence, leading to the crystallisation of the child's separate identity. He describes this process as cognitive differentiation between the self and its context (Honneth 1996, 100). He identifies the mother or father as a person who is fundamentally important for the child but whom the child is unable to fully influence or control. Therefore, the child acquires knowledge about its dependence and becomes disillusioned about its opportunities. The child transitions from absolute dependence to relative dependence, begins to concentrate more freely on the various types of the mother's care, and tries to obtain them. As illustrated by Jessica Benjamin, this leads to efforts to meet the needs of the child through these methods of care, to the struggle for recognition of the needs of the child (Benjamin 1988). If a parent gives a child responsive care through a relationship of love and, thus, provides it with comprehensive support, the child acclimatises to the world, develops the ability to compete in it, and acquires confidence in the world and itself. The ability to grow independently is derived from a child's trust in a caring parent who enables the child to gradually become independent. This facilitates the process where the child separates from the parent and can become increasingly aware of and shape its own identity. The child's decoupling provides the caring parent, in turn, with a lesser degree of interdependence and greater autonomy. In this sense, love is a complex relationship of recognition between parent and child, in which the physical and psychological needs and emotions of the child are recognised and in which the child's universal characteristics, shared with other children, and its specific and particular characteristics, peculiar to that concrete child, are appreciated. This relationship of love is mutual, even though the needs and emotions of the parent are fulfilled in a specific way, depending on his identity as an adult individual.

However, the psychological interpretation of misrecognition has its limits, as noted by Nancy Fraser and several other authors (Fraser and Honneth 2003). While Fraser acknowledges the fact that some kinds of misrecognition may stem from problems that social psychology and psychoanalysis can identify and help to remove, she insists on the need to focus on the political reasons for misrecognition encountered in the private sphere. This argument is reminiscent of the proposition that "the personal is political", widespread in feminist theory. For example, Carole Pateman rejects the division of problems into the private and public spheres because, traditionally, based on this distinction, liberal theory has ignored injustices in the private sphere and centered solely on the public sphere (Pateman 1989; Pateman 1888; Benjamin 1988). This approach reproduced, and even created, inequalities between the status of women and men. Therefore, feminist theory requires that attention be focused on the private sphere and that the same importance be attached to this sphere as has been enjoyed thus far by the public realm (Young 2020, 134–185). The feminist proposition above was popularised, in particular, at the end of the 1960s by the pivotal feminist movement figure, Carol Hanisch, in her text "The Personal is Political" (Hanisch 1971). It is not true that she refuses a psychological exploration of misrecognition in the private sphere of life.[4] The main idea of her premise, however, is that many problems and injustices facing women in the private sphere are not rooted only in the private sphere and that they should ultimately be solved, primarily, as political issues. This is because these problems are often caused by the political order but have so far largely not been regarded as political and have been treated as the private problems of individual women. Therefore, it is necessary to change the problematic conditions and not adjust to them. Hanisch states that women do not need therapy in the first place, i.e., private therapy. She does not diminish the importance of psychological studies of the private sphere but only assigns it a secondary place in the hierarchy of analysis because she primarily strives to have more significance attached to overlooked political solutions. Similarly, Honneth and other authors do not deny the political sources of various injustices that exist in the private sphere.[5] They believe that injustices in the private sphere must be addressed as political issues if they are political, as psychological issues if they are psychological, as cultural issues if they are cultural, etc. Such a complex standpoint is also adequate for critical theory, which must also be feminist

---

4   Of the feminist authors that focus directly on a psychoanalytic analysis of the primary plane of recognition concerning the public sphere and the overlapping thereof, see, for example (Chodorow 1989).

5   For an interpretation of the limits of Honneth's position, see Young (2007b, 189–212).

because it cannot ignore assorted gender misrecognition. Therefore, it might be said that every critical theory must reflect these issues. Similarly, it is necessary to combine critical theory with the criticism of misrecognition made by other marginalised groups (Hondagneu-Sotelo, Avila 2006).

The complex approach of critical theory should be cautious towards approaches which, in social and political theory, do not thematise the causes of misrecognition and are limited to psychological sources; nor should it overlook the psychological problems absent from political causes. As far as combined psycho-political issues are concerned, the psychological difficulties that individuals must confront politically are of a dual nature. First, they may be based directly on political causes and deform the psychological aspects of the personality. Secondly, inadequate bonds of mutual recognition on a mental plane, specifically in the area of intersubjective relations, could block the further development of these relationships of recognition at other levels, including the political level, namely in the area of civil society and the state. What is needed, then, is a complex approach that examines both sources of problems and that, moreover, must focus the political and psychological analysis – in a general form – on core universal characteristics shared by all individuals and – in a concrete form – must guide such analysis according to the life goods of particular individuals or particular groups of persons.

Although Fraser rightly draws attention to political misrecognition, she maybe underestimates the psychological and combined forms of misrecognition which have both political and psychological sources. She does, however, make one important remark. She points out that psychological theory could find itself in conflict with *normative* political theory (Fraser and Honneth 2003). Certain facts that are considered obvious in psychological theory may have repressive political consequences. Therefore, it is necessary for psychological analysis to be carried out not only with consideration for the description of the political forms of misrecognition but also following the required political norms which should form conditions for the existence of a non-repressive society. In terms of spotlighting the normative dimension, Fraser is right but at this point, she methodologically follows a path contrary to that which would be fitting. No unanchored isolated political norms resisting descriptive research can be an assessment criterion. The correctness of norms cannot be based primarily on random normativity but on criticism of misrecognition by unrecognised women and others and on the descriptive identification of positive fragments of reality, and only then on their development and addition to the normative concept of recognition. Here, in Fraser, there are problems with the inadequately reflected methodological trichotomy inherent in the establishment and methods of critical theory.

Before embarking on an analysis of recognition at the level of civil society and the political public, I would like to discuss one point which, on the private plane, has provoked hardly any theoretical dispute concerning parent-child relationships but which is a matter of controversy in the context of relationships of recognition between friends and other adult subjects. While it appears already on a private plane, it gains in stature on a public level. The point at issue here is the symmetry and asymmetry of the mutual recognition of persons.

Although relationships of love and friendship between adult individuals are different from the parent-child relationship in many ways, the basic grammar of mutual recognition is analogous. One of the main differences is the fact that the parent-child relationship is a fundamentally asymmetrical relationship, in which the child finds itself in a hierarchically subordinate position in that it is dependent on the parent's care. Despite the child's gradual emancipation, asymmetric elements remain integral to this relationship, even though they may subsequently be tucked under a layer of the autonomous development of the adolescent and, subsequently, the adult individual. It could be said, however, that human beings find themselves in asymmetric relations of dependence particularly in their infancy, but in adulthood she or he has the chance to care for children, the elderly, and other needy persons, so that, from a long-term intergenerational perspective, it is possible to speak of a certain type of symmetry (Young 2007b, 189–212). In relationships between adults, relationships of love and friendship can then be cultivated symmetrically, although their specific realisation depends, of course, on particular cultural patterns of order in society.

Yet the relationship of symmetrical reciprocity contains certain problematic elements. On the one hand, it is important to develop equal relations between persons; on the other hand, it is evident that recognition of the specificity and diversity of another requires a more empathetic approach. The differences between the two positions are clearly visible in the dispute between Iris Young and Seyla Benhabib.

Benhabib, in her reformulating response to Habermas's theory of communicative ethics, defends the universalist conception of egalitarian reciprocity, i.e., reciprocity based on symmetrical relationships between individuals. According to her, this modern conception is present in the required norms we encounter in speech in our everyday dealings. In their dialogue, its actors formulate egalitarian demands on general principles which, together, they would be able to share. Although each of them has different experience and perspectives of interpretation, they can engage in a "generalisation of the other" and strive to reach a consensus.

However, in Benhabib's view, this Habermasean concept is insufficient, and she reformulates it employing her concept which also preserves the perspective of the "concrete other". She attempts to formulate a more complex concept of persons "as generalised and 'concrete others'". (Benhabib 1992, 32, cf. 170) Although it might seem that a choice needs to be made between generalisation and concreteness, she finds a concept that combines both demands. The basis of this synthesis is the idea of the assumption of another's opinion. According to Benhabib, the possibility of egalitarian respect for another in a situation where that other person is generalised requires us to be able to trade places with her or him. The egalitarian universality of the concrete in relationships of mutual recognition is expressed by the sentence: "All communicative action entails symmetry and reciprocity of normative expectations among group members." (Benhabib 1992, 32, 136–137) Iris Young agrees with this position in the sense that the norms of the reciprocal social recognition of persons are present in normative expectations in everyday dialogic situations and, in this respect, they may also serve as a model for moral and political concepts (Young 2007b). However, she thinks that the "concrete other" should be recognised by a more demanding method than by mere uncertain attempts to assume another's opinion. She seeks a concept that deals with the particular differences among people (Young 2007b). Ignoring the unfavourable social and political asymmetric position of others, or their deliberate asymmetric position in terms of their personal identity, could lead to the misrecognition of such persons or to a repressive approach towards them. A lack of sensitivity to another's differences and the ontological impossibility of transforming one's own perspective of a certain social position into another person's perspective, and, ultimately, the negative political consequences of this approach, result in consideration of the need for the participation of another in the relationships of recognition.

Benhabib herself mentions this idea explicitly in relation to Hegel. She writes that what is needed is not our imagination about the situation of the other, but, directly, her or his involvement in the social order: "It is the other who makes us aware of both her concreteness and otherness. Without engagement, confrontation, dialogue and even a 'struggle for recognition', in the Hegelian sense, we tend to constitute the otherness of the other by projection and fantasy or ignore it in indifference." (Benhabib 1992, 32) Although Benhabib is aware of this idea of the mutual recognition of concrete persons, she understands it only in the narrower sense, without further specification, or does not attach greater meaning to it and, therefore, does not use it to redefine her concept of reciprocal recognition.

Iris Young explains the need for asymmetrical reciprocity with her own interpretation of the mutual recognition of persons. Persons recognise each other and recognise the fact that they have a specific perspective and specific interests that cannot be reduced to the viewpoint and interests of someone else. Recognition of persons requires this concrete type of reciprocity because others are an end in themselves and not just the means. (Young 2007) Asymmetrical recognition in relations between people is of considerable importance especially when they are in very different and unequal positions. Young draws on her conclusions primarily in her analyses of inequalities and differences between men and women and in analyses of culturally defined minorities.

3   Political Public Sphere

My investigation into disputes between the symmetrical reciprocity standpoint and the asymmetrical reciprocity standpoint led me to analyse recognition in the public sphere, as this conflict refers to both the private and the public sectors. Now I will focus directly on the public plane of the research (Thompson 2006; Burns 2001, 319–330; Lazzeri and Caillé 2007; Ricoeur 2000; Ricoeur 2007). The analyses here relate to kinds of social and political recognition applicable to the individual, depending on various forms of distinction – according to whether they deal with the universal or particular characteristics of people. While Charles Taylor makes a distinction between the politics of universalism and the politics of difference, Axel Honneth emphasises the difference between universalist equal respect for law in relation to the state and specific kinds of social recognition in the form of solidarity and esteem of performance in civil society (Honneth 1996, 107ff; Fraser and Honneth 2003, 181ff).

Taylor and Honneth's interpretations build on their conceptions of moral ontology and are on both the plane of general quasi-universalist contextualised ethics and the plane of quasi-universalist ethics which analyses the lower form of quasi-universalism demarcated by Western culture in approximately the last three centuries. These two levels, however, are not explicitly distinguishable from each other, so the individual parts of their analyses coincide. In the reconstruction of the positive elements of Honneth and Taylor's theories of recognition, it is also necessary to transform and extend their normative conceptions of moral/ethical realism into the realism of societal development from which it would then be possible to proceed to a specification of the legal, political and other forms of normativity, as I have noted in the Chapter 2 on methods.

Taylor understands the quasi-universalist interpretation primarily as a historical and conceptual explanation of the development of Western modern self (Taylor 1989; Taylor 2007). This is a way of concretising a moral person, conceived here as the self of Western modern person or, using older terminology, as the spirit of modern times. Western identity contains certain constitutive goods which are jointly shared values of most members of Western culture. Taylor examines them through specific historical events and by reference to interpretations in the context of research into the history of ideas. His entire investigation is set in the framework of a reflection on the self-interpretations of persons who grasp events and ideas and use them to shape their own identity. Modern identity here is a series of important quasi-universal self-interpretations clustered around the fundamental constitutive goods of modern Western society. Taylor also articulates a narrative that, through self-interpretations, attempts to demonstrate the self-understanding of members of Western culture. Of course, the formulation of such creative imagination cannot be exhaustive and cannot capture all the nuances of Western identity, but it can cover the major developmental trends, despite their inconsistencies and the limitations of their quasi-universalism.

Taylor paints a grand picture of the historical development of modern Western identity by explaining the "sources of the self". First, he focuses on several major phenomena of modernity that have appeared in recent centuries. The first is "inwardness", by which Taylor means the inner life of the individual. The gradual development of inwardness can be described as the subjectivisation of individuals, that is, the formation of the free individual subjectivity which began to emerge against a background of various collective identities crucial to the identification of person until the onset of modern times. Until then, the inner life of most of the population was not particularly structured and the existing structures played only a marginal role in people's consciousness. The second phenomenon is "ordinary life". Of course, ordinary life was not ignored also in the past, but it remained unarticulated because sufficient importance was not attached to it. Only in modern times, attention has focused on daily human activities, their institutionalisation and rationalisation. However, their increasing importance does not stem solely from the secularisation of certain activities. This can be evidenced in a comparison with the ancient ideal of contemplative and political life. The third phenomenon is the "voice of nature", which, since Romanticism, has indicated a unique human expression different from the unique characteristics of other people. Nature means not only the good natural talents of a particular person but also good socially acquired characteristics, which, however, the individual perceives as his own specific traits. The fourth phenomenon is "subtler languages".

The pervasiveness of language was manifested in various scholarly and artistic forms of expression, the crystallisation of which can be observed mainly from the Victorian period. The post-Romantic period is characterised by the formation of a scientific method of interpretation, a conception of justice with universalist civil ambitions and various kinds of artistic expression.

These and other phenomena formed a value background for the gradual shaping of constitutive goods of the modern era with a specific modern identity. The individual goods of groups of persons and individual people were formed in the value framework of these constitutive goods, which gradually replaced, transformed, or co-existed for some time with the former constitutive goods. The first source of modern identity is disengaged reason. Disengaged reason is a characteristic manifestation of Enlightenment thinking, placing demands on both the freedom of learning and practical activities, especially with moral – even political – ambitions. The subject adopts the intention to approach the outside world through this Enlightenment rationality in an impartial and objectifying manner and strive for allegedly neutral knowledge. There is a parallel and consistency between this approach and the political sphere, where the subject is treated allegedly as an independent actor who, interacting with others, can himself (it was mainly man) set the rules of his conduct, i.e., he acts as an autonomous subject freely determining laws of moral and political action.

The second source of modern identity is expressivism. Human nature is not only perceived as a good starting point and criterion of human action but also – and in particular – as an original expression of a particular individual or group of persons. The unique activities of human beings and their results are an authentic expression of the individual and group self. Expressivity is manifested here in artistic, social and political areas – as the identity of the artist, the nation, etc. Finally, the third source is the "Judeo-Christian tradition". Unlike the two previous sources, this is not a new product of modernity. At least at the beginning of modernism, it was an enduring constitutive good for most of the population in the Western world. Growing secularisation weakened but did not eliminate this constitutive good. Although it conflicted with the other two, the agonising element was also present in the relationship between the other two sources. Throughout their gradual evolution, specific relations of coexistence, complementarity and persisting tensions between these goods were shaped. However, together they constituted a relatively cohesive value unit delivering an identity of modernism that was stable enough to provide a value background for individuals and groups in the environment of fundamental changes in intimate, social and political spheres brought about by the advent of industrial production. According to Taylor, the constitutive goods of modern identity in Western countries in recent centuries can be sum-marised by the mutually contradictory terms "autonomy", "authenticity" and "god". The main bearers of modern changes, however, were the first two goods[6] because the third one did not have a strong impact on the development of the modern era due to the process of secularization even if protestant ethics had significant consequences on capitalism in the West (Taylor 2007).

While autonomy is primarily associated with the requirement of the recog-nition of the universalist characteristics of man as an equal citizen with equal civil and political rights, authenticity is linked in particular to the requirement of the recognition of the particular characteristics of the individual, including esteem of his specific cultural identity and his performance in the economic sphere. Although the definition of modern constitutive goods in this form is widespread, it is not only inaccurate but also misleading. It is precisely because it is so common that it provides a good basis for criticism and redefinition.

Honneth offers his historical and conceptual interpretation of the develop-ment of individual constitutive goods of Western identity which has led to the institutionalisation of a certain order of recognition, and which embodies the value framework of the bourgeois-capitalist societal form of structure (Fraser and Honneth 2003, Honneth 2014). While the development of primary recog-nition in the form of love and friendship is institutionalised in formulae of mutual recognition on the private plane in particular, primary relationships are institutionalised beyond the confines of the private sphere and assume a specific form that is legally codified, such as marriage or the legal concept of parent-child relationships. Typical patterns of intersubjective bonds between groups of persons and between individuals, however, comprised different for-mulae of recognition and misrecognition, namely the legal respect and social esteem of adult individuals concerning the state and civil society (Honneth 1996; Honneth 2014; Schecter 2019).

Honneth and Taylor agree that premodern society, which in the Western world was represented by the estates of the feudal order, was accompanied by the social and legal unequal recognition of individuals and groups primarily based on their affiliation to a particular estate, which in turn is derived primar-ily from the origin, and then the role, they played in society. An individual's estate-based position in the feudal value system was associated with a certain professional honor, which was distributed very asymmetrically. The highest social strata approached the majority of the population in a non-egalitarian

---

6   Cf. this explanation of the constitutive goods of modern society and criticism of their defor-mation and their mutually imbalanced relationship in Chapter 5, Section 2.

manner within a strongly economically and politically hierarchical society. The flip side of aristocratic privileges, pursued by recognition in the form of aristocratic honor, was the serfdom of the lower layers. Then the steady expansion of the bourgeois-capitalist structure disrupted this estate-based order to the extent that, eventually, it almost disappeared.

The transformation of the order of recognition in Western countries from a traditional society to a modern society is interpreted in detail by Peter Berger and Charles Taylor (Berger 1983, 172ff; Taylor 1994; Taylor 1992). A major turning point was the fall of the traditional social hierarchy, accompanied by the delegitimisation of honour in its aristocratic version. While honour was associated, by definition, with the privileges of the feudal order, modern recognition in the form of dignity encompasses a broader group of persons – the burghers. Honour would lack relevance if it pertained to everyone because privileges remain privileges only as long as they can be assigned to a very selectively conceived group of persons. Conversely, dignity should be a manifestation of a different recognition that pertains, anonymously, to all those who enjoy political recognition in a bourgeois-capitalist structure.

The emphasis here is attached to the recognition of civil and political rights. Officially and formally, subjects should become independent members of civil society and autonomous actors of political decision-making. They are expected to take decisions about themselves without superior political authority situated on the upper levels of the hierarchical order. The strengthening of recognition in the form of dignity, thus, paved the way for elements of capitalist form of democratic governance to be established. Efforts to replace particularly segregated honour with more universally conceived dignity became the basis. This transformation of recognition is symbolically carried by the customary use of the civil title "Mr" instead of the hierarchical estate titles (Prince, Baron, etc.).

Several terms are associated, rather haphazardly, with such public recognition and require analysis. Taylor uses the terms "citizen dignity" and even "dignity of human beings". This is underpinned by his view that the elimination of estate honour resulted in the almost complete removal of exclusivity-based recognition and the introduction of recognition on a principle of the inclusiveness of all people. Symbolically, this transformation means achieving the possibility of using the word "citizen". The problem with this idea and terminology is that the terms "citizen" and "human being" here, in fact, originally referred only to a wealthy man. Bourgeois-capitalist forms of recognition were a manifestation of the efforts of a specific group of persons – wealthy men wielding enough economic clout to attempt to oppose aristocratic privileges. The poor and women did not belong to this elite but tried to emancipate themselves in the social democratic, socialist and communist movements. This includes the egalitarian address of "comrade" which was established in opposition to the bourgeois hierarchy of private owners of the means of production. Exploited and marginalised groups of persons, in their efforts at recognition, gradually try to dismantle step by step the segregational conception of political rights and replace it with a fairer concept that also embraces the exploited, the poor, and women. This is the long-term effort at equalisation in a process that, however, has been far from complete. Nevertheless, at least in some respects, it is now possible, in the political arena in the European Union, for example, to refer to all persons or, almost universally, to human beings.

Honneth supplements these considerations at the level of moral reasoning. He believes that the recognition of the individual is based on moral respect for the human being who can use reason to schedule his activities. In this sense, a human being is regarded as an autonomous person, i.e., this is related primarily to rational autonomy. Autonomous rational decision-making on how to act is then accompanied by accountability for such action. The aspect of a person on which attention is concentrated is the moral responsibility of the individual for his free action (Honneth 1996, 114). Because person does not live in isolation but in a community, moral responsibility is applied to other persons. Moral obligations, in abstract form, are mutual liabilities of moral persons. Here, generalised others are the basis of a perspective that applies to all people without discrimination. Everyone is expected to be recognised here in an undifferentiated, equal way, which has positive and negative aspects.

In this part of his reasoning, Honneth makes a leap, switching from moral norms straight to legal norms without articulating general standards which could be specified further in special standards, whether political, legal, cultural, or other. This can be explained either as the expansion of moral norms into legal norms, although these are subject to different institutional requirements, or – and this is his inference – as a narrowly focused interpretation that clarifies only the moral foundations of legal norms. Leaving aside the two versions of moral interventionism, which overlooks the different roles of moral and legal norms and overestimates their connectedness, and building on the interpretation commenced above, concretised by civil requirements, it will be possible to focus on Honneth's other analyses which I consider to be of value. Honneth shows that legal relationships provide cognitive honour, which implies recognition of the capacity for the self-understanding of the individual, and enable us to recognise, institutionally, other persons as autonomously acting beings legally accountable for their actions. These persons, for their part, recognise us as autonomous and assume that we will be legally responsible for our actions. Therefore, legal relationships institutionalise mutual expectations of autonomy and responsibility in relationships of mutual equal recognition concerning the legal order. Mutual respect for persons is based on the acceptance of mutual rights and obligations in legal relationships. In this sense, respect and rights are internally linked, mainly due to a single autonomous individual acquiring rights and obligations.

These are individual rights and individual obligations of persons who are members of a community with a legal order. These rights and corresponding responsibilities, formed in the struggles for recognition, are usually based on group rights, e.g. in the group struggles of low-income social groups for the individual right to vote in the 19th century, subsequently the struggle for women's right to vote, social rights, the liberation of a certain group of persons from colonial rule in a particular territory, etc., and can be specified by group rights, for instance in the case of the positive action in favour of certain marginalised groups of the population, as I explain below.

So far, I have discussed rights as a kind of legal assumptions for recognition; concretisation of the law leads to the specific institutionalisation of legal rights. This means the mediation of legal relationships by the state, a supranational organisation, a municipality or other jurisdiction units. Legal recognition is a specification of the term respect which Honneth reserves for this type of recognition in his theory.

In this regard, an important point of analysis is whether to consider the law a separate sphere of justice or to analyse it in the context of other spheres. Honneth regards the law as an important area with separate characteristics and, therefore, thinks that it needs to be analysed as a separate area. He focuses on it primarily as a sphere of legal respect for persons. He criticises Nancy Fraser for more or less ignoring the struggle for legal equality of persons. While it is true that Fraser does not treat law as a separate sphere, she does analyse it within the scope of several other spheres; first, in the context of socio-economic redistribution and in the field of cultural recognition, and later also in relation to political representation. She explains that law pervades individual spheres and considers her reasoning of the conception of law to be adequate because law is conceived rather concerning both dimensions of justice, particularly redistribution and distribution (Fraser and Honneth 2003) Therefore, in this interpretation the main factor appears to be not whether the law is a separate sphere, but whether and how it enables individual types of struggle for recognition to be pursued, whether and how it facilitates their linkage to various changes in the economy, politics, culture, etc., and whether and how they are enforced by various population groups.

Turning to the causes underlying the motivation to struggle for legal recognition, it is necessary to thematise the historical changes, initially triggered

by the transforming economy which, with the Western expansion of colonialism in Africa, Latin America and Asia and the capitalist advent of industrial
production, increased the influence and role of the bourgeoisie. The brutal
slavery and post-slavery colonial system overlapped with the development of
capitalism which used colonized unfree labour forces and natural wealth in
the colonies. With the rise of industrialization, and resistance against slavery,
colonialism and feudalism, the system transformed step by step into a wage
labour capitalist system which, however, lost its colonial territories much later
(Fanon 2005; Seth 2013). These are translational motifs that have to be stressed.
In this process, output rose, with a corresponding hike in consumption, and
the role of the market in the economy expanded.

In this context, Honneth notes that market relationships required specific
legal norms to regulate the relationships of those to whom the same or equal
rights were to apply (Fraser and Honneth 2003). I may remind Marx, who
claims that the idea of equal rights is economic in origin and its source is the
idea of the identical nature of goods (Marx 1999). In this sense, the equal rights
of citizens are a legal parallel to equal market access to every good traded.
Each specific product can be conceived as an equal good in the sense that it
corresponds to an amount of abstract financial units. The introduction of the
equal rights of the bourgeoisie, compared to the negative discrimination of
the estates, was a liberating step. Therefore, the replacement of feudal unequal
rights by modern equal rights is progress. However, it soon became apparent
that an equal approach to socially unequal groups of persons confirms and
reproduces the situation of the socially weak. Equal rights do not reflect the
specific common characteristics of exploited and marginalised persons and
conceal the advantages enjoyed by advantaged groups of persons. An example
might be a flat (equal) tax (unlike to a progressive tax) which ignores what part
of the taxed amount the taxed persons need, for example, to survive. Equal
rights also act against specific characteristics not only of entire groups of persons but also individuals, some of whom are wealthy and others are not, some
of whom are talented and others are not, some of whom have families and
children and others do not, etc. In this sense, although equal rights can be conceptualised as progressive, they are rights to inequality unless incorporated
into a more complex system of rights which solves inequality. Equal rights have
to be complemented by specific rights which address the specific conditions of
the weaker persons and groups.

Equal rights were originally and are usually conceived as civil and political rights not intended to deal with social issues. The problem is also that
this does not concern only social issues but also the social conditionality of
civil and political rights. Taylor at least calls attention to this issue when he

states: "People who are systematically handicapped by poverty from making the most of their citizenship rights are deemed to have been relegated to second-class status, necessitating remedial action through equalization" (Taylor 1994, 37–38). Therefore, he acknowledges that the "universalism" of civil dignity, from this perspective, does not fully embrace all persons and that social and economic rights also need to be addressed.

Here it is relevant to mention an idea of unconditional basic income which has been experimented with in dozens of countries around the world for several decades, and which can be conceived as an equal social and civil right (Hrubec, Brabec and Minarova 2022). The basic income is paid individually to all people regardless of any of their characteristics, which has positive social consequences and also creates conditions for the democratic participation of citizens in the life of society when, at the same time, it is complemented by specific rights of the welfare state. Moreover, it is not just a measure but a marker of a more just social society, since it implements the principle of "to each according to his or her basic needs". Later, it may be complemented according to "all the needs".

We can clarify the current interpretation by saying that the struggle for legal recognition takes place in the context of two historical tendencies. First, there is the tendency conceived by Honneth as the expansion of rights (Honneth 1996, 170; Honneth 1994a). Various marginalised groups of persons, whether the poor, women, African Americans in the USA, etc., sought – and many are still seeking – their inclusion among equal citizens (Hrubec and Kasanda 2022). As I have already mentioned, however, in light of historical struggles for the recognition of these groups of persons, it would be preferable to employ different terminology, which entails an exploration of the theme from a different angle. The terminology used and the liberal value order were based on a conflict between the legal privileges of the aristocracy, on the one hand, and the legal claims of wealthy men, on the other, not on a conflict also encompassing other groups of persons, who require legal recognition to be formulated with their interests in mind too. Therefore, this was not primarily a dispute between wealthy men, on the one hand, and poor men, women, and other marginalized groups of persons, on the other, as implicitly assumed by the principle of the expansion of rights to other marginalised groups of persons. The legal recognition achieved, more specifically the order of recognition created by the affluent bourgeoisie, therefore, could only partly satisfy the demands of marginalised persons. This recognition charted the requirements of citizens – wealthy men, with other demands subordinated to civil and political requirements. The actual expansion of legal recognition, without having to be redefined based on a specification of the legal demands of marginalised groups, would therefore be insufficient, and would subordinate marginalised groups to the rights defined for the purposes of other, privileged groups' interests.

Honneth also discusses a second method in the historical development of rights, the intensification thereof. The problem here is the disadvantage faced by socially underprivileged population groups, already alluded to by Taylor. There is also the issue of the requirements raised in connection with certain types of equalisation intended to improve the situation of the poor. Recognition is intensified in this respect by the fact that the socially underprivileged seek recognition of social and economic rights, and these rights are gradually enforced and are legally – and even constitutionally – guaranteed. This point of reasoning is, however, still vague because is a fork branching into at least two interpretative paths.

First, it could be said that social and economic rights are another plane of rights, a second generation of human rights that simply complements civil and political rights (i.e., first-generation human rights). Civil and political rights are viewed here as primary rights. The problem with this liberal interpretation is that even if we work with the version where social and economic rights are acknowledged, in the liberal tradition they are usually recognised only for instrumental reasons, as a means to achieve civil and political equality. Social and economic equality does not come into the real equation.

Second, the efforts at social and economic rights can also be grasped in a more critical reading as struggles for the recognition of rights that are either – from the perspective of efforts at social egalitarianism – equivalent to political and civil rights, or – in terms of human survival – even primary rights. From the perspective of marginalised groups of persons, both feudal and liberal terminology is perceived as segregational and, therefore, undesirable. Struggles for recognition here are a struggle for the recognition of the social and economic rights of poor citizens, the recognition of women's rights, the recognition of ethnic, cultural and other minorities, etc. In this second case, social, economic and cultural rights are not instrumentally hierarchically subordinate to political and civil rights, for example, as a condition for the possibility of a political order but are formulated specifically because of them. This is a step beyond liberal requirements and constitutes the socialist formulation of requirements not originally raised by wealthy men and then, other groups of persons.

4   Recognition of Equality and Difference

Considerations about the need for a more adequate conception of legal recognition leads to the re-thematisation of the recognition of the particular characteristics of persons. While the estate recognition of particular aspects of the aristocratic privileged group in the hierarchical feudal structure resulted in the misrecognition of other groups of persons – in that they were excluded entirely from the sphere of recognition or their recognition was deformed, i.e. they were considered inferior persons – efforts aimed at the recognition of particular characteristics in modern society may also have a positive version if variously marginalized groups seek to obtain esteem of their specific characteristics.

Related to this is the second of the approaches to the modern requirements of recognition, which I discussed in relation to national liberalism. Taylor identifies them in trends of political theory and practice which he referred to as the politics of universalism and the politics of differences (Taylor 1994; cf.Young 1990). However, they are of narrower content. These now very widespread labels are not names for generally formulated demands relating to the recognition of universal or particular characteristics but cover a narrower section of requirements, namely the tension between the liberal politics of universalism and the communitarian and multicultural politics of difference. Taylor considers the first model to be problematic and attempts to justify the legitimacy of the second model. However, major reservations can be raised in relation to both models, and there are convincing arguments indicating their inadequacy. Nevertheless, it is worth discussing them because they represent a classic and influential formulation of the problem of the relationship between universalism and particularism in political theory of recent decades.

First, it needs to be clarified that, although the policy of universalism is focused on certain selected universalist human characteristics, most attention is paid to quasi-universalist elements linked to the constitutive goods of Western identity. As I have mentioned in the chapter providing a critique of liberalism, generally speaking, while the policy of universalism is closely related to the constitutive good of autonomy, the politics of difference focuses on the constitutive good of authenticity. On a political level, the politics of universalism were mostly bound to the liberally interpreted autonomy of the individual, associating with this an emphasis on individual rights. The institutional application of this development of the idea of autonomy results in the conception of the independent decision-making of individuals through abstract procedures. Yet can isolated individuals truly act autonomously, without intersubjective interaction in the community? Can instrumentally conceived procedures be alienated in a way in which citizens can and want to take decisions? And are these atomised individuals motivated to participate in self-government and, thus, institutionally to safeguard their freedom? Taylor is not against a modern conception of the world or against individual rights but rejects their deformed shape. He proposes a solution to the maladies of modernity drawing on modernity's own resources.

Against this background, which Taylor formulates as his doubts and reservations about the liberal politics of universalism, he proposes the politics of difference as an alternative. As I indicated, he is not entirely against the politics of universalism but rather against its distorted liberal form and against its reductionism. Here, Taylor builds on his holistically oriented ontology and presents his conception of the individual anchored in mutual intersubjective relationships of interpretations, evaluations and recognition, as I have explained at the beginning of this chapter. This anchorage allows the individual to articulate his authentic identity and to engage in autonomous acts within the community. Taylor complements the situation of the individual in the community with a republican idea, according to which reciprocal relationships of recognition give the individual the incentive to participate in government and, thus, to effect and safeguard his own freedom. This means that Taylor draws on a holistic social theory which results in an individualistic political theory, and calls this aspect holistic individualism. The aim of holistic individualism is not to fall into two extremes: on the one hand, holistic collectivism, and, on the other hand, atomistic individualism, i.e., the excessively collectivist standpoint of Stalinism, for example, and excessively individualistic standpoint of libertarianism and also, to a large extent, liberalism (Taylor 2003, 465–494).

This interpretation, which is based on ontological analyses, also takes on a more concrete form in some of Taylor's objections to the politics of universalism, which he formulates as a backdrop to his articulation of the politics of difference. He shows that the politics of universalism, by placing a one-sided emphasis on a distorted value of autonomy, is limited to the individual rights of merely abstractly conceived human beings and their choice in procedural politics and, thus, suppresses and distorts the value of authenticity and esteem of the unique characteristics of individuals and entire communities, whether minority cultures, entire cultures, or other entities. Accordingly, in his politics of difference, he concentrates on more specific, authentic characteristics that are unrecognised by contemporary liberal politics. Politics of difference facilitate the support of individuals and communities concerning their unique manifestations. Cultural and ethnic minorities, which in the current model of majority democracy cannot oppose disadvantage precisely because they are a minority and cannot even push through their decisions as the actual implementation of their individual rights, may, due to the politics of difference, overcome ignorance and suppression by the majority population and achieve recognition of their specific unique characteristics. While the recognition of the general characteristics of the politics of universalism is, at best, the recognition of persons in their indistinguishableness, the abstract respect of their common aspects, the politics of difference not only attempt to complement such recognition and, thus, appreciate authentic characteristics but also, at the same time, create conditions for the existence of universal recognition, as it prepares common assumptions for the individual rights of abstractly conceived persons.

However, Taylor's terminology may occasionally be confusing. He reserves the term "politics of recognition" for politics of difference because they are based on the philosophy of recognition but denies this term for the politics of universalism because, even though they also work with the concept of recognition, they are based on a different philosophy. On the other hand, Taylor seeks to clarify that the main motif of the politics of universalism – respect for the quasi-universal characteristics of a person – can and should also be transferred to the philosophy of recognition.

More puzzling, however, is the use of the terms, "universalism" and "difference" (Taylor 1994, 41–42). Taylor uses "politics of universalism", "politics of dignity" and "politics of equal dignity" synonymously; he bases his concept of politics on the idea that all human beings are equally worthy of respect. The subject of this recognition is universal human potential, which means a capacity that every person has, in other words, in the sharing of this capacity everyone is equal. This potential is usually linked with "the capacity for rational action", and this is a springboard for the conclusion of autonomous action and democracy, as I have stated above. It is important that the term "equality" here is used in two ways – as an equal approach to people or their equal recognition, and as recognition of the same or equal content of recognition, i.e. that what is recognised is the same or equal. In politics of dignity, this should, therefore, be what I refer to as "equal recognition of equality".

The politics of difference, i.e. the politics of recognition par excellence in Taylor's conception, can share, with the politics of universalism, "equality" in two ways. First, there is the equal recognition of persons, and then, there is also the fact that "universal potential is at its basis, namely, the potential for forming and defining one's own identity, as an individual, and also as a culture" (Taylor 1994, 42). This means that the recognition of difference is the recognition of the same or an equal basis common to all persons, and the recognition of difference or special identity which is the result of man's universal capacity to form his own self. Compared to the politics of universalism, however, the politics of difference emphasise the fact that people and individual cultural, ethnic and other groups of persons differ from each other. Regarding the equal status of persons, the focus of the politics of difference can be grasped as the "equal recognition of difference". Whereas the politics of the equal recognition of equality are concentrated on what people have in common, the politics of the equal recognition of difference focus on what makes them unique (Honneth 1996, 122). However, concerning the unequal negatively discriminatory status of persons, the politics of difference need to be conceived as the "unequal recognition of difference" because this unique difference may be supported, for example, by positive action, which equalises marginalised persons or entire minorities, for example.

The question is whether the recognition of culturally defined minorities should constitute recognition of their equal value in the sense that each value of a given cultural community should have genuine equal value, or in the sense of mere "potential equal value" which means that each culture should be appraised by its basic capacity to create a unique culture, regardless of whether this created culture has or has not been developed sufficiently to be of equal value. If individuals, in politics of the equal recognition of equality, are recognised also in terms of the recognition of their capacity for the equal potential to act rationally, which does not mean that this is how people actually act in the majority of cases, we could incline towards recognition of the potential equal value of groups of persons defined culturally or cultural minorities.

Another problem, which is related to the previous one, is the already indicated questioning of actual universalism in the politics of universalism. The reality of quasi-universalism is not just that the individual quasi-universalist characteristics of a person are limited only by a given culture, defined by a group of persons from a European or Western culture, for example. It also lies in the fact that the individual quasi-universalist characteristics of a person are mostly implemented within the limits of individual nation-states. Therefore, the object of recognition here tends to be only the quasi-universalist characteristics of the given majority community of a nation state (or a smaller unit), which, however, are relatively particular values, although, in their main features, they may be based on the general quasi-universalist characteristics of a person from Western civilisation in a given historical epoch, or on fewer more general quasi-universalist characteristics that a given culturally defined group of persons shares with other territorial areas beyond the borders of the nation state. In this respect, the politics of universalism, on the one hand, and the politics of difference, on the other, do not stand against each other in terms of recognition. Rather, two particular politics, differing only in that one is an effort by mainstream society, while the other is an effort of a minority, are intertwined here.

In this light, we could address the previous problem of the potential or actual value of a culturally defined community or group of persons in such a manner that we also question the criterion of the value of majority society. An adequate solution appears to be a definition of the criteria under which this or that group of persons will be granted specific group cultural rights which are effectively also granted to the majority. The criterion for the acknowledgement of recognition is, then, usually sought in the number of persons who raise cultural requirements, and in a balance between the realisation of majority culture and minority culture, or minority cultures in the plural. This proposal encounters the refusal to recognise group rights by authors, who mostly subscribe to a liberal approach with individual rights, complemented by an appraisal of cultural membership or other culturally defined supplements to the liberal concept of individual rights (Kymlicka 1996; Kymlicka 1991). Politics, then, remain focused on the individual exercise of demands but the state or region or city may attempt to impartially assess and support all cultural demands of all individual members of the population. Nevertheless, this solution runs up also against the problem that someone will have to lay down rules on the thematisation of these or those cultural circles to be addressed by state administration, and such rules will be defined by one or another culture, i.e., not impartially. The issue of the recognition of groups of persons remains, accompanied by the need to tackle problems linked to the recognition of not only individual, but also group, rights.

Another theme comprises, on the one hand, shifts related to the assimilation or subordination – to the majority – of minority persons and entire groups, and, on the other hand, their exclusion and segregation, whether in the form of ghettoisation or expulsion from the country. The central position between these extreme poles is integration, i.e. the primary requirement of recognition, in a given country, of the fundamental constitutive goods of the majority society, i.e. constitutionally formulated values and interests, and the requirement of basic knowledge of the language, the ability to communicate to the extent that a person can take part in the life of the given society insofar as he or she is able to follow constitutional values. A conflict arises when, in the interests of integration, values are disseminated that directly limit cultural differences, e.g., bans on displays of religious symbols in the form of Christian crosses or the veiling of Muslim women with headscarves or burkas. The requirement of group cultural rights and the balancing thereof between different communities representing different quasi-universalist values, taking into account the values of the Indigenous people of a country – the majority and the minority – is a sort of guidepost that should be developed further in particular conditions, and cannot be dictated as a universal solution for all cases. The exact specification takes place in a particular way in the concrete society.

Closely related is the issue of migration, which has multiple sources. Most relevant in recent times are emigration due to war conflicts, economic and social inequalities, politically repressive regimes, and natural disasters, including the effects of climate change. An adequate understanding of migration should be based on a conception of the relations between the different structures and actions of subjects in national and transnational interactions, and not in terms of allegedly 'fully determining' institutions or 'free' migrants. The reflection should take into account not only the problems of the national borders that are both contested and reinforced by migration but also the more complex local, regional, macro-regional and transnational relations of global capitalism that are the conflictual space of mobility. Unjust economic and political transnational structures, often produced by Western corporations and governments, create and reproduce the exploitation and poverty of people in developing countries. This has migration consequences which, in the future, without addressing the causes in the countries where migrants come from, could lead to the destabilisation of developed countries as well. Migration policies and concepts should not only refer to current migration waves as the mainstream media and politicians do but also to a medium- and long-term approach to migrants facing unstable and unjust conditions.

Moreover, the unequal conditions in capitalist societies do not allow the full realization of even the already acquired rights, and even some rights may come into conflict with others, as in the conflict between minority rights and majority rights, in the suburbs of French cities, for example. The inequality here often stems from the situation of migrants leaving developing countries, as these countries have often been exploited by Western countries for a long time. This requires a transnational multidimensional social, economic, political and cultural theoretical analysis and corresponding practice.[7]

The current interpretation of the recognition of the unique characteristics of individuals and communities has been concentrated almost exclusively on cultural or ethnic differences. The inadequacy of Taylor's conception of politics lies in this reduction even though, on a general plane, it also allows for application to the economic sphere, for example.[8] While so-called identity politics often rests precisely on cultural, ethnic, or gender reductionism,

---

7   See the discussion between the various opinions on this subject by J.H. Carens, Mae M. Ngai, Jean Bethke Elshtain, Linda Bosniak, Douglas S. Massey and others (Carens 2010; Carens 2015).

8   Nancy Fraser takes a different approach from Taylor and Honneth to the recognition of the unique and universal characteristics of human beings. She uses the concept of recognition only to appreciate the cultural characteristics of the individual and communities (in contrast to socio-economic redistribution, she discusses cultural recognition), and thereby twists Taylor's tendency, but in her analysis of cultural recognition, she places an emphasis (unlike Taylor) on the status order (Fraser and Honneth 2003).

recognition of difference can be reformulated as recognition focusing on all of the spheres. Each of them is bound to a certain material basis, which is subject to distribution and redistribution.

The implementation of the egalitarian ownership of internal and external sources should be grasped as a condition to engage in recognition in the sense in which I discussed ownership in the Chapter 5, devoted to a critique of liberal theory. The starting points are the removal of the criticised barriers of ownership, which exclude or significantly restrict ownership among economically marginalised groups of persons, the development of existing positive elements of the economic structure and the implementation of normative models of "participatory economics", "economic democracy" or another alternative, socially oriented model based on citizens' specific practical struggles for recognition and justice (Albert 2003; Schweickart 2011; Schweickart 1992, 9–38). Citizen structures of participatory budgeting and entire complex participatory structures are a way to do this, usually promoting social development trends and creating the conditions for them (Silveira and Silveira 2015). Other elements of this development include public infrastructure networks, public banks, cooperatives, including complex structures like Mondragon, for example. There is room here for the implementation of democratic socialism, socialist democracy, and other models such as market socialism. In these models, strategic issues are the main focus rather than the complete planning of all issues.

Honneth attempts to conceive social esteem – which originally, in an estate society, determined the adversely discriminatory legal recognition of individuals in a repressively hierarchical manner – in connection with the problematic transformation thereof in the emerging bourgeois-capitalist order, and to place it in a relationship with the Weberian idea of the impact of protestant ethics on the development of capitalism. In this idea, esteem of the work performance of the individual becomes established, along with the gradual secularisation of original religious justification of the value of work. In the newly forming normative conception of values, a primary factor should be the economic recognition of persons based on their individual performance, not based on their social origin and affiliation with this or that estate. Part of estate honour is in a sense 'meritocratized'. Ideally, the social esteem of persons is based on their individual achievements (Fraser and Honneth 2003, 135–159). Individual persons should be treated equally, and differences should be derived only from their different work performance (Honneth 2014). This is the promise of a meritocratic approach that has the ambition to address this one performance aspect of recognition which should be complemented and balanced by other aspects.

The principle of performance has played and continues to play a certain role in capitalist countries and it was used also in state socialism in Central and Eastern Europe but, in both the systems, it has been diminished. It has only been revitalised in countries that have introduced socialist market economies. It should be stressed that, in Western countries, the recognition of work in the form of performance esteem is not liberated from the hierarchical structure of society. This is because the meritocratic equality declared in the approach to performance esteem is burdened with an ideological interpretation of performance.[9] The individual types of activities are unfairly appreciated not only according to the fading esteem of the activity of the main power actors from the estate society but also according to the extent to which they are associated with the main subjects in struggles for the recognition of performance. Since these subjects, from the beginning, have been the bourgeoisie, i.e. predominantly wealthy white men, it was the activities they carried out that were regarded, in particular, as performance. The structure of esteem, therefore, mirrors the values promoted by the main actors of industrial and post-industrial capitalism. The raising of children and housework, work performed by lower classes or strata of the population, and activities carried out by immigrants and other marginalised groups of persons are undervalued, if appreciated at all. For example, the social benefit of work performed mostly by women on maternity or parental leaves is severely undervalued and, in some countries, it is not financially rewarded at all. Then, women and other caring persons are dependent on the financial security of their partners, grandparents, friends or non-profit organisations (which are mainly focused on supporting single mothers). At issue here is primarily the inadequate or absent financial redistribution by state or other institutions. In cases where the said undervalued activities make the transition from the unpaid to the paid sphere, power relations and other negatives are also reproduced. Women and other caring persons are also denied social non-financial esteem, which is reflected in the given society's collectively shared values promoted by dominant groups of persons. In Western societies, these tend to be wealthy men (Hochschild 2003).

Structural changes in the context of late capitalism in Western societies, as pointed out by Honneth, are bearers of transformation which further enhance the hierarchisation of work performance evaluation (Honneth 2002). However, in the last decades, he almost has not processed this proposition concerning the transformation from national capitalism to transnational capitalism which

---

9   Ideological abuse of recognition or, rather, pseudo-recognition also poses a threat to other types of recognition (Honneth 2007b, 323–347).

has resulted in even greater hierarchisation of the value system of performance esteem (Sklair 1995; Sklair 2001; Robinson 2004; Harris 2008). The bearers of this transformation are transnational actors, whether individual owners, managers, politicians, highly qualified specialists, multinational corporations or international financial institutions which use advantages of both national and transnational capitalism. However, I will discuss the issues arising in this context in more detail later in this book.

The contemporary recognition of performance incorporates several approaches to recognition which, only as a whole, allow for discussion of the esteem of work performance: first, equal esteem of the contribution of an individual's work (efficiency); second, hierarchical (i.e. unequal) esteem according to the recognition of performance by the main actors of the bourgeois capitalist society, i.e. mainly wealthier male owners and entrepreneurs; third, hierarchical (i.e. unequal) esteem based on the residual hierarchical esteem of activities by the power actors of estate society, i.e. mostly wealthier men who possess external property influential in a hierarchical feudal society; and, fourth, hierarchical (i.e. unequal) esteem according to the recognition of performance by the main actors of transnational capitalism, i.e. especially owners and managers of transnational corporations and international financial institutions.

Although the interpretation of the esteem of work performance is the most typical contemporary form of appreciating difference, it does not cover the full breadth of the recognition of features and expressions distinguishing individuals and groups of persons from each other. Generalisation of Honneth's argument into the form in which he used it in his early writings allows (Honneth 1996) for the articulation of other forms of recognition of differences. Recognition of authentic expressions distinguishing individuals from each other can be clarified as the specific esteem of the individual aspects of individuals in intersubjective relationships insofar as such individuals share a set of significant values, against which background they can appreciate each other. Whereas, in the esteem of performance, conditions underpinning demand for such performance from other subjects were expected, in the esteem of the more general individual contribution of other people and society it is necessary to conceive this element of esteem of a unique contribution more complexly.

The direction followed by Honneth's considerations could suggest a dynamic component of recognition, i.e., the developmental potential of social esteem with two tendencies currently pursued: individuation and equalisation (Honneth 1996, 160–170). Individuation is the possibility of the further concretisation of the recognition of unique expressions of a particular individual or group. Recognition becomes more specific concerning individual expressions and individual subjects. An individual can expect recognition relating directly to her or his own expressions, which she or he may freely and creatively associate with other people or various communities. Equalisation means the possibility of greater equality, not in the sense of an identical method or identical degree of esteem, but the identical or equal opportunity for the esteem of the unique expressions of individuals and groups. Social esteem would be equally accessible to all people.

Shared values and interests of community serve as a criterion for measuring an individual's specific contribution to objectives esteemed by society and rated positively in its members. Although modern society is pluralised and is broken down into many communities which themselves may also provide recognition, the basic value framework across society remains common to them because without it there would be disintegration. As value pluralism is a precondition of modern heterogeneous societies, struggles for the recognition of specific characteristics, skills, expressions and achievements of individuals and groups of individuals take place here, and the esteem of authentic characteristics is realised in a more complex way by social sharing in various communities, overlapping into society as a whole (Honneth 1996, 124; Fraser 1997, 69–98). Members of an adequately ordered community hold in mutual esteem their unique benefits for the community and, at the same time, manifest understanding for specific negative situations in which certain individuals find themselves and show solidarity with them. Honneth argues that "'solidarity' can be understood as an interactive relationship in which subjects mutually sympathise with their various ways of life because, among themselves, they esteem each other symmetrically" (Honneth 1996, 128). Solidarity is related to

TABLE 5   Updated forms of recognition with emphasis on more demanding normativity

Forms of recognition	Primary relationships (love, friendship)	Legal relationships (rights)	Economic relations (performance)	Social relationships (solidarity)
Mode of recognition	Emotional support	Cognitive respect	Work contribution esteem	Social sharing
Dimensions of personality	Needs and emotions	Responsibility	Efficiency and effort	Characteristics and abilities

social sharing here. This argument in a broader sense can be used not only for the recognition of individuals but also for understanding the dynamics of the development and coherence of entire groups of persons and their mutual solidarity based on social sharing, as I illustrate in Table 5 on updated and more differentiated forms of recognition with an emphasis on developing more demanding normativity. Honneth's three forms of recognition are here redefined into four forms in line with developmental tendencies, which is also related to his analysis. I reformulate the issue more systematically in the Conclusions of the book.

In summary, the recognition of difference in the form of social esteem, thus, should lie in the mutual recognition of the unique characteristics of persons and social groups concerning the specific positive and negative positions in which specific individuals are to be found. Based on my analyses, it is possible to discuss here not only the equal recognition of difference but also the unequal recognition of difference, not in the sense of the negative discrimination of persons, as occurs in a society of estates or in the case of gender, racial or ethnic negative discrimination, but in the sense of the positive action concerning disadvantaged persons or solidarity with persons in a negative position or situation. I will discuss the overall breakdown of the individual kinds of recognition again at the end of the book where I reformulate a table of principles of recognition and justice. This will build on my redefinition of the positive elements of recognition from a social and economic perspective and from a political and cultural perspective.

From a longer-term empirical perspective, I conclude the chapter by highlighting the main developmental tendencies of struggles for recognition and, more generally, for justice, which have been overlooked by the authors analysed in many of their partial analyses. First and foremost, although the modern era was primarily shaped by capitalism, as a consequence of its development, it has gradually begun to be punctured by socialist demands since the French Revolution. The Paris Commune, the revolutions in Russia and the subsequent experiments launched in Europe, Asia and Latin America after World War II, and the various versions of indigenous and adopted socialism in the post-colonial period after the independence of African countries are milestones in this development, which, however, failed in most countries. Meanwhile, in the decades after World War II, the welfare state established itself in Western countries, and these emancipatory tendencies culminated in the anti-racist struggles of African Americans, civil and social movements, and the student revolt of the 1960s, although in parallel these countries asocially exploited the cheap raw materials and labour of developing countries. Then, the gradual emergence of neoliberal capitalism began experimentally with the Pinochet coup and became established in Western countries from the 1980s onwards. After the collapse of the Eastern Bloc, this process resulted in neoliberal and liberal triumphalism from the 1990s onwards, later also with neoconservative manifestations. However, the expansion hit its limits in the 2008 financial and economic crisis, with the consequences we are living in now.

Every new system in human history, including feudalism and capitalism, has needed more trials and errors to take hold. The ups and downs belong to the historical process of social learning. The various socialist currents have also gone through a process of updating and learned from their own experiences as well as liberal and conservative ones. But while some of these currents have resigned their foundations and adopted liberalism or conservatism with only fragments of earlier more demanding social demands as the maximum possible achievement, other currents have retained their foundations and have started to re-develop and update themselves through innovative and hybrid experiments.

Dilemmas of Transnational Recognition

> Global social and economic processes bring individuals and institutions into on-going structural connection with one another across national jurisdictions. Adopting a conception of responsibility that recognizes this connection is an important element to theorizing global justice.
>
> IRIS MARION YOUNG

∴

Compared to analyses of local and national recognition, analyses of recognition beyond the borders of a jurisdiction or nation are not yet sufficiently detailed and require a more challenging approach. If, within the framework of critically focused theory, we were to reflect on issues concerning matters between national and global recognition, we must again recall the formative influence of the Frankfurt School's classic texts focusing on the critique of Western civilization, in particular *Dialectic of Enlightenment* by Theodor W. Adorno and Max Horkheimer (Adorno and Horkheimer 2007). In the chapter on critical theory paradigms, I characterized this work as an important shift in the initial standpoint of the Frankfurt School, which placed considerable hope in social emancipation. The horrors of the Second World War and the pathological features of society in Germany, Italy, the Soviet Union and other Western countries, however, transformed the views of Adorno and Horkheimer a decade later. Their historical and philosophical interpretation identifies the negative factors of the rational manipulation of external and internal nature as a source of the pathological development of civilization from antiquity to the present.

Dialectic of Enlightenment contains not only a position of cultural pessimism and overall problematization of technical rationality, but also an approach to social criticism, at whose birth this text was present (Honneth 2000b, 116–127; Honneth 1994b, 9–70). Important elements of Adorno and Horkheimer's analysis of the negative tendencies of civilization can also be understood as a broader framework of Honneth's interpretation of the critique of disrespect. Although Honneth did not follow up on the skeptical consideration of these long-term historical processes, he draws on a "world-disclosing" type of critique of social pathology and on the reformulated articulation of developmental trends that are detectable in the moral grammar of social conflicts based on fighting the disrespect of individuals and groups in the shorter timeframe of the past few centuries (Honneth 1996; Fraser and Honneth 2003). The concept of the polemical relationships of disrespect and recognition between states is one of the specifications of this concept of social conflicts. Honneth's analysis of the order beyond nation-states has not been fully developed yet, it has opened many very relevant and provocative questions (Honneth 2015, 265–285; Fraser and Honneth 2003; Honneth 2007, 197–217).

Analyses of the struggle for recognition of the poor need further conceptual distinction between the different relations crossing state borders. If we divide these topics into classic international issues and current transnational and global issues, Honneth's analyses have still been developed primarily only on the category of international order.[1] He makes a classic differentiation into individual states, and examines particularly states in the international context, while analyses poverty separately. We might talk of the concept of international order here, as he himself uses the term "international" as a synonym for "interstate" (Honneth 2015).

That is not to say, however, that Honneth wishes necessarily to attribute normative priority to states and the relations of recognition between them, and that it is necessary to examine his position simply within the theory of national and international relations. His general social theory also analyses a surplus of normative validity (Honneth 1996, 2014) which is expected to correspond to the developmental tendencies of the patterns of recognition. Thus, his theory should also include the trends of transnational and global development of recognition of the poor in developing countries. Of course, this raises considerable attention and questions among scholars who analyse the concept of international order (Buchanan 1999), or proceed beyond it also to the macro-regional and global levels (Fraser 2010).

In the first section of this chapter, on the metatheoretical plane, I will follow up on the interpretation of realism discussed in the chapter on critical methods and specify it with regard to the issue of the legitimacy of states by explaining how it differs from the concept of utopian realism in liberal political philosophy. In this context, I will focus on the fundamentals of Honneth's concept of recognition between states, and then I will dwell on the necessity of recognition for each state, including an analysis of the relationship between

---

1   Honneth makes a classic differentiation into individual states and deals particularly with states in the international context. He does not deal with relations between peoples, as it is done by Rawls, for example.

the state and political and cultural recognition. In the second section, I will formulate the dilemmas of the concept of interstate recognition in view of social issues of the global processes and in relation to the concept of the individual in a community, after which I will discuss Heins and Pogge's transposition of the patterns of recognition from the national plane to the international and global plane. In the third part, I will focus on developmental trends in transnational recognition in its various forms. In the fourth section, I will discuss macro-regional integration, with a focus on integration processes on the border between internationalism and suprarationalism. Especially in the last section of the chapter, I will deal with the European Union because my explanation in the last chapters analysed mainly European and Western themes, while I will focus on non-Western and global frameworks especially in Chapters 9 and 10. In those chapters, I will study also macro-regions which are formed by the whole civilizations and cultures.

1   Interstate Recognition

Before addressing the proper issue of recognition between states, it is important to deal at least briefly with a meta-theoretical concept of realism, and distinguish Honneth's concept from other ones, especially from Rawls's, which is discussed in this context as well and mentioned also by Honneth. There seems to be a certain similarity between Honneth and Rawls because both share a kind of realism, although more detailed specifications show that the two concepts of realism differ. While Rawls (1999, 4, 5–6, 16–17) gave up a connection of normative theoretical and empirical kinds of research and focused only on normative constructivism, he accedes at least formally to one version of a concept of realistic utopia, which, on the one hand, transcends reality with the certain normative vision and, on the other hand, limits normativity by the realistic applicability of its design. His concept is designed for "reconciliation" with the social world, which for Rawls means that it is proven that there is a real possibility of the certain kind of society and politics, even if it is not based on the struggles for justice in reality but only in Rawls's individual vision.

Although Rawls keeps to this formulation of a realistic utopia, in the background of his reasoning lurks another idea which, while not directly included in his definition of a realistic utopia, is an integral component of his political theory. At play here is not merely a pragmatic consideration of feasibility trying to avoid more demanding requirements of the people and to establish a compromise solution in real politics. His version of a realistic utopia includes the element of civil legitimacy as well. This element is also close to Honneth's concept of moral realism at first sight. However, unlike Rawls, Honneth does not concentrate only on the practical application of normativity into the framework of problematic legitimacy of a momentary time cut, but he views it systematically within the framework of his concept of moral realism (Honneth 2003: 238–247) which enables his theory to draw on the long-term social struggles (i.e., the last centuries) and their normative demands for legitimacy in general. He develops not only a conception of the synchronic spheres of recognition but also, and mainly, a conception of the diachronic, historical development of patterns of recognition (2014). From this point of view, Honneth's concept of realism can extend beyond a description of the situation between states in the momentary time cut and target a normative articulation of long-term tendencies of struggles against misrecognition between states.

As for the longer conceptual history, Honneth follows Hegel in many respects (Honneth 1996), as is well known, but takes a different path in recognition between states (Honneth 2015; 2007) because Hegel associates recognition only with the claims of nations as yet unrecognized, i.e. nations which do not yet feature as actors in international relations (Hegel 1991). However, Honneth is aware that, while the pursuit of recognition is a common part of the vocabulary of individual governments or states, consideration of this vocabulary urges a more cautious approach toward the use of the concept of recognition in international relations. Moreover, while purposefully rational arguments about relationships between states prevail in theoretical considerations dealing with international relations, the term recognition is used in a different sense in the sphere of theory in international law than that intuitively perceived and implemented in philosophical tradition associated especially with existentialist connotations. It is important that the definition of the state, in international-law discourse, whether theoretical or practical, usually requires not only people (a population), territory, and a government but also the ability to enter into relations with other states, which implies one or the other kind of external recognition by other states (Buchanan 1999; Naticchia 1999).[2] The struggle for recognition here goes beyond the scope of psychological interpretation which concentrates on the relations between human individuals or smaller groups of persons.

To specify the kinds of recognition between states, it is relevant to see Honneth's polemic with Hans Kelsen (1941) when Honneth (2015) questions

---

2   Cf. Buchanan's analysis recognizing the legitimacy that a state receives from other states based on fulfilling certain criteria of justice. Disputation with this approach is offered by justification recognizing legitimacy from a pragmatic point of view by Naticchia (1999, 242–257).

his reduction of recognition to descriptive registration of the fact of the existence of one state by another state. Although Kelsen grasps legal recognition as a reciprocal act between two or more entities, he perceives recognition in a relatively narrow sense of cognition, i.e., only as an act of a government acknowledging the existence of another state. This is not an active volitional relationship with another, but only confirmation of a fact. However, as recognition requires the real possibility of a decision and not just a confirmation of the status quo, according to Kelsen this is not re-cognition but mere (one-off) cognition.

While this Kelsen's interpretation is considered unconvincing by Honneth, he finds an adequate interpretation in one of Kelsen's (1941) distinctions – the distinction between legal and political recognition. While legal recognition as mere cognition is effectively no recognition for Kelsen, he considers "political" acts of recognition, through which governments positively or negatively relate to the governments and citizens of other countries, to be understandable and real. He takes the term political recognition to mean roughly what Honneth calls recognition in general.

More specifically, political recognition can be grasped as part of Honneth's broader concept of recognition that also includes legal recognition (Thompson 2006). Although political recognition can also be viewed as specific, it is also a more fundamental concept than legal recognition as, in a more detailed interpretation, it becomes evident that a legal relationship to other states is not possible without constantly assuming political recognition in the sense of obtaining affirming responses to efforts at official recognition of the collective identity of the state. Individual states need not only the legitimacy of their citizens, but also the legitimacy of the outside world beyond their borders. States receive neither of these types of legitimacy entirely automatically and permanently. In this regard, states, even those already recognized, are struggling for their recognition all of the time. This argument also applies to authoritarian states where the people have no real opportunity to participate in the running of the state. These states, too, if they do not wish to rely only on violence in the internal and external contexts, must strive for the certain legitimacy among their citizens and other countries. Furthermore, given that absolute violence is both unsustainable and pragmatically inefficient, each state works with legitimacy to a greater or lesser extent. In this sense, however, it would be more accurate to speak of the recognition of the legitimacy than, generally, of political recognition, which may include a wider range of recognition. However, as I have noted above, states also need long-term recognition, not only current legitimacy.

Honneth touches on yet another form of recognition sought by states, such being unofficial recognition (as opposed to the above-mentioned more official recognition) on both cultural and diplomatic planes. He refers to this as the symbolic space of meaning which creates the context of official political recognition. This kind of symbolic recognition is often implicit but no less significant. In fact, it is more fundamental. It is not purely purposefully rational action aimed at the pursuit of power and certain goods but a symbolic act that contains normative requirements which are based on the specific expectations. Therefore, it is impossible here to make a clean cut between strategic action and social action of a symbolic nature. This interconnection is not a haphazard and auxiliary explanation but corresponds with the above concept of interlinking the descriptive and normative aspects of recognition. This is also evident from military recognition, which, by contrast, is strongly linked with power and which may be symbolically manifested in conflict situations only by tacit recognition, i.e., tolerance in the form of the absence of military intervention.

Thus, the struggle for recognition between states may be perceived as long-term efforts aimed at respect developed from the perspective of members of the community of the state or, indirectly, their political and cultural representatives home and abroad. According to Honneth, such efforts struggle for recognition of a particular group of persons which, thus, takes on a specific bond of reciprocity, both within the group and with external entities providing recognition. These relations are not unidirectional since recognition is a reciprocal relationship, even if the parties can assume asymmetrical positions (Wallace-Bruce 1994).[3]

2   Transcending Interstate Recognition

I will focus on dilemmas contained in Honneth's concept of relations between states, the dilemmas that are characteristic problems of similar concepts for

---

3 It is illuminating to see that there is no fundamental conflict between the constitutive theory of statehood, which is based on the recognition of a state by other states, and declaratory theory, which eventually assumes some, though not perhaps political, recognition by other states. This is evident in the 1933 Montevideo Convention on the Rights and Duties of States, where the explicit political existence of the state, in one sentence, is regarded as independent of recognition by other states but, in other sentences, certain forms of recognition are assumed, in the matter of conserving peace by "recognized pacific methods", for example. Cf. Wallace-Bruce (1994).

other authors as well. At the same time, I will point out the potential that Honneth's theory of recognition offers for the redefinition of the concept of interstate recognition and, more generally, international relations and global interactions. Although Honneth has yet to develop his concept of recognition in this direction, he presents arguments underpinning such development. In Chapter 6, I set out the background in my polemical analysis of the concept of international relations, which I will now try to specify. I will pay attention to the difference between international and global theories, as well as to the conservativist reasons preventing theorists of international relations from advancing from an international theory toward the direction of a global theory. My perspective does not mean a resignation on international issues but an inclusion of international relations into the broader global context, which is very important, especially for the global development of the last decades.

Both Rawls and Honneth are prevented from developing a more adequate theory by the fact that they underestimate the negative impacts of economic and financial global interactions. A concept of international relations is limited here because it is not able to cross relations between states and address the important problems of global capitalism. Many authors point out the influences on national social, economic, political and cultural phenomena in society caused by various problematic global, especially economic and financial, interventions that can substantially and rapidly worsen nation-states circumstances, such as standard of living, and can significantly compromise national and international justice (Robinson 2004; Sklair 2001; Harris 2016; Linklater 2007, 1998; Delanty 2009; Fraser 2010). As I mentioned in the interpretation of the dispute between international, cosmopolitan and global justice in Chapter 5, a social theory, which would include analyses of the developmental transition from the theory of international interactions to global interactions, is more compelling than the traditional concept of international relations, which underestimates, or even ignores, the economic and other global pressures and struggles for global justice.

However, even if Honneth's theory shares these shortcomings with the mainstream international theory, he offers a basis for overcoming them. While the mainstream (i.e.: liberal) theories of international justice (be they formulated by John Rawls or other theorists), suffer from deeper social philosophical deficits, Honneth presents a way to transcend them by his theory of recognition. It can be illuminated by the problem of justice. The guaranteeing of justice and rights, including justice within international law, requires a certain political responsibility and solidarity, and therefore also identification with the political community (Honneth 2000d). The key to identification with the community is basic good in the form of relations of mutual recognition. Honneth (2000d: 27–28) observes:

> Hegel, in contrast to Rawls, does not assume that this 'basic good' is a good in the narrow sense, something which ought to be divided and distributed according to a just standard; rather, it seems that Hegel wants to advocate the idea that modern societies can be just only to the extent of their ability to enable all subjects to participate in this 'basic good' equally.

According to Honneth, although Rawls rightly opens an issue of the good in distributive social justice, he does not understand its foundation in the basic good of relation of social recognition, which is a prerequisite for any other goods and also justice in general (Taylor 1985b, 1995).

Honneth is right when he stresses that if individuals were more rooted in the mentioned basic good, i.e., if they were involved in relationships of mutual recognition with others in the local community, they could be better integrated into relations within the national community relations and could demonstrate solidarity therein. Then, it is possible to add, they could smoothly go beyond this framework and, in solidarity, align themselves with the macro-regional or continental intercultural community on the higher level and the largest global community on the highest level as well. This version of the global theory develops half-forgotten elements of Hegelian philosophy establishing universalistic characteristics of community. Although Honneth builds on Hegel's concept of recognition and community, he follows the more traditional version of his concept of international interactions and does not envisage a kind of a neo-Hegelian concept that would transcend the boundaries of international politics and analyse various transnational and global issues, as some other contemporary authors do (Fine 2003a, 2003b, 2007; Burns 2013; Buchwalter 2013; Vincent 1983; El-Ojeili, Hayden 2006).[4] Therefore, the potential offered by Honneth's general theory to a theory of global justice has not been used by him yet.

The main problem I find with Honneth's concept is the underestimation of transnational and global interactions causing the drastic poverty mainly in

---

4 If a cosmopolitan theory was not based on the relations of mutual recognition of persons within a community, it would suffer the same problems as traditional international theories. Neo-Hegelian defenders of cosmopolitan justice overcome the nationalistic explanatory framework and articulate a cosmopolitan potential of Hegel's theory which is present in his critique of cosmopolitanism alienated from the community, i.e., his critique of -ism in cosmopolitanism.

developing countries, including millions dying from hunger every year. This approach, which consequently leads to a certain reification of the nation state, prevents him from grasping major evolutionary dynamics taking place above the plane of nation states especially during the last decades, because transnational and global economic forces and conflicts significantly influence economic, political, legal, social and other national orders. It creates anti-global protests and movements, including populist nationalist and xenophobic trends which, however, have not blocked the long-term transnational military interventions, global financial speculations and business interconnections despite occasional protectionist measures. If Honneth disregards this relevant aspect, he cannot sufficiently develop his thoughts on the criticism of transnational and global economic and social conflicts, pathologies and injustice, and also cannot address the position of the West in the global framework of agonic intercultural relations. Despite these problems, Honneth's establishment of an analysis of the order beyond the nation state in his theory of recognition provides an excellent starting point but he has not used it yet.

The similar line of reasoning with this global intimation is followed by Volker Heins (2008a), who tries to apply it to three of Honneth's types of recognition. In his study, he tries to extend Honneth's theory in the global way but, while his main intention is good, the realization is not successful. Based on Honneth's three-dimensional theory of recognition, he inferred arguments for the transition from recognition within a national framework to global recognition, and he incoherently draws on certain elements of international theory at the same time. It is more or less the mechanical transmission of Honneth's ideas from a national level to a global plane, regardless of the different basis of the theory and the context. Looking at Honneth's theory, which belongs to the sphere of nation-states, and his analyses of international relations, we can ask if there is a parallel between the kinds of recognition at national and international level. We can explore whether and how such identification beyond the nation state is possible in the unchanged form of Honneth's three kinds of recognition: love and friendship, equal respect and rights, esteem and performance. While Honneth himself does not undertake such an analysis, Heins attempts to do so by transposing these three differentiated spheres into international and global relations.

Just as Thomas Pogge redefined John Rawls' *A Theory of Justice* by the transnational extension of the national principles of justice, focusing mainly on the global poor, Heins (2008a) makes a transnational extension of Honneth's patterns of recognition formulated in his book *The Struggle for Recognition*

(1996).[5] As is clear from the title of Heins's article ("Realizing Honneth"), this parallel with Pogge ("Realizing Rawls") is intentional and acknowledged. Heins (2008a), like Pogge (1990, 2002), shares the main ideas with the author of the original theory he is developing, and elaborates on them in an area beyond the framework of the nation state (Burns, Thompson 2013).

However, there are serious limits to this parallel resulting from the different bases of Rawls's and Honneth's theories. Liberal theory and Critical theory have, of course, different starting points and bases. It can be said that, although Honneth and Heins agree with Rawls and Pogge on the idea of the need for distributive justice, Honneth and Heinz criticize the mainstream theory of distributive justice, including the Rawlsian theory, for deforming the social relations among human beings, which occurs as a result of ignoring the patterns of mutual recognition. However, when it comes to issues of transnational or global justice, this parallel is apt. Heins's efforts are aimed at the global transfer of Honneth's recognition patterns that would determine the moral expectations of individuals in mutual relations of love, rights and esteem in a transnational environment. He does it even if he is aware that the institutional framework that would provide a backdrop for the mechanic application of Honneth's three principles of recognition in the international arena is very weak and specific.

The kind type of recognition – in the form of love and friendship – seems to be at first sight scale-neutral in relation to the territorial extent. This is borne out by the various forms of love carried across borders, whether formally unregistered long-distance relationships, marriage between partners from different countries, and so on. However, the automatic transmission of patterns of recognition from a national to an international and transnational level, as proposed by Heins, is not possible. For example, the child sponsorship he refers to does not fit into the category of recognition in the form of love, which in Honneth's analyses at national level relates to intimate and emotional relationships between a small number of people. Although this kind of adoption resembles the traditional parent-child relationship, it is primarily an important relationship of charity or solidarity with people living in a state of insecurity and poverty, particularly in the developing countries, and not a relationship of family love. We have to see that a child sponsorship is a borderline category relationship on the boundary of Honneth's first and third type of recognition. Thus, it requires a specific articulation which would formulate the new

---

5   Heins intended to "'globalize' Honneth in the same way as Thomas Pogge was able to globalize Rawls". Cf. Thompson's investigation of Honneth's three spheres of recognition beyond the state without a global transposition of Honneth's spheres (Thompson 2006).

important transnational and global patterns of recognition, and the mechanical transposition of the patterns of recognition is not possible. I would like to stress other problematic relationships, specifically transnational care practices which, in the form of immigrant nannies and domestic workers, cause mothers from less developed countries to leave their children and seek work in richer households in developed countries. This is the transnational exploitative deformation of interpersonal relationships which, in a significant, but more parentally detached manner, benefits only one party, i.e., the employer, and does not constitute the development of transnational love (Ehrenreich and Hochschild 2003; Parrenas 2001). In connection with the motto "the personal is political", it could also be said that "the personal is global", but as a problem rather than part of an articulated sphere of recognition (Hochschild 2005; Robinson 2006). These complications are also evident in other examples of Heins's transposition. The inclusion of these examples in Honneth's theory, if it were theoretically possible, would require substantial reformulation (Honneth 2003, 135ff).[6] However, Heins does not undertake this. He also disregards the fact that other forms of recognition on the first plane, such as friendship, are already realized at international and transnational level to some extent and are compatible with Honneth's theory. Friendship may, but need not, take the form of traditional friendship based on personal contact, and it may also be a virtual friendship in various forms of the widespread social media.[7]

The second level of recognition – legal recognition – is regarded by Heins (2008a, 15–16; 2008b) as territorially highly specific.[8] While he does not consider the institutional anchoring of the first level of recognition to be problematic territorially, legal recognition is institutionally closely related to the territory of the nation state, in particular because of the enforcement of individual rights by the government institutions. Although he also considers human rights, he points to the possibility of their limited application due to a lack of institutional support. If human rights do not become part of the constitutions of nation states, they must be regarded more as manifestation rights only, the strength of which lies primarily in their political and diplomatic significance.

---

6 Honneth's redefinition of his original interpretation of recognition in the form of love in the sense of the possibility of the further normative development of this form of recognition facilitates the development of considerations in this transnational direction.

7 These interactions can be realized in various ambivalent forms, from e-mail exchanges to daily interactions in social networks such as Facebook, MySpace, WeChat, etc.

8 The more detailed elaboration of an analysis of the legal sphere of recognition is performed by Heins primarily on the examples of children's global rights, human rights, and intellectual property, but his articles also offer more general arguments about the global order (Heins 2008a, 141–153).

The promotion of human rights in international relations can at least draw attention to problems and demand solutions in the spirit of the internationally accepted Declaration and the related international agreements. According to Heins, delineating this sphere of influence determines the limits of human rights.

The end of the Cold War and the political opportunities that this opened up led Honneth (2007a) to promote the need for the moralization of world politics. He argued in favour of strengthening the importance of human rights and the possibility of the legal enforcement thereof which he later – in his paper on recognition between states – specifies mainly by developing arguments in favour of pre-legal presuppositions of the legal arrangement. As Honneth started his analyses of recognition beyond nation state by articulating this kind of legal recognition, his focus on human rights issues is the relevant topic in an analysis of his theory; even if, in his later analysis (2014), he did not stress a legal sphere of recognition as his first focus. Heins's point of view is limited in that human rights are bound only to states, and international institutions extending beyond states with their international, macroregional and global activities are underestimated. As I will show, transnational and global elements in the application of human rights, especially extraterritorial recognition, should be added to the overlaps in the international framework, not only by macroregional and global institutions, but also through nation states. In this respect, Heins underestimates legal recognition in international and global relations.

According to Heins (2008a: 16f), the third type of recognition, which includes forms of esteem and solidarity, is deficient at international and transnational level because, beyond the nation state, it does not have an adequate parallel (Heins 2008c); specifically, there are insufficiently developed global values to form a basis for this third type of recognition. The greatly unequal financial valuation of work on a transnational scale disrespects people who make a claim to the meritocratic valuation of work. There are only exceptions in particular sectors, such as some services, which promote certain transnational standards, but tend to introduce unfavourable working conditions. As a result of comparisons of work remuneration, in recent times there has been a greater push aimed at demanding higher wages for workers, at least in some sectors, such as agriculture, or in the struggle for gender equality. One might ask, however, whether it would be fruitful to focus more on criticism of the current conditions and on an interpretation of normative transnational and global expectations currently manifested and promoted in these struggles for recognition.

To sum up Heins's mechanical transposition of patterns of recognition from a national level to international and transnational levels, we can say that he regards the different levels of recognition as transposable: the first kind of recognition (love and friendship) smoothly, the second kind of recognition (legal recognition) partially, and the third kind of recognition (esteem) in an uneasy way. All three types of recognition specific for a national level in Honneth's theory, however, according to Heins's opinion, occur to a greater or lesser extent in internationally and transnationally institutionalized patterns of recognition.

3   Transnational Recognition

Now I will move on from the problematic attempts to transcend the concept of national and international recognition to the articulation of a more appropriate approach that is able to realize this transcendence. I have thus far focused my objections to Heins's transposition only on particular issues within each type of recognition. However, I think that his main problem is deeper. The fundamental problem is his ahistorical approach to the patterns of recognition. As Heins copies Pogge's transposition of Rawls's theory, he also gratuitously follows his ahistorical approach to the principles of justice. While an ahistorical approach is typical for liberal theory, it is entirely inadequate for Critical theory, especially in Honneth's version. Honneth explicitly conducts a detailed analysis of both the synchronous and diachronic (historical) dimensions of the patterns of recognition. Furthermore, for him, the analysis of the historical aspect is not just an accessory, but a highly important and fundamental part of his methodology and significant for Critical theory in general. And since Heins's static transmission of the patterns of recognition from the national level to the international plane does not reflect the historical developments in institutional structures of recognition at international level, it is unable to provide an interpretation of the structure of patterns of recognition at international and transnational levels. Therefore, Heins's transposition is not in fact an elaboration of Honneth's theory of recognition but contradicts it methodologically and, thereby, also in the content in the end.

Honneth (Fraser, Honneth 2003, Honneth 1996, 2014) is aware of the difficulties of such a transposition and does not even attempt this. Therefore, whereas he considers three levels of recognition in the local and national communities, he does not accede to this on the plane of international relations because he sees there is no support for it. He knows that they are similarities between the national and international levels but there is a specific development of specific spheres of recognition beyond the boundaries of nation states. What is more, in the different conditions of international relations, he takes the view that it is not currently possible to rely on the necessary social institutions.[9] At the international level, therefore, Honneth concentrates on the general recognition of states and specifically on the recognition of the personality of states. From this perspective, his analysis of recognition between states can be considered an inspiring but underdeveloped contribution to the analysis of the contemporary widespread misrecognition beyond the borders of nation states.

While Honneth's analysis offers mainly a model of three patterns of recognition in the Western context, Heins attempts to transpose this model, in a Western-centric way, into the global arena without analysing the formation of patterns of recognition in other (non-Western) cultures and their intercultural interactions. This absence of the cross-cultural aspect is another serious deficiency in Heins's analysis.

Despite the overall problematic approach which he prefers, his analysis keeps in some aspects with Honneth (2007) when he shows that legal recognition offers a (quasi-)universal hope for future global recognition even if he more or less reproduces Honneth's basic structure of legal recognition from the national level. However, there is in fact the real international and global potential of legal recognition because the long-term establishment of the international legal structures already represents the certain good institutionalized values and structures shared by individual states and other actors. Nevertheless, the articulation of this form of recognition needs to be subjected to further critical analysis and the patterns of recognition beyond the borders of the nation-state need to be identified more finely than Heins has done.

Efforts to develop and reformulate Honneth's analyses of recognition beyond states require the mapping of the historical developmental trends which are articulated through the ambivalent contemporary economic, political and legal orders. Although Honneth did not analyse transnational and global conflicts and their resolution directly much, the focus of his writings shows that he is inclined to think that legal relations on an international level, especially human rights, are more developed compared to the other two spheres of recognition, i.e., the sphere of personal relationships and the sphere of esteem and performance (Honneth 2014, 304–328). While social and economic relations are not institutionalized much at the global level, since *Universal Declaration of Human Rights* and other relevant legal documents, legal relations offer at least a formally hopeful normative basis that may relate to the other two

---

9 A similar argument, again on a metatheoretical plane, is developed by Honneth in his response to Nancy Fraser's chapter on post-Fordism, post-communism, and globalization in their already mentioned joint work on redistribution on recognition (Fraser and Honneth 2003).

spheres as well, even if these legal issues are derived largely from social and economic relations. More precisely, it can mean that, according to Honneth's opinion, the institutionalization of recognition in the remaining two spheres is in a normative way currently developed much less in international and transnational space, and therefore, in terms of moral and societal realism, it provides a weaker basis for important normative connotations, even though it has already started to come more to the fore in the struggle for recognition.

Nevertheless, the third and the second sphere of recognition are not entirely separate from one another in this context. At an international level, legal and cultural recognition is interdependent because legal relations are not completely separated from the cultural status of nation states. Legal relations retain certain cultural connotations of a politics of difference and characteristics of recognition, which is typical for this area, including use of the term recognition in both the traditional (hierarchical) and the post-traditional (equitable) senses. For example, recognition of the sovereign status of a new state by existing states is a legal act, the intercultural component of which is reflected in the acceptance of another, in the acceptance of the different entity by states from other cultural or civilizational circles.

Legal recognition beyond state borders, however, contains its own internal structure. So far, I have distinguished between international relations with their law, on the one hand, and transnational and global relations with their law, on the other. Nevertheless, the transnational and global structures of law should be broken down more finely into several basic types (Koskenniemi 2006; Koskenniemi 2001; Joyner 2005). First, it should be noted that, as in history, various transnational orders have been created step by step in response to the conquest of new lands and their colonization; even today, following the mapping of new economic activities, there is a process of both the enforced corporate and legitimate implementing of various new legal rules that provide a framework for business transactions in particular. As these economic transactions take place in a forming transnational and global investment environment, those who execute them exploit deficiencies or even the absence of standard legal regulations and introduce pragmatically minimum legal rules that are convenient for them. Individual economic and financial corporations carry out their activities often unregulated by national or international law, or only with small corrections. In this context, we speak of neoliberal economics overtaking law and politics. Contracts concluded between economic corporations often bypass standard legal rules of individual nation states or the rules of less extensive international law. This type of transnational legal rules, against a backdrop of "business ethics", is called *lex mercatoria* (Hatzimihail

2008, 169–190.), business law, which has its origins in the conventions of medieval Western European economies.

Where rules cannot be enforced by legal coercion, alternatives are only various kinds of ethical responsibility for the consequences of economic activities. However, the various forms of "corporate responsibility"[10] are often only corporate investments to increase competitiveness by fostering a good corporate image in the media. Since all of these attempts at "soft regulation" of the transnational economy through various advertising versions of ethics have been too weak, at least for the time being, attention must focus primarily on rules enforceable by the legal authorities.

Western corporations often take advantage in unjust global interactions that depend on cheap labour in the Global South. Honneth aptly mentions here that many people in Western countries have been freed from the concerns of daily subsistence through the globalization of markets, the number of people responding to advertisements of consumer goods has increased, and modern mass consumerism has taken hold in Western countries (Honneth 2014, 198–222). Honneth, however, does not analyse in a more complex way social and economic injustices in global interactions, and he focuses his transnational conclusions primarily on the European space, as the last sentence of his book *Freedom's Right* demonstrates (Honneth 2014, 334).

An influential attempt to catch up with the transnational and global economy comprises, at least to some degree, processes developing legal recognition, where, like political integration, two basic types can be distinguished: internationalization and supranationalization, or international and supranational integration. International law includes rules that apply to relations between nation states and other actors, such as intergovernmental organizations, international corporations and individuals. International law is firmly linked to their formulation and enforcement by nation states. The difference between international law and supranational law lies in the fact that a supranational law, created by nation states, may pursue norms which weaker separated nation-states and international law cannot do. While it is true that the supranational legal system and supranational institutions of recognition are not yet well developed, and, insofar as they are applied at all today can be found almost only on a macro-regional level (although some of their elements also appear to a limited extent at a global level), the very existence of supranational entities

---

10   The Caux Round Table, for example, is an organization created by an international network of persons whose aim is to promote the ethical practices of contemporary society, and more specifically to reinforce ethical standards acceptable to multinational corporations.

and their legal codification shows the inadequacy of theories which are limited only to international law but ignore mostly supranational law. It should be noted, however, that the transnational and global economy transcends not only national but also macro-regional territories, hence the possibilities of macro-regional integrated units are necessarily limited in the absence of a legal solution at global level. Although the macro-regional legal units are currently relatively strong regulatory powers and need to be analysed, it would be inadvisable to overestimate their ability to square up to global economic, financial and other challenges. Assuming that they do not become a "fortress" and continue to be open to various aspects of global interactions and integration, the macro-regional level of regulation remains another, albeit stronger, plane of organization, the actual fulfilment of which cannot be realized until the establishment of a more just order on a global level.

4   Macro-regional Interactions

I will now discuss efforts to create supranational legal recognition which is already taking place in processes of the gradual integration of macro-regional units that are integrated economically, politically, etc. I will focus on concepts of legally institutionalized supranational bodies at the macro-regional level, particularly on the European Union in this section, and I will attend to supranational structures on a global level later. I cannot follow much the critically oriented theories of recognition here because they have tended not to pay too much attention to macro-regional integration.

In referring to macro-regions, I mean not only the emerging supranational bodies formed in the gradual integration of multiple individual states, which is often a long dialectical process with many stages of integration and subsequent partial disintegration. I also have in mind large, economically strong countries that have a comparative advantage in that, due to their size, they can partly withstand the pressure of large economic actors in global capitalism. Nation states, such as Brazil, Russia, India, China (the "BRIC" countries but not much weaker South Africa, for example) and the US, are themselves already macro-regional bodies with a strong economy, a large population holding similar interests and values, and vast territories, whose individual provinces or states, however, are quite different from one another, and whose governance, in some cases, is more independent than the common governance of certain states drawn together in recent times into the new super-national bodies, such as the European Union. Another type of supranational integration is the economic and other connections of some former colonial powers with their former colonies which are dominated by the population of the former colonial power,[11] or subordination of former colonies based on the real economic and financial links of certain superpowers with their former colonies and struggles against this subordination and for creation of new independent macro-regional units.[12] All these types of macro-regions now play a significant role in the process of redefining their mutual (mis)recognition and, thus, transforming the current virtually unipolar world order into a multipolar and multilateral world order.

Although transnational bodies, in certain instances, can be conceived as the result of the integration of autonomous nation-states, the case of India and other similarly integrated countries represents a different kind of macro-regional body. The arrangement of these countries was long viewed by Western authors as an anomaly that does not fit into the otherwise dominant type of interpretation and the reality of state formation, i.e., the concept of a sovereign state, as classically interpreted in modern European philosophy. Western theory of absolutism formulated absolute sovereignty or monopoly sovereignty as a reaction to any kind of sovereignty that was shared, regardless if it was free or unfree or if it was in the past or contemporary (Rudolph and Rudolph 2010, 557). As a result of conflicting developments in society and the growing fears of a violent war of all against all, Hobbes advocated subordination to an absolute sovereign in the interests of survival. The defense of absolutism and absolute sovereignty presented in Hobbes's *Leviathan* was then reformulated by Rousseau into the legitimization of the sovereignty of the people, while absolute state sovereignty was preserved. The idea of the nation-state is based on this indivisible sovereignty (Hobbes 2017; Rousseau 1998). Various forms of limited or shared sovereignty in federalism and other multinational bodies were treated as exceptions and backward forms of development. While the colonial expansion of European countries was not aimed at granting sovereignty to their colonized territories sovereignty, ultimately, the European countries unintentionally began to spread the idea of a sovereign state to Africa, Asia and the Americas, where, later, in the postcolonial period, it was partly applied in practice. The concept of a fully sovereign nation-state, however, received and implemented in non-European countries – often only formally – to a much lesser extent than that admitted by the Western-centric claim to the universal validity of this concept.

---

11   One current example would be the links between the United Kingdom, Canada, Australia and other countries, with the Queen as a formal head.

12   The example are countries in West Africa which struggle against the French neocolonialism these years.

The problem with the theory and attempts at the practice of a fully sovereign state is the belief that this type of statehood is generally a higher level of development, which overcomes the split, shared and negotiated sovereignty of earlier (pre-modern), more complex multinational state units, which were typified by authoritarian and hierarchical characteristics. Nevertheless, the replacement of the king by the people did not always coincide with the transition from shared sovereignty to unlimited sovereignty. The fact that this often happened, however, was not a matter of necessity but was solely due to the historical constellation. The sovereign state acquired the form of what was sometimes an absolutist authoritarian state, and other times a democratically oriented state. Both the authoritarian and the democratic version of the state, however, also have a more complex formation with shared sovereignty: an empire, on the one hand, and a democratic federation, on the other. Importantly, while monopolistic state sovereignty is characterized by uniformity, the shared sovereignty of a federal state has plurality and heterogeneity. Strategic sovereignty is similarly partial because it focused only on key elements of self-sufficiency of countries and regions; I will analyse it in Section 3 of the next chapter.

As I have shown, the modern liberal emphasis on the individualistic concept of the citizen, who, as a wealthy man, should be sovereign in his decisions and actions, tended towards an association with the concept of the atomized individual. Parallel to this separation of man is the concept of the monopolized sovereign nation state, as developed in Western countries, also including separating and isolationist connotations of sovereignty not shared with anyone. Furthermore, the reduction of sovereignty to the sovereignty of an ethnically homogeneous territory became, problematically, a widespread criterion, often only implicit, for the demarcation of the boundaries of states in European history. This isolationist approach also contributed to the creation of concepts of ethnic cleansing and racist repression.

In contrast, the concept of the individual in relations of mutual recognition in the community, within the framework of other communities, corresponds with the concept of the shared sovereignty of various communities. An example of this is India which, before, during and after British colonization, never embraced the concept of completely separated sovereign states; rather, it was and is characterized by varying degrees of federal order.[13] Yet India is

---

13   Before British colonialism, India implemented a complex structure of provinces that
      oscillated between regional kingdoms and subcontinental empires which the British
      government largely took over, but its attempts at a centralist concept of the state under
      the British crown were unsuccessful. The dispute over sovereignty also continued after

no exception. Brazil, Argentina, Russia and other non-Western states exhibit similar characteristics, although in some cases sometimes they overlap with authoritarian elements in the conduct of politicians. Although shared sovereignty entails a likelihood of greater internal disputes, it also allows for the mutual recognition of diverse population groups and paves the way for multi-ethnic and multilingual federal bodies.

Of the newly forming macro-regional units in a single territorial area, integrative tendencies – both negative and positive – are most developed in the European Union.[14] Although the European Union is already a supranational body, its implementation continues to remain on the borderline of international and supranational integration with a federalist perspective. Due to the terminology of European studies, this is a conflict primarily between an inter-governmental and neo-functionalist approach, although supranational integration may also be based on other theories (Rosamond 2000).[15] The European integration also has its roots in transnational tendencies in the economy and social norms, specifically integration trends, which in recent decades have resulted in an ambivalent form promoting a *lex mercatoria* of a neoliberal type, on the one hand, and, on the other hand, legal standards that limit law of this type through the promotion of social and economic rights of citizens and attempts to overcome the democratic deficit by strengthening participatory institutions.

Further understanding of the theoretical interpretation requires a more specific analysis. The current dispute over the European Union reflects the process of European integration which is part of the contemporary transformation of relations between the national, European and global structure. In this altered context, the enlargement and consolidation of the European Union is different in nature from European cooperation in the post-war decades. However, once

---

independence. Nehru's efforts at unified sovereignty in the name of social transformation are understandable but Gandhi's support for shared sovereignty opened up the opportunity for grassroots participation by rural communities, thus achieving mutual recognition between different linguistic and ethnic communities which also included elements of social recognition. Although the further development of India was complicated, the country has maintained a system of shared sovereignty to the present day, which enables it to stand its ground very firmly as it strives for recognition in global economic and political competition (Majeed 2009; 2004).

14   In the following, for the sake of simplification, I will use the terms Europe and European mainly concerning the European Union.

15   Many authors mistakenly grasp supranationalism only from a functionalist standpoint as they do not take account of other teleological theories. Moreover, a teleological interpretation need not be conceived only as a descriptively prognostic approach but may also be considered within the scope of normative theory.

again there are questions as to what extent this is the genuine and autonomous desire of Europeans to establish a greater or lesser degree of integration into the institutionalization of patterns of recognition and to what extent it constitutes economically forced regional and continental adaptation and reproduction under the influence of private companies coupled with modification of the international constellation. Attempts to answer these questions lead to discussions about how the process of integration in the European Union is democratically formed. This paves the way for reflection on the current state of transition, which is characterized by a combination of two elements. First, this stage is characterized by a partial shift from the democratically oriented structure of individual nation states to their weakening in a post-democratic regime which arises from the fact that multinational corporations, international financial institutions, global financial speculation, the main world superpower and other factors limit the recognition of citizens in terms of their democratic decision-making in individual states. Current developments on a supranational level of the European Union, while painful and with occasional twists, are peaceful within the EU for the time being when compared to often the conflictual formation of nation states in the past as well as to contemporary foreign armed interventions of the EU's countries. However, if the aforementioned global post-democratic tendencies were to intensify and reactions to them were illusory attempts by weakened nation-states at a nationalist solution to the situation under the transnational corporate influences, part of which tends to be limited to intergovernmental corrections, further development could follow an armed conflictual trajectory also within the EU.

Second, this era has been typified by political powers gradually expanding onto the European level, giving rise to the possibility for the fuller political recognition of citizens through efforts to establish a democratic decision-making structure that could steadily assume other community, confederal, federal, or similar features and thus breathe life into hopes vested in the transition from the European pre-democratic or semi-democratic state to a democratic and socially or socialistically oriented state. Put simply, while the role of democracy in each country is diminished on account of current global pressures, the European Union as a whole is only just starting to develop its supranational democratic structure in this era. Therefore, the weakening of democracy in nation states and the post-democratic economic trend needs to be compensated by the gradual transformation of the European pre-democratic state into a fully democratic European decision-making structures with the corresponding European powers – which is a difficult process because stakeholders of transnational corporations and the North Atlantic interdependence have already co-opted European integration in a significant way. That is why there are protests against a continuation of the integration of the EU in this non-democratic and asocial way now.

It is important to realize that the idea of creating an integrated, just Europe and its gradual crystallization does have a long tradition, but it is only the recent period since the political changes in Central and Eastern Europe and the global expansion of capitalism since 1989 that the current ambiguous and problematic dynamics of the Union have arisen. Although the post-socialist countries' accession to the European Union gave them the opportunity to actively join in the formation of the European area, as a result of the afore-mentioned current situation in the European Union various causes (especially socially disadvantaged) population groups legitimately feel that they are suffering from both socio-economic and a democratic deficits, i.e. a deficit arising from the inadequate recognition of citizens in relation to their real opportunity to participate in the formation of the European Union. Regardless of whether democratic decision-making in the late-capitalist society is being undermined by an inadequately developed supranational political structure or by other factors, the European Union should clearly not be alienated from citizens and should, instead, embody their normative ideas about political, social and other recognition in the community in which they live. These standards should be part of the foundations of the necessary institutional prerequisites for socially oriented and democratic order at European level because certain equitable structures of society and politics are a requirement of any decisions made democratically.

Since world financial speculations and the influence of transnational corporations have not been successfully regulated even by intergovernmental activities, in the last two decades the broader macro-regional whole has undergone greater reinforcement; this is the result both of the impact of global capitalism and of the subjects who are trying to struggle against such influence by trans-national means. This means that the European Union is not developing solely on the basis of its own internal European logic, which includes both post-democratic elements and efforts to regulate them by a process of democratiza-tion, but also as a defensive response to the external pressures of global forces. The defensive nature of the Europeanization process has two aspects: one is defence against the strong and the other is, unfortunately, protection from the weak. At issue here is the above-mentioned defence against transnational eco-nomic actors, along with the response to the actions of the main global super-power, this is subsequently also reflected in the political and military sphere of individual European states which in these respects are no longer autono-mous but not yet united. Another factor is the building of a fortress to defend against migration and other activities coming from peripheries, especially from developing countries of the global South, which, since the beginnings of colonialism, have suffered the military and economic consequences of interference and dominance by Western countries and have sought to liberate themselves from them.

Of course, the European perspective is not the only way of view these matters. The current global interactions and the position of European Union therein can also be viewed from at least two other important perspectives that are actually internally very differentiated and do not exhaust all aspects but should be mentioned for the sake of the transparency of the main lines of thought. By linking up loosely to established terminology,[16] we might mention, first, the unilaterally oriented position of the USA, which is in the position of the center and struggles for hegemony, wherein global economic, military and political capital is accumulated, and, second, the peripheries of the developing countries in the Global South, which has many different forms but also identical characters shared by such forms whether in the development of cooperation in the social and political sphere, in voting at the UN, or otherwise.

Whereas, until the 1980s, most Western European countries formed a welfare state to address their social contradictions and partly in response to the challenge presented to them by the socially oriented Soviet Union, after the Cold War the US neoliberal model gradually started playing a more prominent role.[17] Therefore, the US perspective became an important model of EU's view on its own position in the global order. However, despite the negative impact of various crises, the US point of view had never experienced the genuinely disastrous consequences of economic and political crises on its territory – i.e., Europe's existential experience in World War II. Despite the negative consequences for other countries and its losses in social and other areas, the US, as the main superpower, was in a position to support its current global order until the 2008 financial and economic crisis. The main reason is not the fact that it was a larger territorially integrated unit with more inhabitants than European states. Key reasons include the fact that the specific concept of the economy of the USA worked based on the economically, politically and militarily pursued relative stability and security of capital deposited in US territory. Investors did not seek only to place their capital in a territory with a sound economy or highest return, but in a relatively safe haven, which the major superpower was,

---

16   These ideas were initially crystallized in dependency theory, an important figurehead of which was P.A. Baran, originally a student within the critical theory circle in Frankfurt/Main. Cf. Baran (1957) and Wallerstein (1974).

17   The requirement of the US's leading role has been formulated by Brzezinski, for example, in his book *The Choice: Global Domination or Global Leadership* (2005).

even after 9/11 and relatively also after the 2008 financial crisis. The USA also attempted to maintain this exceptional position on a global scale in the pursuit of its political, economic and military approach, with the US having the largest military expenditure of any country in the world and a vast global network of hundreds of military bases and other facilities. This creates an unbalanced global order that produces major excesses in military funding and global insecurity, including wars (Rufanges 2021). It has its consequences in the EU. Since the 2022 conflict in Ukraine, there has been a significant partial replacement of the EU's planned strategic autonomy with its interdependence on the USA and NATO.

The current global constellation may also be viewed in terms of the periphery, i.e. people living in developing countries in the Global South. They are faced with major existential problems which Western countries, due to the exploitation of the highly asymmetrical relations of the interdependence of individual states, sometimes directly created or continue to create, while other times they only compound such problems with other complications.[18] Poverty is not the only problem; many people also view, for instance, various foreign interventions in the territory of their states as misrecognition and demand a global remedy.

This perspective may provide some guidance that could help citizens of the EU to grasp their problems prompted by the current global tensions as global problems. In this context, however, the European Union could inadvertently walk into the role of a semi-periphery which is tempted to misrecognize key global issues related to the periphery and imitate the center, for which the global regime has been so far advantageous.[19] This arrangement of real and potential crises and wars, however, threatens not only the developing world but also the population of the European Union as well as the USA. It entails drastic social inequality and destruction of the European social model, as well as democratic decision-making, which is also diminished in the European Union by post-democratic tendencies. This is a challenge for the realization of economic and political democracy.[20]

---

18   See above, Chapter 6.

19   Especially since "the US war on terror", the 2008 financial crisis, and the 2022 conflict in Ukraine, there has been a struggle between relative independence and interdependence of the EU to the USA (Borradori 2004; Hrubec 2022).

20   The economic crisis has prompted debate on the supranational regulation of financial operations, for example, specifically the introduction of a Europe-wide tax on financial transactions (the Financial Transaction Tax, otherwise known as the Robin Hood Tax), to prevent financial speculation. At the same time, a fund would be created that would be capable of financing solutions to various financial crashes. Although the European Parliament has already passed the tax (see http://www.europarl.europa.eu/en/headlines),

Claudia Ritter believes that the current post-democratic tendencies could be eliminated if people in the European Union were recognized as citizens, if they could vote and publicly express their sympathy not only with the entrenched political parties, which cling to the center of public attention thanks to their established status and financial support from private and public sources, but also with various groupings of civil society which often lack financial backing but enjoy a certain legitimacy and the support and interest of people in their activities (Ritter 2006, 192–203). Citizens should make decisions on political legitimacy and justice, as well as on social cohesion and justice. In these reflections on the possible development of this as-yet-only pre-democratic plan, Ritter considers an important question to be how to formulate the concept of the European citizen in terms of the European political order, which has a polycentric and multilevel structure (Bache and Flinders 2004). Therefore, Ritter forges a link in particular with the theories of social groups which have already tackled this type of structure and stresses that group recognition is also important. Therefore, democracy requires the social, economic, political and cultural recognition of those subjects to which it applies, and also requires recognition of their collective identity. However, such recognition is the result of the long-term formation of social, economic and political justice.

From the perspective of the critical social theory, Ritter considers the mainstream political theory of European integration to be unsatisfactory. Individuals must be viewed not only in terms of political autonomy but also from pre-political, cultural and social perspectives. This requires a certain critical public discourse, in which efforts at the recognition of persons or groups of persons may be made. In this context, Thomas Risse, in his treatise on the European public, tries to tie together the ideas of Habermas's theory of communicative action with the social construct of collective identity and thereby eliminate the one-sided nature of both the identity theory and the theory of communicative action (Risse 2010, Musil 2005, 47–57). This reformulation of Habermas's theory originating in his earlier, more critical period from the position of the theory of socialization of groups attempts to refine the normative and empirical characterization of the European public and contribute to the elimination of undesirable randomness which may arise in the current decision-making model. He examines the European public concerning critical public discourse taking place, especially in the independent media, to which he attaches key

---

the result of the vote was not binding on the individual countries and the practice of financial speculations, tax avoidance, and tax paradises continues.

importance to communication between the state and society, between public authorities and the public, represented by individual private actors.

Unlike Habermas's concept of consensus, however, Risse, in his concept of conflict, considers differences of opinions to be a starting and key component of any democratic order, whether an arrangement of individual nation-states or a European order (Habermas 2013). Differences of opinion increase the incidence and importance of European issues in public debates and are a sign of the emerging European public, just as they were previously a manifestation of the establishment of the national public. Risse's hinted answer to the question of how, concerning this social construct of the supranational community of communication, which arises in the context of European discursive talks, a European value framework is formed, refers us back to a tenet that incorporates communication into the broader framework of the concept of recognition and that was formulated in more detail by Claudia Ritter, i.e. the knowledge that the participants in this community must recognize each other and achieve recognition of themselves as members of the European Union in disputes on European economic, political, cultural and other issues.

•••

Overall, I can say that every state needs economic, cultural, political and social recognition but, in the present global period, this is difficult to realize it in the national and international frameworks. Although existing theories of recognition offer a suitable first approach on how to conceptualize recognition beyond the nation-state, this requires the articulation of tendencies to transnational and global recognition and justice in relation to other subjects, mainly from the Global South. An emphasis should be placed both on the economic processes and their political and cultural conflicts and on legal recognition. New dilemmas in the transition from a unipolar to a multipolar and multilateral world are emerging (Patino Villa 2017; Chumakov 2010). Real possibilities of promoting recognition beyond state borders indicate that it is necessary to rely on the existing international institutionalization of the law and try to transcend and reformulate such institutionalization according to current struggles for recognition and justice addressing both intercultural and socio-economic conflicts.

PART 5

Global Perspectives of Justice

∵

Intercultural Polylogue: Cultural and Political Justice

συλλάψιες· ὅλα καὶ οὐχ ὅλα, συμφερόμενον διαφερόμενον, συνᾷδον διᾷδον καὶ ἐκ πάντων ἓν καὶ ἐξ ἑνὸς πάντα

Graspings: things whole and not whole, what is drawn together and what is drawn asunder, the harmonious and the discordant. The one is made up of all things, and all things issue from the one.

HERACLITUS (B10)[1]

∴

While, in the previous chapter, I dealt with international, transnational and (macro)regional relations especially from a European and Western perspective, in this chapter, I will focus on intercultural and intercivilizational relations and, in the following chapter, on extraterritorial and (macro)regional relations from a global perspective that encompasses multiple perspectives of different cultures, civilizations and societal systems. Following on from my account of the trichotomy of *critique, explanation, normativity* in Chapter 1, it is now necessary to make a clarification of what normativity I have dealt with in the largely descriptive and explanatory part of the book (Part 4) and what I will deal with in the largely normative part (Part 5). On a more detailed reading, there is the interconnectedness of the various elements of the trichotomy by means of the realism of societal development. Since societal realism does not work with arbitrarily constructed norms but is based on norms that crystallize in real struggles for recognition and justice, it is necessary to distinguish between normative patterns that are less demanding and, therefore,

---

1   This ancient thesis has parallels in contemporary Europe, Africa, Asia, and the Americas. Both the European Union and the United States of America are following it, although so far it is more declarative than realised. "*In varietate Concordia*" ("Unity in diversity", first in English as "Unity in Diversity", now "United in Diversity") is the official motto of the EU. The motto "*E pluribus unum*" ("Out of many, one") appears on the obverse of the Great Seal of the USA. This idea also appears in other cultures, e.g. the motto of South Africa is "*!ke e: ǀxarra ǁke*" ("Different people live in unity" in the language of ǀXam); there is the idea of 和而不同 (*he'erbutong*, harmony in difference) in Confucian culture; the motto "*Bhinneka Tunggal Ika*" ("Different, yet united") is in the largest Islamic country in the world, the Republic of Indonesia, etc.

appropriate to explain within the framework of the explanation of reality (Part 4), and more demanding normative patterns in a global setting that may be included in the interpretation of normativity (Part 5).

In the previous chapter (the second in Part 4), I focused on the description and explanation of *existing* relations and law, in particular on the explanation of their limits (critical explanation) and on *the immediate normative overlaps* embedded in these relations (normative explanation). I have focused on *international* issues and on *supranational* issues, specifically at the macro-regional level, particularly in the Western framework, since both these international relations and the transnational process of integration – in the European Union, for example – are realities with elements of normativity that, however, only slightly exceed the reality in question. The elements of international and transnational recognition in the EU are – albeit in an imperfect form – a matter of reality that allows for further normative development, but it is a process whose possibilities of development are limited by the compromises made so far in the capitalist system in question.

In Part 5, which is mainly devoted to normativity, I will focus on forms of justice that are more demanding in their normative requirements. As I will make clear, these analyses will require an intercultural approach to elucidate the development of international and global ordering in light of the different forms of recognition in different cultures, such as Western, Chinese, Latin American, and Islamic, that might document the possibilities and potential grounds for articulating ordering beyond the state. Moreover, it can be added that intercultural recognition can be a kind of global recognition, as it may not only be realized on a macro-regional scale but also on a global scale. In Chapter 10, I will formulate a very specific kind of justice, namely extraterritorial recognition, which, although based on international recognition, goes beyond it and establishes new transnational relations. So far, it has only been implemented in a few cases, but it has the potential for real development, existing above all as a strong normative requirement. The more demanding demands, specifically of market socialism economy, also have greater normativity. There is further potential in a broadly conceived global justice which I will address primarily in relation to a concept of the global state in dealing with global hegemony, authoritarianism, and war at the end of my exposition in the last section of Chapter 10. What all these kinds of recognition and justice – intercultural, intercivilizational, extraterritorial, alternative macro-regional, and global – have in common is that they possess a stronger normativity.

1   Intercultural and Civilizational Polylogue

There are frequent intercultural conflicts in the present global context which is characteristic of an increasing number of interactions of people from different cultures from the fields of economy, communication or other types of cultural interaction. This does not always mean a state of war. Conflicts take on diverse forms from the cultivated to aggressive ones (Arnason 2003). Although the confrontation of cultures and civilizations leads towards the polarization and culmination of the conflict, the intercultural and intercivilizational dialogue attempts to contribute to their mutual recognition and justice.[2]

These forms of conflict resolution did not develop as separate thought entities but stem from the development of mutual conflict relationships between people and the requirements for their resolution. The process of misrecognition of certain groups of populations in the long-term historical perspective causes their justified dissatisfaction and articulation of their claims for recognition. At the same time, some types of injustice might be initiated by artificial conflicts which are invoked for the purpose of the legitimization of particular power structures or for the purpose of unjust economic and other interests. Despite the fact that some confrontations between cultures are fictional because they are forced upon people without any essential connection with the reality, a possibility of 'self-fulfilling prophecy' has at least a partial influence on the transformation of these conflicts into serious confrontations. The example may be the conflict between the West and Islam after 9/11 or disputes between the USA and Russia, and the USA and China these years. The interactions are then formed as a complex of fictitious and real conflicts.

People react critically to the disadvantages and other forms of oppression which they face, and, in this way, they map the individual problems that need to be resolved. In the background of their experienced reality, they notice positive fragments of reality and try to develop them. In a relatively favourable environment, the criticism of current forms of misrecognition and attempts to correct them may be realized in the form of a cultivated intercultural dialogue. The notion of conflict then includes the notion of consensus which may assist the direction towards the desired final state.

The intercultural dialogue attempts to identify the current social norms through critical discussion and create new ones that might be shared by individual cultures in a universal way. Because the communication does not

---

2   On the value of the role of dialogue, or in other concepts, communication on recognition see
     Dallmayr (2010); Taylor (1992); and Fraser and Honneth (2003).

concern only *two* cultures and therefore a *dia*-logue in the literal sense, it is more precise to talk of a *poly*-logue.[3]

Here we can conceptually relate to the *polylogue: forum for intercultural philosophy*, which is an association that carries out philosophical debate across nations and cultures. However, since the term dialogue is already well established and is not limited to its literal meaning of just two actors in a discussion, while the term polylogue is used only by a limited number of experts, it is possible to use the first term as well. After all, the problem does not only refer to the debate in intercultural philosophy itself but also to the broader – interdisciplinary and public – formation of intercultural dialogue, polylogue, recognition and justice.

Intercultural efforts to achieve transcultural consensus can take place in different discourses. One of these is transnational and global ethics (Stepanyants 2007, Sullivan and Kymlicka 2007; Wiredu 2005). People in different macro-regional cultural circles create moral rules that have the quasi-universalist character of contextual ethics. Indeed, the claims of the application of these contextually defined ethics are largely only macro-regionally contextual, although some segments of these ethics are applied with global ambitions: Western secular, Christian, Chinese, Muslim, Hindu ethics, to name only the most widely used, each of which, of course, has many variations (Küng 1998). The analogous discourse can also be a political or legal one, for example, or interactions and discourse between multiple modernities (Eisenstadt 2002).

The aim of this chapter is to contribute to uncovering the assumptions of intercultural polylogue with respect to just norms and practices that are or could be shared by all cultures. Such norms and practices, which also have considerable power implications, are, of course, not only the subject of hopes for consensus but also the source of many conflicts. If we identify the potential candidates for these norms and practices, we can say that the most shared at present are various kinds of human rights, which, however, often suffer from the imposition of non-consensual particularistic versions of them. It can be noted that one of the important ways in which people have tried to resist their disempowerment and injustice is through the promotion of human rights across cultures and civilisations, be they social, economic, civil or other rights. The fundamental problem is not that people in some cultures reject human rights a priori but that they often assert different human rights than people in other cultures and civilizations, or that they assert the same rights but in

---

3 See The Forum for Intercultural Philosophy *Polylog* that holds a research discussion across nations and cultures (http://polylog.org) and also the *polylog* magazine *Zeitschrift für interkulturelles Philosophieren*.

different interpretations. The ideological abuse and imposition of certain political rights is a frequent problem, for example. Therefore, efforts to struggle for human rights require a formulation of human rights that is not imposed on anyone and that comes from the "bottom" of each culture and from the mutual relations of recognition between people from different cultures. But I conceive of human rights here only as a representative example to be used in my analysis of global norms.

In this section, I will briefly discuss dispute and polylogue; in Section 2, I will focus on the intercultural and intercivilizational nature of the dispute over justice; in Section 3, I will concentrate on human rights, building on the previous discussion; and in the last section, I will touch on human rights legal documents. Such an interpretation, which is a contribution to the formation of unity in plurality, is not entirely self-evident, since most people's attention is either focused only on intercultural dialogue and issues of plurality of cultures, or only on general norms (such as human rights) and issues of the universality of civilization for all human beings. Attempting contact between the two discourses can be read as part of eliminating the frequent ideological abuse of human rights that distorts intercultural recognition and its outcomes in the form of planetary agreements on commonly shared human rights and the conditions for their realization in the struggle against cultural hegemony.

The discourse or polylogue which is the subject of my analysis contains two fundamental elements. The first one relates to the forming of a dialogue 'from below' from the perspective of various cultures and their relationship within human civilization. The second element is in the form of universal human rights which may be the outcome of this type of dialogue. This kind of approach, which is gradually formulated and subjected to many comments from individual cultures, could be the unifying and universal element (An-Na'im 2002; Gyekye 2004). In short, the objective is to reach a commonly shared 'trans-cultural' consensus through inter-cultural means in order to replace the current supra-cultural situation which is not universally accepted.

What does it mean to talk about the dialogue which is supposed to be inter-cultural? The adjective may be initially read as an umbrella term which covers the relationships among individual cultures or civilizations or culture/civilization circles. This definition raises the question about the relationship between the words culture and civilization. The preliminary answer might be to define them as synonyms but under the condition that the limits and any possible misunderstandings are clarified before using these terms. Their frequent interchanging is not only the case in the Western languages. For example, there is also the Arabic word umran, which has a prominent place already in the teaching of Ibn Khaldun from the 14th century, which can be translated either as civilization or as culture (Khaldun 1989).

Some authors prefer to use the word civilization rather than the synonym approach. Yasuaki Onuma presents this term as more appropriate because the word culture may be interpreted also in a restricted sense in which it speaks only about artworks and works with an aesthetic function (Onuma 1999, 103–123). This is certainly correct. Moreover, aside this interpretation, another use of the word culture exists which is bound only by one type of human rights which is cultural rights. Also, in this case, the word cultural is conceived in a limited sense which is concerned with the broader issue of the intercultural conflict about human rights, including the cultural rights (Kroeber and Kluckhohn 1963).

The word civilization is likewise not used in one sense only. On the one hand it is designated to the whole human civilization in the entire humanity while on the other hand it is designated to just one of the civilizational or cultural circles (Benjamin 1973); it is used for example in relation to the Western civilization or culture or the Chinese world. The first mentioned meaning of the word civilization has its origin in defining a specific stage of development of society or culture (Diamond 1997). Civilization is trying to overcome the primitive stage of cultural development. It begins to essentially defer from a primitive culture at the moment when it becomes characterized by the complex organization of its society. Whereas primitive societies seem to be relatively static, civilizations are characterized by the process of development. It is possible to speak in detail about the gradual development from hordes to tribes and chiefdom to state and super-state formations. The criteria of differentiating between these types of cultures has taken into account population density, patterns of colonization, relationships between relatives or relationships within the society, the intensification of food production, the introduction of the division of labour and egalitarian or centralized types of decision making, informal or legal conflict management and so on. The trajectory of development had previously only its regional character, and its various historical stages were analysed in far more detail than the complex planetary trajectory. Once the civilization stage of development of the majority of cultures spread on the planet, the discussion was concerned with one civilization of the whole humankind. Therefore, from the point of view of this explanation, the development proceeds from cultures to civilization. This process also allows the discussion about progress or regress.[4]

---

4   See Adorno and Horkheimer (2007; orig. 1944), for example, and compare it with the alternative interpretations of Toynbee (1934–1961) and Elias (2000).

This interpretation is also compatible with the relating of civilization to the practical-technical sides of a society although the term 'culture' is then used in the opposite sense, that is not as more primitive but more developed product of a society. The distinction between culture and civilization is based on defining civilization by the technical dimensions of the society such as script, urbanism and so on. Culture is then ascribed, sometimes not without difficulties, to the more refined role related to values and humanistic ideals (Tönnies 2005; Spengler 2006).

The disadvantage of this way of defining the word civilization, as used with regards to individual participating civilizations (Western, Chinese, and others) is that it does not allow for discussion about inter-civilizational dialogue with cultures that did not reach the civilization stage of development. Dialogue is then reduced only to the discussion amongst technically developed civilizations and other cultures are left in power dependence on them or in other kind of dependence relationship.

Moreover, the use of only one word civilization in the plural as well as the singular sense has a tendency to contentiously erase the difference between the cultural (plural) and the cosmopolitan and global (singular) meanings. These multiple meanings have their consequences for intercultural and trans-cultural discussion. The use of the word civilization in the plural sense may implicitly cling towards a discussion which omits the acknowledgment of differences of individual cultures, and which aims towards a unifying approach. This approach then defines cultures with an emphasis on one civilization of the whole of humanity only. This kind of approach is usually not an embodiment of a true universalism which in the intercultural dialogue of a desirable and non-imposing manner tries to unify the current positive elements of individual cultures while also suggesting universally acceptable elements which could be voluntarily shared between individual cultures. It is more often the case of an imperialist point of view, whether reflected or not, which under the heading of civilization promotes one culture over another. The history of colonialism and the forms of colonialism which were legitimized by *European universalism* or more preciously by *pseudo-universalism* are its unfortunate consequences (Wallerstein 2006; cf. Seth 2013). The meta-theoretical viewpoints commit the same transgression which without the contribution of other cultures and from the viewpoint of one culture, attempt to dictate which social concepts, values and so on, are relevant and eventually should be considered as universal. All these approaches are usually defined as cultural imperialism (Said 1994; Kögler 2005).

One way of preventing these kinds of problems is firstly to retain the wider sense of the term civilization, that is to use it only in the singular sense for defining the whole of human civilization and secondly to define the term *culture* by its plural connection with individual societies. The word culture might be seduced to various partial conceptions as I already mentioned, from culture as a collection of artworks, to cultural aspects of various areas, cultural rights, for example, to cultures that have not developed into complex civilizations and which have not the use of technology, and also to cultures as a synonym of civilizations. Despite this wider notion, it is always various partial entities and not culture as a singular whole which is under consideration because culture is not usually thought of as an all-human culture but rather as various cultures or cultural plurality. Here we might refer to Majid Tehranian who, in his analysis of civilization and resolving of its conflicts, says that it is more adequate to analyse one human civilization and many human cultures (Tehranian 2007). However, the disadvantage of this approach is that it does not reflect the fact that various civilizations use the term civilization to refer to themselves and, thus, use the term in the plural. It is fair to say that the differently defined concepts of culture and civilization can, with sensitive definitional handling of problematic issues, arrive at a similarly good interpretation in terms of content.

We should reject fixating purely on one of these categories in this case, on civilization in a singular sense or on culture in plural sense. It is necessary to acknowledge both, the differences of individual cultures and civilizations as well as the common values which bring humanity as a whole into one civilization.[5] The key is that in this definition it is possible to respect plurality of opinions and to work 'from below' of individual cultures and civilizations and aim towards their interconnectedness in one human civilization. There is a continuous exchange between the social constructions of these terms.

One of the previously mentioned problems, which arises in connection with cultural imperialism, is the cultural particularism. Regarding its content it often promotes the same values as cultural imperialism but, in its opposition, it openly advocates its specifically non-universal viewpoint. Due to the fact that the advocates of cultural *particularism* emphasize essential differences of individual cultures, they frequently tend towards the opinion that individual cultures cannot reach commonly shared values and therefore they cannot in certain respects unify in one civilization and the community of human beings. The absence of the potential universal consensus predetermines this viewpoint, together with the cultural imperialism, to the confrontation of cultures. In this respect the word culture as well as the world civilization has the

---

5   In similar types of discussions within the framework of the national state, it is usual to differentiate between the politics of recognition or difference and the politics of universalism or equality; see Taylor (1994).

negative connotations because they both can refer to *Kulturkampf* or the *Clash of Civilizations*.[6]

While placing an emphasis on insurmountable differences between individual cultures, the advocates of cultural imperialism and cultural particularism frequently perceive cultures in a segregate way, as historically enclosed units and unchangeable given entities. Individual cultures are here conceived as specific essences (Wallerstein 2006). However, the essentialist view is disturbed by efforts to construct not only random elements of intercultural consensus based on the current partial overlapping of various cultural values, but also by elements of such a transcultural consensus which requires openness of individual cultures towards partial re-definition of their values. The intercultural dialogue does not accept the essentialist view. The essentialist view is confronted by the critique of generalization of cultures and the emphasis on the gradual formation of cultural patterns as social constructs which means the rejection of the transcultural essentialist view (Samson and Smith 1996). Rejection of the essentialist view should not on the other hand lead towards the relativist view which is at the same time a resignation concerning the non-contingent transcultural consensus.

The conception of cultures in the intercultural and transcultural dialogue also requires a more exact identification of the cultural subjects of the dialogue. In relation to Lawrence Blum, the three categories can be distinguished, although none of which have to be designated definitely and can transform in time (Blum 1998; Ingram 1998). Firstly, it is possible to speak of *an individual* who is formed by a particular culture and civilization or *an individual* with a particular cultural and civilizational identity (identities). Secondly, we may discuss *a group of individuals* specified by particular culture and civilization or *group* with particular cultural and civilizational identity. Thirdly, we can analyse an entire *culture* and *civilization*.

The first category of the subject is not in the centre of attention in the intercultural dialogue because the dialogue primarily follows relationships between larger cultural units than individuals. The relationships at the individual level are certainly also important though, in the conflict of entire cultures, millions of individual persons do not enter into discussion but rather the representatives of people who can promote their individual and group interests. Nevertheless, it is important to make sure that the representatives of individual cultures do not represent just their own view and their own culture

---

6 Authors who develop these thoughts use these words often as synonyms. See Huntington (1996) and compare it with an alternative interpretation by Senghaas (2007).

only marginally. But also, in the case when the representatives are successful in representing their culture, they should not represent the mainstream of their culture more predominantly; it is obviously desirable to acknowledge the minority streams as well. This opens the question of a *multi*-cultural dialogue within the *intra*-cultural framework between the majority and minorities, between men and women, and so on (Taylor 1994; Senghaas 1998). Intra-cultural conflicts also largely relate to social conflicts. As mentioned by Yash Ghai in the context of East-Asian economies, a particular territory does not offer just one access to rights, but the heads of companies stress other laws than unionists, and minorities emphasize other laws than the members of the majority, etc. (Ghai 1999). Within the framework of intercultural dialogue, it is important to remember these significant socio-economic factors.

The other category which is formed by culturally formed groups of individuals includes in a more restricted sense the majority of the population of France, for example, and in the broader sense, the majority of the entire Western population. It is the population of the European Union, the USA and other countries that have similarly specified cultural, economic and political systems, such as Canada, Australia and so on. A similar type of discussion could be initiated in relation to Islamic minorities in France and in the European Union in general. Although this is not a general rule, these minorities are often culturally related to the majority of another country: the Turkish minority in Germany is culturally related to the majority in Turkey, for example. Minorities and majorities of course cannot be considered as fixed and the ratio between the minority and the majority may significantly transform in time or even reverse its course.

The third category, which is formed by entire cultures or civilizations (which, however, does not mean closed essences), includes the creations of culturally defined groups, from artworks to various social customs and finally to the whole life in the society, which is a collection of various social, political, legal and other entities. In the wider context and from the long-term perspective, it is also possible to add population to these creations which may be considered as a cultural product of itself. Population as it stands does not perceive itself as an object but asserts itself primarily as a creating subject that gradually forms cultural customs, rules and objects in interaction with the related environment.

What would it mean to refer to the third category in an intercultural dialogue which means the entire cultures? Charles Taylor speaks of entire cultures when he expresses the need to recognize a cultural value of cultures which is required not only for a dialogue but in particular for their own life. He says that we should analyse and recognize the equal value of cultures (Taylor 1994). In

Taylor's interpretation, the recognition of equal respect to different cultures is analogous to the recognition of the equal dignity of individuals.

The question remains whether or not it is appropriate to apply an equal approach to individuals, which we implement in relation to their common characteristics, humanity or citizenship, for example, also for the recognition of cultures (Blum 1998). This approach to cultures seems problematic for two reasons. The first is the gnoseological argument about the difficulties in measuring the value of individual cultures. In order to evaluate the Afro-American culture or the Roma culture, for example, it would mean to consider them as some kind of totality to which we attribute a specific measurable value. The second argument relates to the difficulty in comparing the value of individual cultures even if this value was measurable. This does not mean the tendency towards relativism but only the acknowledgement of the problems of comparing entire cultures. The claim for value stems from justified and histori-cally founded fears of dismissive Euro-centric or today more of a West-centric approach towards other cultures. One of the sources of this problematic approach is based on the thorough evaluative comparison of cultures which often led to the conclusion that the Euro-American culture is superior to other cultures.

If we abandon these kinds of rigorous cultural comparisons and try to re-define Taylor's formulation by focusing primarily on the equal recognition of *groups of people* which are defined by a particular culture, there is a chance that we also rid ourselves of the dismissive West-centric attitude. Then, it will be possible to better understand the requirements of the politics of recogni-tion. It is also necessary not to slip towards an interpretation which homo-geneously ignores various groups of individuals with diverse cultural identity, or to the approach which uses exact techniques of measurement and subse-quently sorts them into hierarchic categories.

These kinds of arguments lead back to the second category of the subject, i.e., to groups of individuals, whether they are small communities in the posi-tion of a minority or larger communities in the form of a majority or even entire 'cultures', although here it is cultures in the sense of groups of individu-als and not cultural entities which are not *defined* by human subjects.

Groups of individuals may at the same time have two basic requirements which are often connected with legal requirements: one is the claim for their recognition as subjects with different cultural identity which will not be ignored, and the second requirement is the claim that these groups as subjects of a dialogue and action are recognized by others as equal to other groups. Although this kind of conception of subjects of intercultural dialogue is not entirely ideal and requires a certain amount of reformulation which is not necessary for the purpose of this text, nevertheless, this approach is more suitable than the approach which talks about entire cultures or civilizations without a recognition of the groups of individuals. In the contemporary global age when national states struggle for keeping their position, to adopt a politics towards culturally defined groups of individuals is a politics which is generally more farsighted than the current obsolete stance of international law which is almost entirely fixated on national states.[7]

2 Dispute on the Universalism of Human Rights

In continuity with the explanation which I offered above, it is possible to say that the connecting element between the *cultures*, which are primarily tied to groups of individuals formed by individual cultures and civilizations, and the *civilization* in terms of the entire humanity is the *inter-cultural* polylogue. The significant characteristic of the intercultural dialogue is the effort to find certain *trans-cultural* characteristics in common which might be shared by all cultures and civilizations and, therefore, by the entire human civilization. The effort to agree on certain commonly shared fundamental norms makes human rights a significant topic (Maritain 1949).[8] Currently, in the matter of human rights – given their many different interpretations – both controversy and consensus prevail.

Before moving on to specify the potential consensus on a particular version of human rights, it is important to distinguish between how the term 'right' is used by recognition theorists and how it is used within legal discourse (Honneth 1996; Honneth 2014; Fraser 1997; Fraser and Honneth 2003). While legal theorists write often exclusively about basic rights, legal experts also focus on issues of the legal order, civil society, criminal law, commercial law, tax laws, etc. As there has not yet been a precise reformulation of recognition theories

---

7 It is important to add that recognition should aim not only towards contemporary components of groups of individuals but also towards the entire historical experience of these groups. To recognize only the present components of the group of Afro-Americans, for example, would omit the historical experience of racism and the resistance against it which forms part of the Afro-American identity which should not be forgotten if an effort to fully include Afro-Americans into the whole of society is taken seriously. Compare with Blum (1994; 1998, 56).

8 The conferences on the 60th anniversary of the Universal Declaration of Human Rights took place especially within the framework of various activities of the UN under the heading of *Dignity and Justice for All of Us*: http://www.ohchr.org/EN/UDHR/Pages/60UDHRIntroduction.aspx.

into legal concepts, it is necessary to point out the difference between "recognition rights" and "legal rights". Both types of rights share the same intention, as both are constructed to ensure mutual recognition of human beings. Recognition rights are claims to rights that create the social conditions necessary for the very establishment of legal rights. In other words, the moral and social claiming of rights is the condition for legal rights which can then put those social claims into practice. Therefore, these two types of rights are interdependent. It is only after this clarification of terms that we can move from recognition rights to legal rights, in this case specifically human rights and how people from different culturally defined groups can potentially agree on them.

In this intercultural debate, we often encounter two extreme positions. Given that on one side stand the essentialists and on the other side the relativists, the discussion is analogous to the debate on cultures, as mentioned previously. The essentialists as well as the relativists present some convincing arguments, though their fundamental views are questionable (Ignatieff 2001). For essentialists, human rights are not a mere creation of human beings, but they have a deeper origin. According to the essentialist view, human rights are natural which means that they naturally belong to all human beings or that their origin is divine, etc. All these kinds of views, however diverse in their argumentation, relate to a questionable opinion that states that human rights have a natural essence that has to be discovered and spread across all cultures.[9] However, cultures are made not only by nature but also by people.

However, just like the essentialist position, the relativist position is also controversial. The relativists justifiably point out the fact that the formulation and promotion of human rights were and are given by their particular selection which was made by one group of individuals or another. This pseudo-universalist selection is usually promoted as a universal collection of rights and implemented against other norms that are shared by other cultures. The norms of the past were enforced similarly in various colonialist expansions, for example, of which European colonialism was probably the most famous as well as its pseudo-universalism of human rights (Wallerstein 2006). Contemporary practices of global capitalism are, in this respect, followers of this legacy. Various culturally tinged fundamentalisms in various parts of the world are then the other side of the same coin. This pseudo-universalism must be rejected on the same basis as cultural imperialism.

---

9   If this conception of human rights was *intra*-culturally suitable to a certain community in which it developed and if it was not forced by them upon other communities, the shortfall of such a conception would lie 'only' in the fact that it would not be a case of *human* rights or the rights belonging to all human beings.

Nevertheless, the objective of essentialists to achieve universal rights is worth following if it is not based on particularism which is not shared by others. In this respect, the relativists fail. It is not possible to deduce from the various present failures as the relativists do attempt, the impossibility of a consensus on universal values and therefore the necessity of relativism. The possibility of a social construct of universally shared rights that have their bases in various cultures remains here, and likewise, the many attempts directed towards its achievement through the intercultural polylogue. The pseudo-universalistic misuse of human rights meanwhile confirms the power of the idea of human rights because it is an example of the fact that various groups of individuals feel it useful to mask their particular interests behind the widely accepted view of human rights. On the other hand, the positive contribution of relativism is its acceptance and respect of cultural plurality. But if we do not want to end up in the relativist indifference to genocides, cannibalism, torture and other brutal approaches to human beings, we must admit that recognition of other persons should contain certain limits that should not be overstepped.

The formulation of commonly shared limits of this kind presupposes mutual understanding between the participants of the dialogue (Schmied-Kowarzik 2002; Holenstein 1999). Every language or languages of individual cultures have their own specific features which are not shared by other cultures. This does not mean that the dispute is absolute and that there is no space for mutual inspiration and overlapping of categories that might be articulated for consensus on a specific issue.[10] These overlapping and universally shared categories may be considered as social constructs which follow on from similar approaches to similar problems which are encountered by various cultures; they could also be cultural universals (Wiredu 1996) or speech universals (Holenstein 1998; Holestein 1985), if we use the terms of Kwasi Wiredu, and Elmar Holenstein. Whatever the basis of this is, there are long-term circumstances for socially created universals on a global scale due to the fact that none of the larger cultural circles are isolated and they do influence each other. At least since the 15th century, there has been a significant world expansion of the West which was in return influenced by an unequal relationship by cultures that the West encountered. The globalization trends of recent times only encouraged these encounters between cultures. This fact is not the evidence of a kind of shared unity; nevertheless, it is a testimony of at least an awareness of common problems which cannot be ignored. Despite the fact that the list of these problems is by no means identical in all cultures, there are certain

---

10   For the conclusions of these thoughts, see Taylor (1999).

overlaps. Although the hierarchy of these issues is not identical between cultures, it is the subject of the discussion itself which can lead to particularly fruitful results. One of these outcomes is a definite level of consensus in regard to designating a group of human rights.

Moreover, an important aspect of human rights is not just their formulation but also their active implementation in history. In view of this fact, it is important to realize that equivalents of particular types of human rights were in practice in various non-Western cultures in the past which were often eliminated by Western colonization. The interpretation of the development and implementation of human rights therefore require letting go of illusions about a leading civilization role from one of the civilizations, namely the West. This should not mean a resignation from articulating human rights also from a Western point of view which should input into the intercultural discussion but not as the main contributor.

In the effort to arrive at consensus within the framework of intercultural dialogue, it is necessary to distinguish between at least four types of models of arrangement which are discussed in the dialogue. These models contain various views on cultural, political, social, and economic arrangements.

First, it is possible to try to achieve the least demanding model – *modus vivendi*, which will ensure a certain consensus in the current power structure. This model is usually part of practical-political thoughts and compromises. Second, it may be possible to try to achieve the *intercultural model* which recognizes the differences of various cultures while searching for the consensus on *fundamental* human rights as a boundary of acceptable tolerance. This model is more demanding than modus vivendi because its normative conception reaches beyond the current power structure of the participants in the dialogue, while it is less demanding than the collection of *all* human rights. The achievement of desirable consensus on a collection of all human rights will require overcoming the double meanings of human rights definition. Third, it is possible to recognize other cultures with tolerance although, within the framework of our culture or in a narrow framework of our nation, we can have a more specifically defined idea of human rights which may not be shared by other cultures and nations. In relation to this, it may be said that the welfare state has been forming since the World War II as a consensus of social democrats and Christian democrats in the Western European states and its followers hope that it might be eventually accepted in some versions in some other parts of the world. At the same time, there are also other political conceptions within which make claims for their legitimacy, significantly more demanding social/socialist and democratic arrangement structure than the one realized up to now in the conception of human rights regime in the European Union or the USA, for example. Fourth, within the framework of each culture, each nation or each minority unit, there are various social groups and individuals that prefer their own so-called comprehensive model which is based on specific philosophical, religious or other views.[11] They do not try to force this model on other communities and individuals, and they are aware of the fact that it is not shared by all the people. They nevertheless may present this model to others and attempt to justify its persuasiveness. These four models of relations between culturally defined groups of persons may emphasize consensus on the basis of now given overlapping values and practices between groups of persons, as well as on the basis of their transformation or integration, and on the basis of innovative creation of new values and practices.

Therefore, if we try to reach more than the modus vivendi (the first model) we will approach the intercultural model (the second model). Here it is important that each party to the dialogue or polylogue has a real opportunity to offer a proposal that can be universally shared in the intercultural shaping of transcultural norms. The proposals should then be discussed with a view to adopting a common proposal. Since it would be wrong to formulate transcultural human rights in intercultural dialogue as only an offshoot of Western national law or Western-conceived international law, it is important that we are not only open to a global reformulation of particular positions and to proposals coming from other cultures, systems and countries, but that we also engage in argumentation on the four levels mentioned above with appropriate models of organization and from different perspectives of dialogue (Brown 2000).

Although participants in dialogue, who build consensus through various disputes, often prefer to start with a modus vivendi, and then, gradually move on to other, more demanding forms of agreement, it is not advisable to completely avoid presenting all-encompassing positions, which often play a crucial role for their proponents, but which we know in advance are likely to remain shared only by some participants in the dialogue. Revealing all-encompassing moral, philosophical or religious positions can serve to improve understanding between the participants and optimise consensus building. Rawls enumerates several forms of public presentations of all-inclusive positions which, although not included in public reason, he nevertheless gives them a certain space by articulating them. Habermas speaks in relation to these public displays of the need to accept the burden of translation between all-inclusive and public opinions, a burden that should, of course, be shared fairly by all participants

---

11   Rawls distinguishes between comprehensive doctrines and political conceptions which look away from comprehensive doctrines; see Rawls (1993a, 11 nn).

in the discussion. This accommodating stance can aim at more demanding forms of mutual recognition and justice, which I will now proceed to discuss in relation to concepts developed by A. Honneth, X. Wei, D. Wong, D. Bell, C. Ihara and other authors.

3   Plurality of Cultures and Civilizations

It would be erroneousness to identify the basis of human rights solely within Western civilization and declare the Western authors such as John Locke, John Stuart Mill and others as their only creators. The universal characteristics of human rights can be found in various cultures in which the requirements for action of people were being formed in the course of the historical development of moral, philosophical, religious and other systems of norms. Despite the fact that the discourse on human rights was gradually formed in a Western context since the 16th century in connection with the American and the French revolutions, the development of various kinds of rights of human beings has a significantly older tradition amongst many cultures.

The search for some kind of implementation of human rights in the Western culture was often connected with references to the Westphalian era of national states. The national framework of Western thought was the solution for both dominant streams of thinking: the republican thinking on legislation for the sovereignty of people as well as the liberal thinking on the rights of private individuals against despotic rulers and oppressive majorities. These thoughts may be interlinked in one interpretation which connects the public autonomy of state citizens with the private autonomy of private individuals in a concept of autonomy of persons. Jürgen Habermas explains the relationship between both parts of autonomy within the context of human rights which he conceives as an institutionalization of 'communication conditions' under which we can form a political will (Habermas 1998). The sovereignty of the people gives foundation to democracy and to rights which are interlinked into reciprocal conditioning in the form of private and state autonomies. At the same time, Habermas is also aware of the contentious attempts of Western implementation of worldwide democracy which is apparent from ambivalent comments on this topic (Habermas 1998).

A similar approach, but from a different perspective, can be seen in Axel Honneth's interpretation. While his article on the politics of human rights echoes a projective democratizing optimism of the 1990s, in his later works we find more cautious formulations that develop a more widely accepted position (Honneth 2007a, 197–217; Fraser and Honneth 2003). More authors have undergone the similar development. In the post-1989 atmosphere, it seemed obvious, especially in the Western countries, that democratisation tendencies along Western lines were almost a worldwide trend but it later turned out that this was a West-centric illusion.

Multiple concepts of democracy which cover areas of democratic socialism, socialist democracy, social democracy, democratic centralism, democratic populism, Christian democracy, and various versions of Islamic democracy as well as the resistance to forceful and frequently mere rhetorical implementations of democracy beyond Western borders, in the case of the war on Iraq, for example, lead many of its present advocates to cautiousness (Cohen 2006, 226–248). First, it is hoped that the norm of democracy can be accepted through polylogue as a universal model, provided, of course, that we consider it in a general form that can incorporate very different interpretations of democracy and other participatory models. Second, it is possible to work with a different just model on a global scale, leaving the model of democracy to the countries in which it is at least partially implemented. According to Joshua Cohen, who himself deals with an idea of deliberative or discursive democracy, democracy cannot be implemented globally as part of human rights without violating the principle of tolerance, as it represents a demanding political institutional model that may not now be shared by all. He thinks that democracy demanded by justice requires more than human rights (Cohen 2006, 226–248; cf. Bell 2006; Bell 2000). For this reason, he does not yet include democracy among the basic human rights that should underpin tolerant intercultural coexistence. It could be a more modest global model expressed in fundamental rights, i.e., a model based on membership and participation of persons in political communities. This model would, therefore, not include the entire institutional democratic set-up but would include the right to freedom of expression, to assembly, to various social and economic rights, etc.

The emphasis on intercultural dialogue and tolerance of diverse regimes is presently stressed by various authors, by John Rawls, for example, in his conception of international rights based on the law of nations (Rawls 1999). He pursues the coexistence of Western democratic societies with societies that, although they do not have a democratic establishment, are nevertheless decent regimes that gain their legitimacy within a consultative hierarchy that allows for popular participation. This kind of coexistence answers questions such as: why should it be appropriate to implant democracy in the indigenous populations of uncontacted tribes in the Amazon, for example, whose members desire their own model of order which they participate in shaping in various ways and which they consider legitimate? This in no way implies that repressive regimes are being promoted. In the framework of tolerance and intercultural dialogue, we can consider as important the fundamental human rights that give citizens the possibility to live and participate in decision-making and create the conditions for the legitimacy of the regime. From this perspective, democracy may be part of a broader set of rights but not part of basic human rights. However, it is good news for me, a democrat, that many authors from different cultures subscribe to an intercultural dialogue and democracy even though their definition of democracy is often different from mine.

So far, my interpretation has been to define rights that are specific to the Western context rather than rights that are universally shared. The question, then, is what might be the more specific content of an intercultural type of model (i.e., the second model) by which to aim at defining a value framework for human rights. This content is not to be found in Honneth's optimistic reading of his texts from the 1990s that I have mentioned but it can be seen at a deeper level in his interpretation in which the foundations of the model of mutual recognition in a community are present, which I have discussed in the chapter on recognition, following Honneth, Taylor, Fraser, Young and other authors. The foundations of this model do not lose their persuasiveness in terms of potential congruence with models based on other cultures. Axel Honneth states that human rights are presently mostly perceived not only as the conditions for communication but as claims when persons recognize each other to arrange the necessary social, economic and civic conditions of their respect or dignity (Honneth 1996). They are at the same time related to the requirements for the rules of a solidary community of people (Taylor 1989; Al-Jabri 2011). The principal definition of these claims for all is a condition for realization of the human existence. People need a guarantee of at least several types of fundamental human rights for the realization of human existence within the framework of the community.

The key value of community which operates based on mutual relationships between members of the community is stressed also by authors from various cultures, civilizations, and societal systems, although they answer some questions differently. I will give a few examples here, which are not intended to offer an exhaustive account but to illustrate the basic lines of argument from selected positions that are making a stronger claim for attention. I will look at non-Western alternatives, especially in Asia, Latin America and Africa, in more detail in my next book, in a sense one could say in the second volume.

Some Latin American authors (Pereira 2013) develop a critical conception of justice (*justicia* in Spanish-speaking countries and *justiça* in Brazil), and particularly of recognition (*reconocimiento* and *reconhecimento*) in interpersonal relations in a community (*comunidad* and *comunidade*), albeit with a specific but similar meaning to the one I have just expounded in this section and in Chapter 7 on local and national recognition. Latin American culture has been and continues to be shaped to this day by indigenous influences as well as by European and African influences. Since Latin America and the Caribbean involve more than three dozen countries, it is important to see the connections in regional and macro-regional groupings and cooperation. In recent decades, there have been the most prominent social and civic movements and two emancipatory tides of governments (Lampter 2023), which I will refer to in the next chapter. While the transcultural congruence of Western needs, interests and values with those of Latin America is considerable, given the intertwined historical development of European and Latin American societies, there are also significant differences in various aspects.[12]

Now I want to turn to the example of China, which I will also discuss in the next chapter. Chinese socialist authors emphasize the social and economic conditions of community, Wei Xiaoping (Xiaoping 2010), for example. There is also a continuity with the concept of community in the traditional civilization there, particularly in the last two thousand years, although Chinese civilization is much older (Nolan 2019). It is not only the historical specifics of Confucian culture that have developed in China, Korea, Japan and other countries of East Asia but also the increasingly important contemporary position of China and other Asian countries influenced by Confucian culture (Bell 2008a; 2008b). The emancipatory elements and interpretations of Confucianism, which are free from various outdated relations, can be built upon here.

C. Ihara characterises the relationships between individuals in the Confucian community as various forms of recognition which take the form of self-respect, respect for others, human dignity, and equality (Ihara 2004, 27.; cf. Rosemont 2004, 49–71). Here, recognition of the human dignity of human beings is based on membership in the community, with self-education leading to self-improvement being conceived as part of the education and development of others. The Confucian ideal of community together with the ethical concept of social roles and the emphasis on harmonious relationships are principals which, from a Confucian perspective, could stand at the forefront of rights and which could serve the promotion of humanity. According to D. Wong, both types of traditions: such as the law orientated ones as well as the community orientated ones need such a concept of community which would be able to offer a creative problem-solving approach to the relationships of

---

12   From the point of view of critical theory, the work of Enrique Dussel, for example, is a close inspirational interpretation; see Dussel (2003; 2009); Alcoff and Mendieta (2000). Compare with the African perspective which also emphasizes community and the other concepts mentioned above (Kasanda 2018; Mbembe 2017; Mbiti 1990; Fornet-Betancourt 2004).

people while 'not losing face' (Wong 2004, 31–48). It may serve for resolving conflicts in human relationships and so prevent the contentious legal decision-making process about correctness at court proceedings. It is possible to speak of community anchoring of rights in this respect, following the older tradition.

The basis is an intersubjective concept of the Confucian virtue of *ren* (仁), humanity, which can also be translated as recognition, kindness, or goodness, and which is the central term and value, or one of the main members of the group that includes also justice (仁义, *renyi*; traditionally written 仁義) and ceremony (礼/禮; *li*) (Zhang 2002). The conception of humanity "has in its character the pictogram of man in relation to the other, it is a category of relating, of personal relating, it is the *agens societas*" (Kral 2005, 107). The humanity of *ren* is an internal characteristic of human being, and the relations to others *li* bring an external moment. These characteristics are followed by a relationship that acknowledges the other person. Recognition of 认 (*ren*; traditionally written 認)[13] of the other person brings recognition 承认 (*cheng' ren*) or 认可 (*rengke*), which has both an epistemological meaning in the knowledge or identification of the person, and a social meaning, namely, regarding the other as having certain characteristics, which implies a kind of appreciation. The mutual recognition of persons then creates "harmony in differences" 和而不同 (*he' erbutong*) in a "harmonious society" 和认社会 (*che-sie she-hui*; traditionally written 和諧社會) (Chan 2005, 2–6, 14–34).

The emphasis on the community is faced by the strong individualistic tendencies of some Western liberally orientated theories. The authors following the Confucian culture similarly to Western communitarians criticize excessive evaluation of *individual* rights. Henry Rosemont, on the one hand, mentions that if the most fundamental human rights are to be considered the individualistically conceived political rights, it would be difficult to anchor the idea of human rights in the Confucian tradition (Rosemont 2004). On the other hand, he states that it is possible to incorporate human rights into the Confucian concept of the membership of human beings in the community.[14] Liberal authors realize this partly in intercultural dialogue too.

Ihara states that, from a Confucian point of view, the individuals' rights are valuable especially at a time when it is necessary to use them in the context of the degradation of communal relationships (Ihara 2004, 11–30). The

---

13   The word *ren* (to recognize) is transcribed officially in pinyin in the same way as the above *ren* (humanity); however, in Chinese, it is pronounced in the second (rising) tone, while *ren* meaning humanity is pronounced in the fourth (falling) tone.

14   This is realized also by more and more Western authors within the discussion on intercultural dialogue; see Rawls (1999, 72ff), for example.

virtues such as relationships based on recognition should play the primary role according to J. Chan while the legislation mechanism should support this role only in the case of it failing to function (Chan 1999, 212–237). This concept is certainly not unusual even to the socially orientated streams of Western theory and praxis. According to various Confucian authors, the mainstreams of Western thought and praxis may find a consensus with Confucianism on the subject of human rights (Bary and Tu 1998; Angle 2002).[15]

The important thing now is to articulate the basic elements of the Chinese community in the institutional patterns of intersubjective relations that exist today (the synchronic model) as they have been established throughout history up to the present, much as I have discussed the Western models in previous chapters (Hrubec 2021). The contemporary Chinese modern synchronic model is compatible with certain Chinese long-standing historical institutional patterns of intersubjective relations in the community, the importance of meritocracy in education and work, for example (Bell 2016), at the level of family, society, state and economy. The contemporary societal system, called socialism with Chinese characteristics, is characterized by both regulated markets with strategic planning and a combination of private and public ownership. It is a specific model which, at the same time, it is capable of cooperating with different models. Here, the anchoring of relations between people in the community is based on the intersubjective constitution of subjects who are not defined atomistically but in relations of reciprocal recognition in relation to their duties and rights in the community, i.e., similar to other civilisations, including the West.[16]

In ancient Chinese feudal society, three spheres of social relations can be identified: the family, the state, and the world. From the first sphere, the sphere of economics has been gradually separated historically. It is also possible to conceive of a separate sphere of society, which is also based on the family, and which has gradually adopted certain aspects from other spheres. In summary, it can be said that today five basic spheres of institutionalised relations can be captured in this model: the family, society, the state, the economy, and the world community (humanity).

The basis of the institutionalization of these relationships lies in the private sphere, in family relationships, i.e., in relationships between parents and

---

15   Compare also with conservative Confucian interpretations which do not reach such a consensus; see primarily Jiang Qing (2013).

16   A relevant comparison can be made with Axel Honneth's recognition theory (Honneth 2000c; 1996), which explains the institutional patterns of social relations in Western countries, see Chapter 7 and also Chapter 8 of this book.

children (孝; xiao), between siblings, and between partners in love and kinship relationships. It is this area that has long played a fundamental role in Chinese civilization. Education for meritocratic action has its origins in the family, leading to a great emphasis on and appreciation of education in Chinese culture, but also in East Asia in general.

It also involves institutionalised relationships in community and society, specifically in friendships, intersubjective relationships between members of different generations outside the family, relationships between neighbours, etc. Here we can see both the egalitarian and meritocratic contribution of people to the wider society, which is grounded in community, and the solidarity of people towards each other.

The third kind of relationship can be mapped in the legal and political sphere at the level of the state. Here we are dealing with an arrangement in which egalitarian conditions for democratic participation at the local level are based. For the implementation of politics and law at higher levels, the aim is a meritocratic arrangement and a consultative system ensuring mutual recognition between citizens and representatives of power who are supposed to ensure that the needs and interests of citizens are met. In a sense, it is also considered a modernized concept of the mandate of heaven postulating accountability and legitimacy of government that must be exercised for the benefit of citizens, their interests and needs.

The fourth type of relationship is the economic sphere, characterized by the attempt to implement a work ethic with meritocratic contributions by citizens in an environment defined as market socialism economy, i.e., regulated markets and strategic planning, on the one hand, and a combination of private and public (state, provincial, municipal, etc.) ownership, on the other – with the aim of achieving more solidary results. Eradicating absolute poverty was already achieved and raising the living standards of all people is still the goal of development. Taking a comparative view, it appears that the high valuation of meritocracy in China (and East Asia in general) is associated with a work ethic that can be seen as a parallel to the Protestant work ethic in Europe which gradually spread from Protestant areas and became the majority accepted model of work recognition in the West.

Fifth, institutionalised relations have their specific continuation in the global community, i.e., beyond China in various international, transnational, macro-regional and global interactions. Policies implemented within the framework of international law and other legal institutions that China emphasizes should ensure both legal equality and respect for difference within that equality, as well as graded modes of accountability, in which the United Nations, including the Security Council, plays a significant role. We can identify here relations of international and global solidarity in development aid and cooperation and, more recently, in tackling global climate change employing China's ecological civilisation project and other related concepts (Yang and Jiang 2018; Pan 2016), as well as relations characterised by meritocratic efforts to achieve international and global recognition which primarily concern state actors. Various efforts to develop these conditions are often hampered by various foreign national, transnational, macro-regional and global distortions by a range of oligopolies and their political exponents.

Building on this interpretation and on a similar interpretation in Chapters 7 and 8 of developments in Western countries in a comparative way, the current state of the spheres in different cultures can be summarised in relation to the degree of institutional development of national and transnational relations in Table 6. The table provides only a basic brief overview at three levels, although transnational relations are, of course, of several kinds, including intercultural relations. The development of norms in the three territorial scales (national, regional, global) is indicated by the size of the circles: a smaller circle indicates less development, a medium circle indicates medium development, and the largest circle indicates the most extensive development. The degree of this unfolding of interactions at different scales is also relevant for further interpretation in Chapter 10 of this book.

In Islamic culture, too, there are parallels to the above concepts that are important for intercultural recognition and justice (عَدَالة; al-'adalah or al-'adl in Arabic). Cultural and civilisational values here are very much tied to religion. Iranian culture represents a distinct, long-standing tradition, at the same time, the one that also shares commonalities with other Islamic countries (Hrubec 2009; cf. Dallmayr and Manoochehri 2007). From the point of view of the Arab Islamic region, which, although it does not encompass the entire Islamic world, forms a central part of it, relations between individuals are dealt with in the context of a community (أمّة; ummah), which means not only

TABLE 6   The degree of institutional development of national and transnational relations linked to the four spheres

	Family	Society	State	Economy
national	O	O	O	O
regional	.	o	o	O
global	.	.	o	O

the community in general but also and above all the community of persons focused on Islam, i.e. the Muslim community. This community can be conceived, first, on a local level as a village, second, on a more complex level as an Islamic nation, i.e., a community of believers (*ummat al mu'minin*), within an individual country or, third, within the community of all Muslims (Göle 2006). Since the concept of *umma* is also used in the sense of a community without Islamic characteristics, it can also be used in a global sense, e.g., in the United Nations (UN, *Al Umam Al Muttahida*). In the Qur'an, we find, in this context, verses that still have a prominent place in the lives of today's Muslims: "May you become a community that calls for good, enjoins what is fitting and forbids what is reprehensible." (The Qur'an 2008, 3:104).[17] A more literal translation reveals connotations that are also important from the point of view of recognition: "May you become a community (*ummah*) that calls for good, commands the recognized (معروف; *ma'ruf*) and forbids the disapproved (*munkar*)."

The recognition of women's rights including citizens and social rights, which are discussed more frequently in relation to the Islamic culture, might be promoted with a successful result too, as argued by Adbullah Ahmed An-Na'im.[18] This might be possible if cultural and religious communities are placed in a more advantageous position rather than if the search of the solution to problems operates only on an abstract level. Norani Othman states that an experience of many active groups of women demonstrates that, in their everyday conflicts, a development was achieved by utilizing specific cultural paradigms (Othman 1999; cf. An-Na'im 2002; Göle and Ammann 2006). This does not in the least mean surrendering the secular state. Common approaches shared by Western and non-Western women's movements consist of anchoring in the framework of current societal system from which prejudices stem and against which the struggle takes place (Jaggar 2005, 55–75). From this point of view, the optimal concept of human rights is in accordance with Islamic values and is founded in *idzhtihad*, i.e., the critical re-evaluation of Muslim canonical texts which can also include *sharia*, or a critical approach in general. It is very important to stress here that this approach and similar concepts in other cultures are relevant to a critical conception of recognition of persons in a community. Without this critical approach, the community could suffer, as is sometimes the case, from traditionalist as well as contemporary repressive approaches to individuals and social groups. *Ijtihad* provides members of the

---

17   Following Abdul Majid Daryabadi's translation. Compare Sura 3, Verse 104 with related
      Sura 3, Verse 110 as well as with Sura 9, Verse 71.
18   On the interconnectedness of religious, cultural, and political discussions in the secular
      state see An-Na'im (2005, 56–80).

community with the opportunity to address misrecognition, either directly or indirectly.

The significant measure of human rights lies also in their social and economic dimension which is their material basis. Yash Ghai states that conditions of certain approaches to rights are material relations which means social-economic relations although we may often observe a time difference that is necessary between reality and ideology (Ghai 1999, 241–263). In case of Asia, he points out the effect of global interactions on the material situation of people and, in this way, also on understanding of the rights and their practical implementation. Leslie Sklair analyses two crises in relation to global inter-actions, the class polarization, on the one hand, and ecological problems of unsustainable development, on the other (Sklair 2009a). According to Sklair, both crises are connected with the culture and ideology of consumerism which directs the dynamics of global capitalism. Against these crises, he places culture and ideology of human rights in which he sees a potential of justice for the solution of these crises. Human rights are conceived as rights which also have a social and economic dimension from which democracy benefits.

A similar topic from a different perspective is formulated by Jeffrey Flynn who also talks about the material conditions of intercultural dialogue. He argues that it is necessary to overcome the usual focus of intercultural dia-logue. He concerns with the wider social and economic context in which inter-cultural dialogue takes place on the one hand, and on the other hand, with duties, especially with social and economic human rights (Flynn 2009, 59–77). Intercultural dialogue might arise with more difficulties in the situation of the extreme poverty which rules many people especially in developing countries. Only the abolishment of poverty will enable legitimate formation of institu-tions which could operate in the global scale.

Such an approach requires a concentration on the socio-economic precon-ditions of intercultural dialogue, that is, on the issues that specify relations within the community. However, this brings us to the metatheoretical level of interpretation where it is necessary to address who decides on the content of the socio-economic preconditions of the intercultural dialogue and in what dialogue. However, the solution, like the decision in the intercultural dialogue itself, should not be the imperial dictate of a limited small group of persons. We should avoid imperial practices and should co-create the concept of human needs and universal qualities together with people from various cul-tures and societal systems, including the global poor. Failure to incorporate their viewpoints into a common concept would mean the absence or pretense of consensus and the passing off of mostly Western-centric considerations as supposedly objectively identified needs of all human beings.

An adequate theory would be a critically focused theory of social justice that conceives of dialogue as only a slice of relationships of mutual recognition and emphasizes the starting point in a critique of specific modes of misrecognition that exposes contentious issues and, then, articulates solutions. However, it should be borne in mind that efforts to find consensus between groups of people defined by different cultures and systems are only one kind of pursuit of justice. Thus, while some transcultural consensus on certain norms can and does emerge, struggles for justice in the social and economic spheres have their own dynamics of development and cannot be reduced to momentary intercultural consensus, even though it is significantly influenced by that consensus. Long-formed perspectives should arrive at intercultural consensus on the basis of the realism of societal development. The basic social needs of human beings and the social rights associated with them can be adequately articulated on the basis of the realism of societal development which is based on the long-standing struggles for justice of social groups who are denied the fulfilment of these needs, including their rights. Nevertheless, this will be analysed in Chapter 10, which will also present the concretization of rights in relation to legal documents.

David Miller discusses a similar problem when he distinguishes three main ways in which human rights are legitimized (Miller 2007, 168f): first, legitimation through practice, whereby agreement on human rights is assessed through their application in practice. One can focus on the main legal documents and on their signing and ratification by individual states, or assess their implementation, to see cursorily what consensus exists on them. It is also possible to look for consensus on the standards relied upon by different governmental and non-governmental human rights organisations and assess their implementation. Second, consensus can be found through overlapping consensus, i.e., consensus through the overlapping or intersection of sets of different norms. Large cultural circles that contain different secular or religious norms may find consensus on certain basic norms that they share. Here it is possible to identify the philosophical, theological or cultural sources of these norms, which may have different kinds of justification in different cultures, and it is also possible to seek a common justification of at least the basic commonly shared norms of humanity. Third, one can look for common foundations that are inherent in all human beings across cultures, or focus on norms of community with a shared future for humanity. Identifying the basic human needs that relate to human survival and life could enable consensus to be reached on the fundamental rights of all human beings.

These are not haphazard ways; each of these paths to legitimation has a sophisticated argument, although the degree of their overall persuasiveness may vary.[19] From the perspective of a critically oriented social theory, it is useful to make these models complementary. The first kind of clarification, which is associated with achieving consensus in the practice of rights, may be able to provide and further generate a first point of reference that comes from below the critique of the non-fulfilment of rights, and can be evaluated in two other ways. Building on all three approaches, it will be possible to start from practical struggles against injustice and for justice, and attempt to both find and shape overlapping values across cultures and systems and to identify universal human needs and characteristics together.

4   Common Norms for Humanity

Since the responsibility for the promotion of human rights is still with individual states but, at the same time, they are only partially able to guarantee the promotion of human rights in the era of global interactions, it is necessary in the current post-Westphalian era to examine and promote human rights and other norms from the level of local communities through national and international levels to the global level. Meanwhile, in terms of long-term historical development, it can be said that the current legal system contains various emancipatory elements that can be developed to contribute to the establishment of a transnational legal system on a global scale. International law, as Martti Koskenniemi says, has historically evolved from an instrument of apologia of a given political regime into a utopia (Koskenniemi 2001; 2006). The turn from apologia to an increased sensitivity to international issues came at the end of the 19th century, and from then on international law emancipated until the 1960s. Thus, an analysis of the growth and decline of international law shows that this trend in the development of international law did not even last a century. Moreover, even this relatively short period was not without its twists and turns. While the transition from sovereignty to internationalism was realized, it began to collapse when it lost the support of the great powers before the World War II. After World War II, many countries revitalized international law, established the United Nations, and drafted and adopted important legal documents. However, the original more ambitious aspirations were not fulfilled because of the Cold War. Where hopes remained, they mostly turned into mere utopia.

---

19   An exemplary case of the first legitimization is (Beitz 2003, 44). The second legitimation is promoted in a distinctive way by Rawls (1993a) and Taylor (1999, 124–144). A third kind of legitimation is elaborated by Sen (1999) and Nussbaum (2000).

The decolonisation process after the World War II confirmed this trajectory. The UN's attempts to eradicate poverty in the Third World have not been very successful because legal commitments to significantly improve the global distribution of resources through public international law have not been taken very seriously by developed countries of the First World. In short, the UN Charter has not become an effective planetary constitution.

In the early 1990s, after the end of the Cold War, statesmen and jurists of different countries tried to revive the institution of international law. However, before these steps could meet with success, after 2001, hope once again turned into disillusionment. However, this outcome was not only due to inappropriate political decisions after 2001. It was part of the evolution from international relations to global relations, which exposed the weaknesses of the international legal order in the context of global economic forces.

Global economic pressures fragment international relations and law. The absence of a transcending legal perspective weakens the application of international law and renders it particularistic. While this is not a reason to abandon this legal project, it is necessary to reform it transnationally. As Koskenniemi argues that today we do not face a question whether or not to be global and cosmopolitan but only a question of what kind of cosmopolitanism we should choose (Koskenniemi 2001, 515).

The proposed view so far necessitates raising the more empirical question about the formation of a legal document such as the Magna Charta for the community of the whole of humanity. Within the framework of current international law, the one of these legal documents is the well-known *The Universal Declaration of Human Rights*. The lesson taken from the World War Two led to the creation of the UN and the establishment of the UN Commission for Human Rights in 1946, which was already from the outset concerned with a proposal for the universal declaration of human rights. Initially, the representatives of 18 states participated, while a group of 8 individuals from Australia, Chile, China, France, Lebanon, USSR, Great Britain, and USA participated on the formulation of the Declaration. The Secretariat of UN subsequently prepared the proposal on the basis of these formulations which were the foundation for further discussions and proposals for changes from other Member states.

The declaration was accepted in 1948 at the UN General Assembly in the presence of 58 Member states from more cultural circles. 48 of them voted for its benefit, 8 abstained, and the representatives of 2 states were not present at the vote.[20] It is therefore possible to say that although the original proposal

---

20   Declaration was approved on 10th December 1948 in Palais de Chaillot in Paris; General Assembly Resolution 217 A (III), 1948.

was created by a group of individuals that was not sufficiently representatively composed of the representatives of many nations and various cultures and systems of the whole world, the following discussions and approval of the document were already achieved by a relatively complex even if not exhaustive representation.

The text of the Declaration is a result of an attempt to formulate binding norms that could be shared across individual nations, cultures and societal systems. Due to the fact that representatives of various cultural circles participated in the formulation of this Declaration with an endeavor to find common norms, it can be considered almost as a transcultural result of intercultural dialogue. It certainly is not a perfect result that would fulfill all requirements placed on intercultural representation and on transcultural consensus. Nonetheless, it is possible to talk about one of the first few articulations of global standards. In the age of planetary, military and other types of aggressive interactions, such an intercultural vision for transculturally shared norms is an act of considerable significance. Transcultural norms provide a common normative foundation which should be the starting point in supporting the abolition of various military and other types of conflicts.

Although the Declaration is not legally binding, it became the basis for the creation of several legally binding documents. Let's mention at least the International Covenant on Economic, Social and Cultural Rights and the International Covenant on Civil and Political Rights.[21] Both Covenants were approved by many states in the UN General Assembly, and they were both more or less equally ratified into the present times by the majority of the states.[22] Other legal documents further specify and supplement these Covenants in relation to various social, economic, cultural, political, citizen, environmental and other rights (Sklair 2009a).

Various rights must be sufficiently defined against each other. In this respect, the UN promotes three fundamental characteristics of human rights: universality, indivisibility, and interdependence. I would like to stress especially the

---

21 Covenants were approved in 1966 after almost 20 years of the preparatory process within the framework of the UN and they came into force 10 years later in 1976, after the necessary ratification process (The International Covenant on Economic, Social and Cultural Rights 1966, 1976; The International Covenant on Citizen and Political Rights 1966, 1976).

22 The number of states that ratified the International Covenant on Economic, Social, and Cultural Rights was 171 by July 2020, and the number of states that ratified the International Covenant on Citizen and Political Rights was 171 by June 2022; see (Ratifications and Reservations: http://www2.ohchr.org/english/bodies/ratification/4.htm); as for the economic, social and cultural rights see (Ratifications and Reservations: http://www2.ohchr.org/english/bodies/ratification/3.htm).

importance of the fact that the economic, cultural, civil, political, and social rights, if presented in alphabetical order, are mutually conditioned and supported. However, it does not yet guarantee a consensus on exactly what rights to promote and what kind of relationship should exist between these rights. A typical example is the conflict between social and political rights or the conflict between individual rights and the rights interconnected with living in the community. This conflict is apparent in discussions between Global West, on the one hand, and Global East and Global South, on the other, as well as among individual countries.

It is essential to realize that ratified human rights in international documents are, so far, a claim which has not yet quite been achieved. That is exactly why we talk about *fundamental* human rights which should be fulfilled and achieved first. At the same time, it is necessary not to give up on the discussion about the more extensive collection of human rights which has already been defined in international documents. The accomplishment of human rights requires the support of a collection of fundamental human rights which can receive stronger support and thus wider implementation. It will be easier to move from the fundamental human rights to the wider collection of human rights and possibly to their redefined and gradually specified form. This is nonetheless a complex matter and challenging topic for the discussion.

Extraterritorial, Strategic, and Global Interactions: Social, Economic, and Security Justice

Everyday forms of resistance make no headlines. Just as millions of anthozoan polyps create, willy-nilly, a coral reef, so do thousands upon thousands of individual acts of insubordination and evasion create a political or economic barrier reef of their own.

JAMES C. SCOTT

•••

Crossing the river by touching the stones (摸着石头过河)

• •
•

In this chapter, I will focus on justice primarily in terms of a normative concept of economic and social justice concerning the implementation of redistribution and property beyond the nation-state. Particularly, I will first concentrate on the articulation of the extraterritorial recognition of social-rights-holders for the international and transnational level of justice by addressing the misrecognition of the socially weakest group of people in the global context, i.e. the global poor.

Pursuing justice in the contemporary global context must deal with the issue of *mis*recognized rights-holders and *un*recognized rights-agents. One of the reasons right-holders are misrecognized is that rights-agents are not specified precisely in relation to their obligations in the new economic and legal arrangements under global capitalism. If we want to help solve the problem of global injustice and develop a political alternative to the contemporary order, we have to define properly whose obligations have to be prescriptive, be it nation-states, transnational corporations (TNCs) or international financial institutions (IFIs) that have put this structure of global capitalism in place, mainly Western countries. However, as the national parts of this structure, especially in the US, after decades of existence, are to some extent running up against their limits, economic and political representatives in the nation-state are redefining this structure by partial neoconservative closure to external competition and by global economic, political and other conflicts. The dynamics of first pushing neoliberal global tendencies and then partially neoconservatively restricting them is a typical example of the dialectical historical development of opening up and partially closing down in order to push the new structure (or even the whole system) to a higher level. Meanwhile, competition to the Western model has been continuously taking shape during the dynamic process through the BRICS+ countries and other, mainly developing countries in the cooperation of the Global South (Pereira da Silva 2023a, 366–377; 2023b), some of which have brought new ways of eradicating poverty not only through redistribution but also through specific notions of ownership.

In the first section, I will make a distinction between the traditional subject of misrecognition and the global poor, and, in the second section, I will analyse the current legal possibilities for extraterritorial recognition of the global poor. These possibilities can be found in some elements of international legal conventions, most notably exemplarily in the "International Covenant on Economic, Social and Cultural Rights". While pointing to the need for transnational recognition at the regional and global scales, I will emphasize the indispensable role of extraterritorial recognition in the transition from an international to a transnational economic and legal order in the dynamics of contemporary protests against social injustice by the means of the regulation of transnational capital (especially corporations and financial institutions) in an era of global conflicts. Most of the impetus for these efforts in recent decades has come from the subjects of the two left tides (*mareas rosas* in Spanish) in Latin America, particularly social and civic actions with their local and global initiatives. In the third section, I will show an alternative model that, through a transformative revolution, has achieved the full elimination of absolute poverty and a significant rise in the living standards of more than a billion people in one country in four decades. Specifically, this Chinese model is based on a system of public and private ownership and on linking the market and strategic planning. The final, fourth section is based on the fact that the current economic, social and political conflicts in the global context are increasingly difficult to resolve through gradual transformation, they are manifested in economic disputes and proxy wars between great powers in formal and informal macro-regional and networked blocs, and may result in direct military clashes, the collapse of the hegemonic power of global capitalism, or the extension of the supranational order into the global state and its risks in the forms of political homogenisation, authoritarianism, and war. At the same time, I will draw attention to the integral embedding of the potential global state in the process of long-term historical crystallization of human civilization, in which it is part of the characteristics of technological development.

1   An Identification of the Misrecognized Subjects

While analyses of intercultural recognition are concerned with cultural diplomacy how to establish equitable relations between different culturally defined groups of persons and how to find and create transcultural overlaps, analyses dealing with the area of recognition of basic human needs are, in the cases of hundreds of millions of persons mainly in Africa and Asia, concerned with struggles for economic and social survival or at least survival under conditions of poverty (Schweiger 2020). Since I draw on the real protests of social actors in my internal social critique, I begin my normative interpretation by clarifying the position of the misrecognised.

Attempts to eliminate social injustice stems from below, from upheaval of the people. The sources of their resistance against injustice are articulated in the framework of experiences concerning a violation of expected recognition (Honneth 1995: 2; Fraser 1997; Fraser 2003). Misrecognition can be transformed into the motivational basis for criticism and resistance. To identify motivations for change, we have to realize that experiences of misrecognition play a role as catalyst of criticism that can be generalized and transformed into social conflicts and normative claims on various kinds of recognition and equal participation. In this way, we can indicate the logic of social conflicts that explains the dynamic of misrecognition and recognition of the people (Thompson 2006; Burns 2001).

The analysis of the current international legal structures can explain the limits of the expected legal influence of the nation-states abroad. The weakness of the individual ordinary states to apply extra-territorial recognition and control activities of their TNCs and IFIs need not be only the bad news but it could provide motivation for the politics of recognition in order to create supranational and global regulative mechanisms in favour of social justice. It seems to be the dynamics of the historical development from misrecognition unsolved on the national and international levels to the supranational regional and global levels of recognition (McDonald 2006; Mertes 2004; Reitan 2007; SinghaRoy 2004). Social agents affected and dissatisfied by the contemporary solutions of the global social injustice are in the process of becoming the subjects of societal change who ask not only for the development of contemporary national and international instruments of justice but also the development and creation of new global institutional structures (Fraser 2010; Reitan 2007).

As I mentioned in Chapter 6 on the criticism of the current international order, this tide of criticism has its causes. These are not only the great social inequalities and the drastic poverty of many people who can express their dissent through demonstrations and other means but also the loss of life. Millions of people die every year because of poverty-related problems. Let me remind you that one person dies every four seconds because of hunger. The Executive Director of the UN World Food Programme has specified that "In a world of wealth, 9 million people die every year because of hunger" (In world of wealth 2021; Humanitarian organizations 2022). These people usually live not in the rich Western countries of the global North but in the much poorer Global South. Without changing this main point, it can be added that, at the same time, there is a growing number of complex places that could be described as the Global South in the Global North and, conversely, the Global North in the Global South (Comaroff and Comaroff 2012).

The "Millennium Declaration", that was adopted at the Millennium Summit in 2000, formulates main goals focused on poverty, gender inequality, international trade, etc. These targets, developed as the Millennium Development Goals (MDGs), were expected to be achieved by 2015 (United Nations 2013). States planned "to halve, by the year 2015, the proportion of the world's people whose income is less than one dollar a day and the proportion of people who suffer from hunger"; and "by the same date, to have reduced maternal mortality by three quarters, and under-five child mortality by two thirds of their current rates." (United Nations 2014: Para. 19). If the child death rate of 1990 would be diminished, as required, it "would mean *just* 4 million child deaths in year 2015" (emphasis added) (UNDP 2005: 28).

The question could be raised if it was adequate to specify the aim to decrease these deaths only in 15 years. Was it really sensitive only to halve the number of people suffering from hunger? Following Thomas Pogge, we can ask: During World War II, what if the Allies had also planned to only diminish, let us say to halve, the Nazi killing rate in this unobstructed way over 15 years? Would Jews, Roma and other non-Aryans assaulted have survived at all until the mid-1950s? (Pogge 2007; 211–12; Pogge 2002)

However, humanitarian aid in practice is even worse than the modest proposals of the Millennium Development Goals. The above facts on the number of deaths are telling. But it was a positive ambition in 2015 that the 2030 Agenda for Sustainable Development and Sustainable Development Goals (SDGs) #1 began to aim for the elimination of poverty in all forms by 2030 (UN 2015a; UN 2015b). Nevertheless, recent data shows that this goal is unlikely to be achieved even in the case of extreme poverty:

> Given current trends, 574 million people – almost 7 percent of the world's population – will still be living on less than $2.15 a day in 2030, the majority in Africa. In 2020 alone, the number of people living below

the extreme poverty line rose by 70 million. This is the largest annual increase since global poverty monitoring began in 1990.

WORLD BANK GROUP 2022, 14

Of course, a successful protest requires the articulation and means of its demonstration that must be strong enough to be influential. That is the reason why a potential subject of social change existing under the worst living conditions mostly in the Global South is almost invisible. The influential subjects of change are often the relatively poor, who, compared to people in absolute poverty, are already in a better position to become at least partially aware of their position in international or global interactions and to act accordingly.

It is the fact that dying people suffering from hunger and severe poverty are not too visible in the mass media and the majority of the population of Western countries who almost ignore them (Scott 1985) as a specific kind of protesters against the contemporary global system. Their discontent and objectives are not formed into pictures that are apparent in every respect today. In this sense, so far, they did not form an alternative strong enough to compete with the contemporary order. But as soon as we identify normative claims of the global poor who experience social misrecognition, we should not be fixed only to the normative objectives that have already received public expression. I argue that the people get accustomed to expect a form of discontent which is typical of the traditional subject of social and political protest in the West, i.e., the labour movement, the proletariat, and the new social movements that reflect various kinds of activist movements oriented to peace, ecology, gender, minorities, etc. Incidentally, already a term of social movement invites us to implicate a move. However, the masses of people suffering from hunger and severe poverty are tightly bound to the places of their everyday lives and, metaphorically taken, almost cannot 'move' in order to protest while global corporate winners can 'fly' easily. The global poor represent a different kind of movement. It is a protest based especially on everyday local struggles for survival hitherto that are not too visible.

Of course, focusing on the classical and the new social movements is significant. Nevertheless, although a publicly articulated experience of social injustice in the West plays an important role in struggles for justice, it could not be a criterion of global relevance. An application of this criterion would be Westcentric and reproduce the dominant kinds of discontent. It could not come down with other forms of social suffering which should also be a legitimate source of our attention. It would maintain restriction on the current level of articulation of misrecognition. Thus, we should pursue a new criterion of public visibility that would reflect the situation of the global poor.

Drawing a parallel to slaves who were not considered human beings on the part of many people before the abolition of slavery, today those suffering from hunger and extreme poverty in the Global South have not yet really been recognized as a protesting subject in the eyes of the majority of the people. We can say, then, that the global poor, who show their dissent in this way, suffer doubly: first, from their poverty, and second, from the fact that their forms of critique are ignored.

In the debate between Nancy Fraser and Axel Honneth, in which they share many ideas, Axel Honneth is right, on the one side, when he argues that she underestimates social movements other than those that have received public recognition (Honneth 2003, 113–14; Thompson 2006). Thereupon she partly reduces her analysis and aims for the publicly visible present-day social movements. However, on the other side, Honneth does not reflect that Fraser studies the important global issues requisitioning their necessary incorporation into the theory (Fraser and Honneth 2003: 88 ff; Fraser 2010). From this point of view, Honneth underestimates a global scope of analysis. It is important to see that, on the one hand, the theory needs responsiveness in respect of the fact that the dissent of the global poor has not evolved into the manifest powerful and sometimes militant forms that working class movement and the new social movements have demonstrated. On the other hand, an understanding of the discontent of the global poor and their normative claims necessitates a study of the contemporary international and supranational arrangements in order to address the needs of the global poor as well as limits that block them.

My argument is that it is requisite to bear in mind also everyday struggles for recognition, even if they have not received much mainstream public attention, and develop social research of global interactions, especially in light of the global poor. If we accept the premises, first, that there is the fact that millions of people are dying of hunger and poverty related causes especially in the Global South, and, second, that there could be serious protests in the form of the social experience of misrecognition that has not been in the centre of mainstream public attention, we should admit that we have to face one of the biggest protests in human history. Then, the theoretical articulation of this critique has to be sensitive enough to realize the human catastrophe that calls for an international and supranational solution. However, this critique is complicated by the fact that many other marginalised people, such as many discriminated women or ethnic minorities, are not in solidarity with the global poor so far.

Seeing that some kinds of recognition are already embedded in the international legal system, it is necessary to analyse what legal obligations that could help eliminate the catastrophic situation of the global poor are there because it would make no sense to invent something that has been already at least formally guaranteed (Giesen and Pijl 2006; Windfuhr 2005; Koskenniemi 2006; Koskenniemi 2001; cf. Honneth 1996; Honneth 2014; Fraser and Honneth 2003). The demand to strengthen existing international law is, of course, only the first of many other demands. It is only when people find that the "easiest way" of resistance within international law is inconclusive that they invest their energies in developing a new, alternative legal order at the supranational level. Today, people in many countries are criticizing their governments and demanding that they live up to their obligations to respect social rights enshrined in international legal documents. A telling example is the *Social Watch Report* (2023; Social Watch 2006), which is prepared each year by citizens from dozens of countries in almost every part of the world as an expression of global civil protest against the non-fulfilment and violation of social rights in the areas of poverty and gender inequality.

The subjects who have most powerfully articulated the demands of both old and new social movements and the global poor since the beginning of the new millennium have been participants in two left-wing tides in Latin America. These social activists, politicians, ordinary citizens and social researchers have been able to integrate earlier emancipatory tendencies there by organizing participatory budgeting and citizen systems (Silveira and Silveira 2015; Prefeitura Municipal de Canoas 2011) and to create new tendencies by innovative social programs (bolsa familia, etc.) and social structural transformations and by organizing local and global social forums, for example (Wallgren et al. 2022; Conway 2012; Fisher and Ponniah 2003). The World Social Forums, which began in 2001 in Porto Alegre, Brazil, have gradually begun to be held in other countries in Latin America, Africa and Asia, creating a transnational and global network.

While Venezuela, Brazil and Bolivia were the key countries in the first left tide launched in Latin America in 1999, Brazil, Colombia and Cuba have followed Venezuela and emerged as the biggest leaders in the second tide since 2018 (Lampter 2023, 319–334; Sobottka 2023, 304–318; Hrubec 2023, 349–365; Harnecker 2015; cf. Gomis et al. 2021). Venezuela's Hugo Chávez has launched a revolutionary Bolivarian project that builds on the Latin American historical efforts of Zamora, Bolívar and Rodríguez in the 19th century (Granés 2022; Dinušová 2023, 335–348). The international cooperation that built on these efforts resulted in the regional organization ALBA (Bolivarian Alliance for the People of Our America) which seeks emancipatory cooperation and the integration of Latin America and the Caribbean, with Venezuela and Cuba as the most active countries. In addition to ALBA, other regional organisations such as CELAC and Mercosur are important in Latin America.

The second left tide in Latin America, like the first tide, also seeks broader cooperation in the world and participates in the various forms of Global South cooperation. I can mention the enlarged version of BRICS and the Group of 77 plus China which has grown from an initial 77 countries in 1964 to today's 134 developing countries from Latin America, Africa and Asia (Li 2021; The Group of 77 at the UN 2022). This group of nearly two-thirds of the world's countries, together with the new left tide in Latin America, is trying to strengthen social tendencies and cooperation in the world as an alternative to asocial global hegemony.

2   Extraterritorial Recognition: Regulation of the Economy

The current international legal system – despite its negative aspects – contains some emancipatory elements that can be developed and thus contribute to the formation of the just global legal system. One important element that is gaining importance in the promotion of legal justice is extraterritorial recognition. Within the Westphalian system of international relations, the concept of extraterritorial recognition has been used only in a small number of cases that have not affected much either the larger number of persons or the system of international relations. However, last decades, as more economic and financial activities have been acquiring an international and transnational character, the extent to which it is necessary to secure recognition of various rights in the territory of other states increased, i.e., the recognition of rights beyond the borders of the state in the post-Westphalian order. The demand for extraterritorial recognition of various rights beyond state borders represents an effort by critical social and political actors to force states to take responsibility for their actions, for the actions of their citizens, and for the actions of corporations. Let us now consider the possibilities of extraterritorial recognition of social rights to date.

'Poverty is a violation of basic human rights,' argued the United Nations High Commissioner for Human Rights (United Nations High Commissioner for Human Rights, 2008). The Universal Declaration of Human Rights pronounces various rights, together with 'the right to a standard of living adequate for the health and well-being [of persons] ... including food, clothing, housing and medical care' (U.N., 1948: Art. 25, 1), and, in relation to a cross-border reach, it states that '[e]veryone is entitled to a social and international order in which rights and freedoms ... can be fully realized' (U.N., 1948: Art. 28). Basic social and economic rights are legally specified in the International Covenant on Economic, Social and Cultural Rights (ICESCR) (U.N., 1966a).

The Covenant was adopted unanimously by the General Assembly of the United Nations,[1] and it was ratified by majority of countries of the world which have the various cultural, economic and political regimes.[2] The Covenant states that 'in no case may a people be deprived of its own means of subsistence' (U.N., 1966a: Part I, Art. 1, Para. 2), and it recognizes 'the right of everyone to an adequate standard of living for himself and his family, including adequate food, clothing and housing, and to the continuous improvement of living conditions' (U.N., 1966a: Part III, Art. 11, Para. 1; see also U.N., 1991; U.N, 1997a). The Covenant sets out the following obligation:

> Each State Party to the present Covenant undertakes to take steps, individually and through international assistance and co-operation, especially economic and technical, to the maximum of its available resources, with a view to achieving progressively the full realization of the rights recognized in the present Covenant by all appropriate means, including particularly the adoption of legislative measures.
>
> U.N., 1966a, Part II, Art. 2, Para. 1

The specification 'by all appropriate means, including particularly the adoption of legislative measures,' is explained by the UN Committee on Economic, Social and Cultural Right (CESCR) in its General Comment 3 (U.N., 1990b: Para. 8). The comment notes explicitly that, provided human rights are respected, it is politically and economically neutral in a sense that it does not require any particular kind of political or economic system: 'a socialist or a capitalist system, or a mixed, centrally planned, or laissez-faire economy, or ... any other particular approach' (UN, 1990b: Para. 8). Therefore, it depends on each state how it defines appropriate means and legislative measures.

It is useful to compare this Covenant with the International Covenant on Civil and Political Rights (ICCPR), which was adopted on 16th December 1966 and came into force on 23rd March 1976 (UN, 1966b), because the nation-states have to implement the obligations of the latter but they are obliged to pursue

---

1   The *International Covenant on Economic, Social and Cultural Rights* (ICESCR) was adopted by all 105 present votes of the United Nations General Assembly in 1966, after almost twenty years of the drafting process which was based on the work of the U.N. commissions and agencies. The Covenant entered into force 10 years later (1976), after the necessary steps of ratification. For a discussion of various aspects of the economic and social rights, see Craven, 2007.

2   Concerning the Western states, while the E.U. countries and Japan ratified the Covenant, U.S.A. did not do so. Nevertheless, the U.S.A. signed it; therefore, they cannot act against the purpose of the Covenant.

only progressive implementation of the former. However, some obligations of the ICESCR have to be realized not only progressively but uniformly in all the states now. The states must not discriminate, for example, for reasons of race, sex, language or other status (U.N., 1990b: Paras, 1, 3, 5). Sex discrimination is a good example of this. Understandably, poor families in many countries of the Global South invest money in the education of sons rather than daughters because it is more complicated to get a job for educated girls than for educated boys. An investment that makes less profit would even worsen the situation of poor families. However, if the state were to eliminate gender discrimination, then poor families could change their investment strategy in favor of girls. In this way, we can avoid punishing the victims.

The legal obligations of the nation-states are focused especially on agents in their territory and under their jurisdiction. However, in an age of global interactions, both state and non-state actors heavily influence people also beyond their territories in other countries. Countries in the Global South in particular are almost powerless in this context. The Western states have bigger – even if only limited – extra-territorial power and possibilities.

The duties of the nation-states that ratified the ICCPR seem to be focused on human beings who are in their territory or under their jurisdiction. Nevertheless, concerning the ICESCR, it is possible to require also extra-territorial recognition because the scope of action of the ICESCR is not limited in the treaty. Thus, an application of the Covenant's social right can go beyond the territory of a state (see also Coomans 2005; Craven 2007: 71–88).

The ICESCR notes that states should apply the rights 'individually and through international assistance and co-operation,' through 'international contacts and co-operation' and 'international action' (U.N., 1966a: Art. 2, Para. 1; Art. 11, Para. 1 and 2; Art 15, Para. 4; Art 23). Such notes suggest two interpretations. Firstly, a realization of rights *individually* demands more state responsibility. Second, *international* assistance, contacts, action and cooperation allow a less ambitious approach of the state that would only share responsibility with other states. Moreover, the notion of international assistance seems to refer either to offering merely humanitarian aid of the state or to taking part in international humanitarian aid. Nevertheless, even if this general specification of scope of application is not too precise, I will show later that the Covenant is specific enough to assist more here.

The statement is worked out when a territorial scope of the ICESCR is specified by its substantive scope falling within the terms of the right to safe water, the right to food, the right to adequate housing, etc. Concerning the right to water (U.N., 1966a: Arts. 11 and 12), for example, the Committee on Economic, Social and Economic Rights stresses that the states should not impose embargoes that prevent the distribution of water and activities necessary for achieving the right to water (U.N., 2002: Para. 32).

There are three levels of obligations that are imposed on the states: (1) to respect, (2) to protect, (3) to fulfill (in an original proposition, also to assist) which contains obligations to facilitate and to provide (U.N., 1999a: Para. 15; see also U.N., 1989a). As for the third parties, regarding the right to food, the states have obligations to *respect* and *protect* what advocates of the rights and other members of civil society do when they *assist* in the fulfillment of the right to food (U.N., 1999a: Para. 35; see also Narula, 2006). In the spirit of the Charter of the United Nations (Art. 56), ICESCR (Arts. 11, 2.1, 23), and the Rome Declaration of the World Food Summit, individual states have an international obligation to recognize the essential role of international cooperation and comply with their commitment to take joint and separate action to achieve the full realization of the right to adequate food. In implementing this commitment, States parties should take steps to respect the enjoyment of the right to food in other countries, to protect that right, to facilitate access to food and to provide the necessary aid when required (U.N., 1999a: Para. 36).

Therefore, the states are expected to satisfy all three levels of the obligation, at least the minimum level that is necessary for a human being to be free from hunger. While the importance of the World Food Program, UNICEF, the Food and Agriculture Organization, and UNHCR is recognized by the United Nations, the states are responsible in individual and joint ways to cooperate in order to provide humanitarian assistance. In these cases, 'the most vulnerable populations' have priority over the others. It should be applied to assistance to refugees as well (U.N., 1999a: Para 38).

I would also like to draw attention to the fact that social rights under the Covenant could contradict some obligations under various legal regimes that the states also ratified. Moreover, the ICESCR mandate may come into conflict with economic sanctions imposed upon some states internationally and unilaterally, and also by the UN Security Council (White 2007: 89–107). While only the sanctions authorized under the UN Charter by the Security Council could prevail because the UN Charter has priority in cases of conflict, states still have a responsibility for possible negative consequences of their decision to impose sanctions and they have to respect that the parts of the Charter that have a relation to human rights must be applicable also in these cases. The UN Committee on Economic, Social and Cultural Rights recalls that various economic sanctions had a negative effect on the population of the target country. The comments on the right to food and the right to water mention that the states should not at any time impose any embargoes that endanger the supply of water and access to food, including services for securing the water and conditions for food production. It is stated that both food and water 'should never be used as an instrument of political and economic pressure' (U.N., 1999a: Para. 37; U.N., 2002: Para. 32). These statements are fully explicit and show that political and economic motives do not have priority over the right to food and water.

The Committee adopted a special comment (General Comment 8) on the relationship between economic sanctions and respect for economic, social and cultural rights (U.N., 1997b). This says, on the one hand, that the U.N. does not cast doubt upon the necessity of sanctions in appropriate cases but, on the other, that sanctions almost at all times 'have a dramatic impact' on social and other rights (U.N., 1997b: Para. 3). For example, they often cause the maldistribution of food, clean drinking water, pharmaceuticals, the malfunction of education and health systems, can bolster the oppressive elites, etc. The comment emphasizes that 'whatever the circumstances, such sanctions should always take full account of the provisions of the International Covenant on Economic, Social and Cultural Rights' (U.N., 1997b: Para. 1).[3] As an explanation, the comment states that 'lawlessness of one kind should not be met by lawlessness of another kind' (U.N., 1997b: Para. 16).

We cannot think that weaker states in particular would be able to exercise full juridical and effective control in their territories and apply the rights in the face of the powerful capital of transnational corporations, international financial organizations and strong states via an unequal co-operation. William Robinson was right when he argued that a weak ability of individual nation-states to regulate capital accumulation at a worldwide level allows to create the polarization between a poor minority and a rich minority (Robinson 1996: 25). The polarization seems to be a kind of 'the new global social apartheid' which requires a separation of space that enables social control in order to guarantee the small elite both life essentials and a consumption of expensive goods. 'The race to the bottom' creates appropriate conditions for the protest that is in process of formation now. An alternative to the transnational concentration of capital could be a popular project that would also have a transnational character. The grassroots kind of transnational dissent could form a counter-hegemonic bloc (Anheier, Kaldor and Glasius 2006).

The protests against transnational capital and other expressions of discontent show that the global tendencies of the economic system have a flip side, manifested in the involvement of local and national social forces in

---

3 General Comment 8 refers explicitly to mentions sanction imposed upon following countries: South Africa, Iraq/Kuwait, the former Yugoslavia, Somalia, the Libyan Arab Jamahiriya, Liberia, Haiti, Angola, Rwanda and Sudan (U.N., 1997b: Para. 2).

transnational critique. Today we are witnessing two new and strongly contradictory processes, with transnational economic and financial structures, on
the one hand, and transnational social critique, on the other. As is well known,
the corporations, the World Trade Organization (WTO), the International
Monetary Fund (IMF) and the World Bank (WB) have pursued their interests
and policies that brought on losses among the most disadvantaged and poorest
populations. The contributions of adjustment measures and other activities
have initiated popular protests both in the North and the South. The people
protested against a negative impact of various kinds of neoliberalization man-
dated via structural adjustment and other programs on inequality and poverty
in many countries. It is precisely the negative impact on the most vulnerable
part of the population that is the core of this kind of argument and that is discussed in relation to a regulation of TNCs and IFIs.

I do not want to claim that TNCs and IFIs are fully responsible for the severe
poverty of the global poor and for millions of deaths. My argument is that in a
world where the nation states only partially influence TNCs and IFIs, we have
to specify the problem of hunger and the severe poverty in relation to responsibility of TNCs and IFIs. A good starting point for thinking about this kind of
accountability is Iris Young's concept of global justice: "The social relations-
based model of accountability argues that actors are responsible for structural
injustice because their actions participate in processes that lead to unjust outcomes." As for a general responsibility, I claim that any influential actor in the
global context, including TNCs and IFIs, should share legally in the liability for
the global arrangement and its negative consequences. Concerning the concrete suffering and responsibility, at first sight it seems to be reasonable that
TNCs and IFIs should have full responsibility for their actions in the same way
as nation-states and various organizations have; in other cases, if they have
only an indirect influence, they should have only a partial responsibility; and
in still others, if they have no influence, then also no responsibility. However,
the structure of responsibility has to be more complex because it is hard to say
that powerful agents have no influence in the interdependent world. There is
a distinction between what the agent brings about and what it merely allows
to happen, but it does not bring about (Haydar 2005: 312–13; Pogge 2002: 41–3).

Following Thomas Pogge, six basic types of causes of problems and corresponding types of responsibility can be distinguished. First, the political and
economic order legally causes problems: some people are legally prevented
from obtaining food or medicine, for example. Second, the order legally allows
private actors to cause problems: vendors refuse to sell some people food or
medicine, for example. Third, the order coercively and avoidably leads to situations that can cause problems: some people cannot buy food or medicine

because of poverty, for example. Fourth, while the order prohibits private actors' actions that cause problems, it also tolerates them: vendors illegally prevent certain people from buying food or medicine, and law enforcement is inconsistent, for example. Fifth, the order does not help people with accidental disabilities even though it could: people with disabilities cannot access the kind of food or medicine they need under the arrangement, for example. Sixth, the order, although it could help, does not help people with self-inflicted disabilities: people with disabilities do not have access in the arrangement to the kind of food or medicine they need to treat the effects of long-term smoking or other self-harm, for example. Responsibility should be graded according to the order of these scenarios, with the first type of arrangement bearing the most responsibility and the last the least, depending on the extent to which it contributes to the creation of the problems itself or merely fails to prevent their creation.

Leaving aside the more demanding requirements following this model of responsibility, we can now make a demand for at least a minimum of responsibility and ask whether the financial value that most of us in Western countries receive each year in direct or indirect current or historical interactions with developing countries is not greater than the amount of money needed to eradicate global poverty, which is estimated at just one per cent of annual global income. This hypothetical question of minimum accountability cannot ignore also the history of colonial and imperial interventions by Western countries in the developing countries and especially contemporary global economic interventions that need to be institutionally held to account as well.

Let us see what are the contemporary legal obligations concerning these problems (Kamminga and Zia-Zarifi 2000). TNCs are, at least partly, legally limited by powerful states on a domestic level. However, on a supranational level, they are directly regulated by various norms that are mostly non-binding and offering only guidelines that they may voluntarily follow if they choose. The Declaration on the Rights and Responsibilities of Individuals, Groups and Organs of Society is an example (U.N. 1999b). The Norms on the Responsibilities of Transnational Corporations and Other Business Enterprises with Regard to Human Rights are also non-binding, they express only voluntary obligations of TNCs to respect restrictions defined by national and international laws (Norms on the Responsibilities). In the contemporary situation, the relatively effective accountability and regulation of transnational organizations can be achieved only via the strong states' extra-territorial recognition.

It is possible to use an extra-territorial regulation of TNCs and IFIs via states that may and should legally exercise their influence over the activities of transnational organizations in other states. The transnational activities of economic and financial institutions should be accountable through the legal relationship to their home states which are bound by terms of international and global legal contracts, i.e., the development of an extra-territorial application of the international and global norms of social justice is possible. In a host country, particularly in the Global South, where IFIs and TNCs operate, they should be accountable through states where they are incorporated, mainly in the West. This approach helps create a global network of distributive regulation eradicating poverty. It points out the useful fragments of the emerging global legal order of distributive regulation, particularly an extra-territorial recognition of individuals and social groups in foreign countries damaged by the transnational economic and financial organizations. However, now these positive fragments are only part of a limited national/international framework with some supranational overlaps.

It is relevant to mention that while TNCs are non-state agents, IFIs such as the IMF and the WB are in fact multinational or international agents because they are established and organized by individual member nation states. Their actions are mostly transnational. On the one hand, even if TNCs and the IFIs are subjects at least under customary international law and, therefore, have some obligations, nevertheless, they are not legal entities under the International Covenant on Economic, Social and Cultural Rights (ICESCR) and other similar social rights treaties. On the other hand, in the thick version of the treaties' scope of action, we can indirectly impose obligations on them and regulate IFIs and TNCs via the states that signed and ratified the ICESCR and other social rights treaties and are consequently responsible for extra-territorial application of those treaties. Thus, responsibilities of a state beyond its territory should be carried out also in case of a regulation of IFIs and TNCs.

The right to water is a good example. In its General Comment 15 on the ICESCR, the UN Committee on Economic, Social and Cultural Rights notes agreements on trade liberalization, for instance, and requires that it should not curtail the capacity of any country to realize fully the right to water (U.N., 2002: Para. 35). More generally taken, the states as members of international organizations are responsible for their actions concerning the right to water in countries where those IFIs actions take place. This thesis is specified in the comment that says that '[s]tates parties that are members of international financial institutions, notably the International Monetary Fund, the World Bank, and regional development banks, should take steps to ensure that the right to water is taken into account in their lending policies, credit agreements and other international measures' (U.N., 2002: Para. 36; see also Para. 35).

Any activity of citizens, companies and other agents which is taken within the jurisdiction of state parties should not cause a deprivation of any other state to be able to satisfy the right to water for the people who are under its jurisdiction. Thus, it is stated that '[s]teps should be taken by States parties to prevent their own citizens and companies from violating the right to water of individuals and communities in other countries' (U.N, 2002: Para. 33; see also Para. 31).

A similar case is the right to adequate food. IFIS (particularly IMF and WB are mentioned) should focus on the right to food and its protection when they decide about lending policies, measures regarding the debt crisis, etc. Any structural adjustment can take place only if the protection of the right to food is guaranteed (U.N., 1999a: Para. 41; see also U.N., 1990a: Para. 9). Also, the right to adequate housing cannot be compromised by any policies of IFIS (U.N., 1991: Para. 19). At a more general level, it is formulated in the comment on international technical assistance measures which are expected to require that 'protecting the rights of the poor and vulnerable' – in the form of major debt relief – should be a basic aim of the possible economic adjustment program (U.N., 1990a).[4]

Not only the IMF and the WB but also the WTO should be guided by the rule that 'the enjoyment of the right to water is promoted' by their co-operation with the states because the Committee on ESCR takes into account the assistance carried out by 'all other actors' (U.N., 2002: Para. 60). They should incorporate the right to water, the right to food, the right to adequate housing and other rights in their policies. Dealing with the obligations of agents other than states, also the role of WHO, UNICEF, UNEP, UNDP, FAO, ILO, UN-Habitant, IFAD, UNHCR, the Red Cross and non-governmental organizations is recognized as important here.

An application of the ICESCR treaty means in reality, for most of the nation-states, only an innocuous attempt to apply it because interventions of TNCS and IFIS are intense. The International Monetary Fund and the World Bank made some self-reflection and corrections after the 2008 financial and economic crisis but there are not really able to reform themselves and deals with new developments. There is a partial significant exhaustion of the current possibilities of regulation of capital that stem from the older, national level (Sklair 1995; Sklair 2001; Robinson 2004; Harris 2008). At the same time, an attempt to support contemporary legal mechanisms of extra-territorial recognition and

---

4   See also: the *Declaration on Social Progress and Development* (U.N., 1969); the *Convention on the Elimination of All Forms of Discrimination Against Women* (U.N., 1979); the *Convention on the Rights of the Child* (U.N., 1989b); and other U.N. treaties.

create a regulation at the new (supranational) level is being developed. The protests against the transnational capital and other acts of discontent following various kinds of misrecognition show that global interactions of the economic system contain also their reverse face in form of an involvement of local and national emancipatory forces in the transnational changes. We witness the establishment of transnational economic and financial structures, on the one hand, and the beginning of the formation of transnational emancipatory social forces, on the other, which create the strong contradictions and conflicts.

An explanation of the insufficiency of the contemporary international legal mechanisms and emerging attempts of the new supranational and global legal instruments should reflect a transnational potential of social forces in order to avoid a territorial reification, mainly a reification of the nation state and its regulative national and international mechanisms. The transnationalization of the contemporary economic and financial institutions strengthens unwittingly the process of creating motivational conditions in a constitution of the supranational and global legal apparatus. The exhaustion of possibilities to solve the problem of misrecognition on the national level could lead the social forces to claims on a higher, supranational level of recognition.

In other words, before moving to a new, supranational stage of regulation, admittedly, people try to use the possibilities of regulation in the contemporary stage of development and, at the same time, in this way realize its limits. An attempt to use regulations and obligations connected with the individual nation-states requires, first, the identification of recent transnational regulative mechanisms that were not the centre of attention in the past but now could play an important role in the new constellations of the global interdependences. Second, it is important to try to reinterpret and develop these mechanisms in their new empowered role. Third, following limited possibilities of the development of the recent mechanisms, it would probably be necessary to create new supranational mechanisms.

To the extent that transnational corporations, international financial and other institutions are transnational and global, the critical analysis should offer an explanation of the historically evolving distributive regulations from the national to the supranational level and hereby help offer an articulation of claims of the global poor.

Strictly speaking, the current struggles for legal recognition and justice in general try to empower an extra-territorial application of the contemporary legal norms of economic and social rights, and thereby disclose both a limited power and a weakness of the application. The claims on extra-territorial recognition appear to be inadequate demands on a nation-state's solution of the problem but their formulation is important for the explication of social conflicts aiming for a solution in terms of a new supranational stage of legal justice.

The global poor express their dissent by means of their everyday struggles for recognition linked to guaranteeing basic conditions for their survival. An articulation and historical development of extra-territorial recognition of the global poor seem to be an attempt to make the nation-states useful, on the one hand, and an exemplary model that identifies a weak role of the nation-states in the process of empowering transnational economic and international financial institutions, on the other. It shows that it will probably not be possible to solve the problems only through global order with a human face in the form of an extra-territorial 'patch.'

Therefore, it is not enough to explain the extra-territorial possibilities of an application of economic and social rights in relation to the nation-states. It is also necessary to see that contemporary international legal structures are not designed to respond to the IFIs and TNCs forces and to eradicate world poverty, and that new emerging regulative legal structures could be articulated in the supranational space, including not only a responsibility of the nation-states but also a direct responsibility of TNCs, IFIs and other agents.

Finally, we may raise the question, what is the criterion of the creation of new supranational and global legal arrangements. Generally speaking, the criterion could be the ineffectiveness of the nation-states' influence of on the TNCs and IFIs via extra-territorial recognition because the ineffectiveness could motivate the people to struggle for the new global arrangements. At the same time, however, it will be necessary to take advantage of the capacity that states still have and develop it, including applying their capacity for stronger cooperation between states in various transnational, regional and global organisations.

Concerning instruments of the struggle for recognition and justice in general, the question remains open whether they will concentrate on a more or less active or passive, partisan or communicative, hidden or public, easy or complicated approach to formulate an opposition against experienced misrecognition. However, the issue of extra-territorial recognition has to be worked out further in order to articulate a dynamic of the protest against social injustice under globalization.

3   Transformative Revolution and Strategic Structures

While so far I have explained that the struggle for extraterritorial recognition is an effort by the global poor and other marginalized groups to act by using existing legal norms through social movements, civil society and developing countries, which are mostly not powerful enough to influence the rules of global capitalism, in this section, I will focus on the case of a large and sufficiently powerful developing country and civilization that has been able to develop its own strong alternative domestic model while being able to deal with difficult challenges of the model of global capitalism in external relations (Hrubec 2021; Nolan 2019).

I will discuss the model of 'socialism with Chinese characteristics', which, in terms of economic philosophy, is based on a concept that strategically combines public and private ownership and links the market and strategic planning.[5] This model of strategic socialism has made it possible, over the last four decades, to completely eliminate absolute poverty and to substantially raise the living standards of more than a billion people. First, it is necessary to understand this model with its foreign interactions, including its initiatives, especially its global Belt and Road Initiative which is a revitalization of the historic Silk Road and the current largest global initiative in the world. Moreover, in a comparative way, the analysis of this particular model also is relevant to other countries that are developing similar models in their own specific versions, namely Cuba, Vietnam and Laos and partially others[6] (Hrubec 2023).

I begin by explaining the basic motives and principles of China's concept of transformation and opening up to the world starting in 1978; then, I will focus on transformation and opening up using the concepts of transformational revolution and strategic socialism; and finally, I will document the continuation of the historical Silk Road in its modernized update.

Following the methodological account of inert structures (Chapter 2, Section 3), the global poor and their advocates (Chapter 10, Sections 1 and 2) were conceptualised primarily in terms of actors' actions, while strategic arrangements (in this section) is conceptualised mainly in terms of structural change, although, of course, these agents of change act through their government within certain structures and produce various arrangements, including strategic ones. However, the main emphasis in these cases on agency of the poor or structures is obvious. Nevertheless, the structural changes analysed in this section are a case of agency from a government perspective.

---

5   This model is affiliated with a market socialist economy and some authors interpret it also with a concept of NEP (The New Economic Policy) and other similar concepts. What is important is that these are related boundary terms whose constitutive elements overlap partially in different interpretations. Compare (Wei 2010; Long, Herrera and Andréani 2018).

6   There are also international and global limits of these developments (Dominguéz and Rodríguez 2022).

Subjects of change who have advocated for social rights and the global poor have sought to make the most of the existing emancipatory aspects of international and national law structures, specifically extraterritorial recognition, as well as creating the structures of the World Social Forums and other local ones, national and regional forums, and other actors have shaped participatory social programs which has taken place primarily during the two left-wing tides in Latin America.

On the other hand, a version of socialism with Chinese characteristics has been conceived more realistically, so that it could be gradually put into practice as much as possible since the reforms began in 1978 (Wei 2010; Jabbour and Gabriele 2021). The production and trade cooperation between the US and then with other Western and other countries with China, which, thanks to its large socialist centrally organized workforce with a traditionally Confucian work ethic, was built on a structural readiness for convergence that its protagonists developed to their mutual advantage. Chinese workers may have received only unfairly less remuneration and had to work in difficult working conditions at first, but they were able to make great use of it, due to active regulative and social government policies, for the development of the Chinese economy and the gradual significant development of living standards of people in China as well as partly in the world.

In terms of normativity, it can be said that the global poor agenda in most of countries of the Global South is characterized only in selected elements by a greater normative potential, but that, precisely because of its great difficulty, it has so far been problematic to realize more fully. In contrast, the complex structures of the strategic arrangement in selected countries in East Asia were characterised by a more realistic normativity that could be realised in a strategically planned move towards a future more demanding normativity. Therefore, given realism, I will focus the following discussion on both the specific conceptual reflection and, more strongly, on the empirical background that has become a relevant frame of reference in academic and practical discussions on this topic.

As in Western societies, in China, elements of the older historical system that were considered useful have been reformulated and become part of the new modern system.[7] In the case of China's post-1978 development, this was particularly the case with the meritocratic approach (Angle 2012). On the one hand, China continued with the economic and political socialist model that it

---

7   My analysis here is based on my study of the relationship of historical sources to China's contemporary development (Hrubec 2021).

had inherited directly from its predecessors, and, at the same time, it began to modify it fundamentally by deciding, in keeping with historical tradition, to revitalise the selection of students and civil servants and the method of evaluating rural workers on a meritocratic basis.

The transformation of the Chinese model was a major structural change that was shaped by state leaders and implemented by the majority of the local citizens. However, as the personal anchoring of the conception and leadership of this reform is important, it can be said that it was Deng Xiaoping and his associates who began to implement a new specific version of China's development from 1978 onwards. He realised that it was not appropriate to copy another country's system, because every country – and especially every civilisation – is different (Deng 2015). Moreover, he saw the long unfortunate history of the interconnection between the Western system and colonialism. Especially in the 19th century and the first half of the 20th century, Western countries expanded their colonies with the help of military force. These countries collapsed in the fratricidal struggle of World War I and soon after plunged humanity into world conflict a second time. Subsequently, although the Western countries were forced to give up their colonial territories, they did so reluctantly and in the post-colonial period they still sought to dominate the territories of their former colonies, not only economically but also through military interventions.

In China, Deng did not wish to see a Western model combining plutocracy with formal parliamentary democracy. However, he wanted to learn from and be inspired by developments in various countries. He was interested in developments in Asia, specifically modernisation in Japan and the four Asian Tigers, namely South Korea, Singapore, Hong Kong and Taiwan (Vogel 2013). He also sought to learn from developments in the US and the countries of Western Europe, which he saw as the main long-term modernization paths. Subsequently, the experience of the collapse of the USSR, followed by a significant decline in the standard of living of the population, considerable internal instability and the vacating of positions on the international stage, also became formative for him. The Russian scenario was a deterrent and a warning of sorts for China. The Chinese leadership feared that the "shock therapy" recommended by Western countries would far more likely lead to the collapse of the entire system and the disintegration of the country (Nolan 2019). Moreover, even before the collapse of the USSR, he believed that China had to follow its own path, albeit inspired by foreign examples.

Deng began to advocate an approach that would correspond to a new era in Chinese history: reform and opening China to the world. The concept of transformation and opening up to the world (改革开放; kaj-ke khai-fang; gaige kaifang) advocated significant change in both production and trade. China offered mainly its cheap labor and factory capacity, and thus began to form pragmatic economic ties with Western states, especially the United States and Western Europe. The relationship between the internal and external models is an important point. While most developing countries were forced to adopt the Western model in order to be allowed to participate in the global economy at all, China, as a large and strongly organised country, was able to integrate into it while maintaining and developing its own model at the national level.

While each of the international partners in these relationships maintained their own system, some elements overlapped with each other, and new areas of commonality were also created. These interactions also changed the US and European economies. A specific kind of interdependence and the integration of different concepts brought about a new model of transnational and global economy. After all, the deep interdependence of the Chinese and American economies that led to the concept of Chinamerica is illustrated by the recent and current trade and production disputes between the two countries, which would hardly exist with the low intensity of the relationship.

Martin Jacques interprets 1978 as one of the most important years of the 20th century. From a contemporary point of view, it can more strongly be said to have become the most important year yet (Jacques 2018). China has come up with a concept that combines elements of the Chinese and Western economic systems to create a new specific model. In the 20th century, only two years can be named that brought about a new and fundamental economic concept: 1917 and 1978. In these years, new alternatives to the old order were born. However, while the Soviet model built since 1917 went off the scene, particularly between 1989 and 1991 in Central and Eastern Europe and the Soviet Union, the Chinese concept took hold and made China the second largest economy in the world by nominal GDP. By purchasing power parity, China even became the world's largest economy at the turn of 2013 and 2014. Thus, for the first time since 1872, the US lost its leading position. The Chinese economy currently accounts for 18.2% of global output (China's Share of Global GDP 2023).[8]

The bottom line, however, is that this development, which initially necessitated difficult working conditions given the original underdeveloped historical background, as I have mentioned, has gradually brought unprecedented improvements in living standards to more than a billion people in China and many more people around the world through China's international cooperation and trade. This is not just an abstract statistic that ignores the real living

---

8   China's GDP was $150 billion in 1978 and $19.37 trillion in 2023.

conditions of the population, especially the poor. This model has succeeded in lifting 800 million people out of poverty over the last forty years or so since 1978. Considering that China has 1.425 billion people, or 17.7% of the world's population,[9] the Chinese model has achieved a significant improvement in social and economic conditions in the context of the development of human civilisation. At the same time, the government recognises that many people still have to live in modest conditions and, therefore, plans to improve their situation in the years to come.

It is important to identify the guiding principles by which Deng Xiaoping and subsequently other theoretical and practical leaders have approached China's transformation. Deng formulated key principles guaranteeing the stability of the political system and announced a modernisation programme in four areas: agriculture, industry, the military, and science. His key principles took the form of concepts that were based on historical tradition, and then, updated for the modern system. But their deeper meaning is not known to most people precisely because they are not familiar with these historical and updating contexts. One of the familiar concepts was the thesis that one must derive truth from facts, and the other was the thesis that transformation must be carried out in the same way as stepping on stones when crossing a river. These principles are invoked by politicians, researchers and others, particularly in the fields of political economy and economic and political philosophy, even today.

The principle of seeking the truth based on facts (实事求是; *shi shi qiu shi*) appears in the classic work *The History of the Han Dynasty*, which was written in 111. Since then, it has been cited by generations of thinkers and politicians, most notably by Deng Xiaoping in his 1978 speech "Emancipate the mind, seek truth from facts, and unite as one in looking to the future" (Deng 2010). The first reading of the thesis of seeking truth based on facts usually stresses that there is little need to investigate truth in principle and that one should look mainly to the practice of the moment to determine what to do. This is a simplistic view, however, because it would be a relativism that Deng did not advocate. He advocated pragmatism but not unlimited unprincipledness. It was a deeper pragmatic link between theory and practice: principles and flexibility. The measure of truth, then, is practice, as historical methodology demands, and so the concept remains deliberately defined only in general terms. Deng expressed his position as follows, "Only if we emancipate our minds, seek

---

9 According to the Worldometer in 2023 (https://www.worldometers.info/world-populat ion/china-population/).

truth from facts, proceed from reality in everything and integrate theory with practice, can we carry out our socialist modernization programme smoothly" (Deng 2010).

The second principle, which demonstrates the pragmatic assertion and certification of particular concepts in practice, is the historical thesis of crossing the river by feeling the stones (摸着石头过河; *mō zhe shítou guòhé*). It explains the experimental process of moving forward through transformation and opening up to the world after 1978. This famous principle asserts a certain directionality while striving to be able to adapt, and, in a way, it relates to Confucius' classic words from the Discourses (6:23), "The *wise* delight in *water*, the *good* delight in *mountains*. For the wise *move*, the good *stay still*." The above quote illustrates that in Chinese tradition, the study of water dynamics symbolically refers to scholars who act. Crossing the river by touching the stones is not a blind attempt to find the right path. Rather, it is considered an activity for those who are sufficiently educated and meritocratic to be able to experiment.

Both the first thesis, about seeking truth based on facts, and the second thesis, about crossing the river by feeling the stones, imply at first sight an evolutionary, gradualist approach in theory and practice. This sometimes confuses some Marxists who cling to the idea of traditional revolution as the only correct way to rebuild society.

The reality is more complex, however, because social change here has two dimensions. First, Deng knew that socialism in China had not yet developed to the point where it was possible to follow a purely socialist path. He understood the need to complete the development of the economy in various spheres that had never been developed in China. Only then would it be possible to follow a more socialist path. Therefore, the transformational implementation of various economic elements has been part of this era. In this respect, he followed Marx, according to whom the previous system had to be sufficiently developed to move on to the next, more developed system. Otherwise, a regression would occur (Marx 1995). More generally, Marx expressed this with the thesis: "It is not enough for thought to strive for realization, reality must itself strive towards thought." (Marx 2009) In China, then, the missing, developmentally "inferior" elements of the system had to be worked out first in a specifically Chinese way (Tong 2006). Part of Deng's theory is the following thesis:

> We must integrate the universal truth of Marxism with the concrete realities of China, blaze a path of our own and build a socialism with Chinese characteristics ... that is the basic conclusion we have reached after reviewing our long historical experience.
>
> DENG 1984, 3

The Chinese model is not an attempt at ahistorical theory without development. On the contrary, it is a historical theory based on historical and actual development possibilities (Wei 2010; Cohen and Scannella 1997, 38–42).

And second, as I argued in Chapter 2, Section 3, while revolution was previously associated primarily with rapid, violent, unconstitutional and comprehensive change, and transformation with slow, non-violent, constitutional and piecemeal change, a closer study of history reveals that many events that formally fulfilled the definition of revolution did not bring about real fundamental changes, and the situation effectively returned to the status quo after the revolutionary upheavals. Although formally it was a revolution, in reality it was only a transformation. Therefore, we can speak of a revolutionary transformation. In contrast, some other events which at first sight fulfilled more the definition of transformation, in the longer term brought about major revolutionary changes, the changes in the PRC since 1978, for example. It is no coincidence that Deng referred to the economic transformation begun in 1978 as the second revolution (the first took place in 1949). Hence the emphasis on a gradual process of transformation in this particular context does not imply a resignation to larger revolutionary goals (Goodman 2002). It implies, on the contrary, the completion of previous stages of development that have not yet been sufficiently developed, and the promotion of gradual changes with profound, revolutionary consequences.

The beginnings of major reforms in the Chinese economy are linked to changes in remuneration. The desirable level playing field between people in specific reward conditions has in some respects turned into an unmotivating pay leveling that, before 1978, did not sufficiently reward the diverse efforts of individuals and groups. Thus, there was a need to ensure greater productivity by meritocratically introducing greater incentives in order to reinforce pay for work, merit and performance (Wei 2010). The principle of merit-based remuneration, or work done, formulated by several authors, including Ferdinand Lasalle, is typical of the first stage of socialism. The principle of merit is also formally proclaimed by capitalism, although this system is in reality largely based on private property and social status. However, the changes in the Chinese economy have broader coordinates.

In terms of political economy, China's transformation considers two key elements – ownership and resource allocation – in the following way. First, strategic state planning (as well as planning at lower administrative levels) has been complemented by the market. Second, public ownership, especially state ownership, has been complemented by private ownership. This model can be described as strategic socialism because it focuses on strategic elements and not on trying to plan or own everything.

Regarding the combination of private and public ownership, the argument is made that the temporary civilizing tendencies of capital (as distinct from capitalism) must be appreciated. "The simple concept of capital has to contain its civilising tendencies etc. *in themselves;* they must not, as in the economics books until now, appear merely as external consequences. Likewise, the contradictions which are later released, demonstrated as already latent within it." (Marx 1973; cf. Tong 2006) That is, the unleashing of the forces of capital, including private property, has progressive tendencies at first but, at the same time, there are limits inherent in it that will gradually manifest contradictions. Therefore, it is necessary to overcome them subsequently by a further developmental stage.

As for the introduction of the market, Deng stressed that such a move was not incompatible with socialism.

> Planning and market forces are not the essential difference between socialism and capitalism. A planned economy is not the definition of socialism, because there is planning under capitalism; the market economy happens under socialism, too. Planning and market forces are both ways of controlling economic activity.
>
> DENG 1993, 373

On another occasion, Deng said that there is no fundamental contradiction between a socialist system and a market economy (Teng 1985). The market could be added to the planning principle in China quite easily also because it had been regulated and cultivated through meritocratic administration for two long millennia.

The concept of a socialist market economy was officially adopted in 1992. In doing so, the Chinese leadership officially endorsed the changes that had taken place in the economic reforms. A broader concept involving a combination of market and state planning as well as private and public forms of ownership became known as socialism with Chinese characteristics (中国特色社会主义; *Zhongguo tese shehuizhuyi*).

The main focus of the transformation has been on manufacturing for export, which has made China a major global export economy. The Belt and Road Initiative was later able to build on this. Since the late 1990s, under the go out strategy (走出去战略; *zouchuqu zhanlüe*), the government has encouraged Chinese enterprises to invest abroad. The concept of go global has gradually become the main theme of China's overseas interactions.

The transformation of China's economy took hold in a world that was experiencing more complex developments than it was previously anticipated at

Marx's times when he wrote about the sharpening economic and social conditions leading to revolutions. But it was also impossible to rely on the opposite, i.e., on the standard theory of convergence. Nevertheless, the rapid growth of the Chinese economy has enabled some convergence. The question to be answered here is what made this development possible. At the heart of the logic of China's transformation lies the fact that international trade did not take place between two countries with the same system. Western countries, on the one hand, and China, on the other, had different political and economic models. As David Daokui Li illustrates, the fact that the Chinese government was actively involved in managing the economy was a relevant factor in China's rapid development (Li 2018).

In relation to these issues, the Chinese model has included two main features. First, because the government regulated the economy and reinvested heavily in firms, it had a large return on capital; unlike in socially oriented developing countries where more of the finance from oil wealth, for example, was spent directly on citizens' consumption in the short term but little on long-term sustainable economic structural reinvestment which in turn could have provided greater increases in the living standards of citizens who would have been willing to defer their consumption in the short term under undeveloped conditions. At the same time, the government also invested the profits in social development and poverty eradication; unlike in many Western-oriented countries where profits were accumulated in the hands of the wealthiest individuals and large corporations and, then, often spent inefficiently.

But the problem now, according to the Chinese government, is economic inequalities among the people, which represent the opposite problem to that at the beginning of the transition. Of course, the meritocratic approach has its own problems, although in the Chinese system it has brought about a significant increase in the standard of living of the majority of the population and the elimination of absolute poverty. There are projects aimed at improving the status quo, including in areas outside the developed East coast of China, and at developing a more egalitarian approach in the future. In doing so, the emphasis is on China avoiding the middle-income trap that South Korea and Japan, for example, have had to face.

Second, the success of the transformation also rested on the big country effect. The size of the economy matters. China is not just one of the Asian tigers. It has applied a more influential concept, the flying tiger concept. This, in the spirit of Hegel's dialectic of master and labourer, has used the process of learning over the course of history and, in a materialist version of this concept, turned an underdeveloped cheap manufacturing and trading partner into a major country. The complex process of practical learning through reform and opening up of China in this way made it possible to turn the weakness of a developing country in relation to the West into an advantage and to use Western capital and technology for China's development (Li 2018). The continuity with the meritocratic recognition of learning, education and work in the long history of Chinese civilization plays an important role here. This educational process has recently been interpreted as a political philosophy of trust: in selected practice, in theory, in politics and in culture.

One consequence of these transformative processes is the Belt and Road Initiative (the abbreviation BRI; 一带一路; *Yidai Yilu*; literally One Belt One Road), which is an effort to take global interactions to a new level. China modestly describes itself as one of the developing countries, or rather the largest developing country, which deepens relations between countries and regions through the BRI. In doing so, China offers yet a new model of global relations, Global Interactions 2.0. The first version of globalization, which the US and Britain initiated in the 1980s and expanded in the 1990s, not only brought significantly stronger global interconnectedness in various spheres of life but also widespread social problems, economic and political crises, and armed conflicts in many parts of the world.

In its global development, China offers a different model, which, unlike the Western powers, the IMF or the World Bank, does not require cuts in health, education or other areas but instead seeks inclusion and mutually beneficial social cooperation, especially with developing countries. Of course, no project is ideal and, therefore, this one also contains shortcomings that need to be overcome. However, it is not a question of seeking an ideal model but of understanding that many people and many countries support the Chinese model and the BRI because these concepts contribute to economic and social development. Against the backdrop of the problems in the world so far, developing countries in particular identify the Chinese concepts as a positive element of multilateralism that should be supported and further developed through their participation.

The BRI is being built along the old Silk Road from China through Asia to East Africa, Europe and beyond. It represents a contribution to global development that builds on the distinctive long-term evolution of Chinese civilization and other civilizations along the initiative, and on China's transformation and opening to the world in recent decades. Since its announcement in 2013, the Initiative has developed primarily in Eurasia and East Africa but eventually in other regions, including Latin America, making it a truly global project. More recently, we have seen the US unilateralism which, although it has lost much of its hegemony in the world, is still fighting hard to reassert itself. At the same time, China and other countries pursue multipolar and multilateral arrangements, the BRICS+ being a case in point. The BRI, by its very official name, is a plurality or multilateralism of pathways: the Silk Road Economic Belt and the 21st Century Maritime Silk Road (丝绸之路经济带和21世纪海上丝绸之路) with its numerous corridors and projects involving infrastructure and manufacturing capacity, and perhaps also the Polar Silk Road in the future (Hrubec 2021).

There is also a specific pragmatic, materialistic reason behind the creation of the BRI. On the face of it, this is primarily its economic expediency. From the outset, however, the initiative has gone beyond mere economy to encompass many other dimensions of cooperation, bringing connectivity, investment and development to many BRI countries in the areas of economy, research and innovation, security, culture and people-to-people exchanges. People in the participating countries are aware of the results of China's development so far. Developing countries, in particular, take these facts into account when considering their involvement in the BRI.

As the BRI promotes links between different places on Earth, it focuses first on the overall territory, and then, on individual macro-regions and regions of the world. An example is cooperation with Central and Eastern Europe (Hrubec 2017, 34–53) which was created to develop strategic dialogue and cooperation between China and the former socialist countries of Central and Eastern Europe (CEE) and later also Greece. While this cooperation can be conceived of in a narrower sense and on its own, it also forms part of the Belt and Road Initiative in a more general sense, with individual countries further free to join or disconnect as they see fit.

So far, most CEE countries continued to pursue cooperative efforts with Western European Union states and the US, on the one hand, and with China and other countries and organisations, on the other. This will mean a new set of relations with the US, the EU, and the development of relations with the BRICS countries and other larger and smaller states within and outside the BRI.

Many developed countries also see China as a relevant partner for cooperation, although in the last decade the US has been trying to defend its declining global hegemony by revitalising its unipolarism and setting up a bipolarism between China with Russia and other countries, on the one hand (Lukin 2018), and Western countries with states in its sphere of influence, on the other. This has its source in the fact that the US defensively began several years after the 2008 financial and economic crisis and developed a partial closure of its economy during the COVID-19 pandemic through the concept of strategic sovereignty, which became an effort to stand in the conditions of its reduced global economic competitiveness and self-sufficiency. This means that the US will continue to operate globally in some areas (cooperation and competition) and only to a limited extent in others (adversary).

As a result of this partial closure of the US, the concept of strategic sovereignty has been adopted by other powers as well. In China, the element of strategic sovereignty was already present and implemented mainly in the framework of a dual economy (domestic and foreign), as China has a domestic system distinct from the external foreign system. With the new focus on strategic sovereignty, China's economy deals more than before with domestic consumption and opportunities to further raise the standard of living of its citizens. It is, therefore, striving for a balance between domestic consumption and exports. At the same time, it is trying to optimise exports so that it is not overly dependent on the US and other Western countries. Because it stems from the sovereignty in basic and strategic spheres of the economy and satisfaction of the basic and other needs of the population, it also brings an emphasis on strategic public ownership which includes critical infrastructure.

This is also being reciprocated in Western and other countries, especially in the European Union (with the concept of strategic autonomy) and in Russia, not only in the traditional left-wing part of the spectrum but increasingly also in the right-wing, conservative part. The importance of critical infrastructure and other strategic areas of the economy has again become apparent in Western countries during natural disasters, migration waves, the COVID-19 pandemic, and energy and economic crises. At the same time, there is a great deal of political interest in critical infrastructure being publicly owned, or at least under strategically tightened state control, not only for traditional socio-economic reasons but now especially for security and resilience reasons.

These tendencies towards strategic ownership and planning can be seen in terms of economic and political philosophy, regardless of the current tensions between the US and China, as a resignation by Western countries to neoliberal openness in some spheres and as a partial inspiration by the Chinese model, thus, as a partial global convergence in which there is a partial acceptance of the combination of strategic public and private ownership and the combination of strategic planning and the market. The development of this model may be implemented in some countries based on a market socialist economy as in China, and in others on the basis of partial state capitalism as in the USA.

As global changes are not harmonious but conflictual, disputes and conflicts are taking place not only in all the mentioned ordinary areas of the world but also in the Arctic, for example, particularly over raw materials and geopolitical control (Spohr 2020). In the current era, relations between great powers are being redefined and global interactions are changing. Economic, political and armed conflicts can lead to greater territorial fragmentation or, on the contrary, to tendencies to dominate as many parts of the world as possible, or even to global conflict and domination. However, there are ways out and possibilities for a just global order.

4 Overcoming Global Conflicts

The conflicts and dangers of the global state tendencies are linked to both the new technological developments of transport, communication, control, and warfare, on the one side, and unsolved economic, political, military, and cultural struggles against misrecognition on the other. Specifying these problems is a prerequisite for a normative concept of more just and harmonious renewal of post-conflict (post-war or merely fragmented) society in international relations (Cf. Brincat, Lima and Nunes 2012; Derian 2009). Hopefully, in the future, people will live in more local communities, where they will be able to develop participatory producer-consumer organizations based on mutual recognition, equality, justice, and principles of subsidiarity (Sklair 2009a; 2009b; Scheuerman 2012; Delanty 2009; Linklater 2007). Nevertheless, the agents of the global system try to develop their system as much as possible. This can lead to the global state, with its conflicts and dangers of possible world war. And this is the theme of this chapter.

In this section, my main focus will be on both the negative and positive possibilities of the global arrangement and war. Since historical development does not unfold evenly, there is a need to deal with potential global reversals in the form of planetary homogenisation, supranational authoritarian tendencies, and a world war, and to formulate possible normative solutions of just and peaceful arrangement to these.

I focus on the dystopian topic of potential turbulent global trends which opens up considerations of development risks and the normative means of managing these. It would not be enough to analyse only the past and current development trends and their impact on the foreseeable future, it is necessary to indicate the potential outcome of these trends over a more distant timescale. It is also necessary to update and develop in a significant way considerations on difficult future civilisational trends. This means overcoming the inadequacy of the contemporary concept of the international order. It requires a concept of supranational interactions at the level of the whole planet in a substantially stronger integration than that of the global multi-level arrangement, specifically the outcome of integration in a global state. Transnational changes in economic, political and security risks of the global system bring with them the need to react transnationally, and to create not only macro-regional but also global institutional structures which would be capable of eliminating these risks. Global governance, to which no small amount of attention has been devoted in recent decades (Held and Koenig-Archibugi 2005; Held 1995; Held and McGrew 2003), may be only an insufficient weak version of the possibility of a full development into a global state (De Oliveira, Hrubec and Sobottka 2018). And this must be dealt with on a theoretical level.

The real development of an emerging transnational state and various global interactions has advanced to the stage where various forms of a just supranational and global order can be realised. However, with the criticism and demands of many groups of people, the trends have not advanced so far that we can consider the legitimate establishment of a global state (Wendt 1999; 2003; Shaw 2000; Lutz-Bachmann and Bohman 2002; Linklater 2010).

I will focus on the global conflicts and their dangers in the form of the global state from the perspective of a critical theory of global system, based on a concept of the struggle for recognition. While critical theorists of recognition Axel Honneth and Alexander Wendt developed a philosophical basis of social recognition among people in community (Honneth 1996; 2014) and a concept of the global state respectively (Wendt 2003), their analyses have to be reformulated and developed in order to reflect problems of global system, articulated by Leslie Sklair and others (Sklair 2001; Harris 2008; Robinson 2014).

Whereas Axel Honneth works with relatively modest normative future opportunities of the current development and reveals thereby a small emancipatory potential in the development of social recognition patterns, I presuppose a more demanding normative potential, which maps a stronger appropriate critique of the social status quo and the options for a further appropriate future development of recognition. However, on the other side, some authors anticipate such a widespread development of the normative potential of recognition, that they may face the opposite eventual problem: the less proven relationship to the development of the social reality and its social criticism. This can be the case of a theory of recognition developed by Alexander Wendt, specifically his concept of the global state (Wendt 1999; 2003).

A comparison of Honneth's and Wendt's theories of recognition requires in particular a specification of the concept of diachronous development, since their reflections on this point lead to quite different conclusions. In contrast to Honneth, Wendt defends the stronger historical principle of intentional teleology which gives development a more rapid dynamic, namely the establishment of a world state. At the same time, Wendt believes that efforts at security – either by individuals or by whole states – can after reformulation be included in the struggle for recognition category. He maintains that contemporary states may seem in themselves to be relatively stable, but that in a global era and in view of their mutual links that is not the case in reality. The current international order of national states is not sustainable, and it is, thus, necessary to consider what kind of system will replace it. From this perspective, the dynamics of the current development lead to a world state. Wendt explains:

> I argue that a world of territorial states is not stable in the long run. They may be local equilibria, but they inhabit a world system that is in disequilibrium, the resolution of which leads to a world state. The mechanism that generates this end-directedness is an interaction between "struggles for recognition" at the micro-level and "cultures of anarchy" at the macro.
>
> WENDT 2003: 25

Like Honneth, Wendt understands the struggle for recognition as an attempt to mould individual and group interests, this means attempts focused on ideas, but mediated by means of material competition.

Now let us look in more detail at this issue. Wendt first poses the question of whether a global state could be achieved through the mere completion of the internationalisation of political authority that is already occurring in the system, or by reform of the United Nations, the European Union, the International Criminal Court, the World Trade Organisation and other institutions This would mean no institution would have a global monopoly on the use of force. He answers that from the perspective of the concept of the state in the form of the Kantian Pacific federation, such a state would mean only a transitional form, since the system would eventually lead to the monopolisation of force at a global level (Higgott and Brasset 2004; Higgott and Ougaard 2002).

Here the fundamental argument is that the transformation of the present form of the state into a global state will require three major changes (Wendt 2003: 22, 23). First, a world state will require the emergence of a "universal security community" (Wendt 2003: 22). A community of this kind means that the community is based on peaceful and not primarily military resolution of disputes, which presumes that individual states must be able to give up the idea of other states as existential threats. Secondly, the idea of a universal security community is linked to "universal collective security" (Wendt 2003: 22) which is not possible without members of the security community treating threats as applying to all, and also sharing in arranging such security. Thirdly, a world state requires a "universal supranational authority" (Wendt 2003: 23) which would be based on securing a procedure legitimate in the eyes of world society for making decisions about organized violence, which means that states must surrender their absolute sovereignty in this domain.

However, this three-point concept of the transformation of the current form of the state into a global state consists in essence of two points. The first and second points, i.e., a universal security community and the exercise of universal collective security together in effect create a "global common power" (Wendt 2003: 23). The understanding of a global state in its entirety at a fundamental security level is here based on the monopoly on the use of organised violence within a society and recognition of all its members. However, since this is not a transition to an entirely new form of organisation, but merely to a new version of organisation, the main emphasis must be put on the issue of the *new level of the state*. That is on its global characteristic, and also on the *transition* from the national and macro-regional levels to the global level. If, within this framework, we focus on the shape of the global state, there is no need to consider its most developed variants (Haigh 2003; Jones 1999; Nielsen 1987). It is enough to outline a realistically achievable form. A global state may have a decentralised form and be made up of elements arising from the transformation of the current form of the state and its international integration. The existence of a political framework for a universal security community does not require the end of shared autonomy for its individual local units, i.e., states or other entities, indeed they may continue together to develop the existence of the global community. Autonomous local politics and culture can continue to develop even in the event that there will no longer be organised violence under the administration of the local community. Secondly, in principle the armies of local communities may remain the same, since there is no need to create a global army. Armed interventions by the global community would occur as the pre-determined joint interventions of individual country armies or parts of these, as is already the case at regional and macro-regional level today. However, fundamental here would be the subsidiarity of these individual armies to a global intervention based on the global monopoly on organised violence. This does not mean that a global government entirely analogous to national governments would have to exist. Thirdly, a global government would not have leadership under a single person, as at the national level. It could have a more complex collective structure with discussion fora within the global public sphere.

Deudney's argument on the trend towards a global state, the basis for which is a thesis on the *scope* of securing the security of the state, is an inspiration for theoreticians of the global state, Wendt included (Deudney 2000; 1995). Deudney mentions that while earlier states could exist within a limited territory, the development of enforcement technologies has led to a situation in which states are no longer able to ensure their own security. The level of destructiveness of these technologies has achieved such an extent that individual states are no longer able to keep it in check. Generally speaking, if the scope for the use of violence exceeds the previous border of a state, thus increasing long-term conflicts between states, it becomes essential for the state also to increase the extent of its territory, either by joining up with another state or by absorbing it. One can currently focus in on this thesis using Deudney's concepts of a single nuclear world or "nuclear one-worldism" (Deudney 1999; 2000). Nuclear weapons and ballistic rockets have created the prerequisites for the extension of the territorial scope of the state. Just as in the Middle Ages, some states expanded territorially as a result of the invention and application of gunpowder and its associated implementations, now the scope of current enforcement technologies allows and requires exceeding the former territorial extent of the state.

At the same time, the last decade has seen the transcendence of the previous use of nuclear weapons for the purpose of deterring an adversary and has opened up dangerous plans for the real use of this type of weapon in a limited nuclear war, i.e., in limited areas without global escalation (Hrubec 2019, 785–798; Larsen and Kartchner 2014, 3–20). This is the possibility of using smaller nuclear weapons through new technologies that allow more precise mutual control of rival adversaries. High-tech electronic systems that incorporate global communication with big data, precision military navigation and radar, or the internet of things have created the conditions and potential for new applications of nuclear weapons. However, unintended or deliberate expansion of limited conflict into global war cannot be ruled out.

This theoretical interpretation makes new technologies a precondition for the possibility of territorial integration, while historical technological development in general here plays the role of a driving principle stimulating an integrating telos. Nevertheless, this remains merely an external possibility and does not explain the internal conditions with its dynamic of the integrating development of society which depends on struggles for social, economic and political recognition of various social groups. We will find these in Wendt's analysis where he considers two aspects of his teleological clarification of the development of the world state: the first is at the micro level, the second at the macro. An aspect which acts on movement from below to above here has the form of a self-organising process of the struggle for social recognition which is being implemented as a result of technological changes. An aspect which acts downwards from above is created primarily by chaos in recognition in the international space which is so far only partially organised politically and is being institutionalised in legal terms. These two aspects form the internal telos of the security dynamic of development (Wendt 2003: 4).

This exposition can be interpreted as the struggle for social recognition of various social groups within the conflicts of global capitalism against the background of a particular stage in technological development being played out in relatively institutionalised local and national contexts, and in transnational and global conditions which are not for the time being sufficiently institutionalised. Since, in this new period, individual territorial units are no longer fully capable of confronting the military threat from new technologies, able to strike over a wider range of territory than previously, and these units are not able to guarantee the security of their own territory, they must redefine their boundaries in favour of greater global integration and communication. Only in such a framework, limited wars may take place and would not immediately escalate into a global war.

Wendt's concept implicitly accepts the negative aspects of technological development analysed by Horkheimer and Adorno in their classical work *Dialectic of Enlightenment* (Horkheimer and Adorno 2007). However, in contrast to them, Wendt does not go down the road of refusing historical technological development, but on the contrary attempts to develop its positive aspects. Nevertheless, it is not clear from his interpretation why it is necessary to accept dubious technological development. A number of interpretations may be considered.

For the purposes of comparison, one can mention that in his theory Honneth does not incline towards any of these scenarios. Although writing about monitoring the pathological moments in historical development, he does not deal with long-term civilisation technological development, but only with the development of models of social recognition in the modern era, in which he deals mainly with the promotion of positive models of recognition. In recent decades of the development of Western society, Honneth has found ambivalent development, which he calls paradoxes of capitalist modernisation (Honneth 2002). In his interpretation, therefore, this is positive or ambivalent social development and not negative development affecting the technology line directly.

From Wendt's formulations, it may be inferred that he implicitly advocates a thesis on ambivalent technological development, since although critically evaluating both past and possibly dangerous future social developments, nevertheless, he expresses hope for a global state with positive characteristics. Nor need this hope be at odds with the last type of explanation which interprets development as negative. In the 1940s, Horkheimer and Adorno may in the *Dialectic of Enlightenment* (Horkheimer and Adorno 2007), but this analysis was nevertheless focused on interpreting only one negative aspect of their analysis of reason within history.

In spite of this being an aspect to which they ascribed major significance, they did not shut off analyses, albeit fragmentary, of the positive aspects.

In view of the fact that up to now people have not been able to reverse the negative civilisational course of development, it would indeed be a surprise if it were otherwise in the case of the trend towards a global state. But in the knowledge that the options for avoiding further development of the negative aspects of technology are not particularly realistic, one may consider attempts to promote in parallel as many of the positive fragments of reality as possible, and to develop them in a form which would at least avoid some of the current negative aspects, as Bill Scheuerman shows (Scheuerman 2011). Following him partly, I take the view that in this sense one may convincingly cultivate a possibly futile, but potentially self-preservational hope of a positively conceived global state as a last resort. However, this does require that we identify possible risks and the solutions.

Which negative characteristics of a global state might be considered difficult and what might be the normative alternatives to these? First, one must recall the objections of the transnational capitalist state which has been established over the last two or three decades by means of corporations, international commercial and financial institutions and other actors. For the time being, the transnational capitalist state is in the process of formation and is not global. It seeks to subordinate and exploit both the structures of international and transnational firms and institutions, as well as the structures of nation-states (not just Western ones) as its organizational units and the USA as its main centre with the largest military expenditure of any country and with a vast network of hundreds of military bases around the world (Rufanges 2021). In this transnational sense, various imperial structures of the USA and its Western allies are also used (Zhung 2021). Of course, it is a process of conflict not only between national and transnational capital but also between parts of transnational capital which contains many contradictions and competing groups of property and power. At the same time, the promotion of ordo-neoliberalism in the decade following the 2008 crisis has brought with it neoconservative tendencies that reinforce elements of the transnational police and security in the Western world and its peripheries (Robinson 2020; Robinson 2022). NATO is an example of the move towards a transnational state in the military sphere.

Behind the principal problems, which I will now deal with in relation to the degree of danger they represent (homogenisation, authoritarianism, war), stand mainly economic interests, although we must naturally also take into account political, cultural, social and other problems. First, the global state can be called into question in view of the potential *homogenisation* of the global community. The danger here arises from the need or necessity of centralising access to the various component communities of which the global community is comprised. Cultural and political diversity is subordinated to a unifying bureaucratic process striving for ease of administration. The result can be the ideological limitation of cultural and political plurality in the interests of the dominant economic forces.

A counter argument might be the response that a global state will rely only on neutral procedural rules which will not require any specific inclination to particular cultural and political orientations. However, as is well known from the critique of political proceduralism, this counter argument is not convincing. A certain minimum jointly shared political culture and relative economic equality between citizens are a necessary prerequisite for citizens to identify with rules that they are to respect and to act in accordance with them. Thus, a global state requires not only basic legal rules or a constitutional framework, but also their establishment in political culture and economics. All these prerequisites may lead to dangerous homogenising tendencies and to the suppression of the economic autonomy of individual countries mainly in the peripheries of the Global South.

These risks should not be underestimated, a look at the previous history of integration institutionalisations shows us that it is likely that these dangers will arise to a greater or lesser extent (Wallerstein 2006; 2003). Nor however should one overlook attempts to eliminate homogenisation. Just as at national level, there is a subsidiary co-existence of institutions of the national state and institutions at a more local level. In parallel with these the specifics of national and local levels, a global state may, through a federative or co-federative arrangement, exist alongside macro-regional, national and local institutions. A global community may be founded on a multi-level "glocal" arrangement, based on individual local, national, and macro-regional institutions, while retaining individual component cultural and political identities with their particular features in an economically equal environment. Adopting this arrangement means giving up the older idea of the absolute sovereignty of individual nation states or of those macro-regional units today identified as national states.[10] Emphasis must be put on the idea of shared sovereignty, which has for that matter been implemented in practice in the majority of states, whether they acknowledge it officially or not, since the transnational economic and political pressures in a period of global interactions does not allow most states to act in isolation. If they should attempt to act in such a manner, they run into existential problems. The only possible exceptions to this to certain scale

---

10   See Chapter 8, Section 4.

are contemporary macro-regional states, the USA and the BRIC countries, for example. Certain other strong older countries, in Western Europe, for example, in spite of being powers in their own right, are not able to act often in isolation and are forced to act at least partly in concert and to accept elements of shared sovereignty in the EU. This can also be expressed in reverse: every state or macro-region needs to secure its strategic sovereignty, i.e., sovereignty on the fundamental issues of security and self-sufficiency and then, can exercise shared sovereignty in other selected areas with other countries. If, within a global state, there was respect for jointly share minimum legal institutionalisation of basic principles of justice, and if these principles were anchored in various cultural, economic and political needs, interests and values in each country or region and macro-region, there would be the global and subsidiary guarantees and possibility that a variety of models can coexist at lower levels from the macro-regional to the local.

Second, a further and greater danger is the potentially *authoritarian* nature of a global state. The problem here is not only homogenising unification as in the case of the first danger, but the introduction of tyrannical, despotic, or even totalitarian elements. Immanuel Kant and Hannah Arendt have pointed out this risk already (Kant 1997; Arendt 1972). The first stage might be the elimination of politics as understood by Carl Schmitt and his successors (Schmitt 2007). Under this interpretation, the centralisation of power in the hands of a global state would bring about a situation in which no political enemies would exist. According to this interpretation, without any scope for the difference between friend and foe, politics would cease to exist. A greater danger arises from a highly centralised version of the global state and assumes the use of police and military forces in the name of a dictatorship (Robinson 2020), since the politicians of a global state respond to the real or possible danger of chaos or dictatorship by a group or groups by strengthening the powers of the state. Practices introduced frequently or permanently, such as increased surveillance, the limitation of freedoms or the declaration of a state of emergency would here be justified as an appropriate reaction. Then, a global Leviathan would allegedly be a necessary and needed result.

The risks mentioned are possible and some of them indeed are likely. However, Schmitt's questioning of the global state assumes politics only in the categories of a hostile struggle against enemies, and ignores the positive possibility of cultivated debates and disputes over recognition between citizens. Schmitt's concept of the political may indeed be progressively reformulated to retain the idea of conflicts which are necessary to politics, but in the case of the global state, one should rather look at the original version of his concept as a pathological departure from the political and as a repressive attempt to present irreconcilable and violent clashes between foes as the only possible politics.

The objection to the danger of authoritarianism remains, for other reasons. A global state might indeed be the way out of an anti-civic repressive dictatorship which would be suppressed in the name of citizens using authoritarian powers.[11] An authoritarian approach in the name of citizens, which is usually applied at the war times, would be a way out of a transnational or even global *repressive* dictatorship. However, in a situation without the threat of repressive dictatorship and in the absence of a federative or co-federative arrangement with the subsidiarity principle, individual local, national and macro-regional units would be marginalised for no reason. If a global state achieved a strong position, there would be nowhere to run to from its police and military forces, as Arendt points out. The persecution of various groups by the Nazis during the Second World War was not successful largely because Nazism failed to achieve world domination. Cooperation and competition between states and macro-regions are a source of movement and bring about a desirable disturbance of attempts to concentrate power in the hands of the few. However, neither a federative nor confederative nature for a global state with elements of subsidiarity of themselves automatically mean the elimination of authoritarianism. It can only be achieved by the participatory involvement and decision-making of members of the political community. Only their involvement in the various levels of decision-making from the local to the global can eliminate authoritarianism. Participation need not represent the entire system of democratic order, since not all societies on the planet (for example various aboriginal groups such as the Amazonian Indians or the Inuit) prefer this system, nevertheless involvement permits decision-making through a consultative system using the votes of a large number of members of a community, giving legitimacy to the decisions in question. Some current major injustices would be hard to eliminate without global participation. For example, eliminating poverty cannot be achieved without the participation of those affected and without their will, or even against it.

However, such a system must be founded on historically long-term and global establishment of cultural, political, social, economic and other recognition standards based on long-term historical recognition debates. Their basic form would be formulated in a legal framework, in the case of a global state in a

---

11   Compare: "If we are to avoid mass-suicide, we must have our worldstate quickly and this probably means that we must have it in a non-democratic form to begin with. We will have to start building a world-state now on the best design that is practicable at the moment." (Toynbee 1962).

constitutional order, which could limit any authoritarian extremes that might arise from the pressures from various population groups.

Third, the most serious danger of a global state is that it results in *war*.[12] This argument consists of the thesis that any attempt to establish a global police force and/or armed forces must sooner or later result in war since the likelihood of an absolute consensual establishment of forces of law and order is minimal and certain groups will resist sooner or later (Schmitt 2007). Not only groups of people but also some territorial units which will not submit to this planetary enforcement force will resist and will respond with violence to the organised violence of the global state. Such reactions may lead either to limited local and regional wars, or to a world war.

This argument, pointing out a revolt against attempts to establish a global police force and armed forces, is based on the assumption that these forces of law and order are introduced in a manner analogous to the present nation-state which claims a monopoly on violence on its own territory. However, through its federative or confederative order, the global state may be so arranged that it uses, as Wendt proposes, parts of the police and military forces of the individual states, and retains only relatively small executive powers which will be made up of people who come from a wide variety of nations. Although we must consider such a future arrangement realistically and be aware of the possible risks of global armed forces, the current state of affairs where one superpower has a leading role, and several other major powers have a major influence in the UN Security Council is worse than a possible global arrangement with a significantly greater multi-polarity. Whereas today the superpower finances a disproportional part of the world's expenditure on weapons and forces, in the future the situation would be more balanced thanks to a more equal distribution of armed forces across individual territorial units.

The military danger associated with a global state arises also from the way it is set up – gradually, or by revolution. Gradually occurring global challenges could lead to a non-violent gradual establishment – either positively or negatively – of a global state including police and armed forces. However, if a global state was established by a quick violent change and was built on the current authoritarian elements of an already developing transnational capitalist state, resistance to it would naturally be stronger. Nevertheless, if a global state arose only as a just reaction to escalating aggressive conflicts, or even to aggressive local or extended wars, the use of violence might be considered an appropriate reaction by those involved in the establishment of the global state. This

---

12   Cf. with a classic work on just and unjust war (Walzer 1977).

assumption has its basis in human history. Habermas calls this "learning from disasters" (*aus Katastrofen lernen*) (Habermas 1998). He builds on the idea that normally people do not learn the lesson of history or theory, but only after experiencing a disaster are they able and willing to react in a practical way to the challenges of their time. Only the horrors of World War I led to a reflection on heightened international tendencies and to the establishment of the League of Nations. However, some countries never joined, and others withdrew after a period. Its powers were weak; it proved unable to abolish the colonial rule of many countries, nor was it able to prevent World War II. Only the results of World War II, preceded by the Great Depression, forced representatives of the individual countries to set up the United Nations with its greater powers.

One may pose the question of whether there are reasons to believe that humankind will proceed in any way differently than in the past and avoid armed conflict indefinitely. With today's technology, this would mean not only territorially limited wars but also military conflict on a global scale. Are there any reasons to assume that the United Nations can prevent another global conflict? If we disregard the worst-case war scenario, we may similarly ask whether there are any reasons why humanity at the global level should not come to homogenisation and authoritarianism before positive scenarios. It is difficult to respond to these questions and to give convincing reasons. But as in the case of our approach to negative technological development, this should not mean giving up the search or attempts to prevent the negative scenarios, or at least reduce their impact. Even a small hope is still a hope.

The global state is a complex concept with many dimensions. Specifying a global peaceful order requires that we clarify the historical development of the crystallisation of transnational and global critiques of misrecognition and the institutionalisation of recognition. In addition to the historical dimension, we must also take into account economic, social, political, legal, and cultural dimensions. At the same time, it is right to analyse from the assumption that a global state presupposes a global community, but it cannot be limited to a security community. The aforementioned concept of a global state is, focused to the great extent only on global security risks, and the principal legitimacy for the rise of a global state is tied to the resolution of these. It includes a comment on the necessary specification of the political and economic identity of the new territorial unit, so that the new larger territorial unit, in this case the global state, has its own identity and is not composed only of the separate identities of the previous subjects. This presumes that the citizens of individual states progressively become citizens of the world, cosmopolitans, and that they gradually establish the identity of the global peaceful arrangement. But here one should specify what further dimensions such a global order presupposes. This applies not just to the concept of a global state from the standpoint of recognition theory, but to all theories of a global order which attempt to determine positive peaceful aspects of such an order. The formulation of at least some kind of hope within these positive aspects from the perspective of the aforementioned negative and ambivalent global developments requires an articulation of multiple dimensions of the global state in its negative and potentially positive characteristics (Fine 2007; Beck 2006; 1999).

A state that is global only in its extent, but not in its other dimensions (social, economic, cultural, political, legal, etc.) can survive only in a global conflict from whose logic it is conceived. Various versions of wartime order, be they war capitalism, war communism or some other wartime model, can be implemented in period of tense conflict. But after the guns fall silent they are either systematically replaced by peaceful civilian forms of administration, or they attempt to persist. However, after a time they are inevitably removed under the pressure of the introduction of civilian criteria, or they simply implode. The idea of a global state based only on security presumes a too-rapid and problem-free development of global integrational tendencies and the sustainability of these. The concept of development, i. e. the transition from an international order to a transnational and global arrangement, must be enhanced with an analysis of conflict development and peaceful alternative, more refined analysis of the complex historical tendencies of recognition development in its various dimensions. A more detailed working of this analysis and other similarly directed research of international, transnational, supranational and global development trends could be the route to marking out the complex and mutually inseparable strong and weak aspects of the global state. Which on the one hand is a potential threat where it ends in homogenisation, authoritarianism and war, and on the other hand is also a way to eliminate these varying new global dangers. Thus paradoxically, the global state remains both a threat and a hope for dealing with these threats, i. e. a potential of both war and peace. Of course, what particular territorial conflicts might specifically bring about these threats remains a matter of future historical development with randomness to it. In this book, I tried to specify the main lines of adequate argumentation in the basis of a theory of global social justice.

Conclusion: the Principles of a Theory of Global Social Justice

In conclusion, I would like to emphasize the main ideas I have analysed so far and to outline, within an overall explanatory framework, the interrelationships of the various principles of justice I have discussed in different contexts in the three Parts (3, 4 and 5) of the book.

The main purpose of the book was to contribute – just as "one pebble in the mosaic" – to the formulation of the foundations of a theory of society and politics in the contemporary global context, specifically a theory of global social justice. In doing so, I started from a critical perspective of misrecognized persons, i.e., from "below", who oppose antisocial approaches to human beings in theory and practice. I formulated a new foundation for this theory of social justice using the trichotomy of critique, explanation, normativity. The critique of negative phenomena in society not only enables the unmasking of unjust social elements but also identifies significant themes that are subsequently addressed in the explanation of social phenomena, while the explanation of positive fragments of reality then enables their development in normative form. I have identified this trichotomy, whose more complex relations I have developed in the form of explanatory critique, normative critique, critical explanation, etc., in various implicit and partially explicit formulations of critical theory, from its early phase in the 1930s to the present. I have documented that Horkheimer, Marcuse, Adorno, Habermas, Honneth, Fraser, Young, Kosík, and other authors have contributed to particular formulations of this trichotomy and developed their versions of the theory in partially articulated continuity with it. Unlike the authors of other interpretive currents, such as liberalism or libertarianism, these theorists are all aware of the fundamental importance of the critical approach. I have presented a theory that also requires the formulation of other methods that allow for more concrete analyses. First, a transdisciplinary definition of research, in which social philosophy plays an important role in cooperation with political philosophy and the social sciences; second, a conception of the realism of social historical development with several kinds of quasi-universalist value frameworks; and third, a conception of action in structures conceived as processes at several levels of historical analysis, from the interpretation of the actions of individual and group actors, through social and economic institutions to the technological structures of human civilization, including the fundamental devastating consequences for human beings, society, and nature.

The gradual transformation of the paradigms of critical theory in the wake of important paradigmatic turns in contemporary research and society meant the application of trichotomy, first, in subject-object paradigms, and then, in intersubjective paradigms after the practical and theoretical critique of the objectification of human beings as object in the unjust regimes. That is, after the paradigm of work, from whose redefinitions critical theory originally emerged, and the subsequent paradigm of drives, especially sexual drives, elements of trichotomy were present in the intersubjective paradigms of communicative action and recognition. The transformation of the concept of conflicting global interactions into a new role that entails the establishment of a paradigm of global interactions completes the development of critical theory for the time being.

I have applied these founding and methodological specifications of critical social theory to examine efforts to eliminate injustice through struggles against misrecognition and injustice in a global context. First, I conducted a critique of the deficits of the liberal conception of society and politics, which I analysed primarily in the ahistorical and contextual conceptions of liberalism and libertarianism. I have shown that the need to deal consistently with these deficiencies requires a shift from liberal and libertarian theory to an alternative theory of justice. Both theoretical considerations and practical historical experience have pointed to the need for this alternative. It can be recalled that the shortcomings of the liberal order and its inability to withstand the world economic crisis of the 1930s led to its collapse and the imposition of regressive policies with xenophobic, overtly nationalist, and disastrous war consequences. And we do not yet know what the other consequences of the still unresolved neoliberal and neoconservative crisis and the current conflicts will be. I have elucidated alternative theories of justice through analyses of a critical theory of recognition and other critically oriented social theories, and, then, developed them in an intercultural polylogue, a conception of universal rights, social extraterritorial recognition of the global poor, and strategic socialist structures. In my account of liberal, social, and other theories, I have referred particularly to the analyses developed by the seminal authors in these theoretical currents: Rawls, Nozick, Cohen, Fraser, Honneth, Benhabib, Taylor, Young, Wendt, Dussel, Wei, Nolan, Mbembe, and others.

While I have mapped the problems by criticizing the shortcomings of liberal theory, I have opened up the possibility of solving them by means of an alternative theory – critically oriented social theory – which consists of a much more complex analysis of the struggles for recognition and in an adequate conception of the individual in intersubjective relations in a just community.

Now I would like to engage the identification and redefinition of the positive elements of recognition in an outline of principles of social justice theory that can serve as a basic orientation to the issues under study. I will present the principles of justice more systematically from the perspectives to which I have given attention in the book: first, from a social and economic perspective, and second, from a political and cultural perspective. Moral, security, environmental, and other aspects permeate these categories. I will present the following outline of principles of a theory of social justice, for which I offer a more adequate spectrum of principles than liberal theory, in national, transnational, and global frameworks.

Before I elaborate on these principles, it is necessary to ask what role these principles play in a critically oriented social theory. In my account in each part of the book, I have successively analysed various aspects and principles of recognition or, more generally, justice in different contexts according to how the articulation of these principles has crystallised against the background of different critiques of injustice, in explanations of their pre-existing fragments, and in the development of their normative forms. Their formulation and meaning are present in the historical and social frameworks of these very contexts. As I have explained, therefore, unlike liberal theory, critical social theory and similarly oriented social theories do not emphasize isolated principles and do not consider them as crucial, since the chronological and social specifications through which these principles can be identified cannot capture more than an indicative guide to determine the topic. Moreover, in its complete form, as Enrique Dussel follows in the footsteps of his predecessors and summarizes, "Every theory comes later, it is not a priori." (Dussel 2018, 29) For this reason, it is more appropriate to elucidate the principles by outline only (Table 7), rather than to enclose them in slogan-like theses that, then, draw undue attention to themselves. Nevertheless, systematic integration of the principles into a single whole can be valuable, and I will now attempt to offer a basic insight into the issue and the possibilities for further elaboration (in a formulation that starts primarily from below, from a local perspective, from which one then moves on to other levels). Thus, the interpretation primarily serves to systematically break down the principles and not to exhaustively define them. It only remains to add that these normative principles are, of course, not developed symmetrically in society, and, therefore, in explaining them, I emphasize in some cases only political, cultural, social, or economic aspects of the issue.

TABLE 7   Principles of justice

---

1 **Social and economic justice**
    1.1 *Principles of social difference*
        1.1.1 Specific social justice
            1.1.1.1 *Addressing unmet basic social needs*
            1.1.1.2 *Social support for talent*
        1.1.2 Recognition of merit
        1.1.3 Social solidarity
    1.2 *Principles of social equality*
        1.2.1 Equal basic social justice
        1.2.2 Equal institutional social justice
2 **Political and cultural justice**
    2.1 *Principles of political and cultural difference*
        2.1.1 Specific political and cultural justice
            2.1.1.1 *Eliminating basic political and cultural injustice*
            2.1.1.2 *Promoting unique cultural and political activities*
        2.1.2 Recognition of contributions to culture and politics
        2.1.3 Political and cultural solidarity
    2.2 *Principles of political and cultural equality*
        2.2.1 Equal political and cultural freedoms
        2.2.2 Equal institutional political and cultural justice

---

1   Social and Economic Justice

1.1   *Principles of Social Difference*

Starting with social and economic justice, it can be said that the principle of social difference primarily involves three types of differential recognition of persons.

1.1.1   Specific Social Justice

The first two principles of social difference concern specific social justice, which focuses on various special forms of given inequalities that most persons either cannot affect at all or can affect only minimally. It involves supporting people in both their disadvantaged and advantaged positions, which can also benefit other people.

1.1.1.1 *Addressing Unmet Basic Social Needs*

In the case of disadvantage, it is about meeting the needs of socially disadvantaged people who suffer from structural injustices such as poverty, unemployment, homelessness, temporary or permanent disability, etc. The principle refers to the targeted elimination of the negative situation of socially disadvantaged persons by ensuring their security and the fulfillment of their basic social and economic needs, which are linked to their physical and psychological integrity, i.e. by ensuring their protection from harmful interference in the basic realisation of their lives (from murder, rape, torture, etc.) and by providing them with food, water, shelter, clothing, health care, including adequate education, which is necessary for the realisation of the individual's life in a given society.

1.1.1.2 *Social Support for Talent*

The analyses so far in this book have focused primarily on fundamental forms of injustice and the kinds of justice that are related to them. In comparison, social talent support is complementary to these. Recognition in the realm of positive, advantageous status for individuals focuses on supporting persons in society, such as talented students, who, through financial and other support, can develop their talents and benefit not only themselves but also the wider society. This usually involves the provision of scholarships, grants, and other forms of support. An example of the misapplication of the same principle is the continued reproduction of the unjust favouring of groups of people who benefit economically from their unjustified privileged social position. In this context, in recent decades, there has been a so-called re-feudalisation of society, i.e., a greater social hierarchisation.

1.1.2 Recognition of Merit

Another principle of social difference is that of justice in the sphere of inequalities, which are not structurally given to people as objects of more or less passive acceptance, but which people can actively influence by their actions. This is the recognition of merit, which, in contemporary society, mainly takes the form of an appreciation of work or at least the result of work, i.e., recognition of performance. Although meritocracy cannot evaluate the unequal starting positions of persons and their ideological differences in the financial and social valuation of work, it can at least to some extent value, for example, the fact that someone has worked more than someone else, or the type of work they have done.

1.1.3   Social Solidarity

The principle of social difference is also the recognition of persons in situations that resemble specific social justice (relating to the sick, the unemployed, etc.) but, in this case, it is the recognition of persons in situations that do not relate to their basic needs. The legitimacy of the unequal status of people, i.e., the well-being of some and the hardship of others, is also challenged by social conflicts that affect not only the socially weak but also the well-off due to the tensions and dysfunctionality of society. This principle, which contributes to the elimination of social inequalities, is the concept of solidarity with the underprivileged.

1.2   *Principles of Social Equality*

Moving now from principles of difference to principles of equality, two types of social and economic equality can be identified: equal basic social justice and equal institutional social justice.

1.2.1   Equal Basic Social Justice

The principle of equal basic social justice primarily involves the recognition of physical and psychological needs, but unlike the principle of difference (Section 1.1.1.1), which refers to specific, most vulnerable individuals and groups, the principle of equality seeks to provide basic social provision across the board for all persons. While it cannot often provide for specific needs (even of specific groups of people, let alone individuals), it can set basic conditions (for example, through a universal basic income) which, then, need to be supplemented by other types of principles. Just as it is the case with equal access to the fulfillment of basic physical and psychological needs, which are a priority in terms of human survival, so it is concerning other social needs that the priority of equal fulfillment of needs relating to the basic social dignity of individuals or groups of individuals is also a priority.

1.2.2   Equal Institutional Social Justice

The second principle of social equality is about ensuring social and economic justice in a *systemic institutional* way, not only through redistribution, but also, in a more demanding version, through a share of property, including public property, which enables people to self-realise also in the economic sphere. Since the redistribution that other kinds of social principles usually work with is intricately mediated and makes the person still dependent on redistribution, people formulate the requirement to ensure each person an equal claim to external property resources and, thus, also an institutional means (formulated by this principle) to satisfy his or her internal needs.

2 Political and Cultural Justice

2.1 *Principles of Political and Cultural Difference*

The second area in the discussion of equality and difference concerns the political and cultural sphere. Three types of cultural and political difference can be distinguished.

2.1.1 Specific Political and Cultural Justice

Similar to the first two principles of social difference, it is the recognition of persons in cases of elimination of *currently given* inequalities that could hardly be influenced by most social groups and individuals.

2.1.1.1 *Eliminating Basic Political and Cultural Injustice*

The first of these principles is about addressing the existing basic injustice of politically or culturally marginalised persons. Although political justice does not include all persons even today (it does not yet include, for example, immigrants to a large extent), most persons demanding justice are only formally, but not in reality, recognized in most societies. Formally, it is often no longer a question of eliminating injustice in the form of *negative discrimination*, such as racial discrimination, but of *actually* eliminating negative discrimination. In recent decades, recognition of specific political needs has also come to mean justice that focuses on *positive discrimination* or affirmative action towards marginalised people, especially women and ethnic and cultural minorities, who, given existing negative discrimination, would not be helped much by mere equal recognition, as it would only reproduce existing injustices, and therefore seek affirmative action. This includes, for example, the struggle of African Americans for their civil rights, support for the promotion of their greater political representation in various political institutions, the provision of quotas for the representation of women in various institutions, etc.

2.1.1.2 *Promoting Unique Cultural and Political Activities*

Second, specific cultural and political justice is not only about redressing injustice (Section 2.1.1.1) but also about supporting potentially valuable cultural and political projects, be they those of minority or majority populations. Here, grant support for projects (magazines, theatres, etc.) with potential cultural benefits is particularly widespread. However, today this kind of support hardly applies officially to political activities, although political subjects that are legitimised by the majority society as potentially beneficial are supported by the public service media, for example, but often very unevenly and according to ideological criteria, so that it is a pseudo-justice.

2.1.2   Recognition of Contributions to Culture and Politics

In cases of recognition of the contribution to culture, the following is imple-mented similar justice as in the previous case of support for everyday cultural activities, but now not as a potential contribution, but mostly as recognition of an already achieved performance, e.g., appreciation of already written books, realised architectural works, etc. In the political sphere, for example, the practice of financially rewarding already successful political parties that have, for example, made it into parliament or other representative bodies is prevalent, but this reproduces the existing distribution of political parties, and puts small and new parties at a disadvantage. However, support for political entities for their merits, for their inter-election activities, for the successful implementation of an election campaign, and for the promise of a political programme that has been appreciated by the voters in the elections, can also be implemented fairly. This principle applies not only in politics in the narrow sense but also in high state offices (including ministries, etc.), which are closely linked to politics, where people are promoted on merit according to their edu-cational background, their experience, how they have proved themselves in carrying out their tasks, etc.

2.1.3   Political and Cultural Solidarity

Another kind of principle of difference in the cultural and political sphere is equity, which is analogous to the principle of social solidarity. It is not about providing basic needs for the survival or, at best, mere subsistence of culturally and ethnically defined groups of people, as in the case of Section 2.1.1.1, but about reducing the greater inequalities. For example, supporting cultural proj-ects (magazines, festivals, theatres, etc.) of different culturally and ethnically defined groups of people to develop them in the context of other dominant cultural patterns allows for the revitalisation and strengthening of the cultural activities of hitherto disadvantaged groups of people who may find it difficult to survive in the environment of the dominant culture. In the political sphere, affirmative action towards persons from disadvantaged minority groups in cases of elections to various councils can be a similar case, but this time not in terms of fulfilling basic recognition (Section 2.1.1.1) but in terms of solidarity that seeks broader justice.

2.2   *Principles of Political and Cultural Equality*

These principles consist of the universal recognition of persons in their basic political and cultural needs.

2.2.1   Equal Political and Cultural Freedoms

While the cultural and political difference principle (Section 2.1.1.1) addresses disadvantaged individuals and groups, this principle provides equal non-addressive basic justice that also serves as a condition for further cultural and political recognition of persons. However, because it is unable to provide for the specific needs of the most disadvantaged, it must be complemented by other types of principles. In the political sphere, the principle of equality primarily means ensuring the right to freedom of speech, assembly, strike, etc. In the cultural sphere, it may mean the renovation of cultural facilities (theatres, cinemas, etc.), for example. This area also includes the various cultural preconditions of political life.

2.2.2   Equal Institutional Political and Cultural Justice

In contrast to ensuring a certain basic cultural and political equality, the second principle of this kind of equality lies in the recognition of persons in the systemic institutional provision of political and cultural equality. In the sphere of politics, it is the institutionalisation of political (and civil) freedoms, which in a more demanding version means the institutionalisation of freedoms into the system of democratic organisation. It is, for example, a blanket guarantee of the equal opportunity of every individual to be elected or appointed to office and to political positions. However, as in the above cases, a blanket guarantee does not guarantee actual realisation and must therefore be complemented by other principles.

· · ·

Now I will follow up on the analyses I have made by recalling a few relevant points and making additional clarifications as to which normative principles, from the perspective of liberal theory and critically oriented social theory, are currently being realized or have the normative potential for development and realization from a local framework to a global framework, although this account cannot be an exhaustive list of the principles of justice that I have addressed in the various sections of the book. It can be said that Rawls focuses on only a few principles in his liberal theory at the national level, and then only in a reduced form and in a different order of priorities (in the political sphere, Section 2.2.1 and Section 2.2.2; in the social sphere, he analyses partly Section 1.1.3 in his principle of difference). In his political liberalism, however, he then carries out a fundamental reduction to elimination in the area of social justice (Section 1.1.3). In contrast, theories of social recognition, developed each in their way by Honneth, Taylor, Fraser, Young and others, deal with particular aspects and types of recognition of almost the whole range of principles I have examined, but develop only some of them, and in ways that contain various dilemmas. For example, Honneth's analysis of national and local level, according to which the state concentrates on equal recognition whereas civil society concentrates on differential recognition, is too simplistic, and furthermore does not capture equal justice in civil society or differential justice in the state.

I have formulated the analyses of local and national justice so far concerning the context of Western societies and in the intercultural polylogue, trying to both identify aspects and principles of justice in the proposal that could be universally shared and to open up, at least in a first preview, non-Western perspectives (Chinese, Latin American, African, Islamic, etc.). These analyses are intended to enable other Western partners in the intercultural polylogue, as well as partners from other cultures, civilizations, and systems. In Parts 3 to 5, I have attempted to show, through my redefinition, several patterns of justice in turn, which I have now summarized in the above principles (except for Section 1.1.1.2 and Section 2.1.1.2, which are here additional categories in the system of justice).

To recall my analysis of the deficits of international liberal theory, Rawls' international liberal theory emphasizes equal basic political freedoms (Section 2.2.1) and, in a non-Western context, omits more demanding political requirements, including democracy, because of intercultural tolerance (Section 2.2.2). In the social and economic sphere, it marginally provides, contrary to its premises, only limited solutions to the most basic social needs (Section 1.1.1.1), with the intention and aim of achieving a political order that is acceptable from the point of view of liberal theory (in terms of instrumentalizing and limiting social justice for political purposes). However, even this reduced intention cannot be realised, since liberal assumptions are the source of the individual's lack of embeddedness in the community and, thus, his or her weak motivation to participate in the political order, including the resolution of social issues. The deficit is also an underestimation of global economic pressures, drastic global economic inequalities, the poverty of billions of people, and the severe social hardship of hundreds of millions of people. Liberal deficits run into the problems of national liberalism, whose international theory is incapable of addressing social inequalities and other issues that transcend nation-state boundaries. The shortcomings of national theory and the consequent shortcomings of international theory point to the need to move to a global theory.

It is for this reason that I have not emphasized the need for fundamental differences between national and international justice in the social field, but rather, because of the current marginalized justice beyond the nation-state, I seek to highlight the need for contextuality while maintaining a discontinuous version of global justice with an emphasis on social and inter-cultural approaches. At a time of fundamental social inequalities and mass social hardship, the focus should be on connections rather than seeking national constraints on justice. Since national and related international solutions to justice are not sufficient, I have focused on other forms of justice that go beyond the nation-state. Justice beyond the nation-state, then, is not only about a set of principles but also about the levels of the principles of justice on which they are realized. Recognition theory offers a relatively appropriate approach to the notion of mutual recognition between states, but it should also go beyond interstate recognition. The turn to transnational justice, however, cannot be made only mechanically and ahistorically in a critical social theory. I have analysed the historical developments towards justice beyond the state concerning the ethical and legal norms that have been extended so far: mainly concerning supranational integration, in particular to the different versions of macro-regional integration at the intersection of internationalism and supranationalism.

However, I have articulated in particular more demanding normative forms of justice that transcend the nation-state, namely justice of intercultural polylogue, social extraterritorial recognition, and foreign interactions of strategic socialism, in an attempt to extend and transcend international justice. Intercultural justice and social extraterritorial justice demonstrate the transition from international justice to global justice, since, on the one hand, they are based on international arrangements, but on the other hand, they also refer to broader entities than nation-states and require the articulation of new forms of justice. Intercultural and intercivilizational conflicts and their elimination through polylogue between different groups of people open up space for the articulation of transcultural and transcivilizational overlaps and the creation of consensus and mutual recognition of basic political and cultural values. In the current institutions that transcend national boundaries (especially the United Nations), the realization of the demands of justice has so far been limited; at least basic political rights are demanded through Section 2.1.1.1 and Section 2.2.1, some of which, however, are articulated in different interpretations in different political and cultural circles, and justice (Section 2.1.2) is partially realized in the area of cultural heritage recognition (e.g., via UNESCO). Western, Chinese, Latin American, African, Islamic and other formulations of commonly shared values and their legal codification lead to the assertion of various transculturally shared basic human rights in an intercultural polylogue, due to intercultural tolerance only in a very partial institutional form (Section 2.2.2) which institutionalizes in Section 2.2.1. Thus, the assertion of real demands for the rejection of interventions in political systems – which also refers to the institutional form – means to some extent that the plurality of political systems is respected (although in practice these interventions still occur).

Alongside these *political and cultural* dynamics of development, I also highlight the *social and economic* dynamics of struggles for justice in the area of extraterritorial recognition of social human rights developed by socially misrecognized groups. Struggles for social and economic justice are more developed as they seek to meet basic survival needs. In my analysis of extraterritorial social justice, which transcends conventional international relations by the transnational scope of legal recognition, I have emphasized in particular the elimination of the deprivation of basic social needs (Section 1.1.1.1 with references to Section 1.2.1), which in current practice is mostly only partially realized via humanitarian aid actions in cases of famine, etc. At the same time, however, I have opened up extraterritorial justice to the social actions that are necessary to eliminate social inequalities in development aid (Section 1.1.3 and potentially also other principles). Criticism of inequality in the economic sphere is directed primarily at the very unequal recognition of workers' performance in developed and developing countries (Section 1.1.2). For the time being, however, the principle that provides an institutionalised solution to externalisation (Section 1.2.2) has not been implemented at the international and global level, although the criticism so far already opens up space for the formulation of demands for the application of this principle. However, at the macro-regional level, strategic external ownership for the purpose of equality is already conceived as public in some cases within a large country that is also a civilization.

Concerning the order of the principles, I can state, in relation to the dialogue models, that in terms of the third and fourth models mentioned above, which are linked to my values, I would consider it desirable to implement all the principles in parallel, but I believe that their order should correspond to the demands of the persons who, in the practical struggles for social, intercultural and other justice, seek to implement them. Such a determination of order can only be made concrete in the context of an analysis of the long-term historical tendencies of the development and crystallization of kinds of justice, as I have tried to show in the course of my exposition in the chapters of the book. From this perspective, it can be noted that the principle of basic social needs that are related to survival (Section 1.1.1.1) should take precedence, even in a global context, for example, over a principle that only ensures greater equality (Section 1.1.3). For analogous reasons, in the context of struggles for justice for the global poor, principle Section 1.1.1.1 should take absolute priority over all other principles. In sum, since justice grows primarily out of a critique of injustice, the order in advancing the principles usually takes into account the (social, economic, political, and cultural) kinds of principle of difference first, and those that ensure basic justice (Section 1.1.1.1 and Section 2.1.1.1). However, the other ranking is a complex issue that needs to be addressed in more detail by further analyses and comparative readings of the individual analyses in each chapter, which cannot be replaced by a mere enumeration of principles.

•••

The principles listed in Table 7 can be developed at different territorial levels, which for simplicity can be defined into at least three types: national, transnational or (macro)regional, and global. However, they contain a more complex structure that also includes local, intercultural and other levels and aspects that I have analysed in this book. I have explored these issues with an emphasis on identifying problems and starting points in Western countries, Latin America, Africa, and China. In doing so, I have focused on the relationship between pluralism and universalism from a cultural and political justice perspective, looking at the interconnection between the two themes, namely, the interplay between acting within the plurality of the intercultural and intercivilizational polylogue, on the one hand, and the structure of universal rights, on the other. Then, from the perspective of the pursuit of social and economic justice, I focused on the identification of the global poor and social movements in Africa and Latin America as agents of social change and on their efforts to extraterritorially recognize the global poor within international law. While these changes are still in their early stages of development, the structural changes implemented via the market socialist economy in China with its strategic domestic and global interactions have made significant inroads and are co-shaping the multilateral world order. As these social structural changes have brought about the lifting of hundreds of millions of people out of poverty and pursued further development, many countries of the Global South have recently been cooperating with China and other BRICS countries. However, unipolar and bipolar tendencies promoted globally by the US and unresolved potential global conflicts are still catching up. Depending on these trends, it is important to monitor threats of macro-regional and global homogenization, authoritarianism, and war. This also brings us, in an escalated global form, to potential environmental collapse which is a threat also in smaller conflicts than a world war. In sum, in the very long run, intercultural, extraterritorial social and strategic (in)justice has been undergoing a gradual evolution (which, of course, takes place in a non-linear way, with different dimensions coming into conflict with each other) from international (in)justice to (in)justice at the macro-regional, transnational and global levels.

The book intends to contribute to conflict resolution and post-conflict ordering in a new era in the pursuit of global justice. Overall, in my articulation of the basic moments of a theory of global society and politics, I have attempted to contribute at least in part to the articulation of efforts to promote global social justice, whether they be alternatives of democratic socialism, socialist democracy, or other such alternatives that draw on critical social theory and other sources from different parts of the world.

From different perspectives of historical interpretation, however, one must also ask whether and to what extent such a theory, even if linked to practical struggles for justice, can help promote justice in practice in the present or only in structural or systemic change in conflict and post-conflict situations. As I have already suggested above, historical experience to date demonstrates the sad awareness that the redress of human affairs is usually not yet very much carried out based on critical deliberation about their existing and desirable arrangements but only as a result of lessons learned from disasters. The constancy of human genetic makeup and cultivation over twelve thousand years of human civilization has not yet brought about significant desirable change in conflict resolution but rather has led to technocratic control of internal and external nature. Genetic manipulation, automation, and artificial intelligence can be expected to influence humanity's conflict evolution in many ways. Meanwhile, critically oriented social theory is becoming a marginal phenomenon in times when people submit to injustice, either out of resignation or in the odd hope that everything will be resolved later in some cataclysm. Unfortunately, it seems, to speak with Hegel, that it is usually only via war that people face "the stabilisation of finite institutions; just as the blowing of the winds preserves the sea from the foulness" (Hegel 1952). Regional conflicts and wars, or even a world war, can lead to the establishment of a global dictatorship, the elimination and replacement of which by global justice would in the future require a theory of global social justice capable of offering both a critique and explanation of the situation and a normative schedule for further development. A critically oriented theory, according to Marx, will only be able to specify and apply itself when it meets social and economic practice: "The weapon of criticism cannot, of course, replace criticism of the weapon, material force must be overthrown by material force; but theory also becomes a material force as soon as it has gripped the masses" (Marx 2009). It should be jointly formed and shared by people from all parts of the world, including Latin America, Asia, Africa, Europe, and North America.

References

Adorno, T.W. 1941. „Veblen's Attack on Culture". *Studies in Philosophy and Social Science*, IX, 389–413.

Adorno, T.W., Frenkel-Brunswik, E., Levinson, D., and Sanford, N. 1950. *The Authoritarian Personality*. New York: Harper.

Adorno, T.W., Horkheimer, M. 2007. *Dialectic of Enlightenment*. Stanford: Stanford University Press.

Albert, M. 2003. *Parecon*. London: Verso.

Alcoff, L.M., Mendieta, E., eds. 2000. *Thinking from the Underside of History. Enrique Dussel's Philosophy of Liberation*. New York – Oxford: Rowman and Littlefield.

Ali, T. 2008. *Pirates of the Caribbean: Axis of hope*. London – New York: Verso.

Al-Jabri, M.A. 2011. *The Formation of Arab Reason. Text, Tradition and the Construction of Modernity in the Arab World*. London: I.B. Tauris.

Allen, A. 2016. *The End of Progress: Decolonizing the Normative Foundations of Critical Theory*. New York: Columbia University Press.

Allen, J. 1998. "The Situated Critique or the Loyal Critique? Rorty and Walzer on Social Criticism". *Philosophy and Social Criticism* 24, 6, 25–46.

Angle, S.C. 2002. *Human Rights and Chinese Thought: A Cross-Cultural Inquiry*. Cambridge: Cambridge University Press.

Angle, S.C. 2012. *Contemporary Confucian Political Philosophy, Toward Progressive Confucianism*. Cambridge: Polity Press.

Anheier, H., Kaldor, M., Glasius, M. eds. 2006. *Global Civil Society* No. 7.

An-Na'im, A.A. 2002. *Cultural Transformation and Human Rights in Africa*. London: Zed Books.

An-Na'im, A.A. 2005. "The Interdependence of Religion, Secularism, and Human Rights. Symposium Talking Peace with Gods", Part 2. *Common Knowledge*, 11, 1, 56–80.

An-Na'im, A.A., ed. 1992. *Human Rights in Cross-Cultural Perspectives: A Quest for Consensus*. Philadelphia: University of Pennsylvania Press.

Apel, K.O. 1993. „Das Anliegen des anglo-amerikanischen Kommunitarismus in der Sicht der Diskursethik". In M. Brumlik, H. Brunkhorst, Hrsg., *Gemeinschaft und Gerechtigkeit*. Frankfurt: Fischer, 149–172.

Archibugi, D., Held, D. 1995. *Cosmopolitan Democracy: An Agenda for a New World Order*. Cambridge, Polity Press.

Arendt, H. 1972. *Crisis of the Republic*. Harcourt: Mariner Books.

Arnason, J.P. 2003. *Civilizations in Dispute. Historical Questions and Theoretical Traditions*. Leiden, Boston: Brill.

Arnason, J.P., Hrubec, M., eds. 2016. *Social Transformations and Revolutions*. Edinburgh: Edinburgh University Press.

Atwood, M. 2005. *The Penelopiad.* New York: Knopf.

Bache, I., Flinders, M., eds. 2004. *Multi-level Governance.* Oxford: Oxford University Press.

Baker, C.E. 2002. *Media, Markets, and Democracy.* Cambridge: Cambridge University Press.

Balibar, É. 2011. „Structure. Method or Subversion of Social Sciences?" *Radical Philosophy*, 165, Jan/Feb, 17–22.

Baran, P.A. 1957. *The Political Economy of Growth.* New York, Monthly Review Press.

Barry, B. 1995. "John Rawls and the Search for Stability". *Ethics*, Vol. 105, No. 4, July.

Barry, B. 1999. *Theories of Justice.* Berkeley: University of California Press.

Bary, T. de, Tu, W. 1998. *Confucianism and Human Rights.* New York: Columbia University Press.

Bauman, Z. 1989. *Modernity and the Holocaust.* Ithaca, New York: Cornell University Press.

Beck, U. 1992. *Risk Society.* London: SAGE.

Beck, U. 1999. *World Risk Society.* Cambridge: Polity.

Beck, U. 2005. *Power in the Global Age: A New Global Political Economy.* Munich: Polity Press.

Beck, U. 2006. *Power in the Global Age: A New Global Political Economy.* Oxford: Polity.

Beitz, C. 1979. *Political Theory and International Relations.* Princeton: Princeton University Press.

Beitz, C. 1999. International Liberalism and Distributive Justice, *World Politics* 51.

Beitz, C. 2003. What Human Rights Mean. *Daedalus*, 132, 1, 36–44.

Bell, D. 2008a. *China's New Confucianism. Politics and Everyday Life in a Changing Society.* Princeton, Oxford: Princeton University Press.

Bell, D.A. 2000. *East Meets West. Human Rights and Democracy in East Asia.* Princeton: Princeton University Press.

Bell, D.A. 2006. *Beyond Liberal Democracy. Political Thinking for an East Asian Context.* Princeton, Oxford: Princeton University Press.

Bell, D.A., ed. 2008b. *Confucian Political Ethics.* Princeton – Oxford: Princeton University Press.

Bell, D.A., *The China Model: Political Meritocracy and the Limits of Democracy.* Princeton: Princeton University Press 2016.

Benhabib, S. 1992. *Situating the Self.* New York: Routledge.

Benhabib, S. 1996. Toward a Deliberative Model of Democratic Legitimacy. In S. Benhabib, ed. *Democracy and Difference. Contesting the Boundaries of the Political.* Princeton: Princeton University Press.

Benhabib, S. 2002. *The Claims of Culture: Equality and Diversity in the Global Era.* Princeton: Princeton University Press.

Benhabib, Seyla. 1986. *Critique, Norm, and Utopia.* New York: Columbia University Press.

Benjamin, J. 1988. *The Bonds of Love. Psychoanalysis, Feminism, and the Problem of Power.* New York: Pantheon.

Benjamin, N. 1973. Civilizational Complexes and Intercivilizational Encounters. *Sociological Analysis*, 34, 2, 79–105.

Berger, P. 1983. On the Obsolescence of the Concept of Honour. In: Hauerwas, S./ MacIntyre, A. (eds.), *Revisions: Changing Perspectives in Moral Philosophy*. Notre Dame: University of Notre Dame Press, 172–181.

Bible. Grand Rapids: Zondervan (2019).

Birken, L. 1999. Freud's "Economic Hypothesis": From Homo Oeconomicus to Homo Sexualis. *American Imago*, 56, Winter, 4, 311–330.

Blum, L.A. 1994. "Multiculturalism, Racial Justice, and Community: Reflections on Charles Taylor's 'Politics of Recognition'". In L. Foster and P. Herzog, eds. *Defending Diversity: Contemporary Philosophical Perspectives on Pluralism and Multiculturalism*. Amherst: University of Massachusetts Press, 175–205.

Blum, L.A. 1998. "Recognition, Value, and Equality". *Constellations*, 1, 53–57.

Boron, A.A., Klachko P. 2023. *Segundo turno. El resurgimiento del ciclo progresista en América Latina*. La Habana: Editorial de Ciencias Sociales.

Borradori, G. 2004. *Philosophy in a Time of Terror: Dialogues with Jurgen Habermas and Jacques Derrida*. Chicago: University of Chicago Press.

Bourdieu, P. 1977. *Outline of a Theory of Practice*. Cambridge: Cambridge University Press.

Brierly, J.L. 1963. *The Law of Nations*. Oxford: Clarendon Press.

Brincat, S., Lima, L., Nunes, J., eds. 2012. *Critical Theory in International Relations and Security Studies*. London and New York: Routledge.

Brink, B. van den, Owen, D., eds. 2007. *Recognition and power: Axel Honneth and the tradition of Critical Social Theory*. Cambridge: Cambridge University Press.

Brown, C. 2000. „Cultural Diversity and International Political Theory: From the Requirement to 'Mutual Respect'?" *Review of International Studies* 26: 199–213.

Brumlik, M., Brunkhorst, H. 1993. *Gemeinschaft und Gerechtigkeit*. Frankfurt: Fischer, 149–172.

Brzezinski, Z. 2005. *The Choice: Global Domination or Global Leadership*. New York: Basic Books.

Buchanan, A. 1999. "Recognitional Legitimacy and the State System". *Philosophy & Public Affairs* 1: 46–78.

Buchwalter, A. 2013. "Honneth, Hegel, and Global Justice". In T. Burns, S. Thompson, eds. *Global Justice and the Politics of Recognition*. London: Palgrave Macmillan, 23–47.

Buck-Morss, S. 2009. *Hegel, Haiti, and Universal History*. Pittsburgh: University of Pittsburgh Press.

Burchill, S., Devetak, R., Linklater, A. et al. 2001. *Theories of International Relations*. London: Palgrave.

Burnham, J. 1972, orig. 1941. *The Managerial Revolution*. Westport: Greenwood Press.

Burns, T. 2013. "Hegel, Cosmopolitanism, and Contemporary Recognition". In T. Burns, S. Thompson, eds. *Global Justice and the Politics of Recognition*. London: Palgrave, 64–87.

Burns, T., 2001. "Recognition Versus Distribution: Three Works on Equality". *Contemporary Politics*, 7, 4, 319–330.

Burns, T., Thompson, S., eds. 2013. *Global Justice and the Politics of Recognition*. London: Palgrave.

Carens, J.H. 2010. *Immigrants and the Right to Stay*. Cambridge, MA: MIT Press.

Carens, J.H. 2015. *Ethics of Immigration*. Oxford: Oxford University Press.

Chan, J. 1999. "A Confucian Perspective on Human Rights for Contemporary China". In J.R. Bauer, D. Bell, eds. *The East Asian Challenge for Human Rights*. Cambridge: Cambridge University Press, 212–237.

Chan, Kwok-bun. 2005. "Prologue: Chinese identities, ethnicity and cosmopolitanism", "Rethinking Chinese ethnicity". In Kwok-bun. Chan, *Chinese Identities, Ethnicity and Cosmopolitanism*. London, New York: Routledge, 2–6, 14–34.

Chase-Dunn, Ch., Lerro, B. 2013. *Social Change: Globalization from the Stone Age to the Present*. Boulder: Paradigm Publishers.

"China's Share of Global GDP. Percentage share of global GDP in 2022". *World Economics*, 2023. https://www.worldeconomics.com/Share-of-Global-GDP/China.aspx (visited June 15, 2023).

Chodorow, N., *Feminism and Psychoanalytic Theory*. New Haven: Yale University Press 1989.

Chumakov, A.N. 2010. *Philosophy of Globalization*. Moscow: Maks Press.

Cohen, G.A. 1992. Incentives, Inequality, and Community. In G. Peterson ed., *The Tanner Lectures on Human Values*, Vol. 13. Salt Lake City: University of Utah Press.

Cohen, G.A. 1995. *Self-ownership, Freedom, and Equality*. Cambridge: Cambridge University Press.

Cohen, G.A. 1999. Expensive Tastes and Multiculturalism. In: R. Bhargava, K.B. Amiya and R. Sudarshan, eds. *Multiculturalism, Liberalism and Democracy*. New Delhi: Oxford University Press, 80–100.

Cohen, G.A. 2000. *Karl Marx's Theory of History*. Oxford: Oxford University Press.

Cohen, G.A. 2001. *If You're an Egalitarian, How Come You're So Rich?* Cambridge, MA: Harvard University Press.

Cohen, G.A. 2008. *Rescuing Justice and Equality*. Cambridge, MA: Harvard University Press.

Cohen, G.A. 2011. "Freedom and Money". In: G.A. Cohen, *On the Currency of Egalitarian Egalitarian Justice, and Other Essays in Political Philosophy*. Princeton University Press, 166–200.

Cohen, G.A. 2012. Rescuing Conservatism. In: G.A. Cohen, *Finding Oneself in the Other*. Princeton: Princeton University Press, 143–174.

Cohen, G.A., M. Hrubec. 2009. Dvojí odkaz Karla Marxe. *Filosofický časopis*, 57, 5, 751–759.

Cohen, G.A., M. Scannella. 1997. Interview. *The Philosopher's Magazine*, 1, 38–42.

Cohen, J. 2003. "For a Democratic Society". In S. Freeman, ed. *The Cambridge Companion to Rawls*. Cambridge: Cambridge University Press.

Cohen, J. 2006. "Is there a Human Right to Democracy?" In Ch. Sypnowich, ed. *Egalitarian Conscience: Essays in Honour of G.A. Cohen*. Oxford: Oxford University Press, 226–248.

Cohen, J.L., A. Arato. 1992. *Civil Society and Political Theory*. Cambridge, MA: MIT Press.

Comaroff, J., Comaroff, J. 2012. *Theory from the South. Or, How Euro-America is Evolving toward Africa*. London: Paradigm Publishers.

Conway, J.M. 2012. *Edges of Global Justice: The World Social Forum and Its 'Others'*. London: Routledge.

Coomans, A. P. M. 2005. 'Progressive Development of International Human Rights Law: The Extraterritorial Application of the International Covenant on Economic, Social and Cultural Rights'. In Windfuhr, M. ed. *Beyond the Nation State: Human Rights in Times of Globalisation*. Uppsala: Global Publications Foundation.

Craven, M. 2007. "Violence of Dispossession: Extra-Territoriality and Economic, Social, and Cultural Rights". In M. Baderin, R. McCorquodale, eds. *Economic, Social and Cultural Rights in Action*. Oxford: Oxford University Press.

Dallmayr, F. 2010. *Integral Pluralism: Beyond Culture Wars*. Lexington: The University Press of Kentucky.

Dallmayr, F., Manoochehri, A., eds. 2007. *Civilizational Dialoque and Political Thought*. Lanham: Lexington Books.

De Oliveira, N., Hrubec, M., Sobottka, E., eds. 2018. *From Social to Cyber Justice. Critical Views on Justice, Law, and Ethics*. Porto Alegre: PUCRS, and Prague: Filosofia.

Dean, J. 2001. "Cybersalons and Civil Society: Rethinking the Public Sphere in Transnational Technoculture". *Public Culture*, Vol. 13, No. 2, 243–265.

Decker, O., Türcke, Ch., eds. 2019. *Autoritarismus. Kritische Theorie und Psychoanalytische Praxis*. Giessen, Psychosozial-Verlag.

Delanty, G. 2009. *The Cosmopolitan Imagination. The Renewal of Critical Social Theory*. Cambridge: Cambridge University Press.

Deng, Xiaoping. 1982. Opening Speech at the Twelfth National Congress of the CPC (September 1, 1982). In: Deng Xiaoping, *Build Socialism with Chinese Characteristics*. Beijing: Foreign Languages Press.

Deng, X. 1984. "Opening Spech at the Twelfth National Congress of the CPC" (September 1, 1982). In Deng. Xiaoping, *Build Socialism with Chinese Characteristics*. Beijing: Foreign Languages Press.

Deng, X. 1993. *Document*. Beijing: Renmin Publishing House.

Deng, X. 2010. "Emancipate the mind, seek truth from facts, and unite as one in looking to the future". In *Selected Works of Deng Xiaoping* (Volume II, 1975–1982). *Marxist Archive* (orig. Oct. 13, 1978). https://www.marxists.org/reference/archive/deng-xiaoping/1978/110.htm [visited July 16, 2022].

Deng, X. 2015. *Selected Works of Deng Xiaoping (1965–1982)*. Beijing: ICP Intercultural Press.

Derian, J.D. 2009. *Critical Practices in International Theory*. London and New York: Routledge.

Deudney, D. 1995. "Nuclear Weapons and the Waning of the Real-State". *Daedalus*, 124, 2, 209–231.

Deudney, D. 1999. "Geopolitics and Change". In M. Doyle, and J. Ikenberry, eds. *New Thinking in International Relations Theory*. Boulder: Westview Press.

Deudney, D. 2000. "Regrounding Realism". *Security Studies*, 10, 1, 1–45.

Diamond, J. 1997. *Guns, Germs, and Steel: The Fates of Human Societies*. New York: W.W. Norton & Co.

Dinušová, D. 2023. "The Trajectory of Ideals in the Revolutionary Processes of Latin America". *Human Affairs*, Vol. 33, No. 3, 335–348.

Domínguéz, E., Rodríguez, R.R. 2022. "There and back again: United States policy towards Cuba in the 21st century". *International Journal of Cuban Studies*, Vol. 14, No. 2, 309–342.

Dussel, E. 2003. *Philosophy of Liberation*. Eugene: Wipf and Stock Publishers.

Dussel, E. 2007. *Política de la Liberación. Historia mundial y crítica*. Madrid: Editorial Trotta. (2011. *Politics of Liberation: A Critical Global History*. Norwich: Hymns Ancient & Modern Ltd.)

Dussel, E. 2009. "A New Age in the History of Philosophy: The World Dialogue Between Philosophical Traditions". *Philosophy and Social Criticism* 35, 5, 499–516.

Dussel, E. 2018. "Las tres configuraciones del proceso político". *Cuadernos Filosóficos / Segunda Época*, Vol. 14, 18–29.

Dworkin, R. 1981. "Equality of Resources". *Philosophy and Public Affairs*, 10, 4, 283–345.

Ehrenreich, B., Hochschild, A.R. 2003. *Global Woman*. New York: Metropolitan Books.

Eisenstadt, S.N., ed. 2002. *Multiple Modernities*. New Brunswick: Transactions Publishers.

Elias, N. 2000. *The Civilizing Process: Sociogenetic and Psychogenetic Investigations*. London: Wiley-Blackwell.

El-Ojeili, C., Hayden, P. 2006. *Critical Theories of Globalization*. London: Palgrave MacMillan.

Elster, J. 1989. *The Cement of Society. A Survey of Social Order*. Cambridge: Cambridge University Press.

Fanon, F. 2005. *The Wretched of the Earth*. New York: Grove Press.

Fasenfest, D., ed. 2022. *Marx Matters*. Leiden: Brill.

Fichte, J.G. 1971. "Grundlage des Naturrechts nach Prinzipien der Wissenschaftslehre". In: *J.G. Fichte: Werke*. Hg. I.H. Fichte. Bd. 3. Berlin: Walter de Gruyter. Known in the English translation also as *The Science of Rights*.

Fine, R. 2003a. "Kant's theory of cosmopolitanism and Hegel's critique". *Philosophy and Social Criticism*, Vol. 29, No. 6, 609–630.

Fine, R. 2003b. "Taking the 'Ism' Out of Cosmopolitanism". *European Journal of Social Theory* Nov., 4, 451–470.

Fine, R. 2007. *Cosmopolitanism*. London: Routledge.

Fisher, W.F., Ponniah, T. 2003. *Another World is Possible: Popular Alternatives to Globalization at the World Social Forum*. London: Zed Books.

Flynn, J. 2009. "Human Rights, Transnational Solidarity, and Duties to the Global Poor". *Constellations* 16, 1, 59–77.

Fornet-Betancourt, R. 2004. *Crítica intercultural de la Filosofía Latinoamericana actual*. Madrid: Trotta.

Foucault, M. 2018. *La pensée du dehors*. Montpellier: Fata Morgana.

Franco, P., Marsh, L. 2015. *A Companion to Michael Oakeshott*. Philadelphia: Penn State University.

Fraser, N. 1990. "Rethinking the Public Sphere. A Contribution to the Critique of Actually Existing Democracy". *Social Text*, No. 25/26, 56–80.

Fraser, N. 2009. "Feminism, Capitalism, and the Cunning of History". *New Left Review* 56, March–April, 97–117.

Fraser, N. 2010. *Scales of justice: Reimagining political space in a globalizing world*. New York: Columbia University Press.

Fraser, N., 1997. "From Redistribution to Recognition? Dilemmas of Justice in a 'Postsocialist Age'". In: N. Fraser, *Justice Interruptus*. London and New York: Routledge 11–40.

Fraser, N., Honneth, A. 2003. *Redistribution or Recognition? A Political–Philosophical Exchange*. London, New York: Verso.

Fraser, N., Hrubec, M. 2004. "Towards global justice: An interview with Nancy Fraser". *Czech Sociological Review* 6, 879–89.

Fraser, Nancy. 1996. *Justice interruptus: Critical reflections on the 'postsocialist' condition*. New York: Routledge.

Freeden, M. 1998. *Ideologies and Political Theory. A Conceptual Approach*. Oxford: Clarendon Press.

Fromm, E. 1936. "Sozialpsychologischer Teil". In M. Horkheimer et al., eds. *Studien uber Autoritdt und Familie. Forschungsberichte aus dem Institut fur Sozialforschung*. Paris: Alcan, 77–135.

Garnham, N. 1999. "The Media and the Public Sphere". In C. Calhoun, ed. *Habermas and the Public Sphere*. Cambridge, MA: MIT Press.

Ghai, Y. 1999. "Rights, Social Justice, and Globalization in East Asia". In J.R. Bauer, D.A. Bell, eds. *The East Asian Challenge for Human Rights*. Cambridge: Cambridge University Press, 241–263.

Giddens, A. 1984. *The Constitution of Society. Outline of the Theory of Structuration.* Cambridge: Polity Press.

Giesen, K.G., Pijl, K. van der., eds. 2006. *Global Norms in the Twenty-First Century.* Newcastle: Cambridge Scholars Press.

Gilens, M., Page, B.I. 2014. "Testing Theories of American Politics: Elites, Interest Groups, and Average Citizens". *Perspectives on Politics*, Vol. 12, Issue 3, Sept., 564–581.

Göle, N., Ammann, L., eds. 2006. *Islam in Public.* Istanbul: Istanbul Bilgi University Press.

Gomis, M., Cepeda Másmela, C., Fransson-Quenoz, F., y Durez, A., eds. 2021. *América Latina: Ciclos socioeconómicos, 1990–2020.* Bogotá: Pontificia Universidad Javeriana.

Goodman, D.S.G. 2002. *Deng Xiaoping and the Chinese Revolution: A Political Biography.* London and New York: Routledge.

Granés, C. 2022. *Delirio Americano. Una historia cultural y política de América Latina.* Bogotá: Taurus.

The Group of 77 at the United Nations. 2022. *G77.* https://www.g77.org/ (Visited June 22, 2022).

Gutmann, A. 2003. "Rawls on the Relationship between Liberalism and Democracy". In S. Freeman, ed. *The Cambridge Companion to Rawls.* Cambridge: Cambridge University Press.

Gyekye, K. 2004. *Beyond Cultures: Perceiving a Common Humanity.* Washington: Council for Research in Values and Philosophy.

Habermas, J. 1973. "Labor and Interaction: Remarks on Hegel's Jena Philosophy of Mind". In J. Habermas, *Theory and Practice.* Boston: Beacon Press.

Habermas, J. 1981. *Theorie des kommunikativen Handelns.* Frankfurt/M.: Suhrkamp.

Habermas, J. 1987. "The Entwinement of Myth and Enlightenment: Max Horkheimer and Theodor Adorno". In J. Habermas, *The Philosophical Discourse of Modernity.* Cambridge, MA: MIT, 106–30.

Habermas, J. 1989. *The Structural Transformation of the Public Sphere. An Inquiry into a Category of Bourgeois Society.* Cambridge, MA: MIT Press.

Habermas, J. 1991. *Erläuterungen zur Diskursethik.* Frankfurt/M.: Suhrkamp.

Habermas, J. 1992. *Faktizität und Geltung. Beiträge zur Diskurstheorie des Rechts und des demokratischen Rechtsstaats.* Frankfurt/M.: Suhrkamp.

Habermas, J. 1995. "Reconciliation through the Public Use of Reason: Remarks on John Rawls's Political Liberalism". *Journal of Philosophy*, Vol. XCII, No. 3, 109–131.

Habermas, J. 1998. *Die postnationale Konstellation.* Frankfurt/M.: Suhrkamp.

Habermas, J. 2009. "Arbeit, Liebe, Anerkennung". *Die Zeit*, 16. Juli.

Habermas, J. 2013. *The Crisis of the European Union. A Response.* Oxford: Polity.

Habermas, J. 2015. *The Theory of Communicative Action.* Vol. 1, Cambridge: Polity.

Haigh, S. 2003. *The World State: Polity or Condition?* Australasian Political Studies Association Conference. Hobart: University of Tasmania.

Hampton, J. 1997. *Political Philosophy.* Boulder: Westview Press.

Hanisch, C. 1971. "The Personal is Political". In S. Firestone, A. Koedt, eds. *Notes from the Second Year: Women's Liberation*. New York: Radical Feminism.

Hardimon, M.O. 1994. *Hegel's Social Philosophy. The Project of Reconciliation*. Cambridge: Cambridge University Press.

Harnecker, M. 2015. *A World to Build: New Paths toward Twenty-First Century Socialism*. New York: Monthly Review Press.

Harris, J. 2008. *The Dialectics of Globalization: Economic and Political Conflict in a Transnational World*. Cambridge: Cambridge Scholars Publishing.

Harris, J. 2016. *Global Capitalism and the Crisis of Democracy*. Atlanta: Clarity Press 2016.

Hatzimihail, N. 2008. The Many Lives – and Faces – of Lex Mercatoria: History as Genealogy in International Business Law. *Law and Contemporary Problems*, 71, 3, 169–190.

Haydar, B. 2005. Extreme Poverty and Global Responsibility. In: Barry, C., Pogge, T. W. eds., *Global Institutions and Responsibilities*. Oxford: Blackwell, 312–313.

Hazony, Y. 2022. *Conservatism. Rediscovery*. Washington: Regnery Gateway.

Hegel, G W F. *Philosophy of Right*. Oxford: Clarendon Press 1952. https://www.marxists.org/reference/archive/hegel/works/pr/philosophy-of-right.pdf (Visited June 12, 2023).

Hegel, G.W.F. 1969. *System der Sittlichkeit*. Hamburg: Meiner.

Hegel, G.W.F. 1991. *Elements of the Philosophy of Right*. Cambridge: Cambridge University Press.

Hegel, G.W.F. 2010. *Philosophy of Spirit*. Oxford: Oxford University Press.

Hegel, G.W.F. 2018. *Phenomenology of Spirit*. Cambridge: Cambridge University Press.

Hegel, G.W.F. 2019. *The Phenomenology of Spirit*. Notre Dame: University of Notre Dame Press.

Heins, V. 2008a. Realizing Honneth: Redistribution, Recognition, and Global Justice. *Journal of Global Ethics* 4, 2: 141–153.

Heins, V. 2008b. Human Rights, Intellectual Property, and Struggles for Recognition. *Human Rights Review* 9, 2: 213–232.

Heins, V. 2008c. *Nongovernmental Organizations in International Society. Struggles over Recognition*. New York: Palgrave MacMillan.

Held, D. 1980. *Introduction to Critical Theory. Horkheimer to Habermas*. Cambridge: Polity Press.

Held, D. 1995. *Democracy and the Global Order: From the Modern State to Cosmopolitan Governance*. Stanford: Stanford University Press.

Held, D., Koenig-Archibugi, M. eds. 2005. *Global Governance and Public Accountability*. Oxford: Blackwell.

Held, D., McGrew, A. 2003. *Governing Globalization. Power, Authority and Global Governance*. Cambridge: Polity Press.

Held, V. 2006. Liberalism and the Ethic of Care. In V. Held, *The Ethics of Care. Personal, Political, and Global.* Oxford – New York: Oxford University Press.

Heywood, A. 2021. *Political Ideologies.* London: Bloomsbury Academic.

Higgott, R., Brasset, J. 2004. Building the Normative Dimensions of a Global Polity. *Review of International Studies*, 29, S1, 29–55.

Higgott, R., Ougaard, M. eds. 2002. *Towards a Global Polity?* London: Routledge.

Hobbes, T. 2017. *Leviathan.* London: Penguin Classics.

Hobsbawm, E. 1996a. *The Age of Revolution: 1789–1848.* New York: Vintage.

Hobsbawm, E. 1996b. *The Age of Capital: 1848–1875.* New York: Vintage.

Hobsbawm, E. 1996c. *The Age of Extremes: A History of the World, 1914–1991.* New York: Vintage.

Hobsbawm, E. 2021. *On Nationalism.* Little: Brown.

Hochschild, A.R. 2003. *The Commercialization of Intimate Life. Notes from Home and Work.* San Francisco – Los Angeles: University of California Press.

Hochschild, A.R. 2005. Love and Gold. The Global Care Chain. In L. Ricciutelli, A. Miles, M. McFadden, eds. *Feminist Politics, Activism and Vision: Local and Global Challenges.* London and Toronto: Zed and Innana Books.

Holenstein, E. 1985. *Sprachliche Universalien: Eine Untersuchung zur Natur des menschlichen Geistes.* Bochum: Brockmeyer.

Holenstein, E. 1998. *Kulturphilosophische Perspektiven.* Frankfurt/M.: Suhrkamp.

Holenstein, E. 1999. *Menschliches Selbstverständnis.* Frankfurt/M.: Suhrkamp.

Homer. 1999. *Oddysey.* London: Penguin Classics.

Hondagneu-Sotelo, P., Avila, E. 2006. "I'm Here But I'm There. The Meaning of Latina Transnational Motherhood". In M.K. Zimmerman, J.S. Litt, C.E. Bose, eds. *Global Dimensions of Gender and Care.* Stanford: Stanford University Press, 254–265.

Honneth, A. 1988. *Kritik der Macht: Reflexionsstufen einer kritischen Gesellschaftstheorie.* Frankfurt/M.: Suhrkamp.

Honneth, A. 1990. *Die zerrissene Welt des Sozialen. Sozialphilosophische Aufsatze.* Frankfurt/M.: Suhrkamp.

Honneth, A. 1994a. „Die Soziale Dynamik von Missachtung. Zur Ortsbestimmung Einer Kritischen Gesellschaftstheorie." *Leviathan*, Vol. 22. No. 1, marzo, 78–93.

Honneth, A. 1995. "The Limits of Liberalism: On the Political-Ethical Discussion concerning Communitarianism." In A. Honneth, *The Fragmented World of the Social. Essays in Social and Political Philosophy.* Ed. Charles W. Wright. Albany: State University of New York Press, 231–246.

Honneth, Axel. 2000a. "Rekonstruktive Gesellschaftskritik unter genealogischem Vorbehalt. Zur Idee der 'Kritik' in der Frankfurter Schule". *Deutsche Zeitschrift für Philosophie* 48, 729–37.

Honneth, A. 2000b. "The Possibility of a Disclosing Critique of Society: The Dialectic of Enlightenment in Light of Current Debates in Social Criticism". *Constellations*, Vol. 7, Issue 1, 116–127.

Honneth, A. 2000c. *Das Andere der Gerechtigkeit*, Frankfurt/M.: Suhrkamp.

Honneth, A. 2000d. *Suffering from Indeterminacy. An Attempt at a Reactualization of Hegel's Philosophy of Right*. Amsterdam: Van Gorcum.

Honneth, A. 2001. *Leiden an Unbestimmtheit. Eine Reaktualisierung der Hegelschen Rechtsphilosophie*. Frankfurt/M.: Reclam.

Honneth, A. 2003. *Unsichtbarkeit. Stationen einer Theorie der Intersubjektivitdt.* Frankfurt/M.: Suhrkamp.

Honneth, A. 2005. *Verdinglichung*. Frankfurt/M.: Suhrkamp.

Honneth, A. 2007a. "Is Universalism a Moral Trap? The Presuppositions and Limits of a Politics of Human Rights". In A. Honneth, *Disrespect. The Normative Foundations of Critical Theory*. Cambridge: Polity Press, 197–217.

Honneth, A. 2007b. "Recognition as Ideology". In: B. van den. Brink, D. Owen, eds. *Recognition and Power Axel Honneth and the Tradition of Critical Social Theory*. Cambridge: Cambridge University Press, 323–347.

Honneth, A. 2008. *Reification. A New Look at an Old Idea*. Oxford: Oxford University Press.

Honneth, A. 2014. *Freedom's Right: The social foundations of democratic life*. New York: Columbia University Press.

Honneth, A. 2015. "Recognition between States". In N. de Oliveira, M, Hrubec, E. Sobottka, G.A. Saavedra, eds. *Justice and Recognition. On Axel Honneth and Critical Theory*. Porto Alegre: PUCRS, Prague: Filosofia, 265–285.

Honneth, A. 2020. *Die Armut unserer Freiheit*. Frankfurt/M.: Suhrkamp.

Honneth, A., ed. 1994b. *Pathologien des Sozialen. Der Aufgabe der Sozialphilosophie*. Frankfurt/M.: Fischer Verlag.

Honneth, A., Hg. 2002. *Befreiung aus der Mündigkeit. Paradoxien des gegenwärtigen Kapitalismus*. Frankfurt am Main: Campus.

Honneth, A., Hrubec, M. 2007. "O kritice a uznání. Rozhovor s Axelem Honnethem", in: A. Honneth, ed. *Zbavovat se svepravnosti.* Prague: Filosofia, 317–330.

Honneth, A., Jaeggi, U., Hg. 1977. *Theorien des Historischen Materialismus*. Frankfurt/M.: Suhrkamp.

Honneth, Axel. 1996. (orig. 1992) *The struggle for recognition: The moral grammar of social conflict*. Cambridge: Polity Press.

Horkheimer, M. (Regius, H.). 1934a. *Dämmerung. Notizen in Deutschland*. Zürich, Oprecht & Helbling.

Horkheimer, M. 1930a. *Anfänge der bürgerlichen Geschichtsphilosophie*. Stuttgart: Kohlhammer.

Horkheimer, M. 1930b. "Ein neuen Ideologiebegriff?" *Archiv für die Geschichte des Sozialismus und der Arbeiterbewegung*, 15, 33–56.

Horkheimer, M. 1931. "Die gegenwärtige Lage der Sozialphilosophie und die Aufgaben eines Instituts für Sozialforschung". *Frankfurter Universitätsreden* 37. Frankfurt/ M.: Englert & Schlosser.

Horkheimer, M. 1932a. "Hegel und das Problem der Metaphysik". In *Festschrift für Carl Grünberg zum 70. Geburtstag*. Leipzig: Hirschfeld.

Horkheimer, M. 1932b. "Vorwort". *Zeitschrift für Sozialforschung*, I, 1/2, I–III.

Horkheimer, M. 1932c. "Bemerkungen über Wissenschaften und Krise". *Zeitschrift für Sozialforschung*, I, 1, 1–7.

Horkheimer, M. 1933a. "Materialismus und Metaphysik". *Zeitschrift für Sozialforschung*, II, 1.

Horkheimer, M. 1933b. "Materialismus und Moral". *Zeitschrift für Sozialforschung*, II, 2.

Horkheimer, M. 1934b. "Zum Rationalismusstreit in der gegenwärtigen Philosophie". *Zeitschrift für Sozialforschung*, III, 1.

Horkheimer, M. 1935a. "Bemerkungen zur philosophischen Anthropologie". *Zeitschrift für Sozialforschung*, IV, 1, 1–25.

Horkheimer, M. 1935b. "Zum Problem der Wahrheit". *Zeitschrift für Sozialforschung*, IV, 3.

Horkheimer, M. 1936. "Egoismus und Freiheitsbewegung". *Zeitschrift für Sozialforschung*, 5, 2, 161–231.

Horkheimer, M. 1937. "Der neueste Angriff auf die Metaphysik". *Zeitschrift für Sozialforschung*, VI, 1, 4–51.

Horkheimer, M. 1938. "Montaigne und die Funktion der Skepsis". *Zeitschrift für Sozialforschung*, VII, 1, 1–54.

Horkheimer, M. 1939. "Die Juden und Europa". *Zeitschrift für Sozialforschung*, VIII, 1/2, pp. 115–137.

Horkheimer, M. 1941a. "Notes on Institute Activities". *Studies in Philosophy and Social Science*, IX, 1.

Horkheimer, M. 1941b. "Art and Mass Culture". *Studies in Philosophy and Social Science*, IX, 2, pp. 290–302.

Horkheimer, M. 1941c. "The End of Reason". *Studies in Philosophy and Social Science*, IX, 3, 366–388.

Horkheimer, M. 1941d. "Preface". *Studies in Philosophy and Social Science*, IX, 3, 365.

Horkheimer, M. 1968. "Nachtrag". In A. Schmidt (Ed.), *Kritische Theorie* [*Critical Theory*]. Bd. 2. Frankfurt/M.: Fischer, 193.

Horkheimer, M. 2002a. "Traditional and Critical Theory". In M. Horkheimer, *Critical Theory. Selected Essays*. New York: Continuum, 188–243 (orig.: "Traditionelle und kritische Theorie". *Zeitschrift für Sozialforschung*, VI, 1937, 2, 245–294).

Horkheimer, M. 2002b. "The social function of philosophy". In M. Horkheimer, *Critical Theory*. Continuum; https://www.marxists.org/reference/archive/horkheimer/1939 /social-function.htm (orig. In *Studies in Philosophy and Social Science*, VIII, 1939, 3).

Horkheimer, M., Adorno, T. 2007. *Dialectic of Enlightenment*. Stanford: Stanford University Press.

Horkheimer, M., Marcuse, H. 1937. "Philosophie und kritische Theorie". *Zeitschrift für Sozialforschung*, VI, 3, 625–647.

Horkheimer, Max, Theodor Adorno. 2007 (orig. 1947). *Dialectic of enlightenment*. Stanford: Standford University Press.

Hroch, M. 2000. *Social Preconditions of National Revival in Europe*. New York: Columbia University Press.

Hroch, M. 2015. *European Nations: Explaining Their Formation*. New York: Verso.

Hrubec, M. 2011. *Od zneuznani ke spravedlnosti*. Praha: Filosofia.

Hrubec, M. 2017. "Innovation in Understanding and Cooperating the Macro-Regions: The Potential of Promotion of the „16+1 Cooperation" and the Belt and Road Initiative". In Huang Ping, Liu Zuokui, eds., *How the 16+1 Cooperation Promotes the Belt and Road Initiative*. Beijing: China Social Sciences Press, 34–53.

Hrubec, M. 2022. "Strategic Sovereignty". In Z. Liu, B. Dordevic, eds. *The Connectivity Cooperation Between China and Europe: A Multi-Dimensional Analysis*. London and New York: Routledge.

Hrubec, M. 2023. "Strategic Socialism. The Updating of Cuba's Model". *Human Affairs* Vol. 33, No. 3, 349–365.

Hrubec, M., "Threat of Limited Nuclear War". *Critical Sociology*, Vol. 45, No. 6, 2019, 785–798.

Hrubec, M., Brabec, M., Minarova, M. 2022. *Basic Income in the World*. Prague: Epocha.

Hrubec, M., ed. 2021. *Global China*. Beijing: Foreign University Press.

Hrubec, M., ed. *Between Islam and the West*. Prague: Filosofia 2009.

Hrubec, M., Kasanda, A., eds. 2022. *Africa in a Multilateral World*. London and New York: Routledge.

Hrubec, M., Višňovský, E., eds. 2023. *Towards a New Research Era. Global Comparison of Research Distortions*. Boston and Leiden: Brill.

"Humanitarian organisations estimate one person dying of hunger every four seconds". 2022. *Reliefweb* 20 September. https://reliefweb.int/report/world/humanit ian-organisations-estimate-one-person-dying-hunger-every-four-seconds (Visited May 20, 2023).

Huntington, S. 1996. *The Clash of Civilizations and the Remaking of World Order*. New York: Simon & Schuster.

Ignatieff, M. 2001. *Human Rights as Politics and Idolatry*. A. Gutmann, ed. Princeton, Oxford: Princeton University Press.

Ihara, C.K. 2004. "Are Individual Rights Necessary? A Confucian Perspective". In K.L. Shun, D.B. Wong, eds. *Confucian Ethics. A Comparative Study of Self, Autonomy, and Community*. Cambridge: Cambridge University Press, 11–30.

Ingram, J. 1998. "Comment on Lawrence Blum". *Constellations*, 1, 5, 69–73.

Intergovernmental Panel on Climate Change Press Release. 2018. 8 October, 2018/24/PR, Geneva.

"In world of wealth, 9 million people die every year from hunger, WFP Chief tells Food System Summit". *World Food Programme*, 21 September 2021. https://www.wfp.org /news/world-wealth-9-million-people-die-every-year-hunger-wfp-chief-tells-food -system-summit (Visited June 10, 2022).

Jabbour, E., Gabriele. A. 2021. *China. O socialismo do seculo XXI*. Sao Paulo: Boitempo.

Jacques, M. 2018. "Cambridge scholar lauds reform and opening-up while underscoring West's ignorance of nation". *Global Times*, Oct. 28, https://www.globaltimes.cn /world/China-Europe/index8.html (visited July 20, 2020).

Jaggar, A.M. 2005. "'Saving Amina': Global Justice for Women and Intercultural Dialogue". *Ethics and International Affairs*, Vol. 19, Issue 3, Dec., 55–75.

Jay, M. 1996. *The dialectical imagination. A history of the Frankfurt School and the Institute of Social Research 1923–1950*. Boston: Little, Brown and Comp.

Jiang Qing. 2013. Eds. by Daniel Bell and Ruiping Fan. *A Confucian Constitutional Order: How China's Ancient Past Can Shape Its Political Future*. Princeton: Princeton University Press.

Jones, C. 1999. *Global Justice. Defending Cosmopolitanism*. Oxford: Oxford University Press.

Jones, J.M. 2023. "Social Conservatism in U.S. Highest in About a Decade". *Gallup*, June 8.

Joyner, C.C. 2005. *International Law in the 21st Century. Rules for Global Governance*. Lanham, Oxford: Rowman and Littlefield.

Kamminga, M. T., Zia-Zarifi, S., eds. 2000. *Liability of Multinational Corporations under International Law*. The Hague – London – Boston: Kluwer Law International.

Kant, I. 1997. *Perpetual Peace: Essays on Kant's Cosmopolitan Ideal*. Cambridge, MA: The MIT Press.

Kant, I. 2017. *Metaphysics of Morals*. Cambridge: Cambridge University Press.

Kasanda, A. 2018. *Contemporary African Social and Political Philosophy*. London and New York: Routledge.

Kelsen, H. 1941. "Recognition in International Law: Theoretical Observations". *The American Journal of International Law*, 35, Oct., 4: 605–617.

Kennedy, P. 2010. *Local Lives and Global Transformations: Toward World Society*. London: Red Globe Press.

Kennedy, P. 2017. *Vampire Capitalism, Fractured Societies and Alternative Futures*. London: Palgrave Macmillan.

Kenover, J.M., Price, T.D. 2013. "A new approach to tracking connections between the Indus Valley and Mesopotamia: initial results of strontium isotope analyses from Harrappa and Ur". *Journal of Archaeological Science* Vol. 40, Issue 5, 2286–2297.

Khaldun, I. 1989. *The Muqaddimah: An Introduction to History*. Ed. N.J. Dawood. Princeton: Princeton University Press.

Kocka,J.,Offe,C.Hg.2000.*GeschichteundZukunftderArbeit*.Frankfurt:NewYork:Campus.

Kögler, H.H. 2005. "Recognition and Difference. The Power of Perspectives in Interpretative Dialogue". *Social Identities*, Vol. 11, 3, May, 247–269.

Kojeve, A. 1947. *Introduction á la lecture de Hegel*. Paris: Gallimard.

Kojeve, A. 1980. *Introduction to the Reading of Hegel. Lectures on the Phenomenology of Spirit*. Ithaca, London: Cornell University Press.

Kosík, K. 1968. "Naše nynější krize." *Literární Listy*, 128–138.

Kosík, K. 1993. *Století Markéty Samsové*. Praha: Český spisovatel.

Kosík, K. 1997a. *Předpotopní úvahy*, ed. E. Červinková. Praha: Torst.

Kosík, K. 1997b. Lumpenburžoazie a vyšší duchovní pravda. In K. Kosík, *Předpotopní úvahy*. Praha: Torst, 93–104.

Kosík, K. 1997c. Všechna moc vychází z imaginace. In K. Kosík, *Předpotopní úvahy*, ed. E. Červinková. Praha: Torst.

Kosík, K. 2004. *Poslední eseje*, ed. I. Šnebergová, J. Zumr. Praha: Filosofia.

Kosík, K. 2012 (orig. 1963). *Dialectics of the Concrete. A Study on Problems of Man and World*. Cham: Springer.

Kosík, K., 1958. *Česká radikální demokracie. Příspěvek k dějinám názorových sporů v české společnosti 19. století*. Praha: Státní nakladatelství politické literatury.

Koskenniemi, M. 2001. *The Gentle Civilizer of Nations: The Rise and Fall of International Law 1870–1960*. Cambridge: Cambridge University Press.

Koskenniemi, M. 2006. *From Apology to Utopia: The Structure of International Legal Argument*. Cambridge, New York: Cambridge University Press.

Kotz, D.M. 2017. *The Rise and Fall of Neoliberal Capitalism*. Cambridge, MA: Harvard University Press.

Král, O. 2005. *Čínská filosofie. Pohled z dějin*. Lasenice: Maxima.

Kroeber, A.L., Kluckhohn, C. 1963. *Culture: A Critical Review of Concepts and Definitions*. New York: Vintage Books, Random House.

Küng, H. 1998. *A Global Ethic and Global Responsibilities: Two Declarations*. London: SCM Press.

Kymlicka, W. 1991. *Liberalism, Community, and Culture*. Oxford: Oxford University Press.

Kymlicka, W. 1996. *Multicultural Citizenship*. Oxford: Clarendon Press.

Laclau, E. 2018. *On Populist Reason*. London: Verso.

Laclau, E.,, Mouffe, C. 1985. *Hegemony and socialist strategy: toward a radical democratic politics*. London: Verso.

Lambertini, M. 2018. "A New Global Deal for Nature and People Urgently Needed". In M. Grooten, R.E.A. Almond, eds. *WWF 2018. Living Planet Report – 2018: Aiming Higher*. Gland: WWF, 4.

Lampter, M. 2023. "The Two Pink Tides in Latin America. Contemporary Global Prospects". *Human Affairs* Vol. 33, No. 3, 319–334.

Langman, L., Lundskow, G. 2016. *God, Guns, Gold and Glory. American Character and Ist Discontents.* Boston and Leiden: Brill.

Larsen J.A. 2014. "Limited War and the Advent of Nuclear Weapons". In J.A. Larsen, K., M. Kartchner, eds. *On Limited Nuclear War in the 21st Century.* Stanford: Stanford University Press, 3–20.

Lazzeri, C., Caillé, A. 2007. "Recognition Today. Theoretical, Ethical and Political Stakes of the Concept". In J.P. Deranty et al., eds. *Recognition, Work, Politics. New Directions in French Critical Theory.* Leiden, Boston: Brill.

Levi-Strauss, C. 2012. *Tristes Tropiques.* London: Penguin Classics.

Li, David Daokui, et al. 2018. *Economic Lessons Learned from China's Forty Years of Reform and Opening Up.* Beijing: Tsinghua University.

Li, Xing. 2021. *The International Political Economy of the BRICS.* London: Routledge.

Linklater, A. 1998. *The Transformation of Political Community: Ethical Foundations of the Post-Westphalian Era.* London: Polity Press.

Linklater, A. 2007. *Critical Theory and World Politics. Citizenship, sovereignty and humanity.* London and New York: Routledge.

Linklater, A. 2010. "Global Civilizing Processes and the Ambiguities of Human Interconnectedness". *European Journal of International Relations,* 1, 16, 155–178.

Lipkin, R.J. 1995. "Liberalism and the Possibility of Multicultural Constitutionalism: The Distinction Between Deliberative and Dedicated Cultures". *University of Richmond Law Review,* 29, Dec., 1263.

Long, Z., Herrera, R., Andréani, T. 2018. "On the Nature of the Chinese Economic System". *Monthly Review* Vol. 70, Issue 5, October 1, 1.

Löwy, M. 2015. *Ecosocialism.* Chicago: Haymarket Books.

Lukács, G. 1954. *Der junge Hegel.* Berlin: Aufbau Verlag.

Lukin, A. 2018. *China and Russia. The New Rapprochement.* Oxford: Polity.

Lutz-Bachmann M., Bohman, J., Hg. 2002. *Weltstaat oder Staatenwelt? Für und wider die Idee einer Weltrepublik.* Frankfurt/Main: Suhrkamp.

Machonin, P. a kol. 1966. *Sociální struktura socialistické společnosti: Sociologické problémy soudobé československé společnosti.* Svoboda: Praha.

Machonin, P. a kol. 1969. *Československá společnost: Sociologická analýza sociální stratifikace.* Epocha: Bratislava.

Majeed, A. 2004. *Federalism Within the Union: Distribution of Responsibilities in the Indian System.* New Delhi: Centre for Federal Studies, Hamdard University.

Majeed, A. 2009. *Working of the Indian Federal System.* New Delhi: Centre for Federal Studies, Hamdard University.

Marcuse, H. 1930–1931. "Zum Problem der Dialektik", I–II. *Die Gesellschaft,* 7, Berlin 1930, 304–326, and *Die Gesellschaft,* 8, Berlin 1931, 541–557.

Marcuse, H. 1932. *Hegels Ontologie und die Grundlegung einer Theorie des Geschichtlichkeit*. Frankfurt/M.: Klostermann.

Marcuse, H. 1934. "Der Kampf gegen den Liberalismus in der totalitären Staatsauffassung". *Zeitschrift für Sozialforschung*, III, 2, 185–194.

Marcuse, H. 1937a. "Die Krisis der europäischen Wissenschaften und die transzendentale Phänomenologie". *Zeitschrift für Sozialforschung*, VI, 2, 414–415.

Marcuse, H. 1937b. "Über den affirmativen Charakter der Kultur". *Zeitschrift für Sozialforschung*, VI, 1, 54–94.

Marcuse, H. 1938. "Zur Kritik des Hedonismus". *Zeitschrift für Sozialforschung*, VII, 1/2, 55–89.

Marcuse, H. 1940. "An Introduction to Hegel's Philosophy". *Studies in Philosophy and Social Science*, VIII, 3, 411.

Marcuse, H. 1941. "Some Social Implications of Modern Technology". *Studies in Philosophy and Social Science*, IX, 3, 414–439.

Marcuse, H. 1955b. "The Social Implications of Freudian 'Revisionism'". *Dissent*, 2, Summer, 3, 221–240.

Marcuse, H. 1955a. *Eros and Civilization. A Philosophical Inquire into Freud*. Boston: Beacon Press.

Marcuse, H. 1968. "Contributions to a phenomenology of historical materialism". *Telos*, Fall, 4, p. 21 (orig. 1928).

Marcuse, H. 1979. "Triebstruktur und Gesellschaft". In H. Marcuse, *Schriften*, Bd. 5. Frankfurt/M.: Surhkamp.

Marcuse, H. 1987. *Eros and Civilization*. London: Routledge.

Marcuse, H. 1991. *One-Dimensional Man: Studies in the Ideology of Advanced Industrial Society*. Boston: Beacon Press.

Marcuse, H. 2009 (orig. 1937). "Philosophy and Critical Theory". In H. Marcuse, *Negations. Essays in Critical Theory*. London: MayFlyBooks.

Marcuse, H. 1936. "Zum Begriff des Wesens". *Zeitschrift für Sozialforschung*, V, 1, 23ff.

Maritain, J. 1949. *Human Rights: Comments and Interpretations*. New York: Columbia University Press, UNESCO.

Marx, K. 1967. *Capital*. Vol. 1, New York: International Publishers, 505–507.

Marx, K. 1973. *Grundrisse*, Notebook IV, the Chapter on Capital. London: Penguin Books in association with New Left Review (orig. 1958). https://www.marxists.org/archive/marx/works/1857/grundrisse/ (Visited June 21, 2023).

Marx, K. 1995. *The Eighteenth Brumaire of Louis Bonaparte*. Marx/Engels Internet Archive (orig. 1852). https://www.marxists.org/archive/marx/works/1852/18th-brumaire/ (Visited July 22, 2023).

Marx, K. 1999. *Critique of the Gotha Programme*. Marx/Engels Internet Archive. marxists.org. https://www.marxists.org/archive/marx/works/1875/gotha/ (Visited July 23, 2023).

Marx, K. 2009. *A Contribution to the Critique of Hegel's Philosophy of Right*. Marx/Engels Internet Archive (orig. 1844). https://www.marxists.org/archive/marx/works/1843/critique-hpr/intro.htm (Visited July 23, 2023).

Marx, K., Engels, F. 1969. *Manifesto of the Communist Party*. Selected Works, Vol. One. Moscow: Progress Publishers, 98–137 (orig.1948). https://www.marxists.org/archive/marx/works/download/pdf/Manifesto.pdf (Visited July 23, 2023).

Mbembe, A. 2017. *Critique of Black Reason*. Durham: Duke University Press Books.

Mbiti, J. 1990. *African Religions and Philosophy*. London: Heinemann.

McCarthy, T. 1994. "Kantian Constructivism and Reconstructivism: Rawls and Habermas in Dialogue". *Ethics* 105, Oct.

McDonald, K. 2006. *Global Movements. Action and Culture*. Oxford: Blackwell.

Mead, H. 1934. *Mind, Self, and Society*. Chicago, London: University of Chicago Press.

Mead, H. 1982. *The Individual and the Social Self*. Chicago, London: University of Chicago Press.

Meadows, D.H., Meadows, D.L., Randers, J., Behrens, W.W. 1972. *The Limits to Growth*. Exeter: Signet.

Mertes, T. 2004. *A Movement of Movements*. London, New York: Verso.

Miler, J.W. 2017. *What is Populism?* London: Penguin.

Miler, J.W. 2021. *Democracy Rules*. London: Penguin.

Miller, D. 1995. *On Nacionality*. Oxford: Oxford University Press.

Miller, D. 2000. *Citizenship and National Identity*. Cambridge: Polity.

Miller, D. 2007. *National Responsibility and Global Justice*. Oxford: Oxford University Press.

Mlynář, Z. 1975. *Československý pokus o reformu 1968. Analýza jeho teorie a praxe*. Köln: Index.

Monbiot, G. 2018. "As the fracking protesters show, a people's rebellion is the only way to fight climate breakdown". *The Guardian*, Oct. 18. https://www.theguardian.com/commentisfree/2018/oct/18/governments-no-longer-trusted-climate-change-citizens-revolt (Visited June 23, 2023).

Montesquieu, C. de S. 2011. *Persian letters*. Charleston: Nabu Press.

Moon, J. 2003. "Rawls and Habermas on Public Reason: Human Rights and Global Justice." *Annual Review of Political Science*, Vol. 6, 257–274.

Musil, J. 2005. "Social integration: A Neglected Field of Studies in European Processes". In Z. Mansfeldová, V. Sparschuh, A. Wenninger, eds. *Patterns of Europeanisation in Central and Eastern Europe*. Hamburg: Krämer, 47–57.

Narula, S. 2006. *The Right to Food: Holding Global Actors Accountable Under International Law*. New York: Center for Human Rights and Global Justice, Working Paper No. 7.

Naticchia, C. 1999. "Recognition and Legitimacy: A Reply to Buchanan". *Philosophy & Public Affairs* 28 July, 3, 242–257.

Neuhouser, F. 2000. *Foundations of Hegel's Social Theory. Actualizing Freedom.* Cambridge, MA: Harvard University Press.

Nicolacopoulos, T. 2008. *Radical Critique of Liberalism.* Melbourne: re.press.

Nielsen, K. 1987. "World Government, Security, and Global Justice". In S. Luper-Foy, ed. *Problems of International Justice.* Boulder: Westview Press.

Nolan, P. 2019. *China and the West: Crossroads of Civilization.* New York: Routledge.

Nozick, R. 1974. *Anarchy, State, and Utopia.* New York: Basic Books.

Nozick, R. 1981. *Philosophical Explanations.* Cambridge, MA: Harvard University Press.

Nussbaum, M. 2000. *Women and Human Development.* Cambridge: Cambridge University Press.

Oakeshott, M. 1991. "On Being Conservative". In: M. Oakeshott, *Rationalism in Politics and Other Essays.* Indianapolis: Liberty Fund, 407–437.

Oakeshott, M. 1993. *Religion, Politics, and the Moral Life.* New Haven: Yale University Press.

Okin, S.M. 1993. "Political Liberalism. By John Rawls". *American Political Science Review,* Vol. 87, No. 4, Dec., 1010–1011.

Oliveira, N. de. 2010. "Towards a Phenomenology of Liberation: A Critical Theory of Race and the Fate of Democracy in Latin America". *Veritas* Vol. 55, No. 1, Jan/April, 206–226.

Olson, K., ed. 2008. *Adding Insult to Injury: Nancy Fraser Debates Her Critics.* London: Verso.

Onuma, Y. 1999. "Towards an Intercivilizational Approach to Human Rights". In J.R., Bauer, D.A. Bell, eds. *The East Asian Challenge for Human Rights.* Cambridge: Cambridge University Press, 103–123.

Othman, N. 1999. "Grounding Human Rights Arguments in Non-Western Culture: Shari'a and the Citizenship Rights of Women in a Modern Islamic State". In J.R. Bauer, D.A. Bell, eds. *The East Asian Challenge for Human Rights.* Cambridge: Cambridge University Press, 169–192.

Oxfam. 2018. Richest 1 percent bagged 82 percent of wealth created last year – poorest half of humanity got nothing. *Oxfam International,* 22 January 2018. https://www .oxfam.org/en/press-releases/richest-1-percent-bagged-82-percent-wealth-crea ted-lastyear-poorest-half-humanity/ (Visitied May 10. 2023).

Pan, Jiahua. 2016. *China's Environmental Governing and Ecological Civilization.* Berlin: Springer.

Parrenas, R.S. 2001. *Servants of Globalization. Women, Migration, and Domestic Work.* Stanford: Stanford University Press.

Pateman, C. 1988. *The Sexual Contract.* Stanford: Stanford University Press.

Pateman, C. 1989. *The Disorder of Women.* Cambridge: Polity Press.

Patino Villa, C.A. 2017. *Imperios contra Estados. La destrucción del orden internacional contemporáneo.* Bogotá: Penguin.

Paul, J., ed. 1981. *Reading Nozick.* Totowa, NJ: Rowman and Littlefield.

Peffer, R.G. 1990. *Marxism, Morality, and Social Justice.* Princeton: Princeton University Press.

Pereira da Silva, F. 2023a. "On a Genealogy of the Concept of 'South–South Cooperation'". *Human Affairs* Vol. 33, No. 3, 366–377.

Pereira da Silva, F. 2023b. *En busca de la comunidad. Caminos del pensamiento crítico en la periferia global.* Buenos Aires: Gabriel Andrés Kozel.

Pereira, G. 2013. *Elements of a Critical Theory of Justice.* New York: Palgrave Macmillan.

Pogge, T. 1990. *Realizing Rawls.* Ithaca, New York: Cornell University Press.

Pogge, T. 1994. *Egalitarian Law of Peoples. Philosophy and Public Affairs* 23, 3, 195–224.

Pogge, T. 2002. *World Poverty and Human Rights.* Cambridge: Polity Press.

Pogge, T. 2007. "Reframing Global Economic Security and Justice". In: Held, D./McGrew, A. eds., *Globalization Theory: Approaches and Controversies.* Cambridge: Polity Press.

Pogge, T., ed. 2001. *Global Justice.* Oxford: Blackwell Publishing.

Power, N. 2009. *One-Dimensional Woman.* Winchester, Washington: O Books.

Preciado Coronado, J.A. 2021. "Populisms: Inherently Illiberal or Plausibly Democratic? Hybrid Regimes May Offer a Complementary Approach". *Politikon,* March, Vol. 48, 26–46.

"Prefeitura Municipal de Canoas". 2011. *Canoas Construindo o Futuro. A experiencia do Congresso e a Estratégia da Cidade 2011–2021.* Canoas, Prefeitura Municipal de Canoas.

Pugh, J., Kahane, G., Savulescu, J. 2013. "Cohen's Conservatism and Human Enhancement". *The Journal of Ethics,* Vol. 17, No. 4, 331–354.

Rawls, J. 1971. *A Theory of Justice.* Cambridge, MA: The Belknap Press of Harvard University Press.

Rawls, J. 1983. The Basic Liberties and Their Priority. In: S. McMurrin, ed. *The Tanner Lectures on Human Values.* Salt Lake City: University of Utah Press, 3–87.

Rawls, J. 1992. *The Basic Liberties and Their Priority.* The Tanner Lectures on Human Values. Delivered at The University of Michigan. April 10, 1981, 1–87.

Rawls, J. 1993a. *Political Liberalism.* New York: Columbia University Press.

Rawls, J. 1993b. "The Law of Peoples". In S. Shute, S. Hurley, eds. *On Human Rights: The Oxford Amnesty Lectures.* New York: Basic Books, 41–82.

Rawls, J. 1995. "Reply to Habermas". *Journal of Philosophy,* Vol. XCII, No. 3, 132–180.

Rawls, J. 1999. *The Law of Peoples with „The Idea of Public Reason Revisited".* Cambridge, MA, and London: Harvard University Press.

Rawls, J. 1999a. *The Law of Peoples with "The Idea of Public Reason Revisited".* Cambridge, MA: Harvard University Press.

Rawls, J. 1999b. "The Domain of the Political and Overlapping Consensus". In J. Rawls, S. Freeman, ed. *Collected Papers.* Cambridge, MA: Harvard University Press.

Rawls, J. 2000. *Lectures on the History of Moral Philosophy.* Cambridge, MA: Harvard University Press.

Rawls, J. 2001. *Justice as Fairness. A Restatement.* Cambridge, Mass.: Belknap Bress, Harvard University Press, 2001.

Reitan, R. 2007. *Global Activism.* London, New York: Routledge.

Richards, D. 1982. International Distributive Justice, *Nomos* Vol. 24.

Richta, R. et al. 2018 (orig. 1966). *Civilization at the Crossroads. Social and Human Implications of the Scientific and Technological Revolution.* London: Routledge.

Ricoeur, P. 2000. *The Just.* Chicago, London: University of Chicago Press.

Ricoeur, P. 2005. *The Course of Recognition.* Cambridge, MA: Harvard University Press.

Ricoeur, P. 2007. *Reflections on the Just.* Chicago, London: University of Chicago Press.

Riedel, M. 1975. *Materialen zu Hegels Rechtsphilosophie.* Frankfurt/M.: Suhrkamp.

Risse, T. 2010. *A Community of Europeans? Transnational Identities and Public Spheres.* Ithaca: Cornell University Press.

Ritter, C. 2006. "Collective Identities for Political Inclusion in the European Union". In: H. Heit, ed. *The Values in Europe. Constitutional Patriotism and Community of Values in the EU?* Műnster, Hamburg: LIT Verlag, 192–203.

Robinson, F. 2006. "Care, Gender and Global Social Justice: Rethinking 'Ethical Globalization'." *Journal of Global Ethics,* 2, 1, 5–25.

Robinson, W. 1996. Globalization: Nine Theses on Our Epoch. *Race & Class,* 38, 2.

Robinson, W. 2004. *A Theory of Global Capitalism: Production, Class, and State in a Transnational World.* Baltimore: Johns Hopkins University Press.

Robinson, W. 2020. *Global Police State.* London: Pluto Press.

Robinson, W. 2022. *Global Civil War. Capitalism Post-Pandemic.* New York: PM Press.

Robinson, W.I. 2014. *Global Capitalism and the Crisis of Humanity.* Cambridge: Cambridge University Press.

Robinson, W.I., Harris, J. 2000. "Towards a Global Ruling Class? Globalization and the Transnational Capitalist Class". *Science and Society* 64, 1, 11–54.

Rorty, R. 1989. *Contingency, irony, and solidarity.* Cambridge: Cambridge University Press.

Rorty, R. 1997. "Back to Class Politics". *Dissent,* Winter, 31–34.

Rosamond, B. 2000. "Theories of European Integration". Hampshire: Palgrave Macmillan.

Rosemont Jnr., H. 2004. "Whose Democracy? Which Rights? A Confucian Critique of Modern Western Liberalism". In K.L. Shun, D.B. Wong, eds., *Confucian Ethics A Comparative Study of Self, Autonomy, and Community.* Cambridge: Cambridge University Press, 49–71.

Rousseau, J.J. 1998. *The Social Contract.* Ware: Wordsworth Editions.

Rousseau, J.J. 2019. *The Discourses and other early Political Writings.* Cambridge: Cambridge University Press, 115–193.

Rudolph, L.J., Rudolph, S.H. 2010. "Federalism as State Formation in India: A Theory of Shared and Negotiated Sovereignty". *International Political Science Review,* 31, 5, 553–572.

Rufanges, J.C. 2021. *Military Spending and Global Security.* New York and London: Routledge.

Said, E.W. 1994. *Culture and Imperialism.* New York: Vintage.

Sakwa, R. 2017. *Russia Against the Rest. The Post-Cold War Crisis of the World Order.* Cambridge: Cambridge University Press.

Samson, C., Smith, N., eds. 1996. *The Social Construction of Social Policies. Methodologies, Racism, Citizenship and the Environment.* New York: St. Martin.

Sartre, J.P. 1985. *Critique de la raison dialectique,* I–II. Paris: Gallimard.

Sartre, J.P. 2003. *Being and Nothingness: An Essay on Phenomenological Ontology.* London and New York: Routledge.

Sartre, J.P. 2004. *Critique of Dialectical Reason.* London: Verso.

Sartre, J.P. 2021. *Being and Nothingness.* New York: Atria Books.

Scanlon, T. 1977. Liberty, Contract and Contribution. In: G. Dworkin, G. Bermant, P.G. Brown, eds. *Markets and Morals.* Washington: Hemisphere Publishing.

Schecter, D. 2019. *Critical theory and sociological theory. On late modernity and social statehood.* Manchester: Manchester University Press.

Scheuerman, W.E. 2011. *The Realist Case for Global Reform.* London: Polity.

Scheuerman, W.E. 2012. *Frankfurt School Perspectives on Globalization, Democracy, and the Law.* London: Routledge.

Schmidt, A. 1970. "Die „Zeitschrift für Sozialforschung". Geschichte und gegenwärtige Bedeutung". *Zeitschrift für Sozialforschung,* I, (orig. 1932), Kösel-Verlag: Munich, 5*–63*.

Schmidt, H.C., Zurn, C.F., eds. 2010. *The Philosophy of Recognition. Historical and Contemporary Perspectives.* Lanham: Lexington Books.

Schmied-Kowarzik, W. Hg. 2002. *Verstehen und Verständigung. Ethnologie – Xenologie – Interkulturelle Philosophie.* Würzburg: Königshausen und Neumann.

Schmitt, C. 2007. *The Concept of the Political.* Chicago: University of Chicago Press.

Schwartzman, M. 2004. "The Completeness of Public Reason". *Politics, Philosophy & Economics,* Vol. 3, No. 2, 191–220.

Schweickart, D. 1992. "Economic Democracy". *Science and Society,* 56, Spring, 9–38.

Schweickart, D. 2011. *After Capitalism.* Lanham: Rowman & Littlefield.

Schweiger, G., ed. 2020. *Poverty, Inequality and the Critical Theory of Recognition.* Salzburg: Springer.

Scott, J.C. 1985. *Weapons of the Weak.* New Haven, London: Yale University Press.

Sen, A. 1999. *Development as Freedom.* Oxford: Oxford University Press.

Senghaas, D. 1998. *Zivilisierung wider Willen. Der Konflikt der Kulturen mit sich selbst.* Frankfurt/M.: Suhrkamp.

Senghaas, D. 2007. *On Perpetual Peace: A Timely Assessment.* New York: Berghahn Books.

Seth, S., ed. 2013. *Postcolonial Theory and International relations.* New York: Routledge.

Shaw, M. 2000. *Theory of the Global State: Globality as an Unfinished Revolution.* Cambridge: Cambridge University Press.

Shue, H. 1980. *Basic Rights: Substance, Affluence, and U.S. Foreign Policy.* Princeton: Princeton University Press.

Siep, L. 1979. *Anerkennung als Prinzip der praktischen Philosophie.* Freiburg, Munchen: Abber.

Šik, O. 1976. *Third Way. Marxist-Leninist Theory and Modern Industrial Society.* London: Wildwood House.

Silveira, P., Silveira, N. 2015. *Orcamento Participativo de Porto Alegre. 25 Anos.* Porto Alegre: Gráfica expresso, Editora da Cidade.

SinghaRoy, D. 2004. *Peasant Movements in Post-colonial India.* New Delhi: Sage.

Sklair, L. 1995. *Sociology of the Global System.* Baltimore: John Hopkins University Press.

Sklair, L. 2000a. "The transnational capitalist class and the discourse of globalisation". *Cambridge Review of International Affairs*, 14, Autumn, 1, 67–85.

Sklair, L. 2000b. "Media imperialism". In J. Beynon, D. Dunkerley, eds. *Globalization.* New York: Routledge, 28–30.

Sklair, L. 2001. *The Transnational Capitalist Class.* Oxford: Oxford University Press.

Sklair, L. 2002. *Globalization: Capitalism and Its Alternatives.* Oxford: Oxford University Press.

Sklair, L. 2009a. "The Globalization of Human Rights". *Journal of Global Ethics* 5, 2 August, 81–96.

Sklair, L. 2009b. "The emancipatory potential of generic globalization". *Globalizations* 6, 4 December, 523–37.

Sklair, L. 2016. "The Transnational Capitalist Class, Social Movements, and Alternatives to Capitalist Globalization". *International Critical Thought* 6, 3, 329–341.

Sklair, L. 2021. *The Anthropocene in Global Media. Neutralizing the Risk.* London: Routledge.

Sobottka, E.A. 2023. "New Wine in Old Wineskins? Incomplete Democratization in Brazil During the First Pink Tide". *Human Affairs* Vol. 33, No. 3, 304–318.

Sobottka, Emil A. 2013. "Participation and Recognition in Social Research". *International Journal of Action Research*, Vol. 9. No. 1, 124–146.

Social Watch Report. 2023. Montevideo, Instituto del tercer mundo. https://www.soci alwatch.org/annualReport (Visited June 30, 2023).

Social Watch: Batthyány, K., and team eds. 2006. *The Right to Not Be Poor: Poverty as a Violation of Human Rights.* Montevideo: Social Watch.

Solik, M., ed. 2015. *Rozpory a alternatívy globalního kapitalismu.* Praha: Filosofia.

Sparks, C. 2001. "The Internet and the Global Public Sphere". In L. Benneth, R. Entman, eds., *Mediated Politics: Communication in the Future of Democracy.* Cambridge: Cambridge University Press.

Spengler, O. 2006 (orig. 1919–1922). *Der Untergang des Abendlandes. Umrisse einer Morphologie der Weltgeschichte.* München: Taschenbuch.

Spohr, K., Hamilton, D.S., eds., Moyer, J.C. assoc. ed. 2020. *The Arctic and World Order.* Washington, D.C.: Johns Hopkins University.

Sťahel, R., Dědečková, E. 2023. *Current Challenges of Environmental Philosophy.* Boston and Leiden: Brill.

Steiner, H. 1994. *An Essay on Rights.* Oxford: Blackwell.

Stepanyants, M.T., ed. 2007. *Comparative Ethics in a Global Age.* Washington: The Council for Research in Values and Philosophy.

Sullivan, W.M., Kymlicka, W. 2007. *The Globalization of Ethics.* Cambridge: Cambridge University Press.

Svoboda, J., Stech, O., eds. 2012. *Interkulturni vojna a mir.* Praha: Filosofia.

Taylor, C. 1975. *Hegel.* Cambridge: Cambridge University Press.

Taylor, C. 1978. "Hegel's *Sittlichkeit* and the Crisis of Representative Institutions". In Y. Yovel, ed. *Philosophy of History and Action.* Dordrecht: Reidel, 133–154.

Taylor, C. 1979. *Hegel and Modern Society.* Cambridge: Cambridge University Press.

Taylor, C. 1985a. *Human Agency and Language. Philosophical Papers 1.* Cambridge: Cambridge University Press.

Taylor, C. 1985b. "The Nature and Scope of Distributive Justice". In C. Taylor, *Philosophical Papers 2. Philosophy and the Human Sciences.* Cambridge: Cambridge University Press.

Taylor, C. 1989. *The Sources of the Self.* Cambridge, MA: Harvard University Press.

Taylor, C. 1992. *The Ethics of Authenticity.* Cambridge, MA, and London: Harvard University Press.

Taylor, C. 1994. "Politics of Recognition". In: A. Gutmann, ed. *Multiculturalism: Examining the Politics of Recognition.* Princeton: Princeton University Press.

Taylor, C. 1995. "Irreducibly Social Goods". In C. Taylor, *Philosophical Arguments.* Cambridge, MA: Harvard University Press.

Taylor, C. 1996. "A World Consensus on Human Rights?" *Dissent,* Summer, 1.

Taylor, C. 1999. "Conditions of an Unforced Consensus on Human Rights". In J. Bauer, D.A. Bell, eds. *The East Asian Challenge for Human Rights.* Cambridge: Cambridge University Press, 124–144.

Taylor, C. 2003. "Cross-Purposes: Liberal-communitarian Debate." In D. Matravers, J. Pike, eds. *Debates in Contemporary Political Philosophy.* London: Routledge, 195–212.

Taylor, C. 2007. *A Secular Age.* Cambridge, MA: The Belknap of Harvard University Press.

Tehranian, M. 2007. *Rethinking Civilization: Resolving Conflict in the Human Family.* London, New York: Routledge.

Teng, Xiaoping. 1985. "There is No Fundamental Contradiction Between Socialism and a Market Economy. Interview". *Time,* October 23, excerpt: http://www.china.org.cn/english/features/dengxiaoping/103358.htm (Visited May 10, 2023).

The Paris Agreement. 2015. New York: UN Climate Change. https://unfccc.int/proc ess-and-meetings/the-paris-agreement/the-paris-agreement (Visited June 29, 2023).

The Qur'an. 2008. Oxford: Oxford University Press.

Thompson, E.P. 1968. *Making of the English Working Class.* Harmondsworth: Penguin.

Thompson, M. 2016. *The Domestication of Critical Theory.* Lanham: Roman and Littlefield.

Thompson, S. 2006. *Political Theory of Recognition. A Critical Introduction.* London: Polity Press.

Tocqueville, A. 2002. *Democracy in America.* Chicago: University of Chicago Press.

Tong, S. 2006. "Civilizing Tendencies of Capital and Limits Latent within Them". *Academic Monthly*, No. 10., 155-156.

Tönnies, A. 2005 (orig. 1887). *Gemeinschaft und Gesellschaft. Grundbegriffe der reinen Soziologie.* Darmstadt: Wissenschaftliche Buchgesellschaft.

Torres-Spelliscy, C. 2020. "The Most Expensive Election Ever". *Brennan Center for Justice*, November 11.

Toynbee, A.J., 1934–1961. *A Study of History.* Oxford: Oxford University Press.

Toynbee, A.J. 1962. *America and the World Revolution.* New York –London: Oxford University Press.

Transforming our world: the 2030 Agenda for Sustainable Development. 2012. New York: UN. https://sustainabledevelopment.un.org/post2015/transformingourworld (Visited 12, June 2023).

Tronto, J. 1994. *Moral Boundaries.* New York, London: Routledge.

United Nations. 1948. *Universal Declaration of Human Rights.* https://www.un.org/en /about-us/universal-declaration-of-human-rights (Visited June 10, 2021).

United Nations. 1966a. *International Covenant on Economic, Social and Cultural Rights.* https://www.ohchr.org/en/instruments-mechanisms/instruments/internatio nal-covenant-economic-social-and-cultural-rights (Visited June 10, 2021).

United Nations. 1966b. *International Covenant on Civil and Political Rights.* https://www .ohchr.org/en/instruments-mechanisms/instruments/international-covenant-civil -and-political-rights (Visited June 10, 2021).

United Nations. 1989. *Right to Adequate Food as a Human Right* (Human Rights Study Series No. 1). New York, United Nations 1989, United Nations Publication, No. E.89.XIV.2.

United Nations. 1990a. Committee on Economic, Social and Cultural Rights, *General Comment 2*, 02/02/90, International technical assistance measures, Art. 22, Para 9.

United Nations. 1990b. Committee on Economic, Social and Cultural Rights, *General Comment 3*, The nature of States parties obligations, Art. 2, Para. 8, 1, 14/12/90.

United Nations. 1991. Committee on Economic, Social and Cultural Rights, *General Comment 4*, 13/12/91, The right to adequate housing (Art. 11 /1/).

United Nations. 1997a. Committee on Economic, Social and Cultural Rights, *General Comment 7*, 20/05/97, The right to adequate housing.

United Nations. 1997b. Committee on Economic, Social and Cultural Rights, *General Comment 8*, The relationship between economic sanctions and respect for economic, social and cultural rights, U.N. Doc. E/C.12/1997/8, Para 1.

United Nations. 1999a. Committee on Economic, Social and Cultural Rights, *General Comment 12*, E/C.12/1999/5, The right to adequate food.

United Nations. 1999b. *Déclaration sur le droit et la responsabilité des individus, groupes et organs de la société de promouvoir et protéger les droits de l'homme et les libertés fondamentales universellement reconnus* (Declaration on the Rights and Responsibilities of Individuals, Groups and Organs of Society to Promote and Protect Universally Recognized Human Rights and Fundamental Freedoms). New York: Assemblée générale des Nations unies, A/RES/53/144, 8 mars.

United Nations. 2002. Committee on Economic, Social and Cultural Rights, *General Comment 15*, E/C.12/2002/11 The right to water, Para. 32.

United Nations. 2013. *We Can End Poverty. Millenium Development Goals and Beyond 2015*. New York: UN Department of Public Information.

United Nations. 2014. *Millenium Declaration. The Millenium Development Goals Report 2014*. New York: United Nations.

United Nations. 2015a. *Transforming our world: the 2030 Agenda for Sustainable Development*. New York: UN.

United Nations Department of Economic and Social Affairs. 2015b. *Sustainable Development Goals*. New York: UN DESA.

UNDP. 2005. *Human Development Report 2005, Human Development Trends 2005*, Part 9 (5).

United Nations High Commissioner for Human Rights. 2008. *Respect for Human Rights Essential for the Eradication of Poverty*. http://www.unhchr.ch/huric ane/hurricane.nsf/view01/10F59F4258CBC22CC1256DC20049B1DF?opendocument date accessed (Vistited 10 September 2018).

Vallentyne, P., Steiner, H., eds. 2000. *Left-Libertarianism and Its Critics*. New York: Palgrave.

Vallentyne, P., Steiner, H., eds. 2001. *The Origins of Left-Libertarianism*. New York: Palgrave.

Van Parijs, P. 1995. *Real Freedom for All*. Oxford: Clarendon Press.

Vincent, A. 1983. "The Hegelian State and International Politics". *Review of International Studies* 9, 193–205.

Vogel, E.F. 2013. *Deng Xiaoping and the Transformation of China*. Cambridge, MA: Belknap Press of Harvard University Press.

Wallace-Bruce, N.L. 1994. *Claims to Statehood in International Law*. New York: Carlton Press.

Wallerstein, I. 1974. *The Modern World-System*, I–III. New York, London: Academic Press.

Wallerstein, I. 2003. *The Decline of American Power: The U.S. in a Chaotic World*. New York: New Press.

Wallerstein, I. 2006. *European universalism*. New York: New Press.

Wallgren, T., Pyakurel, U., Revollo Pardo, C., Teivainen, T. eds. 2022. *Challenging Authoritarian Capitalism: The Transformative Power of the World Social Forum*. London: Routledge.

Walzer, M. 1977. *Just and Unjust Wars*. New York: Basic Books.

Walzer, M. 2000. "International Society: What is the Best that We Can Do?" *Dissent* Fall.

Walzer, Michael. 1980. *Interpretation and Social Criticism*. Cambridge, MA: Harvard University Press.

Walzer, Michael. 1988. *The Company of Critics: Social Criticism and Political Commitment in the Twentieth Century*. New York: Basic Books.

Wei, Xiaoping. 2010. *Rethinking China's Economic Transformation*. New York: Global Scholarly Publications.

Wei, Xiaoping. 2022. *Karl Marx on Socialist Theory and Practice. Rethinking Marx's Theory of Human Emancipation*. London: Palgrave MacMillan.

Wellmer, A. 1971 (1969). *Critical Theory of Society*. New York: Herder and Herder.

Wendt, A. 1987. "The Agent-Structure Problem in International Theory". *International Organizations*, 43, 3, 335–370.

Wendt, A. 1999. *Social Theory of International Politics*. Cambridge: Cambridge University Press.

Wendt, A. 2003. "Why a World State is Inevitable". *European Journal of International Relations*, 9, 4, 491–542.

White, N. D. 2007. The Applicability of Economic and Social Rights to the UN Security Council. In: Baderin, M. A./McCorquodale, R. eds., *Economic, Social and Cultural Rights in Action*, 98–107.

Wiggershaus, R. 1986. *Die Frankfurter Schule. Geschichte, theoretische Entwicklung, politische Bedeutung*. München: Carl Hanser.

Williams, C. 2010. *Ecology and Socialism*. Chicago: Haymarket Books.

Windfuhr, M., ed. 2005. *Beyond the Nation State. Human Rights in Times of Globalization*. Uppsala: Global Publications Foundation.

Winnicott, D.W. 1965. *The Maturational Processes and the Facilitating Environment*. London: Hogarth Press.

Wiredu, K. 1996. *Cultural Universals and Particulars: An African Perspective*. Bloomington: Indiana University Press.

Wiredu, K. 2005. "On the Idea of a Global Ethics". *Journal of Global Ethics*, 1, June, 1, 45–51.

Wong, D.B. 2004. "Rights and Community in Confucianism". In K. L. Shun, D.B. Wong, eds. *Confucian Ethics. A Comparative Study of Self, Autonomy, and Community*. Cambridge: Cambridge University Press, 31–48.

World Bank Group. 2022. *Correcting Course. Poverty and Prosperity 2022*. Washington: International Bank for Reconstruction and Development/The World Bank.

Wuthnow, R. 1989. "Communities of Discourse: Ideology and Social Structure in the Reformation, the Enlightenment, and European Socialism". Cambridge, MA: Harvard University Press.

Yang, X., Jiang, S., eds. 2018. *Challenges Towards Ecological Sustainability in China: An Interdisciplinary Perspective*. Berlin: Springer.

Young, I.M..1990. *Justice and the politics of difference*. Princeton: Princeton University Press.

Young, I.M. 2000. *Inclusion and democracy*. Oxford: Oxford University Press.

Young, I.M. 2001. "Equality of Whom? Social Groups and Judgments of Injustice." *The Journal of Political Philosophy* Vol. 9, No. 1, 1–18.

Young, I.M. 2002. "Lived Body vs Gender: Reflections on Social Structure and Subjectivity". *Ratio* 15, 4, Dec., 410–428.

Young, I.M. 2006. "Responsibility and Global Justice". *Social Philosophy and Policy*, Vol. 23, Issue 1, Jan., 102–130.

Young, I.M. 2007a. *Global challenges: War, self-determination, and responsibility for justice*. Oxford: Polity Press.

Young, I.M. 2007b. "Recognition of Love's Labor. Considering Axel Honneth's Feminism". In B. van den., Brink, D. Owen, eds. *Recognition and Power. Axel Honneth and the Tradition of Critical Social Theory*. Cambridge: Cambridge University Press, 189–212.

Young, I.M. 2010. *Responsibility for justice*. Oxford: Oxford University Press.

Young, I.M. 2020. "House and Home. Feminist Variations on a Theme". In I.M. Young, *Intersecting Voices. Dilemmas of Gender, Political Philosophy, and Policy*. Princeton: Princeton University Press, 134–185.

Young, I.M., Jalusic, V., Pajnik, M. 2009. "When I Think of Myself as Politically Engaged, I Think of Myself as a Citizen: Interview with Iris Marion Young". In A. Ferguson, M. Nagel, eds. *Dancing with Iris. The Philosophy of Iris Marion Young*. Oxford: Oxford University Press.

Zhang, Dainian. 2002. *Key Concepts in Chinese Philosophy*. Beijing: Foreign Languages Press, and New Haven and London: Yale University Press.

Zhung, Xu. 2021. "The Ideology of Late Imperialism". *Monthly Review,* Vol. 72, Issue 10, March.

Index

www.ingramcontent.com/pod-product-compliance
Ingram Content Group UK Ltd.
Pitfield, Milton Keynes, MK11 3LW, UK
UKHW021855120626
6420IPUK00013BA/221